Loss and Hope

Also Available From Bloomsbury

Interreligious Studies, Oddbjørn Leirvik
The New Comparative Theology, Francis X. Clooney, SJ

Loss and Hope

Global, Interreligious and Interdisciplinary Perspectives

Peter Admirand

Bloomsbury Academic
An imprint of Bloomsbury Publishing Plc

B L O O M S B U R Y
LONDON · OXFORD · NEW YORK · NEW DELHI · SYDNEY

Bloomsbury Academic

An imprint of Bloomsbury Publishing Plc

50 Bedford Square
London
WC1B 3DP
UK

1385 Broadway
New York
NY 10018
USA

www.bloomsbury.com

BLOOMSBURY and the Diana logo are trademarks of Bloomsbury Publishing Plc

First published 2014
Paperback edition first published 2015

© Peter Admirand and Contributors, 2014

Peter Admirand has asserted his right under the Copyright, Designs and
Patents Act, 1988, to be identified as the Editor of this work.

British Library Cataloguing-in-Publication Data
A catalogue record for this book is available from the British Library.

ISBN: HB: 978-1-47252-541-3
PB: 978-1-47426-481-5
ePDF: 978-1-47252-907-7
ePub: 978-1-47252-386-0

Library of Congress Cataloging-in-Publication Data
Loss and hope : global, interreligious, and interdisciplinary perspectives /
edited by Peter Admirand. – 1 [edition].
pages cm
Includes bibliographical references.
ISBN 978-1-4725-2541-3 (hardback) – ISBN 978-1-4725-2907-7 (epdf) –
ISBN 978-1-4725-2386-0 (epub) 1. Suffering–Religious aspects. 2. Suffering.
3. Loss (Psychology)–Religious aspects. 4. Loss (Psychology) 5. Violence–Religious
aspects. 6. Violence. I. Admirand, Peter, editor of compilation.
BL65.S85L67 2014
202'.118–dc23
2013044894

Typeset by Newgen Knowledge Works Pvt Ltd, Chennai, India

Contents

Part 3   Ethical and Interdisciplinary Perspectives on Loss and Hope

Contributors

Peter Admirand is a Lecturer in the School of Theology, Mater Dei Institute, Dublin City University. His *Amidst Atrocity and the Rubble of Theology: Searching for a Viable Theodicy* was published in 2012. He is the Secretary of the Irish Council of Christians and Jews, an Advisor to the Ireland Dialogue Society, and a Board Member of the journal *Religion and the Arts*. He has graduate degrees in English (Georgetown) and Theological Ethics (Boston College) and a PhD from Trinity College Dublin.

Mario I. Aguilar is a theologian born in Chile, the Director of the Centre for the Study of Religion and Politics, and Professor of Divinity at the University of St Andrews, Scotland. He is the author of many works on torture, genocide, and the role of the churches in political conflict including: *Religion, Torture and the Liberation of God* (2013), *A Social History of the Catholic Church in Chile* (9 volumes, 2004–2013), *Theology, Liberation, Genocide* (2009), and *The History and Politics of Latin American Theology* (3 volumes, 2007–2008).

David Burrell, C.S.C., Theodore Hesburgh Professor emeritus in Philosophy and Theology at the University of Notre Dame, currently serves the Congregation of Holy Cross in Dhaka, Bangladesh. Efforts since 1982 in comparative issues in philosophical theology in Judaism, Christianity, and Islam are evidenced in works such as *Knowing the Unknowable God: Ibn-Sina, Maimonides, Aquinas* (1986); *Faith and Freedom* (2004); *Deconstructing Theodicy* (2008); and *Towards a Jewish-Christian-Muslim Theology* (2011).

Francis X. Clooney, SJ, is Parkman Professor of Divinity and Professor of Comparative Theology and Director of the Center for the Study of World Religions, Harvard Divinity School, Harvard University. He is the author of numerous articles and books, including most recently *His Hiding Place Is Darkness: A Hindu-Catholic Theopoetics* (2013); *Comparative Theology: Deep Learning across Religious Borders* (2010); and *Beyond Compare: St. Francis and Sri Vedanta Desika on Loving Surrender to God* (2008).

Roja Fazaeli is a Lecturer in Islamic Studies at Trinity College Dublin. Her PhD is from NUI Galway and one of her main areas of research is in Human Rights. She is a Board Member of the Irish Refugee Council; the Association for the Study of Persianate Societies; the Middle East Studies Association; Amnesty International Irish Section; and founder and member of the Irish Network of Islamic Studies. Published articles include "Contemporary Iranian Feminism: Identity, Rights and Interpretations."

Jude Lal Fernando is Assistant Professor in Intercultural Theology and Interreligious Studies at the Irish School of Ecumenics, Trinity College Dublin. Originally from Sri Lanka, he has been involved in Buddhist-Hindu-Christian-Muslim dialogue under the mentorship of renowned Asian scholar, Professor Aloysius Pieris. He is the author of *Religion, Conflict and Peace: The Politics of Interpretation of Nationhood* (2013). He was also the co-coordinator of the People's Tribunal on Sri Lanka, held at Trinity College Dublin in January 2010 and an organizer of the Bremen Tribunal on Sri Lanka (2013).

Kieran Flynn worked as a missionary in the Niger Delta Area of Nigeria from 1993 until 2000. He produced many books in the local Ijaw language including a translation of the New Testament, *Egberio: Folk Stories from the Niger Delta and Learn your Izon Language*. He has studied Interreligious Dialogue and Islam at the Gregorian University, Rome, and at the Irish School of Ecumenics, Trinity College Dublin, where he earned his PhD. He has recently published *Islam in the West: Iraqi Shi'i Communities in Transition and Dialogue*.

Celia G. Kenny is an ordained minister of the Church of Scotland and has graduate degrees from Edinburgh University and Trinity College Dublin. Having completed a doctorate in feminist ethics at Trinity College Dublin, she is presently a Research Associate at the Centre for Law and Religion, Law School, Cardiff University, where she teaches philosophy of law. She is also working on a project for the European Consortium for Church and State Research.

Rabbi Anson Laytner is the Interreligious Initiative Program Manager at Seattle University's School of Theology and Ministry. He is the author of *Arguing with God: A Jewish Tradition* and *The Animals' Lawsuit against Humanity* as well as numerous articles on subjects ranging from Jewish theology to the Israeli–Palestinian Conflict to the Jews of China. Long active in interfaith relations, Laytner has made his career working with a variety of nonprofit organizations in Seattle.

John D'Arcy May, born in Melbourne, Australia, holds the degrees of STL (Università Gregoriana, Rome); Dr theol. (Ecumenics) (Münster); and Dr phil. (History of Religions) (Frankfurt). He is Fellow Emeritus at Trinity College Dublin; Adjunct Professor, Centre for Interreligious Dialogue, Australian Catholic University; Hon. Research Fellow, MCD University of Divinity; and Adjunct Senior Research Fellow, Centre for Studies in Religion and Theology, Monash University. His publications include: *Transcendence and Violence: The Encounter of Buddhist, Christian and Primal Traditions* (2003).

Fulata L. Moyo is the World Council of Church's Programme Executive for Women in Church and Society and a former General Coordinator of the Circle of Concerned African Women Theologians. She received her doctorate from the School of Religion and Theology, University of KwaZulu-Natal, South Africa, in the area of gender and ecological justice and sexuality in the context of HIV and AIDS. She is a coeditor of *Women Writing Africa: Eastern African Region* (2007).

Alicia Partnoy, a poet and scholar, survived the secret detention camps where about 30,000 people "disappeared" in Argentina. She is best known for her book *The Little School: Tales of Disappearance and Survival,* used as evidence in the trials against genocide perpetrators in her hometown. Twenty years after its publication in English, it was released in Argentina as *La Escuelita* and donated by the government to public libraries in the country. She teaches at Loyola Marymount University and presides over Proyecto VOS—Voices of Survivors.

Joerg Rieger is Wendland-Cook Professor of Constructive Theology at Perkins School of Theology, Southern Methodist University. He is the author of numerous books, including: *Occupy Religion: Theology of the Multitude* (coauthored with Kwok Pui-lan, 2012), *Globalization and Theology* (2010), *No Rising Tide: Theology, Economics, and the Future* (2009), and *Christ and Empire: From Paul to Postcolonial Times.* He is an Ordained Elder, North Texas Conference United Methodist Church.

Steven Shankman holds the UNESCO Chair in Transcultural Studies, Interreligious Dialogue, and Peace at the University of Oregon. He is currently coordinator of the UNITWIN network on Interreligious Dialogue for Intercultural Understanding. Most recently he has published *Epics and Other Higher Narratives: An Intercultural Approach,* coedited by Amiya Dev (2010), and *Other Others: Levinas, Literature, Transcultural Studies* (2010). He has been a Guggenheim and an NEH Fellow.

Felix Wilfred was born in Tamil Nadu, India. He is the president of the international theological journal *Concilium* and is President of the faculty of arts, and Chairman of The School of Philosophy and Religious Thought, State University of Madras. Recent publications include: *Asian Public Theology—Critical Concerns in Challenging Times* (2010) and *Margins: Site of Asian Theologies* (2008). He is also editing *The Oxford Handbook of Christianity in Asia* (2011–2014).

Harry Wu, a native of Shanghai, China, was imprisoned at the age of 23 for being a "counterrevolutionary rightist" and subsequently spent 19 years toiling in the fields, mines, and factories of the Laogai. Wu immigrated to the United States in 1985, where he later testified to Congress about the Laogai. In 1992, he established the Laogai Research Foundation and founded the Laogai Museum in Washington, DC. His books include: *Laogai: The Chinese Gulag* and *Bitter Winds: A Memoir of my Years in China's Gulag.*

Foreword

Philip (Fiszel) Bialowitz

A teaching from the Jewish tradition instructs that "The world is sustained by the breath of schoolchildren." Even when the German authorities—who had invaded the small Polish town of Izbica Lubelski that my family called home in 1939—issued decrees that forbade the schooling of children, parents like mine continued to educate their children with the help of private tutors. These acts of resistance by parents and teachers everywhere were about much more than belief in the power of education. They were about the sincere dedication of both adults and children to the idea of hope.

It was this hope that sustained me when I arrived as a teenage boy at the gates of the infamous Nazi death camp, Sobibór, a mined death camp designed to do nothing but systematically kill hundreds, if not thousands of Jews in the time it takes to watch the evening news, or do grocery shopping. In fact, the world would soon learn that 250,000 innocent men, women, and children were murdered at Sobibór over a period of 15 months. Upon arriving, I assured myself that, after enduring so many terrible experiences in my town, "If they are to kill me on this very day then at least it will be my end and I can have some peace."

In the midst of incredible sorrow, each loss compounded the already raw emotional wounds, that quite frankly, should have crushed me into oblivion, never again able to muster the will to survive and seek revenge, let alone the life energy needed to carry on day to day at Sobibór. If only I could die from bullets, I sometimes thought, then I would have resisted those who murdered my family.

But at the same time, I told myself, "I am only a teenager; I want to live!" As it turned out, my prayers were answered by a miracle. I survived six months of brutality inside of Sobibór, until the day of a heroic prisoner uprising that gave me another chance at life.

The date of the revolt at Sobibór was October 14, 1943. Assigned as a messenger during the uprising, I was able to lure some SS guards into barracks, under the guise that they were expecting to be fitted for leather coats or leather boots. Here, they were axed and knifed to death. This act of resistance paved the way and made it possible for Russian POW Sasha Pechersky's escape plan to be executed successfully. So it was then, that I finally felt some sense of satisfaction. A lifting of the malaise that had permeated my being was now replaced by optimism and a fighting spirit that I employed as a coping mechanism.

And so, after a group of Jewish conspirators secretly killed most of the camp's German SS officers, the two leaders of the camp's underground committee—a rabbi's son named Leon Feldhendler and the above-mentioned Jewish lieutenant from the Soviet Red Army, Sasha Pechersky—climbed atop a table and called out to us: "Brothers! Our moment has come. Most of the Germans have been killed. Let us rise and destroy this place. We have little chance of surviving. But at least we will die fighting with honor. If anyone survives, bear witness! Tell the world what happened here!"

Spurred by these courageous words, most of the camp's prisoners attempted to escape despite gunfire coming from the remaining Nazi and Ukranian guards, in addition to the heavily mined area leading from the front gate to the woods. About 400 prisoners died as a result of the revolt, but about 200 prisoners, including me and my brother Symcha, made it to the forest.

From that day forward, October 14, 1943, I became a Sobibór survivor. While still unsure if I was going to survive the war, I was fortified with the belief that survival was possible, and on the other side, awaited a world of hope for a better tomorrow.

By the end of World War II, we and everyone we knew had suffered the deaths of loved ones, the loss of homes, and other great hardships of life under Nazi and Stalinist oppression. For me, this included the murder of my beloved mother (Bajla), father (Szyja), sisters (Brancha and Toba), and niece (Esterka), among other personal tragedies.

Despite such horrors, though, those of us who survived resolved to build new lives. Amazingly, many of us succeeded. The Displaced Persons camps in which we lived after the war were not always pleasant, but communal life flourished rapidly. We quickly organized into political groups, published newspapers, sang songs of both tears and joy, created art, and carried out the many Jewish traditions, including thousands of marriages, children, and, last but not least, education.

I have dedicated the last decades of my life to fulfilling the promise that I made to Leon Feldhendler and Sasha Pechersky when I was a teenager. I travel the globe bearing witness to the tragedy that I and my fellow prisoners experienced at Sobibór, and to the acts of individual and collective resistance that saved us and countless others over the course of World War II. It is a mission that keeps me young, and helps to sustain the world.

As part of that mission, it is an honor to provide the foreword to this collection of essays, many by or about other survivors of mass violence. Examining the themes of loss and hope, the book is particularly important for its emphasis on interfaith dialogue, remembering, and ethics. Thus, I conclude here with the same words ending my memoir, *A Promise at Sobibór*: "We must remember not to forget."

Acknowledgments

The world is a more hopeful place whenever gratitude is expressed, so let me do my small part.

My deep thanks to this volume's contributors, some of whom had never met me before in person and yet were still generous with their time, support, and talents. That alone gives me much hope, and may I be so generous when the tables are turned in the future.

I want to thank Celia for her initial idea on the theme of loss and hope and then supporting my vision of the book you see before you. *Go raibh maith agat.*

I have been at Mater Dei now for over three years and in Ireland for nine years and am reaching the point where even years are passing quickly (I presume decades are next?) and so a deep thank you to the former President Dr Dermot Lane, the Director Dr Andrew McGrady, the Head of the School of Theology Dr Ethna Regan, my fellow ex-pat Americans in the School: Dr Brad Anderson and Dr Joseph Rivera, my always welcoming Irish colleagues: Dr Gabriel Flynn, Dr Martin Hogan, Dr Alan Kearns, Dr John Murray, and Dr Pat O'Donoghue, and my colleague from the Holy Land, Dr Yazid Said.

I also want to send an especially deep thanks to Mater Dei's Educational and Research Trust which paid for this book's index.

Through an Erasmus Teaching Mobility grant at the Seminar für Katholische Theologie at Freie Universität Berlin, I could not have been treated with greater hospitality and kindness by Prof. Dr Anja Middelbeck-Varwick Schwendener, Prof. Dr Matthias Remenyi, and Dr Markus Thurau—not to mention having a walking tour of Jewish Berlin led by Prof. Dr Rainer Kampling and Sara Han. I am already looking for another excuse to go back.

At Bloomsbury, my sincere gratitude for the support and steady professionalism of Lalle Pursglove and Anna MacDiarmid. I also want to thank my copyeditor, Hema Srikanth, typesetter, Srikanth Srinivasan, and to all the staff at Bloomsbury.

As always, I thank my parents, Peter and Margaret (it was the reverse order last time!). You both give me the means to maintain hope especially when loss threatens.

My children Jack, Christopher, Kaitlyn, and Ryan are nothing but hope to me even as four young kids can also cause loss of patience and free time, and perhaps, sanity. But you are all worth whatever happens, and whatever is lost is repaid in full by your smiles, laughter, and love. And Kelly . . . I can't thank you for reading the book or correcting grammatical errors, but none of this would have happened without you. You help keep me grounded, here playing the rock to my academic balloon (we switch roles in other contexts). The book is dedicated to you.

Introduction: The Certainty of Loss and the Ambivalence of Hope

Peter Admirand

Opening reflection

Lack of hope, like lack of oxygen, kills. But certain kinds of hope can kill, too—though in a slow, paralyzing way. And yet for all of hope's false promises, it is sometimes the only type of surety through darkness, loss, and isolation. Hope, like Midas' touch, seeks to turn everything into a type of gold, to render dreams real, mountains moved, and bliss tangible, even as such bliss may only be a morsel of bread to eat or a moment of respite from another's blow or slander.

Generally, we seek hope and avoid loss, but the latter finds all of us, regardless, and the former may not be always what we most need. Sometimes what is loss and what is hope can be unclear, indistinguishable, or even mixed up. Katherine Boo's candid and devastating portrayal of a slum in Mumbai closes with a depiction tinged with the grime and desperation of poverty and the hope laced to such detritus: "But for now, eleven cans, seven empty water bottles and a wad of aluminium foil rested on a long spit of concrete, awaiting the first child to claim them."[1] Is this an image of hope or loss? The children of the Mumbai slum, pitted in Darwinian survival, see in the waste left by the taxi drivers a means, no matter how fragile, of a better future, or at least earnings to bring home. Another's waste is their only hope.

In Hesiod's *Theogony*, a woman, Pandora, had a jar carrying every kind of evil that escaped, except hope. As classical historian Christian Meier writes: "Hope remained inside the jar. Did Hesiod mean to imply that hope, too, is an evil? . . . or did he want to draw attention, for the first time, to the ambivalence of hope?"[2] Pericles, moreover, refers to the "doubtful hands of Hope" in his funeral oration for those who died during the first year of the Peloponnesian War (431 BCE).[3] Must hope, then, also be tainted with words of doubt and insinuations of malevolence?

This is a book about loss and hope. They are linked because one is rarely estranged from the other. Just as the deepest losses may still contain a glimmer of hope, there is a shadow of loss looming behind every manifestation of hope. Sadly, the realization of any earthly hope will eventually succumb to loss. Ironically this augments hope's value. "What would have become of us all," gulag prisoner Eugenia Semyonovna Ginzburg asks, "if it had not been for that illusory light of that tenacious hope?"[4] The hope, here of the gulag prisons "crumbling," is false from Ginzburg's perspective and yet without that stubborn hope, there would have been no life. And did not those prisons eventually crumble? While tenacious and illusory, hope is also indispensible. As the Dalai Lama remarks: "A human being survives only with hope, and hope by definition implies the thought of something better."[5] Dostoevsky penned something similar in his part autobiographical account of his time in a Tsarist prison in Siberia, observing that "without labour and lawful normal possessions men . . . grow depraved and turn into beasts."[6]

We also know that human beings show their depravity in the perversity of certain hopes. Some have even yearned for the destruction of a people and have acted upon such hope. As Halima Bashir, a survivor of the Darfur atrocities, writes: "And not for one moment had I conceived that grown men could be capable of doing such things to little children. Yet now I had seen it with my own eyes, and I knew that the unthinkable was true."[7] We like narratives that depict a hope seemingly unrealizable coming true for the most deserving: they are the stuff of fairy tales, yet here again we are plunged into nightmares. Hope blind to the reality of loss enlightens the orbs of despair. And hope untethered to ethics unleashes despair and loss for others.

Overview of the book

This book is a collection of new chapters from some of the best and most provocative thinkers and scholars reflecting on the universal and accessible themes of loss and hope. In this regard, I sought new essays by survivors of genocide and state terror, social justice activists and scholars, and academics involved in interfaith dialogue and postconflict reconciliation processes. This work opens with a foreword from Philip Bialowitz, a survivor of the Sobibór death camp during the Shoah. It is a testimony to my fervid belief that the voices of the survivors of such atrocities are essential whenever seeking to formulate anything of worth, whether religious belief, theodicy, lasting love, or here, hope. Should we still hope, and is it ethical to hope, amidst or after atrocities and genocidal ruptures? These are difficult questions that must be asked. Thus, Part One, "Survivors and Victims' Perspectives on Loss and Hope," turns to survivors of mass atrocity and scholars working with such testimonies to seek their interpretations of the relationship of loss and hope. Here we have individuals and groups who have dealt with loss on a massive and often catastrophic scale. Having seen and experienced such horrors, they are in particularly unique positions to reflect upon such themes. Such a section demands an acute awareness of how fragile so much of life can be and calls for a response that transcends any alienating differences within gender, class, religion, race, ethnicity, nationality, or other often nebulous identity-markers. Aware of the extent of such loss and the complicity or failure of hope in such atrocities, the section raises crucial but (often) unanswerable questions.

Alicia Partnoy, a poet and professor at Loyola Marymount University, and also a survivor of the genocide in Argentina, opens Part One. She examines a collective account of fellow survivors and witnesses of that historical rupture and what has enabled many survivors to endure and even laugh. To witness is essential. Partnoy "is convinced that the building of a discourse of solidarity with the victims is what ultimately will empower those who chose to tell and will encourage others to share their experiences."

Harry Wu has spent decades tirelessly promoting the need for the world to be aware and remember the victims of the laogai (reform through labor camps in China), of which he was imprisoned for 19 years. In his chapter he turns his attention to the role of Classicide in Communist China and the losses that have resulted from such false divisions and ideology. Wu's calling for justice and memory is an explicit act of hope despite such searing loss.

Jude Lal Fernando, Assistant Professor in Intercultural Theology and Interreligious Studies at the Irish School of Ecumenics, presents an account of mass atrocities in Sri Lanka and how truth claims get subverted by those with vested interests. While facing such losses, Fernando, an academic and activist for peace in Sri Lanka, presents a way forward for a more truthful account of the recent violence and a way for the hope of justice and recovery to be implemented.

Mario Aguilar, Director of the Centre for the Study of Religion and Politics (CSRP) at the University of St Andrews, Scotland, poignantly depicts the atrocities in his native Chile, examining the key theological question of whether and where was God amidst all that torture and murder of life. His hope is that listening to the voices of victims and fashioning a theology from such voices (or reading their bones), can be a means of hope. As he writes: "In my words they are the loss that brings hope to a broken world."

Roja Fazaeli, Lecturer in Islamic Studies at Trinity College Dublin, presents a story of the hope manifest in the Iranian Women's movement. Having experienced the hatred of some Iranian prison guards while under house arrest, Fazaeli turns to the accounts of fellow Muslim women imprisoned for a range of offences while becoming a part of a movement seeking more rights for women in Iran. As she writes: "They give oppressed women a voice . . ."

Such awareness and experience of loss spur the need for partnership and dialogue because they expose the failures and gaps of much of our actions, laws, beliefs, and rhetoric.[8] Thus, Part Two, "Interreligious Perspectives on Loss and Hope," builds upon the truths and challenges of survivors while laying a foundation for the need to examine key areas within interreligious and secular viewpoints. Such views not only demand careful study and awareness of other positions and possibilities, but deep humility and cognizance of our need for dialogue, ongoing learning, and openness. These are qualities that not only provide solid grounds for hope but are also crucial in facing, responding to, and persevering through losses highlighted in Part One.

Francis X. Clooney, SJ, Director of the Center for the Study of World Religions at Harvard Divinity School, opens Part Two by turning to his extensive research and practical experience in the area of comparative theology, and specifically his study of Hinduism as a Jesuit priest and theologian. Clooney makes a compelling case for the crucial role of hope in the area of interreligious learning, writing: "Hope is compatible with failure, gaps, incompletion, melancholy, and uncertainty, but in the end it expects discovery, recognition, and fruition." This also aptly describes interreligious encounters.

Rabbi Anson Laytner's learned, moving, and deeply personal chapter traces a Jewish response to suffering while facing the question of any viable relationship with God. His candid assessment of a Be-Ing who accompanies him but "who directs nothing" could lead to the liberation of unhealthy dependence on God and so the hope of real relationship, though it may also signal the loss of that relationship. Hope is rarely immured from risk.

Melbourne, Australia, native and Trinity College Dublin Fellow Emeritus John D'Arcy May titles his stimulating and rewarding chapter: "May Buddhists Hope? A Christian Inquiry." As an exemplary case of comparative theology, May's chapter investigates whether one can give a fair assessment of possible Buddhist equivalents of hope while also providing a means for relating Christian to Buddhist eschatology. Grappling with "the rigor of Buddhist non-dualism" is crucial in such endeavors.

Kieran Flynn then draws upon his deep engagement with the Iraqi Shi'a community in Ireland to examine how the Ashura narrative in Shi'ism has deep links with Catholic political and liberation theologies and how each can benefit and strengthen the other. German theologian Johann Baptist Metz's linking of ethics and memory is deemed particularly valuable.

Peter Admirand examines how the still-unresolved pedophile scandal in the Catholic Church should impact Catholic participation in Catholic intra- and interreligious dialogue. He contends that if the documented systematic abuse and pernicious cover-up do not infuse humility and true openness toward the non-Catholic Other, then nothing will. Admirand's chapter tries to locate hope in the opportunity for renewal, repentance, and greater interreligious engagement demanded in light of such scandals.

Part Three, "Ethical and Interdisciplinary Perspectives on Loss and Hope," applies a multi- and transdisciplinary approach linked by ethical analysis on matters of pressing concern today, like human rights, globalization, the economy, and postconflict reconciliation. While neither covering over nor unduly minimizing the extent of losses in our world, these chapters together help to paint a picture of an ethics of hope in the face of such destabilizing losses.

Indian theologian Felix Wilfred, President of the journal *Concilium* and of the faculty of arts at the University of Madras, turns to the hope and resources for reconciliation within all cultures but contends that in many cases, such resources need to be discovered and harnessed to achieve such desired ends. In seeking cultural resources for peace, Wilfred raises important challenges to religious and national identities rooted in claims of exclusive ownership of truth and salvation.

Steven Shankman, UNESCO Chair in Transcultural Studies, Interreligious Dialogue, and Peace at the University of Oregon, focuses his chapter on Lithuanian-born philosopher Emmanuel Levinas and Russian-born novelist and journalist Vasily Grossman. Analyzing their unique ways of thinking God through ethical engagements, Shankman also ties in his experiences teaching these thinkers at a maximum-security prison to a mix of university students and inmates. Thus, in a place dominated by loss, he tries to articulate hope.

Celia Kenny is an ordained minister of the Church of Scotland, a cofounder of the Lamont Centre for adults with disabilities in Cluj, Romania, and Research Associate at the Centre for Law and Religion, Law School, Cardiff University. Kenny brings together insights from ethics and jurisprudence to contend how "the loss of old certainties" can be "the ground of our hope." Embracing pluralism becomes essential in such grounding.

Joerg Reiger, Wendland-Cook Professor of Constructive Theology at Southern Methodist University, directs his penetrating insights on the context of our contemporary global recession. Recalling the liberating message of the Exodus, the Exile, and the healing and challenging words of Jesus and Paul, Rieger seeks to present a true hope rooted in the struggle for economic justice for all. It is a timely and much-needed message.

Holy Cross priest David Burrell, Hesburgh Professor Emeritus in Philosophy and Theology at Notre Dame and an academic leader and lifelong participant in areas of dialogue among the Abrahamic faiths, closes Part Three with a concise and sharp account of the journey from optimism to hope. For Burrell, one can only find and maintain the possibility of hope through facing suffering and loss.

Malawian theologian Fulata Moyo, the World Council of Church's Programme Executive for Women in Church and Society and the former General Coordinator of the Circle of Concerned African Women Theologians, pens the afterword to the book. Weaving scenes of Miss Havisham from Charles Dickens's *Great Expectations*, Moyo reflects upon a shattering moment in her own life—the loss of her husband—and the way she was able to "dare to have strength in pain, beauty in the ashes of loss, and the possibility of light embracing the shadow."

Aims and closing reflections

The aims of the work include the following, to:

1. map signals of hope as they accompany the experience of loss and uncertainty amidst our postmodern (postsecular), globalized context;
2. dissect loss and hope amidst genocide, interstate war, and civil war or conflict;
3. highlight interdisciplinary connections, challenges, and studies that analyze or reflect upon loss and hope;
4. examine loss and/or hope from an interfaith perspective to reveal points of contact and dissonance between and among religious and secular traditions;
5. reframe and accentuate some expressions of past and present loss that bear upon (any hope for) present and future meaning; and to
6. provide rich and diverse reflections upon modes of belief, the human condition, and the search for meaning.

These are noble aims and hopes, even as one knows that the task is to contribute to the discussion and to encourage voices not represented here to join in the conversation. Loss and hope demands global, interreligious, and interdisciplinary perspectives. Boundaries and identities are mixed, hybrid, and permeable.

Fittingly, as a New Yorker living in Dublin, I write these words from Berlin, an emblematic city of loss and hope. Memories of architect Daniel Libeskin's Jüdisches

Museum, among other relevant sights, are thus fresh in my mind. Much can be said about that haunting and moving architectural testimony to the Jewish historical and ongoing role in Germany. Many spaces of the museum abruptly end or consist of empty stretches, what Libeskin calls "voids" and yet the exhibits still resonate with life and hope. One area deserves mention: the 79-foot (24 meter) Holocaust Tower. It is reached via black doors after walking below ground and then along a vast corridor (deemed an "axes of death" with objects from Holocaust victims within the recesses of one side of the wall and the names of the concentration and death camps written on the opposite wall). The space one enters is initially dark and narrow. A sloping, silo-like ceiling reveals a sliver of light from a slanted window and so a possible link with the city above. But the light seems too far away: is its presence a false or inspiring hope?

In Emmanuel Ringelblum's *Notes from the Warsaw Ghetto*, there are many crushing scenes, but one passage is particularly draining with the curse of hindsight. After depicting the ever-worsening conditions of the Jews in the ghetto, a journal entry from June 26, 1942 sings with hope. The outside world has finally heard of their plight. "We have overcome every obstacle to achieve our end,"[9] Ringelblum celebrates. But we know that instead . . .[10]

Helen "Zippi" Spitzer Tichauer, who did survive Auschwitz, once remarked: "It is hard to believe we were so crazy to have hope . . . in the middle of this nightmare . . . living hell. Even sometimes at night during all the gassing and burning pit fires, the burning of bodies, we still had hope. Were we crazy?"[11] One wants to answer unequivocally "no," but ours is a world where even hope is tainted, causing at least a momentary hesitation.

Lastly, consider Jonathan Lear's analysis of the Native American chief Plenty Coup facing the Crow's cultural devastation at the hands of American conquest. Plenty Coup's response to such devastation is what Lear calls a "radical hope" that "anticipates a good for which those who have the hope as yet lack the appropriate concepts with which to define it. What would it be for such hope to be justified?"[12] In other words, one hopes even without the available means or the words to do so. It is a hope rooted in faith, and somewhere crucially, in love. It is present as Plenty Coup continues to live even as his culture is threatened with extinction; while Mumbai slum boys who should be in school instead stretch their weary arms for a wad of aluminum foil; and a mythological woman opens a seemingly harmless jar. Loss may be certain and hope ambivalent, but it is that combination that makes prisons crumble, renewal commence, dialogue thrive, and even mountains move. These chapters seek to contribute to such worthy hopes.

Part One

Survivors' and Victims' Perspectives on Loss and Hope

1

A Collective Testimony by Argentine Genocide Survivors: "The Prison Walls Cry and We Laugh."

Alicia Partnoy

I believe that the most difficult aspect of the task we have tackled is that while writing is essentially an individual act, we are trying to write a book collectively.[1]

Del otro lado de la mirilla

In short, you can always say everything. The "ineffable" you hear so much about is only an alibi. Or a sign of laziness. You can always say everything: language contains everything.[2]

Jorge Semprún

To tell you the truth, they wanted to make us crazy, with a calculated and systematic plan.

Jorge "Corcho" Destéfanis[3]

It is a sunny, winter morning and I'm walking the streets around Parque Lezama in La Boca, Buenos Aires, with Daniel Bas y Mansilla. The former political prisoner—usually a calm and collected fellow—gets excited and points to his right, "Over there, in the Torquato Tasso community center, back in 1999," he enthusiastically explains, "we had the first big gathering! We were expecting sixty of us, about six hundred came."[4] That meeting, he tells me, began a quest to incorporate the experiences of former political prisoners into Argentina's history.

Embracing the need to produce a collective account, and inspired by the writings of Holocaust survivor Jorge Semprún, Bas y Mansilla, along with 150 Argentine genocide survivors, continued socializing, remembering, and writing. They had all shared years in isolation, yet not *disappeared*,[5] at the Coronda penitentiary, a high-security facility in the North Eastern province of Santa Fe. In 2003, their work gave its fruits with the publication of *Del otro lado de la mirilla: Olvidos y Memorias de ex Presos Políticos de Coronda. 1974–1979* (*The Other Side of the Peephole. Things Forgotten and Remembered by Coronda Former Political Prisoners*). Their narratives, collected at a series of *asados* (Argentine barbecue parties) and other gatherings, are seamlessly assembled in a volume that reads like a novel. Three years later, another polyphonic[6] testimonial text similar in its editorial dynamics, but radically different in its tone and content, was published. The writing process for *Nosotras, presas políticas. 1974–1983* (We, Women Political Prisoners),[7] had also started in 1999. Including texts by 112 women jailed by the military dictatorship in Villa Devoto, a high-security facility located in a peaceful neighborhood of Buenos Aires,[8] this project had been initiated by Mariana Crespo, a former political prisoner with active participation in the Liberation Theology movement.[9] Crespo had in turn been motivated by her encounter with a Holocaust survivor, as reported by coeditor Viviana Beguán:

> Around the year 1998, anthropologist Darío Olmo invited some of us . . . to tell him about our prison experiences, since from the testimonials [he and other anthropologists] had collected, they could detect a collective experience that was, for them, of great importance . . . Mariana had just returned from Europe where she had interviewed a concentration camp survivor who had spoken to her about the importance of memory, of writing, of telling . . . She took the proposal into her own hands and called a meeting to write the book.[10]

Beguán continued working on the project after Mariana's untimely death, and *Nosotras* is dedicated "to Mariana (Crespo) and the other dear compañeras who did not see this dream come to reality."[11]

Likewise, *Del otro lado de la mirilla*, whose authors acknowledge the influence of Holocaust survivor Jorge Semprún, is dedicated to the four compañeros who died in Coronda.[12] They are the only prisoners identified by name in the narrative, with photographs and chapters paying tribute to them.

The 2006 publication of *Nosotras* coincided with the proliferation in Argentina of books by former political prisoners. Demonized and censored, when not annihilated by the thousands, dissidents had avoided the public sharing of their prison memories, even after the return to democracy. It is true that Jacobo Timerman's *Prisoner without a Name, Cell without a Number*, and my own *The Little School. Tales of Disappearance and Survival* had enjoyed international recognition in the 1980s. Our books, however, dealt with the secret detention camps where the dictatorship tortured and assassinated thousands of political dissidents, to finally disappear their bodies and deny any knowledge of their fate.

While my own literary rendition of this tragedy was not published in Argentina until 2006, another survivor, Alicia Kozameh, issued there in 1987 the first literary work dealing with prison life: *Pasos bajo el agua*.[13] Years later, María del Carmen Sillato, Carmen Cornes, Margarita Drago, and Graciela Lo Prete chronicled in their own books, life in Villa Devoto.[14] *Nosotras* was the first collective work dealing with that prison experience.

Fewer books yet had chronicled life for male political detainees before the publication of the Coronda narrative: Miguel Angel Mori's *Las rondas y los sueños* alternates a narrative of his life as a political activist with chapters about the Rawson prison in the

South of Argentina. Pablo Bohoslavsky's *Cierta fortuna*, also dealing with the Rawson facility, includes 18 tales about his experience. Both works, like the Coronda book, are conceived as literary endeavors.[15] All chronicle empowering practices that helped prisoners resist the isolation imposed by the regime, and its subsequent destructive effects. However, the collective identity performed in both *Del otro lado de la mirilla* and *Nosotras* is their most clever and successful achievement. It embodies a triumphant defiance of all attempts to erase solidarity.

José Luis Hisi Páez, one of the editorial team members for *Del otro lado de la mirilla*, himself a former prisoner, writer, and college professor, reports:

> In Buenos Aires, compañero Bas y Mansilla found a book that was almost the inspiring totem for the editors: *Literature or Life*, by the great Spanish writer Jorge Semprún. That book helped us understand why we got together so many years after the facts to write the Coronda book! And it reassured us on the path of a literary version.[16]

In *Literature or Life*, Semprún recalls that after his liberation from Buchenwald he initially had questioned the "possibility of telling the story," finally to realize that:

> The only ones who will manage to reach this substance, this transparent density, will be those able to shape their evidence into an artistic object, a space of creation. Or of re-creation. Only the artifice of a masterly narrative will prove capable of conveying some of the truth of such testimony. But there's nothing exceptional about this: it's the same with all great historical experiences.[17]

Those of us who produce and study testimonial texts might differ in our definitions of art, creation, or literature. However, I am convinced that the building of a discourse of solidarity with the victims is what ultimately will empower those who chose to tell and will encourage others to share their experiences.[18] Jorge "Corcho" Destéfanis' words at the beginning of this chapter illustrate the ways we continue building this discourse of solidarity. Hisi Páez had disclosed to me the following:

> I remember something sad about the behind the scenes process around the writing of the Coronda book. Its brightest pages were written by compañero Corcho Destéfanis . . . This guy wrote so beautifully that his was the only chapter that was included in the book without any corrections, by consensus and unanimous decision by all of us in the editing committee . . . It was the chapter with the highest literary value . . . And Corcho was a guy who was not a literary pro . . . That guy was Silvia Suppo's husband. She was recently assassinated in Rafaela. When that happened I found out he had died of an awful illness recently . . . The assassination of Silvia Suppo was "cleared" as a consequence of a robbery, but nobody believes in coincidences: she was an important witness in the trials . . .[19]

The fact that Hisi Páez decides to share this information after the death of Destéfanis and the suspicious assassination of Silvia Suppo, continues building solidarity around him and Silvia Suppo, a survivor and star witness in the trials against the genocide perpetrators. Suppo was assassinated after her testimony sent several of the accused, including a local judge, to prison. Her first husband had been killed inside a cathedral during the dictatorship, and she was also a key witness against the perpetrators.[20]

One anonymous participant in the Coronda narrative explains how both solidarity and a will to resist destruction were at the core of this writing project:

> Yes, I agree that main character needs fleshiness, but when we flesh out this collective character, it must be understood that we were active, that we were political activists: students, peasants, workers, intellectual people . . . On the line of what you said, it can be asked: Who are these fellows? . . . Why are they in these situations? And, what did they do so the dictatorship's extermination plan in the Coronda prison could not achieve that much? . . . These fellows won the battle, even when they lost the war . . .[21]

In another excerpt transcribing the lively conversations among survivors when they decided to write the book, the authors' goal to reach the youth is illustrated:

> I don't know if I have told you this, but this entry, from my notebook . . . is what I remember from my experience, and I started writing it when my children were little, thinking that I was going to show it to them, or tell them . . . what I lived as a political activist in those days. Now they are teenagers and I believe it will be very nice to show them, instead of a notebook, a book written by all of us.[22]

José Luis Hisi Páez elaborates on their strategy and its subsequent success: "We did it in the most entertaining way possible: one of my students' sister, a young eighteen years old woman, read the entire book in a weekend, as soon as it was published! Of course we had a lot of fun writing it too."[23]

The result is 37 short chapters illustrated with cartoonish drawings that depict aspects of prison life, and alternate with photos of the prison facility and the compañeros who died in captivity. The book entertains and captivates readers while painting in excruciating detail life and death inside the Coronda prison. The inscription "Obra Colectiva Testimonial" (Collective Testimonial Work) appears in red letters on the cover, where prison bars reflect on a pupil behind a peephole. Nobel Prize Laureate Adolfo Pérez Esquivel—himself a former political prisoner—writes the prologue, where he highlights the motivation to present a collective testimony: "This book by the former prisoners of Coronda, who decided, after several years, to get together and remember, is a contribution to the collective consciousness. It rescues human values and the ability to resist oppression."[24]

Like Pérez Esquivel and Mariana Crespo, many secret detention camp survivors who subsequently spent years in Coronda, Villa Devoto, and other prisons, had a previous history in a Liberation Theology movement heavily targeted by the military dictatorship. To better understand their perspective, so removed from my own background as an atheist from a Jewish family, I turned to the work of Jesuit priest Ignacio Martín-Baró, a social psychologist and liberation theologian. Father Martín-

Baró was assassinated in El Salvador in 1989, along with five other Jesuits, their housekeeper, and her daughter.[25]

His writings highlight the reasons why dictatorships, both in El Salvador and in Argentina, were invested in the extermination of Liberation Theology leaders and followers. The Christian Base Communities that had engaged Latin Americans in grassroots work in the 1960s and 1970s adhered to what Ignacio Martín-Baró calls the "three most important intuitive truths of liberation theology." In the first place, he writes, "the promotion of life" is a Christian's most important task, and it has to be accompanied by a search for better living conditions for the people. According to this Christian martyr, these goals can be achieved by "liberating the structures . . . that maintain a situation of sin; that is, of the mortal oppression of the majority of the people." His third postulate addresses a preferential option for the poor and the marginalized.[26] What Father Martín-Baró calls "intuitive truths of Liberation Theology" are reworded by Peter Admirand in his chapter "Amidst Doubt, Despair and Destruction," when he proposes to include the voices of genocide survivors "in any theodic attempt": "Liberation theology's preferential option for the poor is a means to ensure that theology is centered on the marginalized and voiceless so that promoting the dignity of every person, formed in the image and likeness of God, is a goal and presupposition."[27]

Before being gunned down by members of the Salvadoran armed forces, Martín-Baró had argued that there were two types of religiosity impacting the relationship between religion and politics: "*vertical* religiosity, which leads to alienation and social submission" and "*horizontal* religiosity, [which] leads to critical consciousness and social liberation." Horizontal religiosity was practiced in the Christian Base Communities that followed the Liberation Theology tenets. Martín-Baró further elaborates: "Faced with the possible 'subversive' effect of horizontal religiosity, the directors of the psychological war in El Salvador have tried to promote forms of religious conversion or membership that contribute to political passivity toward the established order."[28]

While such passivity and submission were undoubtedly the goals of prison authorities all over Argentina, it is interesting to notice the diverging responses produced by survivors in these two books. *Nosotras*, a text that seeks to inscribe women's political participation in a national liberation movement, tiptoes around the religious aspect while male political prisoners discuss religious practices at ease in *Del otro lado de la mirilla*.

My own experience as a Villa Devoto prisoner, my talks with several authors, and a close reading of *Nosotras* led me to conclude that the authors' most empowering strategy was not to concentrate on their own religious beliefs and practices. Instead, they denounced the repressive actions of Hugo Bellavigna, the prison priest whom we had nicknamed San Fachón (Saint Big Fascist). His patriarchal and pro-dictatorial approach corresponded with the official position of the Catholic Church in Argentina.

The women of Villa Devoto constantly challenged Father Bellavigna's strategies, that sought to impose a vertical religiosity dear to the then official church. On the other hand, the Coronda inmates were empowered in their narrative by frequent recollections of their religious praxis during and before their incarceration. Daniel

Bas y Mansilla remembers that several political prisoners, including himself, had been seminarians, and that they would say mass on Sundays from their prison cells, screaming the words through the tiny windows, and risking cruel punishment. "The authorities," he remembers, "wanted to cause isolation, incommunication, and the breaking of any organized structure."[29] The prisoners were indeed so physically isolated, that when they met decades later to work on their book, they would recognize each other by voice since most had never actually met.

However, the Coronda inmates had enjoyed the visits of an exceptional bishop, as survivor José Cettour reports, ". . . I would like to tell you . . . about my experience with the church in Coronda, especially with Zazpe, then the Santa Fe bishop, very courageous, and highly respected by all of us, even though many of us are not believers."[30] Bishop Zazpe is remembered in *Del otro lado de la mirilla*: "He spoke when all kept silent, including so many who had the duty to speak out."[31] Other religious leaders are recognized in the book:

> It is fair to also remember other human rights fighters like the Methodist bishops Carlos Gattinoni and Federico Pagura and the Rabbi Marshal Meyer, who lobbied and risked their lives for us, although they were allowed just to visit us individually. And perhaps some other humble priest or pastor whose memory, unfairly we have not kept.[32]

The courageous presence of Rabbi Meyer is also recorded in *Nosotras*. In Villa Devoto too, he was only allowed to visit some individuals. On the other hand, the official representative of the Catholic church, Father Bellavigna, would spend long hours trying to break the prisoners' spirits. Horacio Verbitsky—arguably Argentina's most important investigative journalist—published the first exposé of Bellavigna in an article he titled "San Fachón." Verbitsky—who has written extensively about the complicity of Church and dictatorship—is today the most visible critic of Pope Francis's role in the 1970s. The journalist reports in a newspaper article that the coup leader, General Videla, revealed in interviews conducted in prison "that the former papal nuncio Pio Laghi, the former president of the Argentine Catholic Church Raul Primatesta, and other bishops . . . advised his government on the way to handle the situation of the disappeared people in captivity." Verbitsky writes, "According to Videla, the Church 'offered its good services.'"[33] With the exception of a few persecuted and isolated bishops, high officials within the Argentine Catholic Church supported a government that is currently facing serious legal actions for kidnapping, disappearing, and appropriating dissidents' children and newborns.[34] Over 100 infants have been recovered by human rights advocates under the Grandmothers of Plaza de Mayo's leadership.

In a recent effort to locate the estimated 400 still missing, the organization's president, Estela Barnes de Carlotto, met with Pope Francis. She asked him to open "the Vatican archives, those of the Argentine church and those of communities like the Movimiento Familiar Cristiano (Christian Family Movement) where nuns received children from the [hands of the] dictatorship and gave them into adoption." After the meeting, Carlotto reported to the newspaper *Crónica* to be happy and moved by his words: "Cuenten conmigo" (Count on me).[35]

This is significant, since a serious accusation against Pope Francis is that he denied in court any knowledge of children's kidnappings during the dictatorship, although Grandmother of Plaza de Mayo Alicia de la Cuadra had personally begged him back in 1977 to help her find her granddaughter born in a concentration camp. In 1988, Emilio Mignone, a lawyer whose daughter was a disappeared catechist, published a book detailing the complicity of the church with the dictatorship and documenting the disappearances and assassinations of those involved in the Liberation Theology Movement.[36] Mignone reported how priests, nuns, and lay people who were involved in the Christian Base Communities were targeted for disappearance, torture, and assassination. The political persecution did not spare bishops like Monsignor Angelelli.[37]

Unfortunately, then Pope Paul VI did not challenge the dictatorship, not even to protect his own bishops. A tongue-in-cheek reference in *Del otro lado de la mirilla* alludes to the lack of papal support for the political prisoners: "I am in my 97th day without outdoor recess and I don't know when I will step foot on the prison yard dust. So many are my faults, the last one to throw bread crumbs to the pigeons, that if the Pope does not send his amnesty, I don't know when I'll leave [this cell]."[38]

Human rights organizations as well as our own relatives persistently knocked at the doors of the powerful in the Catholic Church, who as reported in the controversy surrounding Pope Francis, were at times sympathetic and at times cruel. The language used by a dictatorship that justified genocide by calling dissidents "subversive," "terrorists," or "rebellious," was often mimicked by religious leaders. Another author of the Coronda narrative, Guillermo Daniel Martini, reports:

> What is true is the direct correlation between political "subversive" activism and a previous participation in Christian Base Communities, or the experience many of us had in groups connected to the post-conciliar church. The second aspect, the alliance military dictatorship and fascist ecclesiastic sectors, is obvious and widely recognized.[39]

Because the Coronda prisoners were literally blessed by the presence of Zazpe and other courageous pastors and priests, their book pays constant tribute to their solidarity. Chapter 13, strategically placed toward the center of the book, is devoted to prison chaplain Father Guillermo Exner. He had been removed by the authorities shortly after the 1976 coup. Today he is described as "more worried about the present than about the past, active despite his age, and very involved in current events . . . the suffering of his people."[40] Father Exner tells the interviewers:

> One of the things I really have admired in many is this, for example, those who suffered a lot in prison know whom they should talk to, and they talk to them, and they are normal people . . . It is fair to remember so history does not repeat itself; we are living the history of salvation . . .[41]

This interview's focus on solidarity back then and today, Father Exner's remarks about the former political prisoners, and the fact that the Coronda authors disseminate their memories to teach new generations, illustrate what Gottfried Bloch discusses in his book *Unfree Associations*. Bloch, a psychoanalyst and Holocaust survivor, describes how his experiences in a concentration camp have returned to his memory in a painful, overpowering way, "intruding into present joy . . . magnifying (his) anxieties of tomorrow . . ." He calls them "unfree" associations.[42] He then turns to Heinz Kohut's definition of "the time axis" as the subjective inner sense of the continuity of time within a person's life. He further elaborates:

> Reestablishing such continuity after the kind of traumatic fragmentation I experienced was an important part of my return to a fulfilling life. The continuity of the time axis from its roots in the past connects to the future and relates to fulfilling one's earlier goals. Writing this book has for me completed the reparatory process begun in my analysis thirty years ago.[43]

Bloch's words and journey will undoubtedly resonate with the Coronda authors. We can see the healing continuity of the time axis when the collective voice in their book shares that Steinbeck's novel *East of Eden* "played . . . a decisive role in the preservation of my mental health."[44] He goes on by stating in the present tense a central concept in Steinbeck's work, "undoubtedly we choose every day to be or not to be Cain. To oppress, assassinate or not, our brother."[45] The authors of *Del otro lado de la mirilla* keep choosing solidarity over destruction, and the book abounds in accounts that illustrate their quest. As Peter Admirand reminds us: "To depict only violence and meaninglessness, or focus only on 'wretched' humanity, is to paint an incomplete picture of our world. [Liberation theologian Jon] Sobrino aptly encapsulates this idea with his term 'primordial holiness.' Where many only see exploitation and misery, he points to life and hope."[46]

The Coronda narrative is published and disseminated by a nonprofit organization created by the former prisoners called Asociación Civil El Periscopio. The periscope was indeed a strong symbol of resistance inside the prison, as they share in a radio interview after the book's publication:

> The periscope was our great combat weapon . . . Facing a very hard reality of isolation, much perversion, where they tried to push a person into his most intimate corner, let us say, to bring him closer to mental insanity . . . we had to confront that with what we had, and that meant we had to do something in our cell, to be able to sing, to talk to the compañero in the next cell, to do some gymnastics, to comment about a book, a movie. Then, for that we needed some kind of instrument to detect the guards when they walked into the cellblock.[47]

Former prisoner Ricardo Rivero describes that instrument in the same interview, later transcribed by Miguel Espinaco and published in the blog of another editorial group member, Jorge Pedraza:

> . . . that little device was a tiny mirror held with some bread crumbs . . . to be in turn held by a little stick, something like that . . . we would slide it under the door

of the cell to watch if any prison personnel walked into the cell block . . . it was used like a periscope in a submarine . . .[48]

This so-called combat weapon that by happy coincidence was initially devised by movable-type printing inventor Johannes Gutenberg, joins several other resistance tools in the former prisoners' "arsenal." To help us deal with horror and pain, humor and laughter are also precious instruments for survivors. As a recently published prison anthology from Argentina proclaims in its title: "Laughter does not surrender itself." In their foreword, María Eva Cangiani and Martina Noailles state, "Laughter is liberation because it can make power lose, even when just for a short moment, its function as the manager of fear."[49]

Former Villa Devoto prisoner María Claro, a major force behind the publication of *La risa no se rinde*, gave me the book in June 2013, when a second Spanish edition of *The Little School*—one tailored to be taught in schools—was presented at an event in Argentina's national senate building. In the back cover of "Laughter does not surrender itself," these words are inscribed:

Laughter was one of the main resistance tools for thousands of political prisoners, both "legally" arrested or kidnapped, for the persecuted, exiled, and political activists during the past military dictatorship . . . humor is a fundamental tool in the fight for a better world.[50]

Meanwhile, the former Coronda prisoners continue to disseminate their work and, as they announce in the last paragraph of their book:

The prison walls cry and we laugh . . . simply because we keep walking. [We keep] traveling the narrow surface of the road, in transit between those two worlds, like a symbol that would like to remind us that our journey takes place in the fragile border between life and death, between Coronda and freedom.[51]

They (and perhaps we) feel and act like Jorge Semprún, the Holocaust survivor and Spanish resistance fighter who was a strong inspiration for the Coronda book. In *Literature or Life* Semprún remembers his reaction after his liberation from Buchenwald: "I'm laughing, laughing to find myself alive."[52]

Author's note

My gratitude to former Coronda prisoners Daniel Mansilla y Bas, José Luis Hisi Páez, José Cettour, Jorge Daniel Pedraza, Guillermo Daniel Martini, and others who gave me invaluable information on their collective writing process. I would like to thank Loyola Marymount University for a grant that facilitated this research, and Professor Jennifer Abe, who introduced me to the work of Father Martín-Baró.

2

Classicide in Communist China: A Laogai Survivor's Reflection

Harry Wu

Although excited by the opportunity to share my perspective, I felt slightly apprehensive when I received the request for me to write a chapter for *Loss and Hope*. Owing to the fact that I had been sentenced to life in the laogai (reform through labor camps) after graduating from the geology department of Beijing Geology College in 1960, I had spent much of my adulthood far removed from the demands of academic writing. In fact, during the 19 years I spent in the labor camp, I had virtually no access to pens, papers, or books. The only books that I owned as a prisoner, among them *Les Misérables*, were taken from me in 1966. Prison guards subsequently burned these books in front of me and then beat me until my left arm was broken. From this time until 1979, the year I was released from the laogai, I was totally cut off from all books. Life in the camps was an animal life. Lying, cheating, stealing to survive, I had no morality or sense of social responsibility. I forgot about God.

I spent the winter of 1961–1962 in starvation. An 80-pound skeleton, I spent all day lying in my camp barracks half asleep. Total lack of energy caused my brain to almost stop functioning.

Many memories haunt me. I still feel guilty about accidentally killing my friend Chen Ming. After it happened, I prayed to God for the first time since my childhood. "Who can help me?" I asked. "If I have been bad, then I deserve to die in the Laogai. But I don't think every prisoner here is bad." I yelled to God: "God, why don't you help them? Are you sure you exist? Are you sure you are almighty?" Some answers are not in books.

Nevertheless, because of my limited access to educational materials during these years of intense struggle, I felt somewhat unprepared to write a paper for an academic publication. Although I have since worked at venerable institutions, spent countless hours researching the laogai system and received several honorary PhDs, my background differs significantly from those who have earned a PhD in their respective fields. Nevertheless, I think that my first-hand account of life in a laogai could help advance understanding of this pressing issue in academic circles.

A new vocabulary

In 1993, a *Washington Post* reporter asked me: "What do you want to do?"

I said: "I want to see the word 'LAOGAI' in every dictionary. I want to see the laogai system ended."

Since this interview over 20 years ago, I have often wondered why the word "gulag" is widely understood to refer to the Soviet labor camp system, while the word "laogai" remains largely unfamiliar to the educated public. Does China not have a repressive communist government? Has China not tortured and murdered its own people? I am unable to think of a compelling explanation for this gap in understanding.

Laogai is a normal word in China. Millions of people have been incarcerated in the laogai, and the system continues today. People use this word instead of jail or prison. Everyone understands that this word refers to the Communist Party's prison system, which is designed to control people by using so-called reform through labor.

In addition to the word "laogai," I am perplexed as to why the word "classicide" is not a part of the popular lexicon. In fact, after years of reflection, I think it is equally necessary to add the word "classicide" to standard dictionaries. Moreover, as the operation of the laogai camps served as a primary means through which the Party conducted its classicide, an understanding of this campaign of systematic persecution is essential to comprehending the legacy of the laogai.

The roots of the practice of classicide in China trace back to Mao's lie that his Communist Revolution would save lives and make everyone rich. In order to achieve this goal, Mao asserted that China would first have to abolish two classes: the landlord class and the capitalist class. The resulting violent purges ended in the deaths of millions. Subsequent Maoist policies caused the deaths of an estimated 65 million Chinese people during peacetime. In light of the scale of suffering inflicted during communist purges, we should recognize Mao's systematic persecution of "class enemies" in the same way that we acknowledge Hitler's genocidal persecution of the Jews.

The roots of China's classicide

In order to consolidate power, Mao Zedong implemented a nation-wide ideology aimed at eradicating those who previously held power in China. According to this theory, society is composed of different classes of people who can be divided into two major groups: the exploiting class and the exploited. Mao delineated these two groups so that he could more clearly classify those who held power in pre-Communist China, members of the so-called exploiting class. In order to identify such people, Mao launched a political campaign to determine each person's political and social status. This campaign entailed determining an individual's class status based on the amount of land owned, capital controlled, property held, and income earned (as well as the situation of their family members). Everyone was subsequently designated as a member of the landlord class, the capitalist class, the rich peasant class, the middle peasant class, or the poor worker and peasant classes.

The poor classes were praised for their humble way of life and work ethic. As such, they willingly supported the Communist Party. Meanwhile, the landowners and capital owners—the wealthy, the intellectual elite, and the remnants of Chiang Kai-shek's Nationalist government—were demonized and persecuted as "black classes." Not only did the government seize their property, they were also sent to perform the most difficult and dangerous manual labor in the countryside. Some of these people were beaten to death during various political movements, and many were sent to the laogai.

The Communist Party proclaimed that "class struggle" was necessary for promoting social development and that the ensuing violence was necessary to establish a proletarian socialist state. There were around 20 million members of the landlord and rich peasant and capitalist classes nationwide in 1949. By the end of the 1970s, when the Cultural Revolution had ended, less than 10 percent of this class remained.

"Rightists" and "Black Classes" under Mao

I was sent to the laogai as a result of my background and comments I made at a student political meeting held at my university. Specifically, I criticized the Soviet suppression in Budapest in 1956 and disagreed with the Communist Party members' treatment of common people as second-class citizens. The fact that I was a Catholic in a country that frowned upon religion, Christianity in particular, provided additional justification for my persecution. In the end, authorities labeled me "bourgeoisie-counterrevolutionary-rightist" and sentenced me to the laogai in 1960.

Mao Zedong had stipulated that 10 percent of intellectuals must be "Rightists," which meant that at least two people in my university class had to wear this label. Conveniently, only two others among the 30 students had a negative class background like mine. Unfortunately for my fellow classmates and citizens who were members of the "black classes," a group that managed to avoid persecution during this "Anti-Rightist" campaign, Mao targeted the rest of the exploiting class during the horrors of the Cultural Revolution.

Persecution of the "black classes" raged throughout the Cultural Revolution. On August 18, 1966 in Beijing, Mao Zedong unleashed the Cultural Revolution when he directly called on the "Red Guards" to "make revolution." Under Mao Zedong's direction, the Red Guards incited violence and social chaos. These soldiers of the revolution, mainly comprised of Chinese youth, terrorized class enemies while waving a book titled "Revolutionary Quotations of Mao Zedong." Although this campaign began in schools, it quickly spread to the streets, where these bands of angry youths annihilated "class enemies," the remaining members of the exploiting class. In 1966, from August 18 to the end of September 1, 714 of the "five black elements" were beaten to death. However, there are no statistics indicating how many were ultimately killed or injured, how much property was confiscated, or how many were sent off to the laogai. This kind of annihilation was carried out throughout the country.

Only in the 1980s did the Chinese Communist Party (CCP) make new policies removing "hats," the term for the labels given to different classes of society. This change, however, came too late; nearly all members of the landlord and rich peasant classes in the countryside had been exterminated during the preceding 30 years. To this day, no one has been put on trial for these atrocities.

Classicide as a legacy of the Chinese Communist Party

Since the establishment of the People's Republic of China (PRC) in 1949, China has known only one form of government: the authoritarian communism of Mao. Although China has undergone thirty-some years of major social and economic transformation, the fundamental system of dictatorship established by Mao has not changed. Why is this? I propose that it is because China's communist leaders are deeply afraid of relinquishing power. As notions of freedom, democracy, and human rights are antithetical to their one-party dictatorship, they see meaningful political reform as a threat to their monopoly on power.

The Party of Xi Jinping, Hu Jintao, Jiang Zeming, and Deng Xiaoping is the Party of Mao Zedong. We cannot just forget the crimes committed against humanity over the course of its 64-year history. The world rightfully remembers the horrors of the Holocaust, where around 12 million were murdered by the Nazis, including 6 million Jewish people. Many in the West, however, do not realize that systematic persecution took place on an even greater scale in the People's Republic of China. Under Mao's reign, scholars estimate that 65 million people died of unnatural causes—many of whom were killed because of their class background.

"Genocide," as defined by the United Nations, "involves acts committed with the intent to destroy a national, ethnic, racial or religious group." Importantly, acts of genocide are not limited to killing. Rather, genocide also encompasses mental harm and restrictions on people's rights and freedoms. Although the victims of Mao's purges were targeted for their class background, the brutal and widespread persecution they endured deserves the same degree of international recognition accorded to victims of genocide. Moreover, considering that the political party that perpetrated this classicide continues to govern China, it is imperative that we acknowledge these horrific crimes. Hopefully, increased international recognition will prompt the Chinese people to directly confront the harsh truths of the past, the reality of the present, and the prospects for change in the future.

The laogai as a machinery of Chinese repression

Tyrannical governments require a system of suppression to maintain power. Hitler had the concentration camps and Stalin had the gulag. Similarly, since the dawn of the PRC, Chinese authorities have never hesitated to use forced labor prison camps in their efforts to maintain political control. As noted above, in China, they are called the "laogai," the literal translation of which is "reform through labor." Over time, this word has come to stand for the regime's vast system of politically imposed slavery. Laogai forced labor prisons continue to serve as a vital tool in the Party's efforts to eliminate political opposition.

Mao and subsequent CCP leaders demanded that the laogai produce two kinds of "products": first, the prisoner himself—the "reformed socialist person." This extermination of "thought" is possibly the greatest invention of the CCP. The second kind of product refers to the agricultural, industrial, and consumer goods needed to fuel the nation's economy. "Thought reform," as CCP officials say, is: "the use of forced labor to reform the thinking of criminals and transform them into self-dependent, socialist new men." This is brainwashing! The CCP wants all prisoners, from thieves and murderers to political and religious "criminals," to abandon their political or religious beliefs, reform their "incorrect" social views, and live life according to communist rule. They must either learn to support the Party while in prison or never gain release. Should they dare to voice any public criticisms of the government, they could find themselves locked in prison again.

Remembering the past for the sake of the future

Many Western academics choose to ignore the significance of the laogai, even though it has existed for more than 60 years. The Laogai Research Foundation estimates that since 1949, almost 40–50 million people have been thrown into the laogai. However, all information related to the laogai is treated as a state secret, which means no outsiders know the true number of victims who have suffered under this brutal system.

Ignoring the laogai, however, could have devastating effects. Just as China's economy is now booming, Germany's economy expanded by 73 percent from 1933 to 1937, and most Germans then agreed with Hitler's policies. Meanwhile, foreign businessmen cooperated with German companies. No nation saw any reason to boycott the 1936 Olympic Games in Berlin. Not until 1939, when Germany invaded Poland, did the world realize Hitler's intent. Further, only when people were liberated from the concentration camps did the world begin to fully understand the scale of this atrocity.

Thankfully, we have witnessed the end of the regimes of Hitler and Stalin. In China, however, the world's most extensive system of forced labor camps persists. We cannot condemn the atrocities committed in the camps of Hitler and Stalin and ignore the continuing brutality of the laogai. The United States never dreamed of doing business with the Soviet Union during the Cold War, especially in the fields of science and technology. Yet, business with China is ever increasing, even as the rising global power becomes a major security threat to the United States and other democratic nations.

Capitalism is growing widely and rapidly in China today. In 1978, Deng Xiaoping put aside the communist economic ideology in favor of adopting a capitalist system. However, this was never intended to resemble Western capitalism; it is capitalism under the limitations of a one-party state. As the government controls the land and the market, this market-friendly "communist" regime is not bad for business. Meanwhile, cooperation with foreign companies is at an all-time high and the economy's growth rate is holding strong. Unfortunately, the leadership in Beijing is not only using this money to strengthen its control over the Chinese people, but it is also giving China unmatched bargaining power in its foreign relations.

We now know that capitalism does not automatically give rise to democracy and freedom. In today's China, those with wealth are largely those with political power. Conveniently, the flag of "class struggle" is no longer raised. Having eliminated a large portion of the nation's intellectuals and capitalists, Communist Party members and their offspring have filled the void created by decades of slaughter. Moreover, class divisions in Chinese society have become increasingly apparent. The working class, held up on a high pedestal throughout Mao's reign, is in fact struggling to get by as Chinese government officials get rich from corrupt business deals. Ironically, this new China has been built upon ideals ostensibly detested by Mao Zedong.

Conclusion: Hope

When I was released from the laogai, I went from a small cage into a big cage. I was still monitored, and the stigma of being a former prisoner restricted my social and professional opportunities. It was only when I moved to California that I felt truly free, even though I slept on the street at first. I was truly happy—homeless but free.

I used to walk around San Francisco, going to bookstores. I bought my old favorites, including *Les Misérables* and *A Tale of Two Cities*. I would go to the Catholic churches, too, where some of the priests were Chinese. I spoke with them but didn't tell them my story. In those churches I knelt down and prayed. I was free but I remembered that China was not.

Years later, in 1998, when I was 61 years old, my son was born, I called up Ethel Kennedy, the widow of Bobby Kennedy, and her priest baptized him. I thought I would never have children. He is a gift from God. But my work continues.

China's new leader, Xi Jinping, will not change the existing political system. Have we ever heard Deng Xiaoping, Jiang Zemin, or Hu Jintao publicly condemn Mao Zedong, who died back in 1976? No, because China is not a "former" communist country. Modern China remains under the firm control of the Chinese Communist Party. Although the Party has enacted market reforms, its core ideology is incompatible with freedom and democracy. The continued persecution of political activists and the recent tide of Tibetan self-immolations clearly demonstrate that there has been no meaningful improvement of freedom of expression, assembly, or religion. In fact, the situation is getting worse.

The PRC is now facing an enormous political, ideological, social, and economic crisis. At this critical moment, the people of the world, and particularly the Chinese people, must realize that if China wants to become a free, democratic, and prosperous nation, it must have a clear understanding of its own dark history. Such collective reflection is necessary in order to ensure that we do not repeat the violence of the past. Only after learning from history can Chinese people know what must be rebuilt; only then can they know how to move forward.

The Politics of Representations of Mass Atrocity in Sri Lanka and Human Rights Discourse: Challenges to Justice and Recovery

Jude Lal Fernando

Introduction

Within the legal framework of international law, the representation of mass atrocity is expressed through the categories of war crimes, crimes against humanity, and genocide. However, these conceptual categories are applied within particular political and ideological fields that must be critiqued in order to reach an inclusive representation of truth about mass atrocity. The focus of this chapter will be on the representations of mass atrocity in Sri Lanka and will demonstrate that ideology has determined how truth is perceived and how justice and recovery are envisaged. Approaching this task through a hermeneutic of suspicion allows a more accurate representation to emerge within the political imagination and indicates more comprehensive justice and recovery measures to be pursued.

Death beyond reckoning . . .

According to United Nations (UN) sources, at least 40,000 Tamil civilians were killed in the final phase of the war, lasting just four months (January through May of 2009).[1] Giving testimony at the Government of Sri Lanka (GoSL)-appointed Lessons Learnt and Reconciliation Commission (LLRC) on January 11, 2011, the Bishop of Manner revealed that there are still 146,679 Tamils unaccounted for, a figure he arrived at by analyzing official data issued by the GoSL.[2]

How can the truth about such shocking loss of life, such a staggering number of deaths, best be represented in the political imagination? International law provides conceptual and legal categories, including war crimes, crimes against humanity, genocide, and crimes against peace. The representation of mass atrocity in Sri Lanka within these categories will determine what measures are deemed necessary in terms of justice and recovery.

Is it a war crime?

The three-member UN panel report on Sri Lanka, Human Rights Watch, and the International Crisis Group represent the mass killings of Tamil civilians in the last phase of the conflict as possible war crimes. The United States/United Kingdom/ European Union (EU) also seem to follow the same line of thinking calling for war crimes investigations.

The discourse on "war crimes" in the specific case of Sri Lanka has several distinguishing features:

1. The war is considered an internal armed conflict.
2. Individual rights are prioritized, and limits to the acceptable use of violence are imposed.
3. Emphasis is laid on the culpability of both sides (Human Rights Watch justified the banning of the Liberation Tigers of Tamil Eelam (LTTE) by the EU on the same grounds).[3]
4. The discourse accepts the right of the Sri Lankan state to defend itself and upholds the unitary character of the state (the political field).
5. All forms of nationalism are considered negative.[4]

With the discourse on war crimes in Sri Lanka circumscribed by these ideological markers, it is inevitable that the scope for justice would also be similarly limited. Emphasis is thus laid on the reinforcement of the rule of law and the punishment of perpetrators. While these are important steps to overcome impunity, these do not address the root causes of the conflict. Within this paradigm, recovery becomes an undefined political solution for the victims (Tamils) under the existing unitary state structure. This type of a solution emerges from the inadequacy of the discourse on war crimes that reduces the truth about mass atrocity in Sri Lanka to a breakdown of law and order. Such an approach severely lacks a historical perspective of the conflict in that there is an inability even to call into question the unitary state structure and its ideology that have given rise to the conflict. This approach more or less represents the rationale behind the findings and recommendations of the Sri Lankan government-appointed LLRC report that considers the Sri Lankan state structure as an unchangeable entity and legitimizes war to protect its sovereignty. The difference between the LLRC report and the findings of the other international human rights groups mentioned above is that the latter accuses both parties of war crimes, whereas the former treats violations of human rights by the government security forces as individual and isolated events that do not have a relationship with the chain of command. In this sense what does the discourse on war crimes really mean? It means that war is legitimate to protect the unitary state, but war crimes are not legitimate!

Is it a crime against humanity?

Although the organizations mentioned above do not use the term "crime against humanity," Amnesty International does. The People's Tribunal on Sri Lanka (PTSL or

Dublin Tribunal), held in January 2010, used both terms.[5] In this context, a crime against humanity refers not only to unjustified murder within an armed conflict, but also a crime that has been perpetrated within a widespread or systematic attack directed against a civilian population with knowledge of its outcome. Even though the *material element* is the same, the *mental element,* or the *intent,* differs when considering a crime against humanity, as opposed to a war crime. Michaela Frulli states: "As to the mental element of murder as a war crime, it consists in the intent to kill one or more persons, while the mental element of murder as a crime against humanity not only includes the intent to cause someone's death, but also the knowledge of being part of a widespread and systematic attack on any civilian population."[6]

The Dublin Tribunal asserted that the Sri Lankan conflict was primarily a war against the Tamil people, and pointed "to the full responsibility" of international actors in "providing political endorsement of the conduct of the Sri Lankan government within the context of the 'Global War against Terror.'"[7] By using the words "Tamil people" in its report, the Dublin Tribunal recognized the collective identity of the principle victims, while holding the GoSL mainly culpable for the crimes. Additionally, by going beyond a single-state lens, the excessive internationalization of the Sri Lankan conflict is also acknowledged. The Dublin Tribunal refrains from naming the mass killings as genocide, but recommends further investigation.

How does the discourse on crimes against humanity inform justice and recovery? The Dublin Tribunal sees justice and recovery as a release of political prisoners, addressing the needs of refugees, postwar rehabilitation, and a power-sharing political solution. It also recommends an authoritative Truth and Justice Commission for Sri Lanka (avoiding the word reconciliation), and an independent international commission to investigate the responsibility of the international community in contributing to the breakdown of the 2002 peace process and commencement of war in 2006.[8] Even though some of its recommendations for deliverance of justice and recovery overlap with those of the discourse on war crimes, the Tribunal's approach to mass atrocity in Sri Lanka differs in critical details. The Dublin Tribunal upholds that international humanitarian law was promulgated to protect citizens from their state and lays emphasis on the culpability of the GoSL.[9] It also exposes the complicity of the United States/United Kingdom/EU in supporting the GoSL. The Dublin Tribunal is not legally binding, but it is morally binding, creating a space for an improved political representation of truth and justice.

However, the legal categories of war crimes and crimes against humanity have been applied to Sri Lanka without a historical analysis of the conflict. There is no exploration of the nature of narratives and stories that shape the two main public discourses of the conflict: Sinhala Buddhist nationalism (ethno-religious) and Tamil nationalism (ethno-secular). Even though these legal categories are necessary as preliminary steps to understand mass atrocity in Sri Lanka, they do not sufficiently represent the scope of the conflict, and consequently negatively impact the delivery of justice and processes of recovery. It is therefore necessary to approach political imagination of mass atrocities in Sri Lanka with a historical perspective. This means to recover truth from the perspective of the victims and their resistance to historical oppression as a distinct national group.

Is it genocide?

According to Raphael Lemkin, genocide refers to "the destruction of a nation or of an ethnic group . . . Generally speaking, genocide does not necessarily mean the immediate destruction of a nation, except when accomplished by mass killings of all members of a nation . . . . It is intended rather to signify a coordinated plan of different actions aiming at the destruction of essential foundations of the life of national groups . . ." (Raphael Lemkin, 1944). The UN Convention on Prevention and Punishment of the Crime of Genocide (1948) further clarifies that such actions may be directed at the target group "in whole or in part." The definition of genocide therefore lays emphasis on the *collective identity* of a population and a *coordinated plan of actions* to eliminate them *in whole or in part*. The second session of the Dublin Tribunal, which was held in Bremen in December 2013 (Bremen Tribunal), not only named the mass atrocity a genocide that reached its climax in 2009, but also recognized genocide against Tamils as an ongoing historical process.

The staggering numbers of civilian victims in the Sri Lankan conflict were not only individuals possessing individual rights, but also a distinct group of people with a particular collective identity who possessed collective rights as such. By analyzing the *intent* and *actions* of the GoSL during the war within a historical perspective, the genocidal process carried out against the Tamil people becomes evident. A *coordinated and systematic plan* elaborated through *a series of policy statements, orders, and actions* materializes from the historical backdrop. The primary focus until this point has been on the last phase of the war (January through May 2009). However, in situating the element of *intent* within a historical context, four main periods of the Sri Lankan conflict emerge, without which the genocidal intent of the last phase of war remains obscured.

1. The colonial period (until 1948): The Sri Lankan state was built by the British colonial rulers with a unitary state structure that established the rule of the Sinhala majority. This is the beginning of racism in Sri Lanka, informed by the Indo-European Aryan myth of racial superiority over Tamil and Dravidian cultures.[10]
2. The postcolonial phase (1948–1970s): All postindependence governments have reinforced the unitary state structure and its Sinhala Buddhist ideology (the majoritarian ideology), promoting cultural homogenization throughout the entire island through the apparatus of the centralized state structure. Citizenship rights of Tamil plantation workers were abolished. Sinhala was declared the only official language, and Sinhala settlements were built in Tamil areas as state-sponsored colonies. During these 30 years, Tamil resistance embraced Gandhi's methods, yet nonviolent protests were brutally attacked by racist Sinhala groups as well as state armed forces. Nevertheless, no one was brought to justice, although over 500 Tamils were killed as a result of racial attacks.
3. The era of GoSL–LTTE military conflict (1970s–2002): In the first 30 years of the postcolonial phase, the primary demand of the Tamil resistance was that the Tamils should be incorporated into the state structure as equals. However, as a result of the suppression of the Tamil movement for equal rights as shown above, in the 1970s, a militant nationalist movement evolved under the leadership of the LTTE.

July 1983 marked a turning point in which, according to official figures, over 3,000 Tamils were massacred by racist Sinhala groups with the support of the security forces, police, government officials, and ministers. According to the *British Medical Journal*, at least 215,000 people, mostly Tamils, have been killed in war until 2002.[11] Different estimates suggest that over 1.5 million people have been displaced.

4. The ceasefire period (2002–2006): The Ceasefire Agreement and peace process between the GoSL and the LTTE came into effect as a result of a balance of power being reached between the two parties in conflict. The last phase of the war began in October 2006, leading to another round of shocking violence, characterized by staggering numbers of civilian casualties.

Although *intent* may be seen as an individual psychological state, the dominant *public discourse* connects the individual to the collective *intent*. The *public discourse* of the local agent or perpetrator (as there are also international ones) of mass atrocity in Sri Lanka, that is the Sri Lankan government, is Sinhala Buddhist nationalism, which upholds the unitary character of the state and espouses cultural homogenization. The *motive* behind the *intent* to destroy the Tamil ethnic and national group in part was to protect the unitary state and its Sinhala Buddhist ideology. In this sense, the *motive* underlying the *public discourse* corroborates the genocidal *intent* of the Sri Lankan government.

Motivation and Intent in historical perspective

In the colonial period

Anagarika Dharmapala, the founding father of Sinhala Buddhist nationalism, instigated anti-minority sentiments and riots in the 1910s. The following is an excerpt from a letter he wrote to the colonial government in 1915, opposing the arrests of Sinhala leaders who led anti-Muslim riots: "The British officials may shoot, hang, quarter, imprison or do anything to the Sinhalese but there will always be bad blood between the Moors and the Sinhalese. . . but my loyalty to the British Throne is as solid as a rock . . ."[12]

During the 1930s, the leading Sinhala labor leader, A. E. Gunasinghe, was addressed as a lion by his party. Its official paper resembled the spirit of Hitler's racist ideology, emphasizing the need to keep "Sinhala blood pure" by "avoiding mixed marriages."[13] While in Germany, anti-Semitism was promoted in defense of the "German Aryan race"; in Sri Lanka, anti-Dravidianism was ideologized in defense of the "Sinhala Aryan race." The racialized interpretation of Sinhala identity was reinforced particularly among the working class, resulting in attacks on South Indian migrant workers during the Great Depression.

According to a speech given in 1939 by D. S. Senanayake, who is considered to be the "father of the nation," and who became the first prime minister after independence in 1948: "We are one blood and one nation. We are a chosen people. The Buddha said that his religion would last 5500 years. That means that we, as the custodians of that religion, shall last long."[14]

S. W. R. D. Bandaranaike, who as prime minister in 1956 would declare Sinhala the only official language of the state, made the following statement in 1939: "I am prepared to sacrifice my life for the sake of my community, the Sinhalese. If anybody were to try to hinder our progress, I am determined to see that he is taught a lesson he will never forget."[15]

The era of postcolonial nation-building

The nation-building process was marked with anti-Tamil riots. Most of these riots were instigated with the aim of counteracting the nonviolent demonstrations of the Tamils against discriminatory measures. The following are representative examples of remarks made by Sinhala members of parliament in 1958 after an anti-Tamil riot:

1. "The Tamils will destroy us eventually. Before that happens, I ask that the Tamils be settled once for all"—Pani Illangakoon.[16]
2. "The Tamils are gaining strength in all parts of the country where they are. The Sinhalese are in danger of being liquidated by them"—Sagara Palansuriya.
3. "Destroy them"—Lakshman Rajapakshe.[17]

The era of GoSL–LTTE military conflict

As the Tamil resistance turned militant, articulating a separatist agenda, the first executive president of Sri Lanka, J. R. Jayawardene (1978–1988), stated: "I am not worried about the opinion of the Jaffna people . . . now we cannot think of them, not about their lives or their opinion . . . the more you put pressure in the north, the happier the Sinhala people will be here. . . Really if I starve the Tamils out, the Sinhala people will be happy."[18]

The following statement of the Minister for National Security (1982–1988), who commanded military operations in the Tamil region, reveals the intent of eliminating one of the foundations of the collective identity of the Tamils. "The only way to root out terrorism was to remove the concept of 'traditional homelands (of the Tamils)'"—Lalith Athulathmudali (Vssubramaniam, March 12, 2010).

During this period, one of South Asia's oldest libraries, located in the Tamil region of Sri Lanka and possessing a large number of ancient Tamil manuscripts, was burnt by a group of Sinhalese, who were led by a government minister. The library was revered as the principal cultural symbol of Tamil collective life. During the same timeframe, 53 Tamil political prisoners were murdered by Sinhala prisoners, with the support of the prison guards. The following statement by another president reflects the racial ideology of those who led the Sri Lankan government in the 1980s and early 1990s: "Minorities are like creepers clinging to the Sinhala tree"—D. B. Wijetunge (Vssubramaniam, March 12, 2010).

In September 1998, while on an official trip to South Africa, Chandrika Kumaranatunga said in a television interview: "They (Tamils) want a separate state—a minority community which is not the original people of the country . . ."

The *motivating* Sinhala Buddhist ideology behind the systematic and well-coordinated genocidal *intent* does not reflect an unchangeable essentialist collective mindset among the Sinhalese. This mindset was primarily a historical construct of the British colonial practice that imposed a centralized state structure amalgamating diverse regions into one single administrative unit while propagating the myth of Aryan "superiority" against the Dravidian "inferiority."[19] Existing (precolonial) postcanonical Buddhist texts were translated and reinterpreted in such a way that the Sinhalese were made to believe that the entire island belongs to them and that it has been a centralized state from time immemorial and the others (mainly the Tamils) are "invaders."[20] In this sense, the British *motivation* behind such a construct was strategic as they treated the island of Lanka as a military location to rule India which was the "Jewel of the Crown."[21] In maintaining a strategic location, it was necessary to establish full political control over it and this was achieved by privileging the majority, the Sinhalese, who were in fact a minority in the Indian subcontinent as an ethnic group. This was also accompanied by the idea that, even as the British were colonizing, the Tamils were the invaders and that they "built nothing in Ceylon, but had destroyed what others had built."[22] All precolonial invasions were depicted as Tamil invasions despite the fact that all these were dynastic wars generated by a politics of succession based on conflicts among ruling castes and dynasties within the Indian subcontinent! These wars radically differ in their content and structure from modern national and international conflicts.

Despite the collective experience of historical suppression and repression, the Tamil national movement had transformed itself from a position of helpless victimhood to a collective assertion of nationhood and statehood, especially under the leadership of the LTTE, and created a de facto state in the North and East of the island. By 2002 it is this reality that had considerably weakened the force of the *public discourse* of Sinhala Buddhist nationalism—that emboldens the racist *intent*—as the government's military efforts brought about dire consequences to the country's economy. A negotiated political settlement was seen as the only way forward. The *motivation* and *intent* behind mass atrocities have to be analyzed within this historical perspective; 4 to 6 years after the signing of the 2002 ceasefire agreement (CFA), how did the political/military power of the *public discourse* increase and lead to the destruction of the de facto state of the Tamils killing a large number of its population who decided to live in that state? Did it happen spontaneously, totally as a result of irreconcilable racial stereotypes and local power dynamics as it is often depicted by some western diplomats, the mainstream media, human rights groups, and experts in conflict resolution? According to an analysis made by the International Crisis Group, it is the intransigence of the two main ethno-nationalist forces that have contributed to the intractability of the conflict: "Together the two competing ethnic nationalisms have sapped the ability of governments to develop a consensus for a negotiated settlement and power sharing."[23] Such analysis is based on a single-state perspective that does not recognize the geopolitical context of the conflict.

Last phase of the war . . .

The shocking violence and staggering numbers of victims from the last phase of war are neither the result of a historical accident, nor an isolated set of unfortunate events, neither collateral damage, nor a breakdown of law and order. They are not only the logical consequence of a historical process of eliminating the ethnic and national foundations of the Tamil people by successive Sri Lankan governments, but also a direct consequence of the dismantling of *the parity of esteem* accorded to both parties in the 2002 CFA and the peace process. This dismantling was first done by the United States/United Kingdom and later by the EU (as a result of the United States/United Kingdom pressure). The United States unilaterally decided to hold a key meeting of the peace process in Washington and thereby excluded the LTTE from the negotiating table in 2003. Furthermore, the United States' refusal to allocate funds to the joint tsunami mechanism in 2005 between the LTTE and the GoSL and the EU's ban on the LTTE in 2006 when the United Kingdom was holding the EU chair were crucial steps that were adopted by these major powers in dismantling the *parity of esteem* between the two parties. These steps increased the political power of the Sinhala Buddhist *public discourse* that underpins the existence of the Sri Lankan unitary state. The need to secure the unitary character of the Sri Lankan state has to be analyzed within the emerging geopolitical dynamics in South Asia. These dynamics are formed by two factors: the United States' interest in securitizing South Asia with the invasion of Afghanistan and Iraq, and the competition between China and the United States in forming strategic alliances with the region. India's growing relationship with the United States as opposed to China, and Sri Lanka's close ties with all these powers who support the unitary state, are part of geopolitical dynamics that determined the character of the Sri Lankan conflict.[24] The de facto state of the Tamils with conventional military power and a well-organized civil and political administration—in which over 500,000 Tamils had chosen to live by 2002—had not only weakened the unitary state and its supremacist ideology (*public discourse*), but also caused serious concerns among the above global powers whose main interest was to secure the unitary state structure. In actual effect, the outcome of the political, diplomatic, and military support given by these powers to the GoSL was the reinforcement of the Sinhala Buddhist *public discourse*. This mobilized the Sinhala society and polity toward war by emboldening its genocidal *intent*. This does not mean that the global powers want Sinhala Buddhist nationalism. The main interest was to achieve a territorially unified state with a single political authority.

It is also important to explore the power dynamics among the Western powers, mainly the EU and the United States/United Kingdom, which will throw light onto why the EU supported the peace process initially and why the position of the United States/United Kingdom has been ambiguous from the beginning. Analysis of the geo-strategic importance of the unitary state structure in Sri Lanka and power dynamics among global powers need further discussion that goes beyond the scope of this chapter.[25] However, in recovering the truth about mass atrocity in Sri Lanka, two fundamental questions should be raised: (1) Which comes first in orchestrating the last phase of the war against the Tamils?; and (2) Is it the specific *intent* of the GoSL or the strategic interest of the above global powers that dismantled *the parity of esteem* between the two parties?

Often, the last phase of the war is justified by the GoSL and its international allies as a counter-insurgency war, rationalized within the "global war on terror." They deny the charge of genocide due to the absence of a *specific intent* to destroy a distinct group of people. However, even without articulation of a *specific intent,* the *general intent* remains clear enough. A knowledge-based interpretation of intent[26] illuminates the psychological relationship between the perpetrator and the outcome of his/her actions. As it was argued in the case of Guatemala, could the intent be military (to destroy insurgents), not racist?[27] If the outcome of the massive attacks directed against the Tamil population could have been predicted with prior knowledge and with practicable certainty, such actions can constitute genocide. In other words, engaging in a coercive counter-insurgency war that deliberately terrorizes a civilian population through large-scale military attacks in order to resolve an ethno-nationalist conflict is genocidal in *intent*.

The following statements of Sri Lankan military and political leaders during the last phase of the war, which accompanied *coordinated plans* to attack the Tamil population, reflect both the specific and the general *intents*:

1. "I strongly believe that this country belongs to Sinhalese . . .We, who comprise 75% of the population, will never surrender ourselves. The right to defend the country lies in our hands. Minorities can live here. But they cannot make unjustifiable demands using the cover of being a minority"—Lt General Sarath Fonseka, Commander of the Sri Lankan Armed Forces (September 23, 2008—National Post, Canada).
2. "In any country the administrative powers should lie in the hands of the majority. We cannot prevent it. The majority should have the power in their hands. This country will be ruled by the Sinhalese who represent the 74% of the population"—Lt General Sarath Fonseka, Commander of the Sri Lanka Armed Forces (July 19, 2008, Daily News, Colombo, Sri Lanka).
3. "People who are trapped in Mullaithivu area are just the relatives of the Terrorists. They cannot be considered as civilians at all"—Government coalition partner JHU (Jathika Hela Urumaya—National Heritage Party) Press Conference (January 28, 2009, Colombo, Sri Lanka).
4. ". . . Anything that stands outside the designated safety zone, will be targeted. Be it a hospital, be it civilians, as long as it remains out of the 'no fire zone' it becomes a legitimate target. . . ."—Defense Secretary Gotabhaya Rajapaksa (February 2, 2009, Interview with "Sky News").

These statements clearly reflect knowledge regarding the destructive consequences of the GoSL's actions for the survival of the Tamil people. The UN report revealed that even the designated "safety zone" was heavily attacked.[28] In the aftermath of the war, in May 2009, the Sri Lankan president, Mahinda Rajapakshe, declared in his victory speech: "There are no minority or majority communities in Sri Lanka today. There are only patriots and traitors."

On the international level, in the last week of the war in May, on the same day, the Security Council, the EU, and the White House issued statements that clearly reflected their recognition of the GoSL as the legitimate authority in Sri Lanka. The Security Council and the EU went to the extent of stating that the GoSL has a "legitimate right" to "combat terrorism." The EU welcomed "the commitments" made by the GoSL to "assist" affected civilians. The US president urged the LTTE to lay down arms. After supporting the 2002 peace process at the initial phase—that made attempts to focus on issues of de-militarization, rehabilitation, resettlement, and power sharing—later the international community led by the above global powers clearly demonstrated its political will to support the GoSL and thereby destroyed the space for a negotiated settlement. This was legitimized by the rhetoric of the "global war on terror" and implemented by tactics of counter insurgency warfare that eventually caused the destruction of a large part of the Tamil population, their national foundations, and leadership. Therefore, in recovering truth about mass atrocity in Sri Lanka, it is of paramount importance to go beyond a single-state lens. There is a need to transnationalize truth and look for its international, political, and legal implications.

The geopolitics of genocide: A crime against peace

The *well-coordinated* attack directed against the Tamil people was carried out with the full knowledge of not only the Sri Lankan government, but also the international actors whose voices could be heard through the UN. To name genocide in Sri Lanka is not only legally, morally, and conceptually correct, but also captures the political imagination of the Tamil people who for decades have struggled against discrimination, oppression, and repression. Naming genocide not only has an emotional and symbolic value, but also a political value that seriously questions the ethical validity of the Sri Lankan unitary state structure and its international alliances. The war intentionally destroyed the national foundations of the Tamil people, created as a resistance to a racist ideology and power structure. The Sri Lankan government is culpable for the Tamil genocide, however, the international community, led by the above-mentioned powers, are complicit in it and share responsibility for it.

How would the role of the above powers be framed under international law? Does not its role constitute a crime against peace, which is committed by a war of aggression? In reality had this war of aggression not been orchestrated, the Tamil genocide would have been avoided. In this sense what comes first is the strategic interest rather than the genocidal intent. However, the global actors were aware that their support to the Sri Lankan state would result in genocidal massacres. Furthermore, any recognition given to the Tamils as a nation would destabilize the regional power balance in South Asia. Deliberate steps taken to dismantle the 2002 peace process and the recognition of the Sri Lankan state's right to engage in a war to protect its national boundaries—knowing that there were mass killings—make the global actors complicit in both the crime of genocide and crimes against peace.

Conclusion: Justice, recovery, and hope

What is the relationship between the concept of justice and naming mass atrocity as genocide? Naming genocide effectively establishes and consolidates the political and moral validity of the Tamil demand for self-determination and autonomy in their traditional homeland. However, this form of justice should not lead to an essentialist construction of Tamil versus Sinhala binary identities that will further polarize the two nationalities. Justice is a fruit of continuous, courageous resistance to a fundamentalist state ideology that does not tolerate diversity, equality, and interdependence. Such a fundamentalist ideology does not have perennial or primordial bindings that are unchanging; rather, it was historically constructed within the colonial period and reinforced by Sri Lankan nation-builders and their global allies. Only such a historical and nonessentialist (nonracist) perspective can support recovery in Sri Lanka. It is only by recognizing the Tamils as a nation that the path toward recovery can be opened.

What is the relationship between the concept of justice and crime against peace? The euphoria about the UN Human Right Council's annual sessions in 2012 and 2013 project Tamils as helpless victims and pretends to give them hope. The United States' support given to UNHRC's proposal (supported by India in 2013) for an accountability mechanism for Sri Lanka would not go beyond requesting GoSL to implement LLRC recommendation, which legitimized war to protect the state and reduced human rights violations to the "misbehavior" of individual soldiers. This has been clearly stated in a press conference statement made by Maria Otero, Undersecretary to the US State Department, and issued by the Public Diplomacy Office of the American Embassy in Colombo on February 13, 2012. The word used in the statement is "wartime abuses!" The above-mentioned human rights associations along with a number of international NGOs have issued a statement on February 17, appreciating the United States' call for action! In the aftermath of the war, the attempt made by the United States-led governments to reduce mass atrocity of a genocidal character to mere individual violations of human rights is a clear indication of an ongoing complicity.

It is not only clear that the international humanitarian law has not been applied to represent in a true sense (within a historical perspective) mass atrocities in Sri Lanka, but also that there is a deliberate attempt by the powers who are culpable for crimes against peace to conceal the truth and stifle justice and recovery. In a true sense what has been committed against the Tamils in Sri Lanka is a genocide and a crime against peace. It is also a crime against peace for the whole island whose peoples were attempting a negotiated settlement for different reasons through the 2002 peace process. In examining loss and recovery in Sri Lanka, a single-state lens is misleading. There is a need for a transnationalization of truth without which an independent international investigation would be meaningless. Who could lead such an international attempt? At the least, those countries who are less complicit in the mass atrocity should lead it. In practical terms, this demands a reorientation and a paradigm shift in international lobbying for human rights and a just-peace in Sri Lanka. Justice for crimes against peace could be achieved only by such a reorientation. Amidst traumatic memories of mass atrocities, hope can be found only by learning from history.

Torturing God at the Villa Grimaldi (Chile): Loss of Human Dignity, Hope of Unity

Mario I. Aguilar

In my previous work on postcolonial theology and genocide, I expressed, with sorrow and trepidation, the constancy and symbolic connections between the screams of those to be arrested and the silence of those who are to be tortured and killed.[1] Language, human or divine, does not and cannot express the moment in which a human being feels the absolute loneliness of fear and death and at the same time longs for the love, human and divine, that is absent in a place where she cannot communicate with others and only hears the shouts of the torturers and feels the pain of isolation.

The Senegalese novelist Diop has inscribed the silent daily practices of people who visit the remains of their relatives still unburied as follows:

> Loneliness was also the young woman in black who came almost every day to the polytechnic. She knew exactly which of all the tangled skeletons lying on the cold concrete were those of her little girl and her husband. She would go straight to one of the sixty-four doors of Murambi and stand in the middle of the room before two intertwined corpses: a man clutching a decapitated child against him. The young woman prayed in silence, and then left.[2]

In such places, human beings are separated from each other and reunited in silence; the tortured person does not need to explain; the person who loved them does not need to understand; and the God of love unites all of them in a world of higher values than that of the prison chamber. Silence becomes the means to cope with these horrible moments and later, shamefully later, silence about torture and humiliation by others remains a means to personal dignity until the psyche explodes and everything comes out. Then, narratives of torture and of tortured bodies become embarrassing. The tortured person returns to the world of silence and is able to connect solely with those who were there with him, including those who tortured him. A nonsacrilegious relation of symbolic significance is established between tortured and torturer that impedes a full disclosure because in the analysis by the neuro-psychiatrist Paz Rojas: "to narrate, to speak, would mean to recognize the presence of the ethically unacceptable."[3]

This dehumanizing system that used electricity and violence within torture places in Chile in the 1970s found its counterpart in the theological periphery of love and danger by those who tried to protect the persecuted and in doing so challenged the loss produced by torture and rape with a return to the basic human tenants of solidarity, love, and affection. This theological reflection combines the personal experience of violence and annihilation at the Villa Grimaldi (Cuartel Terranova) in Chile as well as some of the historical narratives of prisoners of this torture camp that in a few years received around 5,000 prisoners.[4]

Theological and historical works on torture have focused on the aftermath of crimes against God and humanity. This chapter examines theologically the moment in which prisoners were tortured with an immediate loss of human dignity. Following the concept of crucified victims already explored elsewhere, this chapter argues that following incarnational principles, God was in the torture chambers not as a companion to prisoners but he was a "crucified" prisoner himself, abused and tortured by those who wanted to kill God.[5] The hope of God's presence among left-wing opponents to the military regime was realized by the unity of prisoners sitting around the rose gardens and the presence of Christians who brought the hope and care of the Kingdom then and for the future to come.

Torturing at the Villa Grimaldi

The Chilean military coup of September 11, 1973 led by General Augusto Pinochet brought with it a systematic violation of human rights and a full persecution against those who had supported the socialist government of President Salvador Allende (1970–1973). Camps of political prisoners were housed at stadiums, police stations, military barracks, and civil buildings. If the initial crush of the pro-Allende supporters was vicious and well-organized (September–December 1973), the creation of a special intelligence body of special forces—a kind of political police known as DINA— brought a systematic hunt for political activists affiliated with the MIR (Movimiento de Izquierda Revolucionario), the Chilean Communist Party, and the Chilean Socialist Party. Those arrested were kept in unknown destinations, not known to the general Chilean population where they were interrogated, tortured, and abused for different periods of time and from where hundreds of prisoners were transferred to their unknown deaths and subsequent forced disappearance. The Villa Grimadi was one of those places. God, however, was at the Villa Grimaldi in the midst of what Peter Admirand has called "the rubble of theology." Thus, the Villa Grimaldi becomes a locus theologicus where in Admirand's challenge to theodicy, "witness testimonies must be given sufficient authority to place all of one's theological doctrine, traditions, and beliefs into question."[6]

Of the 5,000 prisoners who passed through the Villa Grimaldi, 142 are still not accounted for, and today they are listed among the disappeared (*detenidos-desaparecidos*).[7] Most of these prisoners were kidnapped from their homes, from their work, or from the streets by the DINA. The DINA operated a fleet of Ford pick-ups with canvas covers and those kidnapped were blindfolded and already burned with cigarettes on their way to the Cuartel Terranova. In most cases, they had been mentioned by other prisoners under torture or had been deemed to have information about wanted left-wing sympathizers or activists. However, in other cases, such as that of the suspended Catholic priest Antonio Llidó, the DINA kidnapped prisoners from other detention centers, sometimes in direct competition with other security services.[8]

Prisoners' memories of the Villa Grimaldi include the cooler air of the Santiago hills and the noise of the big gates when they were opened. They experienced the landscape of the Cuartel Terranova through other senses rather than through vision. Though sight remains the "privileged sense of the West," the prisoners experienced the Villa through other senses, particularly through the painful reality of feeling their bodies through torture.

Torture by means of electric shocks applied to the genitals, tongue, breasts, teeth, anus, etc. was a norm for all prisoners. The aim of torture was not always to extract information about others. Those prisoners who gave up information quickly raised suspicions with their rapid confessions. In these cases the torturers tried harder so as to verify the information already provided. Viewed in this manner, torture was part of a rite of passage within a liminal stage away from the ordinary life of citizens. During this liminal stage, using Victor Turner's understanding of a formative process of education, prisoners were given the choice of agreeing with the existence of an authoritarian state, or of dying, with the subsequent disappearance of their bodies.[9]

In the Cuartel Terranova, prisoners certainly underwent a process of taming, and those who were returned to their homes and families were supposed to offer a good example to other citizens who might stray from their duties toward the country (*la patria*). However, those who did not give up any information after days of torture by electricity, particularly those prisoners deemed "special" because of their ranks within political organizations, were administered other kinds of torture. Thus,

1. Prisoners were hanged and beaten up for days.
2. They were submerged in dirty water until they experienced a complete lack of air, or their heads were put in plastic bags until they suffocated.
3. Drugs and hypnosis were also used on prisoners.
4. Women were raped in front of their loved ones, sometimes with the help of trained dogs kept only at the Cuartel Terranova.

The length of stay varied enormously. Some prisoners were kept for only a few days while others stayed there for months. Daily life was different for those who were in the tower (*la torre*). Only those who had already been tortured could join the daily routine of cleaning and be given tea and dirty water for meals. Some prisoners, particularly women, cleaned toilets, the officers' mess, the torturers' barracks; they also swept the grounds particularly in summer when the dust spread on the hills of Santiago. Within this landscape of pain, it was difficult to know how many days had passed, and the questions posed during torture were always related to the location of government opponents that the DINA wanted to interrogate. The activities of the Cuartel Terranova continued day and night as prisoners were brought in or were transferred to other locations.

Narratives on the landscape

The Villa Grimaldi read as cultural construction remained during this period "secret," "forbidden," "unspoken," "secretive." Only those that had passed through its gates and survived the experience were able to convey their horrific experiences to the outside world, which for the most part did not believe them. Their testimonies became not aesthetic works of literature but legal testimonies used in the Chilean Courts in order to ask questions about people who had disappeared, and, much later, as legal accusations against those who had created the landscape of secrecy and terror.

Thus, legal narratives allow the contemporary historian and theologian to fill in details of what happened at these landscapes and how they were filled with bodies and lives. Textual narratives express the ethnography of the past, which, within our ethnographic present, suggests patterns and social action. Thus, the reasons for the existence of the Cuartel Terranova are found within the suppression of political dissent in Pinochet's Chile. However, the social breach of community and the wide practice of human rights abuses can only be intimated by looking at some of the cases of prisoners who passed through the landscape previously known as the Villa Grimaldi, some young, some old, men, women, and children. The following biographical text is an example of what was happening within this landscape of secrecy and it illustrates the ethnography of the dead and not of the living.

Felix Santiago de la Jara Goyeneche was 24 years of age at the time of his arrest on November 27, 1974. He was a member of the MIR and a former student of History and Geography at the National Chilean University. Civilians who accompanied his kidnapped girlfriend Sonia Valenzuela Jorquera, arrested him at 7.45 a.m. on Independencia and Olivos Streets, Santiago. At 11 a.m. that day, five members of the military intelligence (Servicio de Inteligencia Militar) searched the house of his mother Eugenia Goyeneche Mora for two hours without finding anything of interest to them.

In December 1974 prisoners at another torture center "La Venda Sexy," located in Irán and Los Plátanos Streets, Santiago, spoke to him between interrogations. On December 16 or 17, another prisoner María Cristina Zamora was brought in to help De la Jara who had an infected wound in one leg. However, it is clear from the testimony of Elías Padilla Ballesteros that De la Jara had already been badly tortured by the time he arrived at La Venda Sexy at the end of November.

De la Jara had been brought to the Villa Grimaldi for interrogation and later, when he became ill, his body was brought back to the Villa Grimaldi in order to be thrown into the sea from a helicopter. His name appeared in an edition of the Brazilian newspaper *O'Dia*, reproduced in Chilean newspapers that reported 59 Chileans who had died in armed internal strife within left-wing Chilean organizations. Despite this news, De la Jara was a victim of a military offensive aimed at killing all members of the MIR. His name appears among those inscribed in the Wall of Names at the Villa Grimaldi (*Muro de los Nombres*).

The presence of God in the torture chamber

Spaces are outlined and created by human beings in order to signify particular human activities. Thus, torture chambers are spaces used by those inflicting torture within larger landscapes of political repression and human productions of inhumanity. As such, these landscapes are somehow temporary, even when jailors and political masters could think that they are perennial creations. The authority and the power advocated by those who order or conduct sessions of torture come from their own personal perception that these spaces are not known by others, that their social existence will prevail changes in society and that their actions would not be discovered or accounted for in the future.

The torture chamber in the Villa Grimaldi of Chile was made of a room where there was a desk, a typewriter, a wall map of the city of Santiago, a couple of chairs, and a steel bed, single or double, linked to a dynamo that through wires could be linked to a prisoner's body. The prisoner was brought into the room from the dungeons (wooden boxes where prisoners were kept) in order to be asked questions about herself, her past, other people connected to her, and her political activities. Questions and answers were typed and recorded in order to gather information that could be linked to other testimonies. Sessions were at random and female prisoners were raped as well as being given electricity shots. Other prisoners were hanged for hours and days with the excruciating pain entailed by this experience; others were beaten or made to suffocate with plastic bags attached to their heads where breathing became shallow and a near-death experience.

It is at this moment in the life of a person arrested and tortured that the prisoner loses complete and absolute control of her existence. The person's will wants to resist and any political activist promises not to give any information away. Nevertheless, the moment of the actual torture and when the noise of the dynamo is heard creates an immediate response of fear because it is only during the first time that the prisoner doesn't know what is going to happen. Fear is used and in-built in this torture script by the torturer because the prisoner knows what is going to happen and fear appears mixed with pain and anxiety and the thought of an endless moment in time that is actually extremely short. This moment in time could be compared, with the limitations and the respect toward prisoners that the metaphor entails, to a root canal treatment by a dentist. The dentist has to drill the materiality of a tooth in order to repair and restore a human tooth—the only problem is that teeth have roots, alive and sensitive to the act of drilling. As a result, the person having the root canal feels pain once the sound of the drill starts. That conditioning, that human reaction to something heard and felt, is the reaction activated in a prisoner who is tortured with electricity, who could be blindfolded and who only listens to the noises around her.

The theological dungeon

It is in the variety of spaces for torture and in the variety of human experiences related to a synchronic moment of madness that the torturer(s) and the tortured encounter each other in an unequal relation. One or several of the torturers have the control of time and space where another human being has no control over his physical body, the senses, or the materiality of the moment but can keep control over two spheres of human experience: the mind and the metaphysical. The mind resists the possibility of giving out information to the torturers and desperately connects with the muscles that produce speech and sound as to block them from speaking about coherent things such as contacts, addresses, plans, past events, future events, or people's gatherings. The torture chamber as a larger reality disappears and the only world that exists is the voice of the torturer and the mind of the tortured. The electricity flows into the blindfolded body and the pain numbs the brain and the sensation is that of a scream that does not come from the mouth but from the inside of the body with a sound that is an utterance of an animal rather than a human scream. If prayers of fear or desperation were uttered when thrown into the torture chamber, they are forgotten as well as the bodily conditionings. The human body soils itself completely while nothingness and "the nothing" appear. This is not a metaphor or a utopian description but the actual sensation of losing one's control of reality while the brain desperately tries to control events by blocking any passage of information.

It is at this precise moment, a moment that could be frozen in time, that one asks "where is God?" If God is there, God can only be present within the theological dungeon. Logically speaking, if God is love, God could only be there supporting the prisoner rather than the torturer. It is at this moment of intense heat when disgusting odors are smelled and when foul words are uttered that the theologian could decide to affirm or negate the presence of God. It would be much easier to decide that God is not present in a torture chamber because places such as dungeons are not sacred and do not represent places where God dwells. The biblical image of the Temple of Jerusalem could be used here as to argue that it is at the temple where God dwells and that in order to connect with God humans have to ascend to the Temple or celebrate the festivals at synagogues or churches. However, I argue that God is present in the places where torture is used as a mode of interrogation and human destruction. I also argue that God is present in the torture chamber as part of a theological dungeon because God was present at the crucifixion of Jesus of Nazareth, assumed by Christians as the Messiah and the Son of God.

Javier Rebolledo recently investigated acts of torture, killing, and forced disappearances at the house of Simon Bolivar Street 8800 in Santiago, Chile, during the Pinochet regime. His mentioning of the presence/absence of God in that house of horror becomes a literary fact that is worth examining here.[10] The book examines the testimony of Jorgelino Vergara, a waiter/servant who worked for and was brought up by General Manuel Contreras, the head of the Pinochet security services (DINA) and who later was transferred to the house of horrors at Simon Bolivar Street. In the introduction to this work, Jorge "Gato" Escalante, states that Vergara "does not live in peace. And very few times remembers God. *God was not there*. In that place where they disfigured faces with fire. Where they erased fingerprints. Where they took golden teeth out with pocket knives and pliers."[11] Later, Escalante writes:

What happens with God? (Vergara) knows that he (God) was not present in Simon Bolivar [detention center]. During those years he (God) was forgotten. "It was better that God would not interfere in my business". His heart (Vergara's) still had some piety. More water to the prisoners in secret. Christmas Eve 1976 (. . .) Now was the time to remember God. Was he afraid of being punished for his evil deeds? Maybe Viva the Virgin of Mount Carmel! There he was among the devotees of the Virgin Mary. Through the streets in Curico, shouting Viva to the Virgin Mary![12]

In this reflection God was not present within the detention camp but was outside in places where his mother, the Virgin Mary, could be seen publicly, and within a mass of people, torturers and tortured, who could acclaim the greatness of the Virgin Mary as protector.

In the case of the Villa Grimaldi, it is clear that less theological reflections exist because most prisoners were agnostics or atheists through their political work while their parents and grandparents could have been practicing Roman Catholics. Every year during Holy Week, members of the Christian communities of Santiago walk toward the place where prisoners were kept and remember through the Way of the Cross, Jesus's arrest and crucifixion in Jerusalem twenty centuries earlier.

On torture

Issues of torture at the international level are regulated by the United Nations' Convention against Torture and Other Cruel, Inhuman or Degrading Treatment or Punishment (1985).[13] Within this convention:

Torture means any act by which severe pain or suffering, whether physical or mental, is intentionally inflicted on a person for such purposes as obtaining from him or a third person information or a confession, punishing him for an act he or a third person has committed or is suspected of having committed, or intimidating or coercing him or a third person, or for any reason based on discrimination of any kind, when such pain or suffering is inflicted by or at the instigation of or with the consent or acquiescence of a public official or other person acting in an official capacity. It does not include pain or suffering arising only from, inherent in or incidental to lawful sanctions.[14]

With this working definition of torture and the possibilities of a critical expansion of this definition, questions about theology and torture can be asked. However, these questions and critical reflections can only at the end be theologically asked through the incarnational lens of the arrest, imprisonment, and torture of Jesus of Nazareth at the hands of the Romans. Questions such as "did Christ expect a violent death?" become not only related to the atonement and the passion of Christ on the cross but to many victims of violence, oppression, and state oppression. They become part of their self-understanding of their relation with God.[15] Nevertheless, in this chapter I am not concerned with what happens before the torturing or after the torturing but I am asking a concrete question that was of concern to the millions who died in the Shoah, known as the Jewish holocaust: where was God at that moment? Peruvian theologian Gustavo Gutiérrez has suggested that the question in context (e.g., in Latin America) is a slightly different question because he was reflecting on the experience of hunger, extreme poverty, disease, and neglect.[16] Aren't those the same experiences of Jews dying in Auschwitz? Maybe the eruption of the third world in theology for the past 40 years has allowed us today to rethink theological categories not only in terms of the Shoah but also in terms of the 1994 Rwanda genocide perpetrated by Christians on Christians. For the purposes of this chapter, the questions seem to be the same because theologically they involve the nature and location of God vis-à-vis the nature and location of a human being.

The summation of the parts and the fragmentation of the whole in context only point to the change of names while the moment of suffering, abandonment, and the cross remains a common diachronical experience by different human beings. Following from this synchronic commonality we can ask: Where was God at the moment when Dr Sheila Cassidy was tortured at the Villa Grimaldi by members of the Chilean security forces? Where was God when thousands of Argentineans were tortured at the camp El Olimpo, later to be drugged and thrown alive from helicopters into the ocean by members of the Argentinean security forces? Where is God when thousands of women are raped in the Democratic Republic of Congo?—raped in a country that today is called "the world capital of rape." These are not different questions but a single question about the locality and agency of God at the moment when God's own son was being tortured and killed in Jerusalem as he exclaimed: "My God, my God, why do you forsake me?" (Mk 15.34). This is a moment in human and colonial history that later would change the perception of many human beings on their own human and colonized history.

Theology as history, the first act

Gutiérrez has argued that the reading of the Bible, for example the passage I have chosen related to the torturing of Jesus in Jerusalem, needs to be historical as well as militant.[17] In making this suggestion and in his reading of biblical texts, Gutiérrez brings the synchronic events of God's salvation into the diachronic sphere of modern and contemporary history by arguing that:

> God reveals himself in the history of the people that believed and hoped in him—
> and this leads us to rethink his word from the viewpoint of our own history. But
> because ours is a true history, crisscrossed by confrontation and conflict, we can
> enter into it consciously and effectively only by steeping ourselves in the popular
> struggles for liberation.[18]

In a short theological summary, Gutiérrez asserts that "the locus of our encounter with the Father of Jesus Christ is the concrete history of men and women."[19] Gutiérrez consistently argues that to bring divine concepts to human beings in order to restore a divine world to the modern world, as done by Karl Barth, does not solve the issue of the presence of God in the history of human beings. For the proclamation of the Gospel is done through the idea of "a weaker God" as pointed to by the prisoner Bonhoeffer.

Thus, what makes a Christian, in Gutiérrez's commentary on Bonhoeffer, is "being caught up into the messianic sufferings of God in Jesus Christ."

God acts in history and it is to history that we must turn in order to understand God's presence or absence, in a world assumed as mature rather than lost, populated by human beings created by God but who exercise their own free will to exercise their agency with God or without God within contemporary events. Those contemporary events have shaped the moments of history in which we can ask questions about torture and about the presence or absence of God within those moments in history. Let us recapitulate on some of the moments of human history that have marked the presence of God and the actions of human beings and the Church in the past few decades.

The collapse of the Berlin Wall, the end of totalitarian regimes in Eastern Europe, the end of the Latin America military regimes, and the collapse of the apartheid regime in South Africa brought a sense of hope to humanity in the early 1990s.[20] As it was felt at the end of World War II, Christians as members of a larger humanity felt a clear hope that atrocities and the suffering of human beings under the hands of other human beings would finally cease. Sadly, this was not the case and the rising of the Cold War after World War II with all its violence and international divisions was replicated after the collapse of the Berlin Wall by the devastating events that took place in Rwanda and the former Yugoslavia. If the Rwandan genocide saddened Christians all over the world because of the fact that Rwanda was the most "Christianized" country in Africa, the events that followed in the former Yugoslavia horrified humanity once again because they took place in Europe. Torture as a mode of interrogation, harassment, human degradation, and as a means of destroying human beings and their dreams was used in all these conflicts and became part of an unspoken given. Thus, it was not necessary any longer to ask if prisoners were being tortured. This was presumed, and so the larger the number of prisoners, the more questions were being asked about the reasons and the perpetrators of mass killings. Within those legal and criminal investigations, dead bodies and mass graves spoke by themselves while those who had survived the killings and were tortured remained living testimonies of genocide and ethnic cleansing.

Questions about God, suffering, and the nature and purpose of the Church were also being asked as it had been after the Jewish Holocaust; however, these questions changed context, from a local to a globalized state of affairs. Beginning with Nuremberg and continuing with the establishment of the International Tribunals for crimes against humanity, states and peoples asked questions about gross human rights violations. Some of those responsible were brought to justice and the case of the arrest of General Augusto Pinochet, the former dictator of Chile, in London brought a renewed sense of hope at the arrival of the new millennium.

This theological investigation related to religion and violence is grounded in the impossibility of doing theology or studying religion without a context. As Gutiérrez has pointed out, theology is "a second act" while praxis/action is the first act, an action that precedes theological thinking and not the other way around. We connect the act of theologizing as "a second step" with the theological indecency of reflecting on actions that are closer to human actions that we do not usually speak about as pointed out by the Argentinean theologian Marcella Althaus-Reid; we connect the context of any theology with the incarnation. For the principle of the incarnation relates not to virtual realities and metaphysical understandings but to the Son of God himself who comes from the Father as Jesus, true God, and truly a human being. This remarkable human being and Son of God was born of a woman, preached the Kingdom of God, was arrested, tortured, abused, nailed to a cross, and killed by his captors. The cross and the location of Golgotha became the context and history of such incarnation to be repeated in other histories, other contexts, and other Golgothas.

Sitz in Leben

This theological reflection started at a particular place, location, and history. The place was the city of Santiago in Chile; the location was a small area of central Santiago, precisely the area close to the Church of St Francis, located at the junction of Alameda Bernardo O'Higgins Avenue with London Street. The history remains united in a diachronic manner because the same church bells rang in the 1970s as in the twenty-first century and had done so every hour of every day for many years. The bells marked the hours for people at the time when clocks and watches were not readily available but they also marked the presence of God within the urban center. Within the 1970s and after the Chilean military coup of 1973 that saw the start of General Pinochet's regime (1973–1990), the bells were heard by prisoners at a house located at number 38 London Street where the security forces and the political police brought prisoners to be tortured, many of whom never returned and were counted among the disappeared.

Bells in this particular context can have different meanings and remind people when they hear them of the warm feeling and the clean linen of a church altar as well as of the days and months spent in captivity at a torture center. Individual signifiers provide a sensorial memory that operates at an individual level creating either trauma or hope, challenging perceptions of torture as a flash-back on social bodies. The flash-backs of torture and imprisonment become personal issues when the totalitarian regimes are gone and the sound of rifles are silenced. Nevertheless, for those who believe in God and for those who are members of the Church, the individual experiences of the past and the present are linked to individual narratives about God and God's presence or absence within such sensorial moments of the past and the present.

If we negate the possibility of God being there, we deny the given-dictum that God knows everything and is everywhere. But most people do not have to ask these questions and others find this an indecent thought, not a clean theological one. It is within this theological investigation that I recall the possibility of avoiding and forgetting God within a moment of complete liminality in which a person is taken to a place, a location, a real location that for other people does not exist, a secret place denied by the authorities and in which those in-charge of prisoners can do whatever they like with them. Most writings of history and theology have focused on the actions before the torturing, mainly on the kidnapping, and the actions after the kidnapping, when a person reappears and legal processes start to defend rights, state, and human, and a battle follows to decide what legally happened.

It is crucial to remember that while the issue of torture has been ignored in the writings of the Latin American theologians, some Latin American bishops such as Oscar Romero of El Salvador and the bishops of Chile in the late 1970s and early 1980s were very vocal about the absolute Christian condemnation of torture as a possible human activity. It is important to remember that the position of the Chilean bishops was not a warning or a denunciation. They publicly excommunicated, that is declared not in communion with the Catholic Church, those Catholics involved in torture in the early 1980s.[21] The Chilean Bishops and Archbishop Romero based their public statements about the abhorrence of torturing for whatever means or ends on Paul VI's address to the United Nations where he emphasized the Catholic Church's commitment to human rights, to the basic rights of all human beings.[22] For in Paul VI's interpretation of Romero's words, he clearly stated that the Church was making her own the voices of "the dead, victims of cruelty, and of those who continue to live, but in terror, under threat, bearing in their bodies the marks of torture, of outrages committed against them."[23]

Archbishop Romero, not always recognized as a theologian, proposed publicly in his four renowned homilies that torture was a reality that he wanted to address from the pulpit and within his public addresses to the Salvadorian nation.[24] He had witnessed the physical damage on some of his clergy who had been arrested and tortured by the Salvadorian security forces and had been extremely distressed when Fr Barrera was killed in 1978 and the related testimony of a political prisoner, Reynaldo Cruz Menjívar, was legally filed and published.[25]

My personal narrative, not necessarily the most wanted one, could have happened in any Latin American city of the 1970s or 1980s but it happened in my native Santiago and the problem is that it happened too often during the years of the military government led by Augusto Pinochet. A car stopped on a street. A person, a human being, a father, a mother, a daughter, a sister, a brother was taken by a group of secret police, quickly moved onto the floor of a car or a pick-up, eyes sealed with sticky tape, hands handcuffed, cheeks burned with cigarettes, eyes filled with violence, terror, and human fear. The car carrying this human being stopped at the gates of an old villa on the foothills of Santiago, previously known as the Villa Grimaldi and during the days of terror known as the Cuartel Terranova. Quickly and blindfolded, the now prisoner is brought to rooms within the main house where the first questions are asked by a member of the secret police before moving the prisoner naked to a room where a couple of steel beds, a typewriter, and an electricity dynamo are located. The prisoner is stripped naked and positioned on the bed with electrodes attached to different parts of the body. As a question is asked, electricity moves through the prisoner's body while the body shakes, the tongue enlarges itself, the mind goes numb, and a full sense of terror engulfs the mind. In this scenario seconds seem hours and the thirst and pain, hell. This, of course, until the prisoner collapses unconscious! This scenario happens once and again and it has less theological or human logic than one could suspect. After a session of torture the prisoner feels completely lost, unwanted, and is in shock—not only physically but also emotionally. The act of torture becomes "bitter memories" in the words of Felipe Agüero, a Chilean prisoner of the National Stadium of Santiago after the 1973 military coup.[26]

Conclusions: The hope of being human

If, and only if, there was any doubt that violations of human rights were systematic rather than isolated abuses of power by individuals, the history of the year 1974 unfolds a grotesque picture of a systematic hunt for the MIR in order to annihilate and destroy human life to the point that the reorganization by the MIR was a myth of utopian proportions. In fact, the MIR was so closely monitored by the DINA that the reorganization became a suicidal operation so that when two *miristas* met, they knew that it could be the last time they did so because they were eventually going to be killed. For example, Luis Muñoz, a member of the MIR who was captured, tortured, and imprisoned but survived, recalled his meetings with another *mirista* who was captured and disappeared, María Cristina Stewart, of whom he became rather fond of but never had the courage to tell her.[27] In December 1973 María Cristina Stewart told him that she had been attracted to him but decided not to make a pass at him because Muñoz was involved with Diana Aron, another *mirista* who was captured and disappeared, and who at the time of her arrest was expecting Muñoz's baby.[28] When Muñoz asked Stewart why she was telling him about those feelings now, Stewart answered: "Because we are going to die. We are going to be killed, Luis; it is only a matter of time and I cannot go with these feelings inside me."[29]

Jon Sobrino SJ has centered part of his theological reflections on the presence of God and the victims, heavily influenced by the experience and theological trauma he suffered when all his Jesuit confreres and friends of the University of Central America (UCA) were murdered by Salvadorian soldiers in November 1988. For Sobrino, God is present in the victims who are crucified; I follow from him in my interpretation suggesting that God is present in all those moments when a person is beaten up or tortured. Sobrino argues that the crucified and the victims are the ones who bring salvation because they are part of a globalized truth of a common humanity.[30] In my words they are the loss that brings hope to a broken world.

In the words of Ignacio Ellacuria, the victims are part of what he calls "the civilization of poverty," poor but trying to live the values of the Kingdom in peace and harmony.[31] It is within such a search for the Kingdom, that the victims are the ones that bring God to a common humanity. They represent the face of God in places where those living outside "the civilization of poverty" cannot go even in their wildest imagination.[32] Thus, the torture chamber becomes a place in which to do theology becomes a "second act" because the first one is to be in solidarity with other human beings who are being tortured.

Previously, the Chilean theologian Ronaldo Muñoz had elaborated on the person of God for Latin America, stating that "the God of the Bible is shown becoming truly involved in our history, seriously taking the part of oppressed individuals and people."[33] As part of his work as a parish priest in the slums of Santiago, he had to listen to testimonies by youth of his parish that in parts read as follows: "Yesterday, God was with Ricardo in the torture chamber, and yesterday his companion in torture was Jesus Christ."[34]

The conclusion to this chapter is quite straightforward, even when these conclusions are indecent and unpalatable as torture itself: God is at the torture chamber not holding hands with prisoners but he/she is tortured and he/she is in liminal places where torture is carried out today. Torture has been clearly defined in international terms but in daily parlance is used to describe other inhuman relations such as the abuse of children, psychological violence, domestic violence, and every act that discriminates, abuses, and uses violence against other human beings. I would like to disagree here with the reflections by William Cavanagh when he suggested that "if everything is torture, then nothing is."[35] Not everything can be labeled as torture but it is worthwhile, I would argue, to explore the psychological torture, relations of power, and psychosomatic harm done, for example to victims of clergy abuse in the same Catholic Church articulated in Cavanagh's sharp and elegant analysis of torture.[36] Thus, after some critical analysis it could be argued that the conclusions might point to other manners of physical and mental abuse. Thus, reflections on ideas of decency/indecency and orderly power over human beings have implications for the current understanding of abuse of children by priests, violence against women in the family, gender violence, human trafficking, and homophobic discourses against human beings of a diverse sexual orientation.

It is a sobering reflection that a liberating theology that arises out of praxis, human and divine, is coming more and more from outside the churches after common experiences of human oppression and suffering, common to Christians, Muslims, Buddhists, Jews, Hindus, atheists, and agnostics. All these reflections on the impossibility of a divine wish for torture could maybe prevent further suffering to human beings as images of the God of all and reiterate the hope that any loss brings with it.

The Iranian Women's Movement: A Narrative of Hope and Loss

Roja Fazaeli

Introduction

The feminist movements[1] in Muslim-majority countries have become some of the most innovative sociopolitical movements of the past decades. The movements challenge the male-dominated interpretation of Islamic laws, and in some countries such as Iran, they have become the new voices of dissent. A wide array of literature has been written on women's rights in Islam,[2] of women's perceived oppression,[3] and in the last decade, of women's self-determination in the form of Islamic feminisms.[4]

The Iranian women's movement has a long history. Its beginnings can be traced back to the late nineteenth century. The past three decades have witnessed a revival in historical studies of the early Iranian women's movement. Scholars such as Parvin Paidar, Afsaneh Najmabadi, Ali Akbar Mahdi, Eliz Sanasarian, Hammed Shahidian, Homa Hoodfar, Nikki Keddie, Mehrangiz Kar, Shirin Ebaid—to name a few—have all written on aspects of the Iranian women's movement from historical, sociological, and politico-legal perspectives, from the movement's beginnings until after the 1979 Islamic Revolution. As Janet Afary observes, after the 1979 Iranian revolution not only academics but also female activists "began to search in the dustbin of history for the origins of feminism in literature and politics."[5] This search is particularly notable in the writing of Noushin Ahamadi Khorasani and Parvin Ardalan. Their book, *Senator: The Works of Senator Mehrangiz Manouchehrian for Legal Rights for Women*, explores the life story of Manouchehrian. By way of her story, this work explores the history of the women's movement in Iran from the postconstitutional era to the Pahlavi Dynasty and including the early period following the 1979 Islamic revolution.[6] More recently Ahamdi Khorasani's book *Bahar Jonbesh Zanan* (*The Spring of Iranian Women's Movement*) published in 2012 gives an intimate account of the movement from Ahmadi Khorasani's personal and yet extremely important perspective.

One forum where women rights activists and reform-minded intellectuals have traditionally voiced their concerns regarding discrimination, and where debates and discussion of religious and secular kinds took place, is that of women's reformist media. The role of women's reformist media has been the topic of many articles and books. Women's magazines such as *Zanan, Farzaneh*, and *Payam-i Hajar* have been thoroughly studied as platforms where women's issues were discussed and religious texts were reinterpreted.[7] These previous studies form the basis for understanding the present women's movement. However, there is a clear paucity in the academic study of Iranian online publications and blogs as sites integral to the women's movement where collective and individual narratives form innovative tools in the fight for equality.

This chapter has two sections. Section I is the study of the new women's movement in Iran with a focus on the One Million Signatures Campaign (OMSC). The campaign is a follow-up to the ongoing efforts by women activists to reform gender discriminatory laws in Iran. It is supported by international scholars and activists such as Shirin Ebadi, Niki Keddie, and Nayereh Tohidi. It intends to collect one million signatures to end legal discrimination against women in Iranian laws, including those that address blood money, inheritance, custody, guardianship, and divorce. These laws discriminate against women in the name of Islam. The women active in the campaign have faced complex restrictions leading to a near halt of the campaign in Iran in particular during Mahmoud Ahmadinejad's second term of presidency (2009–2013). During the past five years, many women's rights activists have been arrested, threatened, and/or exiled. Women's rights activists and advocates such as Shiva Nazar Ahari, Bahareh Hedayat, and Nasrin Sotoudeh remain in prison. With the election of Hassan Rouhani on June 14, 2013, there is renewed hope that the women's movement will once again flourish. Nonetheless women activists have already been critical of the absence of women in Rouhani's newly elected cabinet and there has been no sign of any release of imprisoned activists.

Section II explores the pendulum that is the women's movement in Iran. Swaying from the family (or private) to the public sphere, it leaves women activists in a siege of containment. Women advocate for reform in religious state laws using international human rights law as a measuring rod. While female activists fight for equal rights in the public arena, they are faced with contradictions in their family lives, and some of these contradictions result from discriminatory laws that designate the husband as the head of the household and the maintainer of the family. This is a paradox where the public identity of a female activist does not go beyond her identity as a mother, wife, sister, or daughter within the private realm of the family. It is a lapse from equality to complementarity. When pressured by the government, the male interrogator uses the interrogee's identity as a mother, wife, daughter, or sister to force her to submission by threatening her family's honor, pushing her back to the private realm. Hence the sway of the pendulum has become an instrument of control in the hands of the patriarchs in the family and the Islamic government.

This section also examines a new medium for women's public voices, namely the emerging prison narratives from women rights activists that are published online. These narratives are powerful testimonies of innovation. They give oppressed women a voice and raise questions about the nature of private/state-owned prisons. By giving these testimonies, the women not only defy the state, which has otherwise imprisoned them, but they also create a new space for their activism. Their narratives regularly relate stories of women prisoners in the *band nasvan* (women's ward), some of whom are awaiting the death penalty for having killed their husbands. Their narratives are important as they not only give a humane face to these women who are generally referred to as criminals but also because they critically analyze the reasons these women have resorted to murder. These reasons usually include having been in violent relationships and not having had access to any legal remedies.

Section I: Women's movement and agency in Iran and the One Million Signatures Campaign

The women's movement in Iran has a long history and is comprised of activists from different socioeconomic, cultural, and political backgrounds. Some equate the beginning of the modern women's movement in Iran with women's active participation in the so-called tobacco movement (boycott), which followed after a *fatwa* issued by Haji Hassan Shirazi, a Shi'a cleric in 1892.[8] Women's activism continued throughout the constitutional revolution (1906–1911).[9] During the Pahlavi era (1925–1979), women resisted Reza Shah's forced de-veiling (1936),[10] and they participated en masse in the 1979 Islamic revolution, which yielded the Islamic Republic.

To the discontent of those who supported the revolution, women lost many of their rights after the 1979 Islamic revolution. The 1967 Family Protection Act (FPA),[11] which had restricted polygamy, raised the age of marriage for girls and allowed women the right to divorce, was abrogated. Women were banned from working as judges[12] and the legal age of marriage for girls was lowered to 13.[13] Girls were barred from technical and vocational schools and also from higher education fields such as engineering, agriculture, and mathematical sciences.[14] Some of these laws were progressively reformed. For example, in December 1992 the parliament (*majlis*) passed the Amendment to Divorce Law, which outlawed "registration of all divorces without a court certificate called the Impossibility of Reconciliation."[15] This law obliges the husband to pay his wife *mahr*,[16] *nafaqa* (maintenance) if he intends to divorce her and to financially support her during her *idda*,[17] unless the wife is the one who is initiating the divorce. In that case "she forgoes all her dues in return for her release."[18] Other reforms and amendments included "the appointment of women judges as advisers to the main judge," and enablement of women to be paid for their housework "*ujrat al-mithl*" (wages in kind).[19]

Other discriminations that women faced after the 1979 revolution included the enforcement of a gender-segregated public realm, including school, universities, and the workforce. The imposition of *hijab* was a real setback but nonetheless for some, it was their ticket to the public realm. Traditional families who viewed the Pahlavis as Western and the public mixing of genders as immoral, were happy to allow their daughters to enter the segregated and veiled public realm of the Islamic Republic. Other factors such as the Iran–Iraq war (1980–1988), during which men were forcefully enrolled to fight at the fronts, and the declining economic situation also yielded an increase of women in the public sphere.

The women's movement after the revolution set against a backdrop of a paradoxical society has became embedded in religious and state rhetoric. Women who have the power to reform discriminatory laws are those within the state apparatus, for example women members of the parliament or women presidential advisors.[20] During the reform era (1997–2004), much of the gender talk was intertwined with the politics of the reform movement. Women reformist parliamentarians in particular in the sixth parliament (*majlis-i sheshom*) did fight for women's equal rights; however, these women were not part of a separate women's party but of the reformist camp. Since the conservatives took majority seats at the seventh parliament (*majlis-i haftom*) in 2004 and subsequently in the eighth (2008) and ninth parliaments (2012) (*majlis-e hashtom va nohom*), there has been a shift in the movement, away from political power and the conservative Islamic framework to autonomy and secularity. In the past nine years, the movement has faced many obstacles; nonetheless, despite a clear indication of the movement's shift toward secularity, the importance of solidarity in the movement is highlighted more than ever. As Nayereh Tohidi states, "Women's struggle in today's Iran is primarily a cultural and legal one, which is fought in a historical context rather than a battlefield."[21] Women who are active in the movement, unlike the reformist political groups who in the past have used women's issues as political tools, are not seeking political power but tangible solutions to women's problems.

The OMSC is the new face of the Iranian women's movement based on the 2004 Moroccan model of family law reform.[22] There are many other campaigns that could also be used as examples of the shifting nature of the movement. However, the OMSC is unique in its mobilization, the support it enjoys nationally and internationally, and also as Tohidi further elaborates: "This campaign seems to have surpassed ideological, sectarian and religious boundaries and limitations."[23] She further notes: "This movement has distanced itself from the more prevalent masculine and elitist perceptions that assume only a handful of avant-garde intellectuals, having discovered the 'Whole Truth,' are the sole proprietors of solutions, [and] who through personal sacrifice would impart the knowledge, bring freedom and 'save the souls of the ignorant and oppressed masses.'"[24]

The OMSC has been "initiated by the younger generation of women's rights activists,"[25] who aim to collect one million signatures to demand an end to legal discrimination against women in Iranian laws as outlined above.[26] The campaign is an active progression of the women's movement from the constitutional revolution and a more immediate "follow-up effort to the peaceful protest of the same aim, which took place on 12 June 2006 in Haft-e Tir Square in Tehran."[27] The campaign's goals are multifold. Apart from collecting signatures, the campaigners aim to promote social change through collaboration and cooperation; to identify women's needs and priorities; to strengthen their voices; to increase knowledge; and to promote democratic action through dialogue.[28] The OMSC is becoming "a point of convergence among many groups and individual activists in different parts of Iran."[29] The initial proposed timeline for the collection of signatures was two years. Consequently on the collection of signatures, "legal changes will be proposed through draft legislation prepared by scholars [such] as Shirin Ebadi and presented to the parliament for consideration."[30]

Owing to the pressure exerted on the activists, the collection of signatures has proven more difficult than anticipated. In particular, post-2009, the public collection of signatures as well as other public aspects of the Campaign came to a near halt in Iran. In an interview[31] with one of the Campaign activists, she explained that although the collection of signatures has been dormant for the past few years, nonetheless the Campaign is still ongoing. The activists in exile continue to speak publicly about the Campaign, in lectures, seminars, and public talks. The Campaign website is still active and accessible in six different languages.[32] In addition the Campaign activists are still running workshops in Iran and the active members try to demand change of laws through other means, even if not under the umbrella of the Campaign. It is also important to note that the dormancy of the signature collection is not only related to pressures exerted on the activists by the state but also to the illegitimacy of Ahmadnejad's government after the contested 2009 elections. According to my interviewee, as the Campaign required the signatures to be presented to the *Majlis* (Parliament) to ask for changes to the discriminatory laws, the Campaign activists preferred not to do so during the tenure of a government which they deemed as illegitimate and not elected by the people.[33]

The OMSC uses human rights norms as a yardstick for its objective of attaining nondiscrimination and equality of genders. Although the movement is leaning toward secularity, there is adequate Islamic justification in order not to make the Campaign contradictory to Islamic principle and hence acceptable to the 98 percent Muslim population of Iran. As affirmed by the campaign organizers:

> . . . The demands of the Campaign are not in contradiction to Islamic principles: the demands to reform and change discriminatory laws is not in contradiction to Islamic principles and is in line with Iran's international commitments. Iran is a signatory to the UN Convention on Civil and Political Rights and as such, is required to eliminate all forms of discrimination. Based on these commitments, the government of Iran needs to take specific action in reforming laws that promote discrimination.[34]

The campaign's call is to reform laws that are discriminatory against women. The OMSC supports its claim by referring to the ongoing call for reform of laws by religious scholars like Ayatollah Saane'i and Ayatollah Bojnourdi. According to the activists: "A million signatures supporting changes to discriminatory laws will demonstrate to decision-makers and the public at large that a large segment of the Iranian population is in support of revising discriminatory laws against women and that these demands are not limited to a small segment of society."[35]

Nonetheless, the Campaign has faced severe crackdowns, and many of the activists have been arrested, interrogated, and threatened. Many of those arrested are charged with "being a threat to the national security." Women activists are accused of plotting a "velvet revolution,"[36] whereby "journalists, human rights defenders, intellectual NGO activists and social activists are seen as agents of foreign governments, who are engaged in activities designed to bring about velvet revolutions and overthrow the government."[37]

As mentioned above, although the Campaign has been less active in the past five years, it has continued its activity in innovative ways. With the election of Rouhani in June 2013, there are hopes for the Campaign to renew its public activities.

Section II: Redefining the public and confusing the private

Very few write on women's rights without reference to the public/private schism. As Fatima Sadiqi and Moha Ennaji define:

> The public/private dichotomy is rooted in the Greek legend in which human action takes place in a space divided into the public, or the visible male world called Hermean (the Greek god of communication), and [the] private or the invisible feminine world called Hestian (the Greek goddess of home).[38]

The Hermean space is the public sphere of law and politics, dominated by men and the Hestian space is that of private life of the home and the family, the realm of the mother, wife, daughter, and sister. This section investigates the public/private divide, arguing that even in a country like Iran, the public and the private are not so polarized to be solely male or female spheres. Realms are conditioned by many factors. The public and the private are becoming more and more intertwined. Realms that have historically been designated to men are changing, given the increased female participation in the public sphere.[39] Using the women's movement in Iran and the OMSC as an example, I will demonstrate how women activists, who are wives, daughters, mothers, and sisters, are constantly swayed between the public and the private by the patriarchs of the society and the family.

Most women activists in Iran have at some stage worked within the context of civil society. Civil society as defined by Moghadam and Sadiqi is "the non-state realm of associational life, civility in public discourse, and state-society relations,"[40] which constitutes an indispensable part of the public sphere, a platform for public opinion. As in any other public realm, civil society has historically been a male domain. However, women's participation in the public space has increased, yielding to a large number of women civil society activists. One can therefore say that the civil society has become feminized.[41]

As noted above, the OMSC is a public campaign that stems from the heart of the feminized Iranian civil society. Ahmadi Khorasani argues that "in reality, the One Million Signatures Campaign was borne of a feminine imagination to resist the violence imposed on us by the riot police when they attacked our peaceful rally for equal legal rights on June 12, 2006 in Haft-e Tir Square."[42] The campaign's face-to-face strategy requires women activists (also some of their male counterparts) to infiltrate the public through the private realm. This strategy requires them not only to engage in the rights dialogue with individuals in public spaces but also to go door-to-door to people's houses in order to collect signatures. The OMSC brings to contention "the old school notion of [the] public dominated male realm and the private sphere of women and family."[43] Women in the campaign defy government pressures and are emerging even stronger in the face of arrests and exile. They turn situations such as the prison into new platforms for the Campaign. These activists "are motivated by aspiration for equality and enhanced rights" and they "draw on international standards, conventions, and networks in support of their claims."[44] The government's increased pressure, threats, and arrest of campaigners is meant to strike fear in the heart of the activists, so that they retreat to their homes, to the very place where gender discrimination is most prevalent. Noushin Ahmadi Khorasani depicts the fear that is created by the state: "our lives are consumed with fear. Fear of falling behind. Fear of a conservative government that wants to imprison us in our houses or flats or in cells."[45] In another article she talks about the crisis in which the campaigners find themselves:

> ... since the inception of the Campaign ... members of the Campaign have had the misfortune of experiencing a crisis of some sort on a bi-weekly basis. As a result, we have been forced into a state of fear and anxiety, forced to comfort one another, forced to address the multiple crises at hand, and forced to constantly reassure one another that we are indeed not engaged in any sort of illegal activity—so why is it that we live in such fear? Are we asking for anything more than justice and our basic human rights?[46]

Another type of fear has emerged within the family sphere. Women activists as mothers, sisters, daughters, and wives are also the bearers of their families' honor. The Iranian family, as in other countries in the region, is patriarchal. Valentine Moghadam argues that the "'Middle Eastern Muslim family' has long been described as a patriarchal unit, and it has been noted that Muslim family laws have served to reinforce patriarchal gender relations and women's subordinate position within the family."[47] The family as defined in the Iranian Constitution is the primary unit of the society, noting that: "all laws, regulations, and pertinent programmes must tend to facilitate the formation of a family, and to safeguard its sanctity and stability of family relations on the basis of the law and the ethics of Islam."[48]

The public/private demarcation blurs in suggesting a separation of the private (the family) from the public (the state). A sharp separation does not exist in particular where family law is based on male-dominated interpretation of religious law. As Moghadam deliberates: "Far from being an enclave, the family is vulnerable to the state, and the law and social policies that impinge upon it undermine the notion of separate spheres. Yet the haven ideology persists and is often strategically deployed by state authorities and dissidents alike."[49] The OMSC activists have been pushed back into the "private" by the state (yet the private is regulated by the state), and so they are denied public spaces to hold public meetings and conferences. Women are therefore forced to hold meetings in the basement of their houses and in their flats and apartments. As stated by one of the activists:

> ... When we are denied space to conduct our activities, we have no other choice but to squeeze into our own apartments and homes to hold training workshops. Inevitably the police come to warn our neighbours about the "suspicious" comings and goings in our apartments. You [referring to officials in charge of arrests and

threats] try to sensitize our neighbours, so that perhaps they can carry out your duties in your stead.[50]

There have been instances where the parents of the younger activists have been threatened and warned of their children's collaboration with the Campaign and asked to caution their daughters and hence to keep them in the house.

> . . . Local police stations are brought on as your collaborators, and they work to coerce and threaten parents, so that they can confront their children. You call the homes of Campaign members, and inform their parents about the existence of lists—lists of persons who should be "advised" and list of persons scheduled to be "arrested." Interestingly enough, the police emphasize that parents should not convey these "private" conversations to their daughters; rather, they should advise them and guide them so that they are not deceived by others.[51]

Women activists in general, and in particular those in patriarchal societies, are threatened with their honor and their family's honor. The classical patriarchal view is that the women should be home-makers and should not be looking for equal rights, which could in turn lead to immorality, where girls and boys have sexual relations outside the confines of marriage. A general tactic used by male interrogators is to accuse one of adultery (*zina*). To accuse one of adultery is to bestow the ultimate insult and it permeates the uttermost private spaces. The interrogator who penetrates the interogee's most private space does so to lay an ultimate insult not only to the honor of the female interrogee but also as an insult to the males in her family.[52] Sexuality has become a tool of harassment of political activists, creating mistrust both in the public and the private. As Nahla Abdu writes: "In the context of the colonial state, sexual abuse, harassment and torture are often used as a direct tool for enforcing women's submission, compliance and obedience. They are means enforced to quell women's participation in the resistance movement."[53] However, one can argue that it is not only in the colonial context that women's participation in resistance movements is quelled but in any patriarchal society and in particular in countries where the regimes are authoritarian and theocratic. Women's treatment is exacerbated where one's honor depends on one's perceived piety even as torture, abuse, harassment, and threats are used to silence those who are perceived as an opposition. The state controls women's bodies and sexuality as a mode of political control over the family and the society at large.

I experienced similar tactics as explained above during interrogations in the summer of 2004 in Tehran. During this time my house was raided, my laptop, notes from interviews, and photos, as well as my passports (Iranian and Irish) were confiscated by the intelligence of interior ministry and I was placed under house arrest, which lasted two-and-a-half months.[54] I had somehow found myself in the midst of a wave of arrests of civil activists and webloggers.[55] On the first day of the interrogations, I was asked to collaborate with the Iranian security forces, while during another session I was accused of being an adulterer (*zina kar*). In a later session I was offered tea and sweets and was told that I should consider my interrogator a friend and that I should revaluate who my real friends are. The activists, journalists, and bloggers arrested during the summer of 2004 experienced humiliation, torture, and a few had to make false confessions that were televised. However, talking to women's rights activists arrested between 2005 and 2009, it seemed that most of the interrogations were not as explicit as is usually experienced by political activists. In a sense, regardless of the summons and arrests, at the first instance the interaction of security forces with women's rights activists prior to 2009, in comparison to their interaction with political activists, seems "softer." I agree with Parvin Ardalan's assertion that although women's rights activists, possibly "by virtue of their gender and the nature of their work," are positively discriminated against, nonetheless "the interaction of security forces with women's rights activists and the pressures they exerted on this sector" is delicate and yet complicated and in need of further analysis.[56] This complication is even more apparent now with some activists arrested during or after the post-2009 election protests who are serving sentences as long as ten years. The state authorities have used different techniques in their crackdown of women rights activists. These include threats, raiding of houses and offices, public and private arrests, invitations to collaborate with the security forces, and interrogations of all sorts, which at times may even "include tea and sweets."[57] Another technique used by the state is to create rumors and feelings of mistrust among the activists. They accuse them of being impious and agents of the West. As Ahmadi Khorasani states:

> . . . you start rumors about the ethical, financial, and sexual misconduct of campaign members, about their uncontrollable desire for fame, their relations with foreigners, their perpetration for carrying out velvet revolutions, and other strange and bizarre behavior which seem somehow to surface of their own accord. Of course, there "does" not exist any formal and organized venue through which these rumors are spread. But with the help of these rumors, the public can come to understand that the rights, are in fact, terribly dreadful women starved for attention and fame, in search of asylum in the West.[58]

These strategies—sticks and carrots or good cop, bad cop—are all different forms of state patriarchal control over women employed to weaken the women's movement.

Amidst all of the public/private threats, interrogations, and arrests, a surprising prison narrative has emerged. Prison, which is "a primary site for state control over the targeted population,"[59] is the site where the public and private collide. Since the start of the OMSC, many of its supporters have been interrogated, detained, imprisoned, and exiled. To the dismay of the authorities, these women, in particular those imprisoned, have managed in a short space of time to reshape and redefine the public/private sphere of the prison by bringing to the women prisoners tales of rights, freedom, and the Campaign, and to the public tales of the women prisoners. Women like Mahboubeh and Maryam, whose narratives are depicted below, are redefining spaces.

These prison narratives are important, for while not condoning criminality, they give a human face to women who are generally referred to as criminals while critically analyzing the reasons these women have resorted to murder. This usually includes having been in violent relationships and not having had access to any legal remedies. These prison narratives are a mixture of both loss and hope. Many are told by women rights activists who have found themselves in the same space as women prisoners in the *band nesvan* (women's ward) for disciplinary purposes due to their activism. These narratives collected prior to the 2009 elections shed a new light on the lives of women who have been entangled in a web of violent discrimination that is both legal and cultural and who previously were talked about as victims very rarely. The narratives are powerful and personal. They portray these women as victims of a society where discriminatory laws, patriarchal forces, and violent cultural contexts have pushed women to commit murder. Nahid Keshavarz, who spent 12 days in the notorious Evin prison, describes the women's ward as containing three sections and some 400 women. According to Keshavarz, those who committed crimes connected to drugs make up the majority of women prisoners. After this category there are those who have committed an illicit sexual act.[60] Third in number are those charged with scams, such as bounced checks, and fourth are women who have been charged with murder. The online narratives relate predominately to this last category: women who are charged with murder and awaiting the death penalty. The narratives are powerful and personal. They portray these women as victims of a society where discriminatory laws, patriarchal forces, and violent cultural contexts have pushed women to commit murder.

Maryam, a journalist and a woman's rights activist, is one of the interlocutors of these narratives. She is one of the 33 women who was arrested on March 4, 2007 while protesting the trial of five women's rights activist outside Branch 6 of the Revolutionary Court in Tehran. Maryam and two other young women were then transferred to the women's prison after protesting the lack of medical attention required by a number of women activists arrested. Maryam, who had previously visited the same prison as a journalist reporting on the condition of women's prisons in Iran,[61] narrates her experience as a prisoner:

> . . . I still do not believe that I am back at the women's prison. I am angry since they have separated the three of us from the others without any court case or legal reasoning, but I am so delighted to see the prison again that I have forgotten my anger. I am no more the young journalist who entered the prison with numerous previous arrangements. I am a prisoner, one of the 33 women, some of them are in solitary confinement. Our crime is the desire for equal rights.[62]

Maryam's narrative is emotionally charged. As a blogger she has used the internet as a platform to make public the situation of women prisoners. Monireh Baradaran describes Maryam and her contemporaries as a new generation of political prisoners who have experienced prison differently to others as reflected in their writings, given the freshness and honesty of their narratives. This style of narrative has become a hallmark of the women's movement:

> . . . We enter the room (cell) most of them wake up. Only the 20 years old Leila remains asleep. The rest are above 40 years and a few above 60. One by one, they open their eyes and they look at us as if they felt sorry for us being so young. They

formed a circle around us. Seeking the moment, I began telling them about the Campaign and women's rights. They could not believe that the women whose noise of hammering fists they had heard earlier today are the same journalists, social workers, and lawyers who work for women's rights. We tell them that many of the women who are now in solitary confinement are those working on the cases of Kobra Rahmanpour,[63] Ashraf Kolhar,[64] and Akram Ghavidel.[65] To our surprise they tell us that the woman who body-searched us downstairs was Akram Ghavidel. Apparently prisoners who are well-behaved get to help in the daily running of the prison. This is unbelievable. Everything is like a movie. Outside these walls Asieh Amini works for Akram's freedom and this side of the prison Akram has to take Asiye to a solitary cell, search her and lock the door. I don't know whether to laugh or cry. When I tell Akram, she doesn't believe it: "The same woman who went and saw my child? Swear to god, I didn't recognise her . . . ." Both our bodies tremble.[66]

Another trademark of these narratives is the activists' concern for women's rights. They do not have sufficient access to justice and they do not know their rights. Maryam depicts the women prisoners' lack of rights and their lack of knowledge of their rights:[67]

. . . Many of them are here for months, some for years, without knowing their fate. They don't know anything about the law. They have no lawyers and outside there is no one who cares to follow their case. Some don't have families, some have been abandoned by their families and some others have run away. I understand their pain with all of my being.[68]

Maryam continues:

Everything is like a movie, a scary movie but arresting. I had never even imagined that I could be in front of all these women, whose cases I am so familiar with and each of whose sentences (death) had at one point shaken me to the core. They were all there: Kobra Rahampour, Ashraf Kolhar, Akram Ghavidel, Shahla Jahed and many more whose names I didn't know; their pain was the same old pain of not having rights and not knowing their rights. I told Kobra that there are many who are active in search of justice and freedom for her. She looked at me with kindness and said: "I wish justice was executed for all women."[69]

Apart from a lack of knowledge of the law, the law itself is a hurdle for these women. Some were divorced by their husbands while in prison. When Maryam asks Akram why she killed her husband, Akram replies, "I wanted a divorce. But neither my husband nor the court granted me one."[70]

Mahboubeh, another woman's rights activist, writes about the women on death row whom she met in Evin prison in this way:

"Our husbands are lying in enclosed graves and we are in open graves. We too ceased to live the very day that we killed our husbands." These are the words of a woman who spends her nights on the three-story bed across from me. Her nights are filled with nightmares of the death of her husband—a husband she stabbed to death.

This is Evin prison—the women's ward. Nahid and I do not fully comprehend what national security we have undermined, nonetheless charged with this we spend our days in limbo in the midst of all these women. Ten of the sixteen women with whom we have shared a cell with for over a week, are here on charges of murdering their husbands. These women, having lost faith in a legal system that offers no hope and no protection, weave their days into the darkness of the night that lingers behind the tall walls of Evin. If our laws had the capacity to defend women charged with murder, they would not be here now, spending their time idly in waiting for the day that would swallow them (a term used by female inmates to describe execution day).

These women, they all seem kind and patient to me. They are women forced into marriages they did not choose, women who were forcibly married off at the age of 13 and 14, women whose husbands were chosen by their fathers. One of these women was forced into marriage through physical violence. She asks. "Why doesn't anyone listen to our problems or pains? Where was the judge when my husband forced me onto the streets, into prostitution, in an effort to earn enough money to support his habit of addiction? What is one to do? Which laws were meant to support me? Which laws were intended to save me? Why didn't the judge listen to my pleas? I grew weary. The law provided me with no refuge. I defended myself. Yes! I killed him!"[71]

According to Mahboubeh, many women have similar stories of being in abusive relationships, requesting a divorce that discriminatory laws will not allow, and deciding to take matters into their own hands. The willingness of women prisoners to take an active part in the campaign is another surprising aspect of these narratives:

The female inmate who has now started to record her own experiences in a small diary, pulls me aside and asks: "Can I help you in collecting signatures for the Campaign?" She wants me to use whatever means possible to get her a signature form, so that women who are condemned to spend their days at Evin prison, too can have the opportunity to create change for others. So that with their individual signatures they can bring hope to other women. And this reminds me of the last question asked by my interrogator before I was brought here: "your demands in the Campaign, including banning of polygamy, equal rights to blood money and testimony, are in contradiction to the foundations of Islamic jurisprudence and the foundations of the Islamic Regime. Given these facts, will you continue to ask for changes in the laws?" In response to this question, I wrote: "Yes! I know that our demands are not in contradiction to Islam." And today, after this experience, I am more determined than ever and I write: "I ask for changes to these discriminatory laws. I ask them in an effort to honor the dignity of all the women in my country."[72]

These narratives are clear indications of the extent of how the existing discriminatory laws against women can negatively affect women's livelihood, in some extreme cases driving them to murder. Through the depiction of women prisoners and their lack of knowledge of their rights, these narratives elucidate the necessity of a grassroots reform movement where women are educated about their rights. Such training should be carried out in a rights-based approach, while keeping in mind that international human rights norms are not effective unless implemented at the national level. The ultimate success of the Campaign cannot be measured due to the transitional nature of Iranian politics at the present time, but thus far, the ongoing Campaign has been successful in raising awareness both nationally and internationally of the existing legal discriminations against women in Iran. In addition, both the challenges and the successes of the Campaign can be used as a framework of reference for other women's rights movements in Muslim-majority countries.

The Campaign adopted by the new generation of feminist/activists is bringing to public attention the every-day realities of gender discrimination. The fifth generation of Iranian feminists are dedicated to new and innovative forms of agency such as street action. The campaign situates itself in public and private spaces. The public realm that was traditionally deemed masculine is merging with the feminine. The swaying of the pendulum, which is ultimately a tool of state control, has surprisingly redefined the public/private schism. Through the prison narrative and the reports on the campaign published on the Internet, discrimination faced by women in private has become publicized. However, the challenge arises as to how to hold on to public spaces reclaimed by the movement and how to institutionalize change. The campaign is but a new bridge between the shifting realms, whose foundations are being weakened by the pressures exerted by the state.

Part Two

Interfaith Perspectives on Loss and Hope

The Virtue of Christian Learning from Other Religions: The Substance of Things Hoped for

Francis X. Clooney, SJ

Faith is recognized as central to religious identity and a key factor distinguishing one tradition from others.[1] It seems to some that faith in particular is at stake because it may be threatened by too much learning about other religions; yet faith can also, in some cases, be the motivating force that encourages people to interreligious encounter. Love too has been seen as an incentive and a bridge that can bring people in different traditions together. But little has been said about hope, the third theological virtue, with respect to the interreligious context. In this chapter, I would like to talk about hope in relation to the Roman Catholic attitude toward interreligious learning, specifically in the context of my study of Hinduism. I am concerned specifically with how hope motivates us in interreligious learning.

Are there grounds for hope in interreligious study, that is to say, for its fruition in learning that is both academically respectable and theologically fruitful with respect to the traditions studied? Some would say no. Some remain skeptical simply on the grounds of a lack of evidence that any progress has been made in centuries of such study. Encounters have either been poorly done, or used for the wrong reasons, or properly executed but then titled toward results contrary to original intentions. I will argue for the importance of hope in the realm of interreligious learning, precisely because knowledge and hope are in a substantive relationship, both pertaining to what is real.

According to Thomas Aquinas, hope is a function of the appetitive power, "since movement towards things belongs properly to the appetite" (II.I.40.2), and hope is "a certain stretching out of the appetite towards good." It seeks the good and turns away from evil; it looks to the future, to what is arduous but possible to obtain. For there is, beyond us and not of our invention, a goodness essential to the world—the good and the real are convertible—and even when that good is not yet complete, we can hope to recognize how it is coming to be, approach it, and welcome it. In a theological context, hope is more than confidence or a natural instinct for it manifests the conviction that in our learning we will come to know God more deeply; for God is to some extent knowable, and it is supremely good to know God. This hope is essential in the study of religions as well, if that study is to be productive and useful with respect to Christian faith. In knowledge we find our way into encounter with reality, and at the same time verify our expectations about the world in God's eyes. This is what we hope for, a deep reason why we study religions other than our own.

It is useful early on to distinguish hope from an optimism that expects the best about interreligious understanding, as if things will get better in a straightforward way, ever progressing, thus fulfilling (Christian) expectations. But there is no basis for any simple version of optimism. Optimism, even if well meant, floats across the top of similarities and differences, and flows on regardless of obstacles and unanswered questions. Hope rather is grounded in reality in all its dark and light features; with reference to learning, it discloses what is to be hoped for precisely in actual learning. Hope is compatible with failure, gaps, incompletion, melancholy, and uncertainty, but in the end it expects discovery, recognition, and fruition. We can be hopeful even when what we learn disturbs us and when we do not know what to make of it. We can glimpse and have conviction regarding what we cannot grasp—and yet do not give up on as the destiny to which we are headed. Needless to say, if we forego optimism, we will be spared pessimism as well, the attitude that always, or ever in our day and age, things are always getting worse.

Nor is confidence the same as hope, even if we may be confident that we can learn, and that learning is for the better. But the grounding of this expectation lies in a conviction, in faith, as hope, about the nature of the world and all that is in it, created by God. So we have hope: however difficult learning may be, reality is in ways substantively though imperfectly knowable, from the largest patterns of the universe to the inner subtleties of human nature; all the individual things that can be known about reality cohere, and we can expect that what we learn is integral, the parts cohering and not contradicting one another; what we learn is also in keeping with the unity of God, for there is a convergence of truths with what we know of God; knowing can transform us in deep and salutary ways.

Benedict XVI's reading of hope

For a substantive theological perspective, I turn to Pope Benedict XVI's 2007 encyclical *Spe Salvi*, dedicated to the theme of hope.[2] Benedict begins by asking, "what sort of hope could ever justify the statement that, on the basis of that hope and simply because it exists, we are redeemed? And what sort of certainty is involved here?" (n. 1). Hope is not merely in a positive judgment about our world, but is grounded in encounter with God: "Jesus, who himself died on the Cross, brought something totally different: an encounter with the Lord of all lords, an encounter with the living God and thus an encounter with a hope stronger than the sufferings of slavery, a hope which therefore transformed life and the world from within" (n. 4). This hope in God's promises and deeds is not premised on optimism about the world. Nor is it merely a confidence that the world is becoming what we hope it will be. Hope is real and objective in its reference. It is a social and communal reality, not just "my" hope or merely a subjective mood.

Hope is an attitude about the future that changes how we dwell in the present moment. The Gospel message is not merely informative, but also performative: "the Gospel is not merely a communication of things that can be known—it is one that makes things happen and is life-changing. The dark door of time, of the future, has been thrown open. The one who has hope lives differently; *the one who hopes has been granted the gift of a new life*" (n. 2).[3] Turning to a key passage in the *Letter to the Hebrews*, Benedict argues for the substantive nature of faith in relation to the hope with which it is necessarily connected:

> In the eleventh chapter of the *Letter to the Hebrews* (v. 1) we find a kind of definition of faith which closely links this virtue with hope. Ever since the Reformation there has been a dispute among exegetes over the central word of this phrase, but today a way towards a common interpretation seems to be opening up once more. . . The sentence therefore reads as follows: "Faith is the *hypostasis* of things hoped for; the proof of things not seen." For the Fathers and for the theologians of the Middle Ages, it was clear that the Greek word *hypostasis* was to be rendered in Latin with the term *substantia*. The Latin translation of the text produced at the time of the early Church therefore reads: *Est autem fides sperandarum substantia rerum, argumentum non apparentium*—faith is the "substance" of things hoped for; the proof of things not seen. . . . (n. 7)

Faith is this apprehension and living out now of what God has promised, what is (surely) to come. This faith subsists in things hoped for and promised to us, and so it discloses how the world is objectively and in God. This faith sees God's work in the world as a future event and yet also changes how we live now. It draws the future forward into the present, so that "the present is touched by the future reality," as "the things of the future spill over into those of the present and those of the present into those of the future" (n. 7). It is more than a subjective disposition because even now it gives us "something of the reality we are waiting for, and this present reality constitutes for us a 'proof' of the things that are still unseen" (n. 7). This "materiality" of faith in things hoped for stands apart from other versions of material well-being: "Faith gives life a new basis, a new foundation on which we can stand, one which relativizes the habitual foundation, the reliability of material income. A new freedom is created with regard to this habitual foundation of life, which only *appears* to be capable of providing support. . ." (n. 8). All this affects practice too; in the life of saints "the new 'substance' has proved to be a genuine 'substance'; from the hope of these people who have been touched by Christ, hope has arisen for others who were living in darkness and without hope. In their case, it has been demonstrated that this new life truly possesses and is 'substance' that calls forth life for others" (n. 8).

Hope in the Christian study of Hinduism

That faith has to do with God's real work in the world and thus has a substance outside itself makes a difference in the interreligious context, where a willingness to learn is a sign of Christian hope. Christian hope gives a new value to interreligious learning as ordinarily disclosive of the good in others; whatever difficulties arise in the course of learning, we are intellectually, socially, and spiritually the better for this encounter because God's promises are substantive in what we encounter.

For examples of the kind of study I have in mind, I direct the reader to chapters 6 to 8 of my *Comparative Theology* where I refer to instances of comparative study I had recently (as of 2010) undertaken; namely:

1. An explication of a Catholic practice of interreligious learning that begins in a Hindu temple and concludes in meditations on St. Paul's Christology.
2. An inquiry into the *imago Dei* theme in Christian theologies of Genesis 1 in comparative reflection on a "highest sameness" with God in the *Mundaka Upanisad.*
3. The meaning of "Narayana" as a supreme Hindu name of God, understood in 108 ways, of which perhaps 100 are accessible and should be also agreeable to Christians seeking language about God.
4. Meditation on the three holy mantras of the Shrivaishnava Hindus, with careful attention to their meaning in Hindu theological tradition and, on that basis, how accessible they are to Christians for understanding and even prayer.
5. Reflection on three long hymns praising Hindu goddesses for the sake of an appropriation of them in Christian theological understanding, and subsequently for a reflective comparison with the Virgin Mary as praised in three Christian hymns.
6. Multiple religious belonging as clarified theologically by attention to a medieval Hindu verse, which expressed the view that God accommodates us, speaking and appearing in the terms we can understand and have come to expect.

This list is tedious as a set of examples without any principle that generalizes them and frees us from the details; but this specificity, which cannot be generalized, is the point: hope is in the details, which are reached only by study. In all these projects, I sought to be as scholarly as possible, yet also expectant about finding interreligious theological connections of significance and fruit for the Catholic community. To say that hope grounds my work is to say five things. First, there is a deep and true foundation for interreligious study that is not merely the subjective experience of the student or scholar. Second, we can legitimately, without detriment to faith, expect to "find God present" in what we study, but only by actually finding it there, not by a theoretical insubstantial guess about the other. Third, the Christian/non-Christian distinction does not justify restricting hope to the former while relegating despair and meaninglessness to the latter, as if making objective claims about them simply by knowing something about ourselves. Fourth, such study, progressing by reason and study, with respect for historical and cultural contexts, is properly theological, "in God," grounded as it is in the theological virtue of hope. Fifth, its results are accordingly to be appreciated as illuminative of what God is like. In all of these ways, the study of other religions is constituted as a deeply hopeful, deeply Christian enterprise.

Hope misunderstood as a tool for judging other people's religions

The logic of hope means that learning interreligiously need not be measured as a kind of progress that adds up to an ever better situation. Nor does hope permit a slide into an objectivist Christian reading of the other that permits claims about the other without a commensurate effort to know the other first. Reason guided by hope does not skip past or turn away from the other religions, as if it is possible quickly to catalogue and weigh their worth from the outside. Quick judgments, made without grounding in knowledge, betray a shallow "faith" that operates without deference to hope: as it were, faith without works.

While this chapter is guided by Benedict's teaching on hope, I must note that unfortunately there is a dark corollary to Benedict's teaching on hope, evident already in the words cited earlier, "hope has arisen for others who were living in darkness and without hope": as if Christian hope is mirrored in the objective hopelessness of their situation. When Benedict makes a strong case for the reality of God as that which grounds hope, he finds it necessary, by a kind of symmetry, to argue that (ancient and modern) religions without the named God of the New Testament are without hope. *Ephesians* is used to set the scene for a stark contrast marked by the rod of hope: "Paul reminds the Ephesians that before their encounter with Christ they were 'without hope and without God in the world' (Eph. 2.12). Of course he knew they had had gods, he knew they had had a religion, but their gods had proved questionable, and no hope emerged from their contradictory myths. Notwithstanding their gods, they were 'without God' and consequently found themselves in a dark world, facing a dark future" (n. 2). Benedict contrasts those living in hope and those living "in darkness and without hope," and maps this by a Christian/non-Christian distinction that makes a language of hope seem rather counterproductive in the interreligious context.

Benedict is speaking directly of religions of antiquity, but his point seems intended to extend to modern times as well. Christianity and hope are deeply, even necessarily, interconnected, as hope both gives one a future and allows one to live more fully in the present. He adds, "A distinguishing mark of Christians is the fact that they have a future," and "only when the future is certain as a positive reality does it become possible to live the present as well" (n. 2). The unstated corollary is that non-Christians do not, as non-Christians, have a future, and so cannot properly live well in the present.

But hope matured in hope does not require any such judgment. Instead, it exposes such claims as hypotheses that, no matter how deeply and sincerely grounded in faith, are themselves not yet faith-with-hope. They do not yet exist *in substantia* as real claims about the real world in which we live.

Hope with respect to one Hindu tradition

We need to question the contrast that creeps in—not inevitably, but not unsurprisingly—when hope is preserved as a distinguishing sign of Christian faith. In part such a claim might be a matter of terms—if "hope" is by definition "Christian hope," then there is nothing more to say. But hope is about more than how we use words. Does Benedict really mean that it is generally true that people in other traditions believe and live differently because they are in darkness and they have no hope? Their reality, it seems, would then be lacking in the *hypostasis*, the *substantia* of things unseen. But if hope and the "things hoped for" are substantive and deeply engrained in reality, it might well be observable in the lives of non-Christians. To put it simply, unless we have defined hope as "Christian hope," then what is "out there" should help us decide whether non-Christians live as if God is real to them. The substance is available to those who study, not to those who conjecture favorably or unfavorably.

A single example from my own research on the Shrivaishnava Hindus will serve the purpose here.[4] In his *Essence of the Three Mysteries,* chapters 13–19, the medieval Hindu theologian Vedanta Deshika sketches the behavior of those who have taken refuge with the Lord in a complete surrender of their past, present, and future into God's hands. For those who have surrendered, life is entirely free from grief and anxiety because all is in God's hands, yet still disciplined in accord with what he sees as necessary and presupposed as societal expectations (such as caste) that govern the lives even of people living in accord with God's will. Old structures pertain but with new foundations and purposes. In *Essence* chapter 13, Deshika describes the person who has taken refuge, just as he had previously focused on the discontent (chapter 7) and desperate helplessness (chapter 10) of the person seeking the way of refuge. *Bhagavad Gita* 18.66, known as the "last" or "ultimate" verse (*Charama Sloka*), guides the ethical exposition of the *Essence* in chapters 13–19: "Having completely given up all modes of righteousness, to Me alone come for refuge. From all sins I will make you free. Do not grieve."

The person who has surrendered responsibility to the Lord is free from further duties: "Beginning immediately after taking refuge, the person established in this distinctive means no longer has any connection with anything that has to be done regarding the expected results. By performing just once the part he had to do, he is finished." Because the Lord is now the primary actor on behalf of such a person, she or he can live without anxiety or grief: "The Lord of all, who is independent, whose intentions come true, and who gives the result, is the one who has said, 'Do not grieve.' So [the person taking refuge] should examine his situation: having surrendered his burden he is now a person without any burden. The Lord of all, who has agreed to be the objective means and accordingly has said, 'To Me alone come for refuge,' is also the one who has decided to give the result, saying 'From all sins I will make you free.'" The result of taking this promise seriously is a radical rearrangement of priorities, with a consequent relief and deep joy: "When he sees the Lord who is trusted, capable, and the means, [the person taking refuge] no longer has doubts regarding the accomplishment of the goal, and is freed of any burden. All other means are uprooted and other goals disappear without a trace, and he is like a person with nothing who has received a great treasure without effort, and he rejoices at the prospect of life's supreme goal, that he is now to obtain."[5] Such joy cannot be mandated, but Deshika can highlight its normative value for the person who has taken refuge:

One of the prerequisites for taking refuge is grief before taking refuge. If a person has no grief before taking refuge, he will be lacking a necessary prerequisite for performing it since, by the principle "No cause, no effect," his means will be ineffective. But similarly, when he reflects upon himself after taking refuge, if then he still grieves owing to tepidity regarding the words of his protector, then, by the principle "No effect, no cause," it follows that his performance of the means (i.e. surrender) had been incomplete. In that case, we know that its fruit will be delayed, since he still needs to complete the means. The person who was previously full of grief and who is now free from grief in accord with the prohibition, "Do not grieve," is the one known to have taken refuge properly.[6]

Or, as Deshika aptly suggests in *Essence* 11, the person who has taken refuge is like someone who has transferred responsibility for his or her worldly affairs to a reliable friend, and thereafter sleeps peacefully at night, free from care about the future.[7]

Now unless "hope" really is stipulated to mean only an explicitly Christian hope, then Deshika's exposition seems to mark a life filled with hope, grounded in God's promises and in surrender to God. The hope that drives study and makes us expect to learn about God by studying another religion enables us to recognize something we did not know before, even if we had grounds to expect it: hope is effective in life of a Shrivaishnava after surrender to God, hope as a faith living out now what God has promised for the end time: "Having completely given up all modes of righteousness, to Me alone come for refuge. From all sins I will make you free. Do not grieve." This can be taken as a true sign of God's presence, even if this is a hope that is therefore not simply or merely a characteristic of Christian life. Only an optimist turned pessimist, or someone pessimistic about relativism, would feel warranted in looking at the Shrivaishnava tradition and insisting, "There is nothing there."

Benedict seems to be without hope about other religions in their substance. Without giving any detail about any religion other than his own and that of the ancient Ephesians as commented on by St Paul, he sharply distinguishes those of us who "have always lived with the Christian concept of God" from those "without God in this world":

> Yet at this point a question arises: in what does this hope consist which, as hope, is "redemption?" The essence of the answer is given in the phrase from the *Letter to the Ephesians* quoted above: the Ephesians, before their encounter with Christ, were without hope because they were "without God in the world." To come to know God—the true God—means to receive hope. We who have always lived with the Christian concept of God, and have grown accustomed to it, have almost ceased to notice that we possess the hope that ensues from a real encounter with this God. (n. 3)

In other contexts a Catholic theologian such as Benedict might well insist that God is everywhere in the world and no one is entirely: "without God in the world," but here he chooses to explain Christian hope in part by judging that other religions are substantively defective and hope-less.[8]

The question I am raising about Benedict's judgment on religions has in this context strictly to do with the place of hope in the matter. Does a Christian appreciation of hope and the substantive nature of hope necessarily entail the opinion that non-Christians are without hope, that no substance of hope can be found in the texts and practices of those members of other religions? I suggest that hope tells us that the things of God are coming true, even now and in the substance of who we are, and that no part of the world and certainly no people are merely hopeless. Hope, which is not merely subjective, is not merely a static property that belongs to some and not to others. Hope is not just about Christian things, since in Christ God is already everywhere at work, including beyond Christianity. Hope seeks substance and dwells in the details and does not allow us to judge religions in the abstract, or solely by attention to our own tradition. In this regard hope is closer to love, for like faith and hope, love and hope too are inextricably interconnected. Like love, hope moves beyond obstacles and discovers common ground rather than sharpening the distinction between two groups of people, those with hope and those bereft of it. Benedict's own rich insights into the objective nature of hope, its reality in the reality of God, and its power as a hope for the future in transforming our current reality—all suggest that a more dedicated and attentive look at religions in their substantive particulars is implied by hope and urged on by it.

Despair and presumption as the opposite of hope

It might seem at first that the real opposite to hope is a deterioration of Christian confidence about the truth of Christian faith in the face of what is learned from other traditions, driven by a worry that reckless interreligious learning undermines Christian uniqueness, depriving Gospel promises of their urgency. In this scenario, optimistic scholars become a problem and suffer a crisis, since the search for the optimum may suggest a rivalry in which we lose if they win, or in which we may end up feeling pessimistic about the uniqueness of our faith—first hopeless about the other and then, ironically, increasingly hopeless about ourselves.

But if hope subsists in a substantive claim about the world, it need not reduce to a narrow confidence in one's own tradition as special and superior to the other, particularly as long as such confidence remains in an important theological sense unsubstantiated. But if we are thinking of hope with its substantive claim about the world in God's eyes, then the vices are quite different.

Aquinas reminds us[9] that opposite to hope are two vices, despair and presumption. These are two ways of turning away from the reality of God's world, instead trusting in ourselves and our self-serving narrative of the world. In the interreligious context, *despair* occurs when we do not believe that what God has promised will be found to be true in and after interreligious learning, and when therefore we turn away from that study because our secret lack of hope is the real disease weakening our faith. *Presumption* occurs when we become entirely satisfied with ourselves, forgetting that hope is not self-confidence or a subjective state of being pleased with ourselves, and all the more so by finding, again and again, that by comparison others are lacking. Hope by contrast does not give up on or skip over learning and does not preemptively reduce wisdom to reaffirmations of what we already know. Hope pushes us forth, to find God beyond the bounds of that dimension of the world, however fundamental it necessarily is, that is already marked with familiar signs of Christian faith. The real opposite of hope lies in any relegation of interreligious learning to the margins or to the subjective: pessimism regarding the substantive nature of what can be learned or instead an untested and unsubstantial self-confidence that requires no learning about the other in order to test claims.

If confidence and optimism are not key factors, then the deeper interreligious learning may at first be all the more difficult and challenging. The discovery of great depths in other traditions may do us the favor of robbing us of grounds for presumption and despair about ourselves and our tradition. Interreligious learning—in which there are no easy modes of study, no easy answers—dashes our expectations of success, and of immediate, convenient results. But if we are stripped of such self-confirmation, convenience, and rewards, we will be able to be more hopeful in practice, in study. In hope, the loss that learning occasions and the dismay that accompanies the shattering of our presumptions about ourselves clear the way for a still deeper Christian hope. Faith humbled and strengthened by hope wants to learn more, and then Hindu wisdom (and of course other such wisdoms) will illumine what we and how we learn regarding any given topic. Then we find given back to us, differently, the very beliefs and sentiments we had been suffocating inside versions of faith and hope that were lifeless because too safe, never tested.

Hope and dialogue

Hope then provides intellectual and spiritual conviction in support of a solid and enduring learning across religious borders, a learning that takes seriously who we are, our commitments and capacities, but also respects the religious other substantively, proceeding by detailed attention to another tradition. Hope instigates interreligious theological learning because it expects to find common ground across religious boundaries, "the substance of things hoped for" on both sides of the interreligious border. It demands a commitment to a real learning that does not back away from what is actually learned. *Dominus Iesus*, no liberal tract, makes the point firmly:

> Inter-religious dialogue, which is part of the Church's evangelizing mission, *requires an attitude of understanding* and a relationship of *mutual* knowledge and *reciprocal* enrichment, in obedience to the truth and with respect for freedom.[7] In the practice of dialogue between the Christian faith and other religious traditions, as well as in seeking to understand its theoretical basis more deeply, *new questions arise* that *need* to be addressed through pursuing *new* paths of research, advancing proposals, and suggesting ways of acting that call for attentive discernment.[10]

This comment on dialogue might be extended to include the full range of ways in which we learn interreligiously, for it means little unless we learn with hope and not just a cautious and self-protective faith. Discerning God's will more clearly through study has a price, since such learning is not merely about ourselves. There are messy uncertainties and implications that cannot be predicted in advance, and an outcome that is ultimately in the hands of God; it is not for anyone to close the doors on different plausible openings before they are even considered:

> With respect to the *way* in which the salvific grace of God—which is always given by means of Christ in the Spirit and has a mysterious relationship to the Church—comes to individual non-Christians, the Second Vatican Council limited itself to the statement that God bestows it "in ways known to himself." Theologians are seeking to understand this question more fully. Their work is to be encouraged, since it is certainly useful for understanding better God's salvific plan and the ways in which it is accomplished.[11]

This is a hopeful statement in a document not uniformly radiant with hope.[12] If we do not have faith in the truth of God's promises, the substance of a hope in the promises of God that cannot but be present in the substance of the other tradition too, we may reduce hope to mere certainties. If so, dialogue will be impossible. Pessimism about others, cloaking a sly optimism about ourselves, will occupy the place of hope. It would be ironic and sad were concerns about where interreligious learning might end to preempt the start of that learning, thus reducing the mystery of God at work in all religions to what we are already comfortable with—hope reduced to the comfort zone of our self-confidence.

If grounded in hope, the study of religious traditions other than our own has first of all to be worthwhile in itself, not intimidated by worries about where such learning leads. This in turn requires hope for and about and in those traditions: those believers, whom we begin to understand from a Christian perspective, are not merely in darkness or merely hopeless; even now they are grounded in God's presence and enriched by the coming true of God's promises. The examples I gave earlier simply illustrate a point that applies both to scholarship and to other forms of dialogue: it is hope that makes the encounters possible, and it is in the detail that this hope vindicates the truth of dialogue. Without reducing expectation to optimism or to comfort for the comfortable, hope gives us the grounds for believing that we are better off for studying religions, and that we discover God more deeply in the patient time of our study across religious boundaries.

Interreligious hope in practice

Earlier I mentioned that my field of study is classical Hinduism, which I study as a Catholic theologian. At this writing I have recently finished with another major instance of my approach, a comparative study titled *His Hiding Place Is Darkness: A Hindu-Catholic Theopoetics of Divine Absence* (Stanford University Press, 2013). In it I read the *Song of Songs* with its medieval commentators, alongside some Hindu mystical poetry with its medieval commentators. In studying this mystical love poetry with special attention to the absence and presence of the beloved, my goal is to go deeper into my tradition while also taking another tradition to heart, as a Catholic paying attention to both. The book draws on religious poetry rich in multiple meanings and possessed of no firm conclusions. As such, *His Hiding Place Is Darkness* also manifests my refusal to keep entirely separate dedication to my own tradition and intense interest in another. Allowing the poetry of the *Song* and the poetry of the *Holy Word* to mingle, so to speak, I am suggesting that we can intensify our own spiritual and theological commitments by taking other traditions seriously.

His Hiding Place Is Darkness is not a work of optimism. It is about divine absence, a hiding of God that can be accentuated by the disorientation arising in interreligious study. As such, it does not prove that all religions are converging in an ever more benign climate. Nor is it grounded in the kind of Christian self-confidence that seems robust until it is deflated by the discovery of challenging ideas and spiritual insights in other traditions as well. It is rather a testimony to hope that does not shroud the outcome in optimism or pessimism, but believes that learning will be possible and good and transformative, even when neither the poet nor the theologian can state with sure confidence where things will end up, in a real future, its eventualities not settled in advance. The beloved may be absent for a very long time, after all, and turn up in another, unexpected place. As a scholar I work in hope, expecting to know more of God through my study. Hope puts aside both relativism and exclusivism, standing rather on the firm ground of a conviction that God is at work in the world around us, and in the ideas and words of our sisters and brothers in other religions. And so we are encouraged to great zeal in our scholarship as a manifestation of faith and not a threat to it, a sacrament of love and not distraction from service, and as is most relevant here, a deep enactment of the Christian virtue of hope in interreligious learning:

> We want each one of you to show the same diligence, so as to realize the full assurance of hope to the very end, so that you may not become sluggish, but imitators of those who through faith and patience inherit the promises. (Heb. 6.11–12)

A Healing Process in Jewish Theology: From Passivity to Protest to Peace

Anson Laytner

Part I: Traditional explanations for suffering

I

During the time that my late wife worked at Seattle's Woodland Park Zoo, I saw more than my share of films about life on the African savannah. One set of images stands out in my mind from these sorts of films: a herd of zebra or other such creatures suddenly erupting in terrified flight as a lion or cheetah charges through the herd to single one beast out for slaughter. Then, once the deed is done, the herd returns to its normal munching. The carnivore is an instrument of random terror in the daily life of the herd.

This leads me to realize that human life is not much different. We go to work and live our private lives, but always with a lurking awareness and a silent dread of disease and death. Then someone we know is brought down by some malady, and we offer our condolences and support, we shake our heads, utter private thanks that it wasn't us, and return to living life as normal until the next time. Disease and death are instruments of random terror in our daily lives.

Now the beast does not ask why the big cat chases it as prey but, try as we might, we can never fathom the random terror of disease and death. Curiously, it is life's tragedies more than life's joys that cause most of us to seek meaning . . .

What *is* the meaning of suffering? For generations, humanity has tried to make sense out of suffering; each religion offering a variety of explanations to comfort those in need and in answer to this question.

II

It is very hard to live in a world where random natural terror runs amok. We crave order. In most religious traditions, including those of Asian origin, there *is* the belief that all that happens to us is somehow part of a universal plan, whether that structure is karma or divine providence. According to these beliefs, all that happens to us acquires meaning precisely because it occurs as part of a universal order.

In the monotheistic Abrahamic traditions, God is ultimately responsible for everything. If we believe the Creator operates with a plan, then we must accept whatever happens as God's will, even perceived evils. "Submission" is the term used in Islam, and it applies equally to the Jewish and Christian traditions as well. However, it seems to be human nature to expect only the good from God. But, although some survivors of a plane crash may attribute their survival to God's will, most of us would probably shun the corollary that it must therefore also have been God's will that everyone else perish. At the same time, if we truly believe that God is always in control of everything, what point would there be in doing anything? Why seek medical treatment, a human intervention, when "God" has ordained that you be ill or healthy?

The Abrahamic religions place a special premium on the concept of divine providence: the belief that God oversees and/or controls to some degree everything that happens both to humanity as a whole and to us as individuals. Beginning with the Bible, these faiths teach that God is actively involved in history: selecting individuals through whom to reveal the divine will; intervening in human affairs; testing, punishing, and rewarding individuals and whole nations based on their adherence to divinely revealed moral laws and as part of some divine plan. To that end, it is traditionally believed that natural phenomena, so-called natural evils, are used by God for positive ends. Much effort has been spent to explain two apparently contradictory beliefs, the first of which fits into the second: First, human beings have free will; but God is omniscient. Second, there is one God, who is omnipotent, personal, and perfectly good; but evil exists.

Over the centuries, each faith has developed a number of solutions to this conundrum, so that today a sufferer has a veritable smorgasbord of theodicies from which to choose. Here is a taste of some major ones from the Abrahamic faiths[1]—and may the scholars of religion forgive me for generalizing:

1. Sometimes, the inexplicability of suffering is asserted in combination with an attitude of submission. Individuals are encouraged to place their trust in God's goodness and in God's plan for each of us, even if it includes suffering. Whatever happens, whether good or bad, is God's will and God alone knows why. Therefore, one simply ought to submit to God's inscrutable will and realize that whatever happens is for the best because it is divinely ordained. Having an attitude of "Don't ask" is appropriate because questioning demonstrates a lack of trust or faith in God's plan. There *is* something very comforting about surrendering control of one's life to the divine. It is capable of sustaining inner peace even in the face of great suffering. It keeps our world safe, secure, and predictable even when life's experiences might well suggest otherwise. Perhaps there *is* a divine plan in which both personal and national suffering makes sense. Perhaps the good suffer in this world for sins committed but *are* rewarded in the Hereafter, whereas the wicked may prosper now but will pay later. Perhaps there is "a divine integrity beyond our knowing," but personally, after the Holocaust, I find this response to suffering to be very offensive because what kind of God and divine plan can involve the deaths of 6 million Jews, not to mention millions of other people? What kind of God and divine plan can allow for the untimely death of anyone?[2]

2. Sometimes, suffering is seen as a punishment for sins committed and therefore is seen parentally as a loving discipline—like corporal punishment—meant to redirect one to follow God's ways. One is taught to analyze one's behavior for sin and to accept such suffering with gratitude. In some biblical books, this view was applied both to the suffering of the nation and the individual. This route is preferred by the Jewish prayer book and popular theology. After the Holocaust, for me personally, this response to suffering is simply obscene because it makes of God an abuser[3] and presumes to know the mind of God in this matter.

3. Sometimes, suffering is seen as a test or trial of individual faith, such as Job was subjected to. If one can endure it without losing faith, one will emerge spiritually more refined. Furthermore, it is an honor to be chosen because God only tests those presumably worthy—and God "never gives one more than one can handle." Traditional imagery includes smelted metal, a pruned tree, a clay pot that gets knocked to test its mettle, or a poked fire. Here too, since God only tests the righteous, one ought to accept these suffering with loving acceptance. In the Jewish tradition, this sort of suffering is called "sufferings of love." Again, after the Holocaust, for me personally, this response to suffering is simply obscene because both the test and the reward—not to mention the character of the Judge—pale in comparison to the numbers of dead and the suffering they endured.

4. A Jewish "arguing with God" approach holds to the traditional concept of God but asserts that much suffering happens for no apparent reason and is unwarranted. Therefore, protests can and should be lodged to God against God for these perceived injustices—even if there is no alternative other than to endure them as part of the divine scheme. (More on this in Part II.)

5. A distinctly Christian approach holds that when we suffer, we share something with Jesus, because in human form he suffered as we do. Suffering makes human beings the wounded hands and feet of Jesus. God/Jesus suffers when we suffer. This is comforting in a way, but one has to ask: "So what? What tangible benefit does God's suffering along with us accomplish—although in the long term belief in resurrection means to have hope that all will be rectified in the afterlife (the afterdeath?), a belief that is shared as well by traditional Judaism and Islam?" Nonetheless it still begs the question: "Why did God once intervene actively but not now?"

6. Some Christian denominations embrace the existence of "Satan" as an opposing power to God. Good things come from God; bad things come from the Devil, a demi-deity. Human life is the battleground between two or more cosmic forces.[4] Therefore, one prays to the good God for support and strength against the Bad. As a monotheist, I reject this duality of power—although it is very tempting to see the Nazis and their allies as demons and not humans.

The Holocaust—which for me, as a Jew, remains the zenith of human cruelty to other humans and the nadir of divine activity in the face of immense suffering—poses a challenge to the validity of any of these theories because it applies our concepts of God and prayer, and suffering and providence, to the most extreme of life situations. This is what I call "the Holocaust litmus test": *Whatever your key theological concepts are, they must not only apply to your own life, the challenge is that they also make sense of Auschwitz.*[5] To put it crassly, do you really expect that God will pay attention to mundane, petty petitions—such as supporting your team in a football match (or harder still, to imbue those attending your board meeting with wisdom) when God apparently ignored the prayers of the many people who died in Auschwitz, or in Cambodia, or Bosnia, or Rwanda, or Darfur? If God does not answer the prayers of people in those extreme situations, why should God be expected to answer our minor requests?

For me, the Holocaust has created an irreversible rift between the religious past—and its views on suffering—and the present. I would rather suffer the agony of unknowing than choose to rely on any of these hoary answers.

Part II: Arguing with God—prayers of protest

I

In most of our faith traditions, prayer—by which I mean public prayer—is limited to praise, petition, penitence, and thanksgiving. However, for me, and perhaps for many other people today, these traditional forms of prayer may no longer work the way they did for our ancestors. Simply stated, the stories of God's miraculous interventions into history as recorded in the Bible often stand in stark contradiction to the darker realities of human life ever since. Why then, but not now? Why for them, but not for us?

We cannot have it both ways. The Exodus and the Holocaust—to name the opposing poles, with the one standing for the Biblical experience and the other for historical experience—contradict each other. Either the account of the Exodus from Egypt is true or our experience of the Holocaust is true, but both can't be true without something having to give way. If the Exodus story is accurate, then we ought to question where God's saving power was during the Holocaust. But if our experience of the Holocaust is accurate, then we ought to have no expectations of God and should question our continued adherence to the concept of a God who intervenes in the course of human life and history.

But both cannot be right because that would mean that God apparently acts capriciously. To hold that the Exodus story is true and that the Holocaust experience is also true leaves God open to charges of being cruel and heartless, indifferent to human suffering and injustice, and deaf to pleas for mercy.[6]

The problem is not unique to the Jewish people. I imagine that the contradiction between "Exodus," the human expectation in the divine, and "Holocaust," the actual human experience, resonates with people of many faith traditions and cultures—where and whenever bad things happen to basically good people. This contradiction between expectation and experience has led many people to suffer a sense of alienation from traditional God concepts. If negative feelings like these were part of a human relationship, they would be communicated to the other person in the hopes of gaining understanding and change. But when the troubling party is God, the form of communication is called prayer and, unfortunately, anger and protest generally are considered inappropriate in tone for addressing "our Father in Heaven."

II

In Jewish culture, however, there is acceptance of a tradition of protest, what I call "arguing with God," that goes all the way back to Abraham. In the Tanach/Bible, many people protested and argued with God—Abraham, Moses, Elijah, Jeremiah, Job—either on behalf of the people or for their own sakes. In this approach, because of the Covenant (*Brit*, in Hebrew), the Jewish people have the right, as does God, to take the other party to task if said party is perceived not to be fulfilling the terms of the Covenant. Thus, when bad things happened, God simultaneously could be praised for the miracles of the Exodus *and* reproached and criticized for failing to intervene in the current crisis. In this way, the people's expectation to see God's ultimate justice was affirmed, but their feelings of anger and abandonment also were validated. In other words, this form of prayer endeavored to hold fast to both ends of the contradiction.[7]

Consider the following examples:

As early as the Psalms, in this case Psalm 44, God's great acts in the past are celebrated: "We have heard with our ears, O God, our ancestors have told us what deeds You performed in their time, in the days of old." But then just a few stanzas later come harsh accusations:

> Yet You have rejected and disgraced us . . . You let them devour us like sheep; You disperse us among the nations . . . All this has come upon us, yet we have not forgotten You been false to Your covenant . . . Rouse Yourself; why do You sleep, O Lord? . . . Why do You hide Your face, ignoring our affliction and distress? Arise and help us, redeem us, as befits Your faithfulness.

Words like these are both a protest *and* an argument, or at least one side of an argument. God's apparent inactivity is questioned—but God's power and authority are not—because of the expectation that God *would* respond, that God *would* answer their protest with action.

Jewish suffering over the centuries has made a case for a sustained argument with God, often based on the Exodus precedent. In a rabbinic story (*midrash*) dealing with the destruction of the Temple and the oppression in Roman times, the following complaint was lodged:

> Master of the Universe! You did wonders for our ancestors, will You not do them for us? . . .What a work You performed in bringing them forth out of Egypt and dividing the sea for them! But You have not done anything like that for us! . . . You did it for them, but not for us. . .When will You work a good sign for us? . . . "show us Your mercy, O Lord, and grant us Your salvation."[8]

And, this being *midrash*, with the intent to provide comfort to its listeners, God responds: "Indeed I shall be favorable to you also" and Psalm 85.2 is cited as a proof-text for God's intentions in the future. Anger, complaint, plea, and a word of divine comfort—it was an effective message for the people to hear in those difficult, trying times.

Sometimes the rabbis actually prayed this way themselves. Raba, one of the sages of the Babylonian Talmud, quoted the opening line of Psalm 44 in a prayer for rain and an end to persecution: "Master of the Universe! 'O God, we have heard with our ears, our ancestors have told us, what deeds You performed in their time, in the days of old'—but as for us, with our own eyes, we have not seen it!" Rain came, but Raba was rebuked by God in a dream for his audacity.[9]

Centuries later, during the massacres of the Crusades, rabbi-poets wrote poem/prayers called *piyyutim*, and many of these continued this quarrel with God. In one of these prayers, the author plays savagely on the words of Exodus 15.11: "Who is like You among the mighty (*elim*)?" But he adds one letter to the word *elim* so it becomes *elmim*, with the result that the verse now reads: "Who is like You among the dumb?"

> Who is like You among the dumb, my God? You kept silence. You were silent when they destroyed Your Temple. You remained silent when the wicked trod Your children underfoot . . . We came through fire, water, and flame. They mastered us, stoned us, and hung us on scaffolds. They rode on our heads, but we declared our love for You. We descended into Sheol while living and we were swallowed . . . You are the zealous one and avenger, where then is Your vengeance?[10]

This prayer is all the more audacious because it puns the opening line of a major prayer in the Jewish liturgy that celebrates God's intervention at the Sea of Reeds.

Another example, written during the Chmielnitski pogroms of seventeenth-century Poland/Ukraine, which saw the massacre of at least 100,000 Jews and is considered one of the worst slaughters in Jewish history, demands: "When will the day of the final miracles come? Your sons and Your daughters are given into the hands of an alien nation and Your eyes see! Show us Your miracles as during our Exodus from Egypt!"[11]

But prayers of protest were not always angry. In the eighteenth century, some Jews of Eastern Europe sought a new way to cope with tragedy and created Hasidism, which sought to minimize suffering by focusing on the immediacy of prayer, the presence of God in all things, and the need to live joyfully. The Hasidic *rebbes* (masters) presumed a personal and intimate relationship with God and encouraged their followers to have the same. Protest was part of that relationship with God, but, unlike the medieval arguments, Hasidic arguments were gentler, more loving, and even humorous. Laughter has always been a great antidote to suffering. One of my favorite Hasidic stories concerns the great Hasidic master Levi Yitzhak of Berditchev and a simple tailor:

> On one Yom Kippur, the Rabbi interrupted services to call up a simple tailor before the entire congregation. He asked him to relate his argument with God from the previous day. The tailor replied: "I declared: 'Dear God, You want me to repent of my sins during the past year, but I have committed only minor offenses: I may have kept leftover cloth instead of giving it to my customers, or I may have eaten in a non-Jewish home, where I worked, without washing my hands. But You, dear God, have committed grievous sins: You have taken away babies from their mothers,

and mothers from their babies. But I'll make a deal with You: You forgive my sins and I will forgive Yours!'"

Said the Rabbi, shaking his head: "Why did you let God off so easily? You could have forced Him (to send the Messiah) to redeem all of Israel . . ."[12]

What is striking about this story is the fact that the tailor's quarrel with God took place in the context of an accepting community and an accepting faith. After all, his rabbi asked him to repeat his prayer before the entire congregation—and then chided him for not striking a harder bargain.

And this brings us to the post-Holocaust era. Even now, the Jewish quarrel with God continues, although today it is our poets and authors, not generally rabbis, who continue the tradition. Consider this poem by Frederich Torberg about a Passover seder held during the War:

Lord, I am not one of the just.
Don't ask me, Lord, for I could not answer.
I do not know, you see, why for your servants here
This night is so different from all the others. Why?
The youngest child was happy once
To learn the answer at the table feast:

Because we were slaves in Egypt,
In bondage to wicked Pharaoh
Thousands of years ago . . .

The youngest child who heard all this
Has long since lost his faith.
The answer of old no longer holds,
For next year never came, O Lord,
And the night weighs down heavy and dark.

We still have not wandered across the sand.
We still have not seen the Promised Land,
We still have not eaten the bread of the free,
We still have not done with the bitter herbs.

For time and again in our weary wanderings
Pharaoh has set upon our trail,
Behind us he comes with his bloody henchmen
The carts, O Lord, do you hear their clatter
O Lord, where have you led us to!

You sent us on without a star,
We stand at the shore and stare on high,
O Lord, the flood has not returned,
O Lord, the night is not yet past,
"Why is this night so different from . . ."[13]

As with previous generations, argument and protest are but back-handed ways of affirming the same vision for the world as normative prayer. Once the protest was lodged—and however that argument was made—it was assumed that, at some point in the future, God would make things right. The point is that *if* God had not saved Israel from Egyptian bondage, *then* there would be no expectation that God would save Israel again. But, since it was traditionally believed that God *did* save Israel in Egypt—that God *does* watch over humanity and that God *does* intervene in history—therefore, when experience contradicted expectation, prayers of protest were one response that the people and their spiritual leaders chose to utilize to voice their upset.

III

Perhaps we should try expressing our anger with God when we gather to pray in our respective faith communities and/or when we gather to mourn and grieve over loved ones? Perhaps doing this might be efficacious, if not for God, then at least for us in our pain.

It was precisely this reasoning that led to the one and only occasion on which I personally and publicly called God to account with my own prayer of protest. When my sister-in-law, Jane, died suddenly and tragically of a brain tumor at age 63, I composed a prayer for myself, and for those members of our family and friends, who had trouble accepting what had happened and who could not, in good faith, utter the words of divine praise required of us by the traditional liturgy. It was my intention to speak the truth about things, but even more importantly, I viewed my words as therapeutic or pastoral, meant to begin moving us from anger toward acceptance. That is the reason why, in this prayer, I turn from confronting God to challenging ourselves.

> In the funeral service we pray: "The Rock, His work is perfect; for all His ways are just . . . Righteous are You, Adonai, in taking away or giving life . . . None should presume to question Your judgments. Praised be the True Judge."
>
> *But we do question; we do protest!* Ribbono Shel Olam, Ruler of the World, I call You to task for breaking two of Your own Commandments . . . You have murdered and You have stolen. With this cancer, part of Your creation, You have murdered first (her brother) Michael, and now Jane, cut them down in the prime of their lives . . . And, as if this were not enough, You have stolen. You have stolen precious years that ought to have belonged to Jane. You have stolen years of love and companionship from her, from her husband, from her mother, from her sister, from her children, from her beloved grandchildren, and from her many friends and colleagues. Dear God, it is intolerable what You put us through sometimes!
>
> And yet, what choice do we have? Whatever happens, happens. There is no way to avoid this truth of existence . . . We can only accept and continue on, dealing with our feelings of loss and grief as best we can.
>
> So, dear God, although we must accept what has happened . . . that does not mean that we accept it as Your will. We cannot, we will not, offer words of praise to You if indeed this was Your deed.

But we can offer thanks for the very existence of this wonderful woman, for how Jane touched our many lives in so many different ways: as child, sister, wife, mother, in-law, grandmother, friend, colleague, and therapist. Though her life was too short by half, she lived it passionately, intensely, and we are all better for having had her as a portion of our own life experiences. Her life was indeed a blessing to us all.

For having known her, and for having loved her, and for having been loved by her, we gather now both to honor her memory and praise Your Holy Name. Amen.

The experience of suffering—because it is both personal and collective—is always traumatic. Should people not express feelings of anger, betrayal, abandonment, and injustice? Should people sit on their feelings and pretend that nothing ever happened; that all is well between them and God? Is there not a need—and should there not be a place—for individual and collective prayers of protest and anger? Prayer should reflect reality and God—whatever God is—ought to be able to handle honest communication from the likes of us.

The "arguing with God" tradition, hopefully, is one way to help some people remain engaged and involved in the process of defining their relationship with this traditional conception of a God who intervenes in human life. I believe there can be no true connecting with the God of our ancestors without an accounting, a reckoning; without also articulating our feelings of anger and betrayal and grief in prayer. Today, if we truly want to be honest, not only to God and the Biblical experiences, but also to the Holocaust and our own experience, then perhaps prayers of protest ought to be included in our various worship services. It is both theologically and psychologically sound.

In recent years, the "arguing with God" approach has also gained some currency in the wider Jewish circles and in segments of the Christian world and seen application to a broad variety of situations.[14] David Blumenthal, in *Facing the Abusing God: A Theology of Protest,* utilizes both the accounts of survivors of child sexual abuse and of the Holocaust to make the case for Jewish prayers of protest against a sometimes abusive God.[15] Kathleen Billman and Daniel Migliore, in *Rachel's Cry: Prayer of Lament and Rebirth of Hope*, explore the pastoral and spiritual dimensions of the lament if it were adopted as part of Christian usage.[16] William Morrow, in *Protest against God: The Eclipse of a Biblical Tradition*, believes ours is an age that will see a revival of prayers of protest in Jewish worship—and for the first time in Christian prayer too.[17] Most recently, Peter Admirand, in *Amidst Mass Atrocity and the Rubble of Theology: Searching for a Viable Theodicy* has taken the need for protest global.[18]

IV

Protest has its place and function with a traditional God-concept, but this may not be enough in our post-Holocaust but still genocidal, postadvent of AIDS age.[19] The Holocaust was so traumatic that, for many Jews, it shattered the "blame the victim" mentality for all time and I have seen AIDS do the same on the individual level. For many people, the Holocaust and AIDS have marked the death, not of God, but certainly of their belief in the traditional conception of God and in their expectations of this God.

If we consider letting go of this God-concept, then we may be better able to honor our own experience because the contradiction will have been eliminated. And this returns us to the second option: to affirm that the Holocaust experience is reality and the Exodus experience is illusory. In one way, this is very freeing because then we need not have any expectations of God that fly in the face of our own experience. On the other hand, it is very troubling because it also means abandoning a view of God and a whole system of religious thinking that has served people well for several millennia. Prayer too will need to be reexamined because most prayers are based on an interventionist, supernatural God.

This challenge may also apply to other peoples and other faiths. Many individuals have feelings of anger and abandonment; many question the absence of God's saving presence or protest against God's perceived indifference to their fates. Other peoples and faiths have endured catastrophes of their own as well. For all those stuck between the accounts of our hugely miraculous past and our largely miracle-less present, a new way of conceiving God may be needed.[20]

Part III: Toward a new God-concept

I

When God first appears to Moses, God gives His personal name as "Ehyeh Asher Ehyeh," meaning "I will be who/what I will be," or "I am who/what I am." Sometimes God calls Himself simply "I will be" ("Ehyeh") for short. But God has another, related name, which may be rendered in English as "YHVH," which is used throughout the Bible and in Jewish prayers to this day. This name is called the Tetragrammaton and in Jewish tradition is unutterable, both because it is believed to be God's ineffable name and also because its pronunciation, which only the High Priest knew, was lost when the Temple was destroyed.[21] Personally, I believe YHVH to be the sound of breath entering and leaving our bodies and should be pronounced accordingly.[22]

For Jews, "YHVH" is the deity's name and "God" ("Elohim" in Hebrew) is a job title, related cognately to the generic term for god ("el") and "Allah." But The Name ("HaShem" as traditional Jews routinely call YHVH) also has meaning of its own. The Name's letters represent a combination of the present and future tenses of the verb "to be." YHVH is literally (and grammatically) pure potential, indefinable, and ineffable. The Name suggests that God's essence is forward-looking and future-oriented, as in fact the Torah has God say by way of self-description. In Exodus 3.12–15, in what ought to have been a humorous skit, Moses asks for God's name. Imagine Moses's consternation when God replies that Moses may use the name "Ehyeh-Asher-Ehyeh," meaning "I am who/that/what I am" or "I will be who/that/what I will be," or "Ehyeh" for short.

Judaism traditionally has accepted the premise that God is essentially unknowable. Of course, like any other religion, Judaism then spent much effort trying to define and contain God.[23] But God is always beyond our limited abilities of comprehension; God cannot be contained or controlled, summoned like a genie from a bottle, or confined by our desire to define. We may think we know God in some way through past deeds attributed to God by our ancestors, or through our own experiences, but that should never constrain what God is because God ultimately will be whatever God will be.

Thinking of "God: as "YHVH" is the essence of the First Commandment: not to make any images of the divine. If any single perception of God is given the mantle of absolute truth, whether by virtue of its antiquity or by canonization, it changes form and becomes a humanly sanctified image—an idol, so to speak—for subsequent generations. YHVH—"God"—is beyond all our words, past, present, and future; beyond all our imaginings. Dare we permit ourselves to let "God" be YHVH—can we let "God" just BE?

II

Like many other people, I believe that each and every faith tradition has a claim on "God" and the "truth." Today, the world appears smaller than it once was; we know more about each other than ever before, thanks to advances in travel and communication. Consequently, "God" today is perceived by some to be more universal than any faith tradition ever imagined "God" to be. But, even in the best expressions of traditional religion, the universal God of the Jews is still attached to the Jews; the universal God of Christianity is bonded to the Church; and the universal God of Islam reveals His word only in Arabic—even the "no-God" of Zen Buddhism prefers ceremonies and meditation to be performed Japanese style! However, "God" is beyond these borders of our making. Rather, "God" belongs to us all, however and whatever we perceive "God" to be; no matter how we choose to dress and address the divine.

Because "God" is ultimately unknowable and ineffable, all our theologies are flawed. But they are identically flawed in that they are all limited by our human capabilities to know. Nonetheless, they also all point to a shared truth: That humanity perceives there is "Being" somehow greater than all of us. Each religion has a unique perspective of this "Being" and has built distinctive systems of belief and practice upon that perspective. There is unique validity to each perception of "God" and to all the religious systems built upon those perceptions.[24] This can be a challenge to accept, particularly if one vehemently disagrees with this or that religious perspective—but there are other ways to measure religious perspectives without discounting their perception of the divine.

I often compare "God" to a multifaceted gem, offering many different perspectives for observation. Each faith is capable of describing only a few divine facets—and then arguing with other faiths about which facet is truer—but none can ever know the whole "gem." Our efforts at theology are like the parable of the blind men and the elephant, with each of us having the capacity to describe but one part, or, as the Hindus more charitably say, our efforts are different paths up the same mountain. Our theologies are our metaphysical constructs based upon our perceptions of "God." They are not eternal verities; they do not represent the ineffable One.

Many of us today need to free ourselves from past conceptions of God as we struggle to make sense of suffering. We need the freedom to perceive God in our own ways, to reinvent God, as it were, for our own day and our own needs. It is not "God" we are changing; only our God-concepts. We are only admitting our collective limited ability to "know God."

Just as what we have done and who we have been define us in our relationships, so too the Bible and our respective faith traditions define and confine God. Although our past has a great impact on our present, we still retain the ability to shape our own destinies and also to affect those of the people with whom we interact. Similarly, we need to let go of "God" by letting go of old theological concepts—even cherished, hallowed, time-honored concepts—in order to forge a new relationship with YHVH.

Part IV: And a new theodicy

I

So: How to make sense of suffering with a God of mystery? I start by leaving God out of the equation and build from the ground up. To begin with, we can make sense of suffering simply by observing how we ourselves deal with suffering, that is, how we live it. Life—whatever happens to us—is what it is; but *we* make it what it *will mean* for us. The meaning of suffering is not found by asking "why?" but by asking "to what end?" A pregnant woman endures the pain of childbirth because she knows (or hopes) that something good will emerge, that a baby will be born. But other sorts of pain, physical and emotional, are not so clearly productive. It remains for us to shape or create the offspring of that experience by imbuing it with meaning. Every experience is either a stepping stone or a mill stone, depending on how we perceive it and how we use it.

For many years, I worked with people with AIDS. Many of these men and women were self-destructive prior to diagnosis. Only after learning of their terminal conditions did some of them choose to turn their lives around. They were able to transform their pain into creative, positive energy because their impending deaths gave their lives meaning and purpose. Similarly, after our adult daughter died of leukemia, my late wife was able to transform her near-suicidal grief into renewed life by creating a memorial video for our daughter's two young sons. Finding a new purpose for living is a way to transcend the tragedy of our most terrible personal experiences. In purpose lies meaning and hope for the future.[25]

Our various faiths have numerous martyrs who, although they were physically hurt, did not suffer. They did not suffer because their sense of connectedness with God remained intact. Job, on the other hand, suffered spiritually because he could not reconcile his experience with his understanding of what the divine order was supposed to entail. Job was a righteous man who, after having been afflicted with tragedy and physical suffering, also endured spiritual suffering. (Actually he was doing fine until his so-called friends came to "comfort" him.) This led him to question God's justice. Job suffered primarily because his sense of meaning in life was turned upside down. He could not accept what had happened because it made no sense; he did not have the means to cope with adversity *and* the torment of his friends' insensitivity. As a result, he suffered spiritual alienation—a sense of isolation from God's presence.

Fortunately for Job—and how unlike so many of us!—Job received an answer directly from God. From his revelatory experience, Job learned that (1) what had happened to him was both unjust and unjustified, (2) it was an insignificant part of the greater mystery of creation, but (3) that God cared for him enough to make an appearance. And it was that divine appearance that restored Job's sense of connectedness, even though the lesson learned—that there is no justice manifest in suffering and that what occurs in life is part of something larger than one can ever comprehend—was no comfort at all. The healing for Job lay in his restored sense of connection with God that came as a result of God's answering Job and not necessarily in what God said, humbling though it may have been.

While I no longer hold out for this kind of miraculous intervention, I still hope that YHVH is somehow and in some way present. Quite in line with traditional Jewish thinking, I see the divine in whatever happens in life, both the apparent good and the perceived bad. What I struggle with is the realization that I will never really know if YHVH "cares"—if I may be permitted this anthropomorphization. Lacking this certainty, I nonetheless draw inspiration—and hope—from the ancient speculations about an empathic God: One who suffers when we suffer and who rejoices when we rejoice.[26] And, while I wait and hope for further enlightenment, I realize that it is important to maintain some kind of open channel with the divine through music, meditation, and prayer. All these are vehicles to transcend our human limitations and reach out to the divine.

Prayer's value from this perspective lies in helping reorient ourselves in a period of crisis and turmoil. Interestingly, in Hebrew, the verb "to pray" is *lehitpallel, which* is a reflexive verb—something that one does to oneself. The root of the verb, "palal," means "to judge," which makes the actual translation of prayer as something more akin to *self-evaluation*. Therefore, in theory, when a person "prays," he/she is actually doing an accounting of him/herself, taking stock of his/her level of spiritual development and ability to accept reality as it is. In line with this understanding, prayer is not necessarily directed externally; it is meant to change one's personal attitude. So, when life's experiences disappoint one's expectations, then prayer, traditional and reflexive, including those of protest and anger, are good tools if they help one get to the point of accepting that what is, is.

II

Because I no longer expect a supernatural deity to intervene now or in the future to alleviate or validate suffering, I must look elsewhere for my support. And here, I need look no further than to my fellow human beings, as reliable *and* as unreliable as they are.

For the ancient rabbis, the key operative element in our world was the concept of *hesed*, usually translated as lovingkindness, but also meaning mercy, favor, faithfulness, piety, benevolence, righteousness, and graciousness. From *hesed* come *gemilut hasadim*, or acts of lovingkindness. So important were these that one sage, Shimon the Just taught that they were one of the three pillars upon which the continued existence of the world depended (the other two are Torah and worship), while a later sage, Rav Huna, taught that one who only studied Torah but did no deeds of lovingkindness was like one who has no God.[27] Deeds of lovingkindness are the quintessential, demonstrable acts of Jewish piety and the desire to be holy (like God is holy).[28]

I believe that the concept of *hesed*, or lovingkindness, is universal; it is only articulated differently. I think it is analogous to the concepts of *agape* and *caritas* in Christianity, to *rakhma* in Islam, to *karuna* in Buddhism, to *ren* and *de* in the Chinese Confucian and Taoist traditions, and to *daya* in Hinduism. It may be, along with our various versions of the Golden Rule, the closest thing we have to a universal (global) religious truth. Lovingkindness is the best we are able to offer our fellow creatures, both human and beast. It builds bonds of connection; of unity, love, and trust; and enables us to heal, or to repair, our world.

Life's crises are never easy, but by treating one another with lovingkindness we can help support one another through almost everything. God won't necessarily be invoked to assist from above—and even if invoked, it is unlikely that God will intervene—but YHVH will be present in the love shown, in the joys shared, in the solidarity demonstrated and, if we have the skill, in the peacefulness created.

The factor that determines or limits our choice between love and fear is the ability to trust. In Hebrew, the word for "trust" is more complexly nuanced because it is related to "truth" and "belief" and also to "nursing," "supportive," "reliable," and "faithfulness." All derive from a common root, "a-m-n." (We get the word "amen" from here, meaning "so be it" or "true.") Since the Hebrew words for "trust" and "faith" and "reliability" and "nursing" are all related, then the leap of faith that we must take is to trust ourselves and one another to be reliable and compassionate. Trust is a psychological process, a spiritually transforming experience, and a personal commitment to our individual and collective potential to build a growing force for good in the world. To take this leap of faith and truly to trust other human beings is to begin the process of redemption because it nurtures a sense of hope. For some, this long jump goes even further, extending to the belief—or having faith—that God actively cares for us as individuals, for humanity, and all Creation.

Conclusion

Mirroring the modern cycle of grief, prayer at times should include the expression of anger and other "negative" emotions. "Acceptance" is the penultimate step in the emotional healing process, just before "recovery."

According to the stages of grief construct, most people go through a nonlinear series of emotional/spiritual peaks and valleys that mark their struggle to deal with adversity. Suffering has its stages in which anger is as appropriate as guilt or denial but, for many people, displaying a lack of emotion during times of emotional or spiritual turmoil—and thereby denying their anger, depression, and the like—may actually demonstrate fatalism not faith; not acceptance of what has happened but acquiescence to an apparently abusive power beyond their control. In many of our faith traditions, fatalism is often confused with faith and acquiescence with acceptance. I believe that prayer, at times, should include expression of these "negative" emotions because by expressing all of our feelings and not censoring any of them, we allow ourselves to heal and become whole, regardless of what YHVH/God "does" with them.

The key to providing suffering with meaning is acceptance. When life is taken as it is, one releases oneself from one's expectations for the future and from one's illusion of control. This, it seems to me is the wisdom of "praising God for the good and the bad" because in the "praising" comes an eventual acceptance of whatever happens. However one achieves it, acquiring a sense of acceptance of one's fortune can make suffering endurable, and perceiving a sense of unity with God's presence can provide hope. What happens may be part of God's plan or it may be a random act of natural (or human) terror; that is for each of us to decide. But wisdom and peace come only in transcending events, in seeking the spiritual learning moment in everything, and in striving to remain connected with the divine, however conceived.

To my mind, to believe that nothing comes directly from God is almost the same as believing that everything comes from God. Surprisingly, in my own times of crisis, I found I could almost repeat the words of Job: "YHVH has given, and YHVH has taken away; blessed be the name YHVH"—"What has been given to me has been taken away; blessed is YHVH/Be-Ing." The key, for me, is to accept whatever happens in life with as much equanimity as I can muster and ultimately to make my peace with whatever occurs.

That "YHVH IS" is the only thing I think I can say with any certainty on the subject of God. I now consider God to be much more of a mystery than I ever did, so the qualities traditionally ascribed to God bother me less because I know that they are only attributed to God, not actually God. To be sure, part of me still yearns to confront my ancestral God. I am, after all, one of the Children of Yisra-el, meaning "one who strives with God," and I still wrestle with the God-concepts of my ancestors. Increasingly though, I realize it is not God from whom I am seeking an explanation, but rather from my ancestors' perceptions of God that I inherited as a child. Now I am willing to let God be "the Name," the One who will be what the One will be. Be-Ing in Process of Becoming. YHVH.

I find my comfort—and my meaning—in a Be-Ing who accompanies me in some mysterious way throughout my life's experiences but who directs nothing; a Be-Ing who enables me to determine spiritual meaning in each experience (if I wish to) but who teaches nothing; a Be-Ing who may "listen" when I pray but who does nothing in response. In my Be-Ing's nonaction, I may find strength and solace, but I must rely on myself and my fellow human beings to do on earth that which many have expected, or still expect, God to do for them. As Dorothee Soelle (1929–2003) once wrote: "God has no other hands than ours. If the sick are to be healed, it is our hands that will heal them. If the lonely and the frightened are to be comforted, it is our embrace, not God's, that will comfort them." To which I can only say, "Amen."

May Buddhists Hope? A Christian Enquiry

John D'Arcy May

All hope abandon, ye who enter in!

Dante, *Inferno*, Canto 3

The final and irretrievable loss of all grounds for hope could perhaps be described as the ultimate torment, underlying all the horrors Dante encounters on his journey through hell. This is sufficient indication that in reflecting on hope we are not talking about mere optimism or the "positive outlook on life" purveyed by motivational psychology. We are dealing with an attitude that plumbs the depths of human subjectivity yet which at the same time is cosmic in scope. Moreover, hope, as a concept, is heavily dependent on Jewish and Christian antecedents, whereas it plays no part in Buddhist teaching.

This is not to say that Buddhists do not have a kind of eschatology: from ancient India they inherit an abundance of heavens and hells, whose delights and torments are portrayed at least as vividly as their counterparts in the Abrahamic faiths. In Christianity, as we shall see, the scenarios of salvation and damnation and the final battle between good and evil have not so much Jewish as Iranian roots, which in turn go back to pre-Vedic India. Even for Christians, as many contemporary scholars and enquiring laypeople are finding, while the imagery of heaven and hell is at home in the symbolic language prevalent in Jesus's time, it does not do justice to the full import of his teaching for believers today. In Buddhism, this seems to have been the case from the very beginning: though temples are often illustrated with graphic depictions of the torments of the damned, in the Indian scheme of things neither the bliss of paradise nor the suffering of hell is eternal; beings eventually move on from both to return to the endless cycle of cosmic existence-in-flux known as *saṃsāra*. The most coveted rebirth is as a human being because only humans can achieve ultimate liberation from the law of *karma*, according to which the residue of deeds, including our hiddenmost intentions, inexorably determines our future destiny. It is from this, and the ignorance (*avijjā*) that conceals it from us, rather than from "hell," that we are "saved."

The difficulty in finding a Buddhist equivalent of hope goes even deeper. It can fairly be said that, for Buddhists, hope as presented in Christian scripture and doctrine must seem like a form of delusion, a longing for some future transformation of our human lot springing from desire (*tanhā*, Sanskrit *tṛṣṇā*, lit. "thirst"). But by referring everything back to "me," desire ipso facto confines us within the prison of the self (*ātman*, for Buddhists the primary illusion: that there is a substantial self-existing individual or *svabhāva*). For Humanist and Marxist critics, Christian hope has the wrong object: it is a distraction from living fully in the present and building a better future here on earth.[1] The Buddhist aim of extirpating all desire without remainder (*nirodha*), even the desire of final release from becoming, birth, and death, seems to be more radical, tackling directly the question of loss and detachment.[2]

A story from the Pāli Canon graphically illustrates this dispassionate attitude to trauma and loss. The Buddha is approached by a distraught woman, Visākhā, whose beloved granddaughter has died. Enquiring about the cause of her grief, the Buddha is told of her loss. His response is to prompt Visākhā to reflect on the untold number of bereavements and other troubles that afflict the people of the area. The lesson he draws from this is: if people and things were not dear to us, we would not be sad when we lose them. "Only those are happy and free of care to whom nothing in the world is dear" (*Udāna* VIII, 8). This and many similar stories seem to offer the opposite of consolation: those suffering loss are told, in today's terminology, to get over it, because loss is our common lot.

These preliminary considerations indicate that there are several clusters of themes we must investigate if we are to give a fair assessment of possible Buddhist equivalents of hope. For Christians, hope is the very medium of faith, the outworking of faith in the temporal dimension: "Hope is nothing else than the expectation of those things which faith has believed to have been truly promised by God"; conversely, "faith is the foundation upon which hope rests, hope nourishes and sustains faith."[3] The concept of a promise given in the past and fulfilled in a future yet to come suggests that an awareness of history is fundamental to the Christian conception of hope. Hope points to the outcome of an unfolding story of which we are part, and this in turn prompts us to think about time, for our relationship to time is a crucial component of ethical responsibility, and it is here that we may engage in a phenomenological analysis that Christianity can share with Buddhism. This gives us historicity, narrativity, and temporality as three perspectives on hope that, together, might provide a basis for relating Christian to Buddhist eschatology.

Hope and historicity

The awareness of history and its relevance for the shaping of institutions and ideas— what modern theology called "historicity" (*Geschichtlichkeit*), meaning by this the situatedness of the human in time between memory and anticipation—is a relatively new development arising from the European Enlightenment. Historicity implies a reflexive awareness, a dimension of human subjectivity, a consciousness of being shaped by a determinate past, and open to an as-yet undetermined future. As a methodological tool, historicity gives scope for distancing and objectifying past events as "facts," which at the same time isolates and identifies the observer's standpoint as one among possible others. By the same token, it is a social construct, and this in turn implies that the sense of history and its significance is by no means the same or even present in every culture. The so-called primal traditions of indigenous peoples deal with history through the oral transmission of elaborate stories about culture heroes, whose activities shaped the world and its inhabitants in a kind of continuous present, a time beyond time. This is taken to fall under the category "myth" and is therefore denied any "historical" value in the sense of verifiable fact, yet oral history is the foundation of all historical narrative, as can be seen in cultures to which literacy came late. The long evolution of the Hebrew Bible, with its multitude of genres and its sometimes contradictory accounts of what must have been in some sense historical events, illustrates this process, though it only became fully apparent after controversial attempts to introduce critical methods into biblical scholarship. The conviction that history has religious significance is a fundamental dimension of Christianity's—and the West's—Jewish heritage.

There is a widespread assumption that, if historicity is recoverable with regard to the Jewish traditions that flowed into Christianity, it is entirely absent in the Indic traditions that formed the matrix of Buddhism. This assumption has been criticized and modified,[4] as has the equally simplistic notion that Greek and Hebrew conceptions of history are "cyclic" and "linear" respectively. Von Rad points out that Israel experienced time in a way quite different from ours. It was incapable of abstracting time as an absolute schema of past, present, and future from particular events; indeed, Hebrew lacks a word for "time" in the Western sense.[5] The Greeks, too, though they pioneered the writing of history, knew nothing of historical time as we understand it. As with so many indigenous peoples, it was the great festivals that determined time, not the other way around. Yet as Israel began to realize that its present was preceded by complicated historical developments, it began to think of time as stretching out from a known past to an anticipated future, "historicizing" the festivals in the process; historical time had now become truly irreversible.[6]

The insight embodied in historicity is that there is no such thing as "history" in a pure state, only *interpreted* history, nowhere more so than when we are considering the religious significance of history:

> Christianity is founded upon the history of Jesus, and this particular history establishes criteria according to which Christianity interprets history in the first place. This means: the fact that Christian faith is founded on the history of Jesus does not imply that it is *merely* historical, because in the history of Jesus the transhistorical and transtemporal dominion of God is announced. The legitimation of Jesus and indeed of faith is *not* historical in itself, but derives from an *interpretation* of history supported by faith.[7]

The tensions implicit in this statement were worked out in the nineteenth century "quest for the historical Jesus" and the juxtaposition of a "Jesus of history" to a "Christ of faith."

If historical awareness situates memories and the records of events in interpretative frameworks and contexts of relevance constructed by the interpreter, it is not surprising that in contemporary Buddhism, too, as it enters more and more into the mainstream of historical scholarship and religious pluralism, the question of the relationship between the historical Buddha, the North Indian ruler's son Gautama Śākyamuni, and the transcendental Buddhas of the voluminous scriptures that arose long after his death, comes to the fore. Just as Hinduism's reawakening to its own past was inspired by India's encounter with the West's curiosity about origins and its skepticism of received accounts, Buddhists, in comparable circumstances, soon learned how to parry Christian propaganda with its own weapons. Relations between Buddhists and Christians in Sri Lanka (colonial Ceylon) were often rancorous and sometimes took the form of public debates and polemics.[8] These were almost exclusively doctrinal; but on a more pragmatic level the Buddhists had no hesitation in adopting the methods used so effectively by Christian proselytizers, such as the printing of pamphlets, and in developing an apologetics which claimed that Buddhism from its earliest origins had been all that Christianity purports to be: historical, verifiable, rational, and critical.[9] In the process, Buddhists came to appreciate their own Indian heritage; the sacred sites of the Buddha's life, his enlightenment (*bodhi*), and his death (*parinirvāṇa*), mentioned so often in the canon, were restored and became places of pilgrimage. More ominously, the great chronicles of the island of Laṅkā, the *Dīpavaṃsa* and the *Mahāvaṃsa*, began to be seen, in the light of the nationalisms that sustained Western imperialism, as sources for a Sinhalese Buddhist nationalism and a consequent rewriting of history.[10]

In the West, too, the historical integrity of Buddhism is sometimes compromised. Senior Western Buddhists seem to be becoming increasingly alarmed by the tendency among Western converts to Buddhism, many of them highly educated, to abandon their critical faculties and enthusiastically embrace the quasi-mythical legitimations of their lineages proposed by their Asian spiritual masters. The American Buddhist scholar Rita Gross urges Buddhists to take their own teaching of impermanence (*anicca*) seriously and develop a nonsectarian history of Buddhism that does not cling to culturally determined peculiarities of their traditions.[11]

There is, of course, a sense in which the Buddhist *dhamma* or teaching is fundamentally atemporal. The *saṃsāric* cycle of flux and rebirth is without beginning or end, as is the succession of *kalpas* or world-ages within which it continually manifests itself, each of which brings forth an Enlightened One (*buddho*) to point out the way to liberation from rebirth. Final liberation (*mokkha, mokṣa*) severs all bonds with the karmic process in the reality-beyond-reality called Nirvāṇa, but this, being absolutely unconditioned and beyond the scope of language and conceptual thought, is strictly speaking ineffable; as the *Sutta-Nipāta* puts it with admirable simplicity: "When all conditions are removed / All ways of telling are removed" (*SN*, 1076).

Historically, however, teachings developed over time. As successive Buddhist spiritual movements and schools of thought emerged in India and moved out to permeate virtually the whole of Asia, their adherents had no compunction in producing scriptures to legitimate their particular teachings, often attributing them to Gautama Śākyamuni as the historical Buddha, even though they arose centuries after his death. The Theravāda traditions of south and southeast Asia, notwithstanding the fact that their canon, composed in a Prakrit or local language called Pāli, was written down some five centuries after the Buddha's death at about the same time as the New Testament, claimed to have preserved the original and authoritative teaching (*dhamma*) and monastic rule (*vinaya*). The schools that emerged in the first centuries CE, known as the *Mahāyāna* or "Great Vehicle," therefore needed to make plausible that it was in fact their teachings that fully revealed the *Dharma*, now conceived as the utterly transcendent Buddha-nature itself. The key to this hermeneutical feat was the technique known as skilful or expedient means (*kauśalya-upāya*). According to this, Gautama had deliberately withheld certain advanced teachings because of the limited capacity of his original hearers (meaning contemporary adherents of what was deprecatingly dubbed the *Hīnayāna* or "Lesser Vehicle"), disclosing them only now to disciples and Bodhisattvas of superior spiritual attainments. This is patently evident in the *Lotus Sūtra* with its disparaging remarks about *arhats* or purportedly enlightened ones. It was thus something of a shock when Japanese scholars began to assert that the teachings of the Mahāyāna *sūtras* could not possibly stem from the historical Buddha, with the no less controversial rider that the teachings are true quite independently of who uttered them when or where: doctrinal truth has nothing to do with historical reality.[12]

Notwithstanding this all-pervasive ahistoricity and atemporality of Buddhist traditions, a complex but coherent narrative of the Buddha's life was meticulously preserved, allowing us to reconstruct his deeds and words in their North Indian context with all the abundant detail of personalities and places provided by the Pāli and other Buddhist canons. Though it is generally agreed that it is no more possible to compose a biography of Gautama than it is to write a life of Jesus, the outlines of a "historical Buddha" definitely emerge from the abundance of evidence handed down by oral tradition.[13] Indeed, Gautama has been called the first identifiable personage in an Indian history otherwise consisting of unverifiable legend. It is already apparent that these questions are bound up with the continuity of tradition, the legitimation of authority, and the possibility of authentic development in Buddhism, as are their counterparts in Christianity.

The problem of relating a timeless truth to particular historical persons and events is present, then, though in different terms, in both Buddhist and Christian traditions. The whole thrust of the concept of historicity, especially as it was appropriated by theology, is to show the immanence of the transcendent in the very sinews of historical existence. The significance of the Hebrew prophets consists not in foretelling the future but in recognizing the hand of God in the events of history itself:

> This relationship of correspondence of the prophets to world history is nothing less than the key to understanding them aright; for the new actions of God in history which they perceived were for them on a par with the old canonical historical norms; indeed, the prophets grew in the knowledge that this new historical activity would surpass and therefore more or less replace the old.[14]

This developed into the realization that history was moving toward a fulfillment, a definitive end of world-time in which God's actions within history would culminate, though this would necessarily occur "outside" history.[15] In other words, they "eschatologized" history, thus establishing the Jewish component in the framework for what later became apocalyptic, the visionary portrayal of the final catastrophe that colored the mental world of Jesus and his contemporaries and is most vividly represented in the New Testament by the *Book of Revelation*. Central to this mentality was not only the Jewish idea of Israel as a kingdom under God's dominion but also the Iranian symbolism of the triumph of the "Wise Lord," Ahura-Mazdā, portrayed by Zarathustra as a judgment at the end of time that would separate the evil from the good.[16] This conception is thoroughly dualistic and as such, especially as it was developed in the *Books of Henoch*,[17] it permeates Jewish thinking about the restoration of the kingdom of Israel and shapes the earliest Christian expectation of the imminent end of history. The "kingdom of God" was already among them (Lk. 17.21), and "there are some standing here who will not taste death before they see the kingdom of God" (Lk. 9.27), but its nonarrival as an apocalyptic event constrained the Christians to come to terms with historical existence under the political circumstances of the *Pax Romana*. God's promise to the patriarchs, renewed through the prophets, was fulfilled in the coming of the Messiah, but its final outcome was to be postponed until he came in glory.

The structure of Christian faith thus becomes one of promise and fulfillment, defined by hope: "Hence it is not our experiences which make faith and hope, but it is faith and hope that make experiences and bring the human spirit to an ever new and restless transcending of itself."[18]

The promise revealed to Israel has already been fulfilled in the coming of Christ (*past*), yet it is still awaiting fulfillment in the final judgment at the end of time (*future*). The Christian life of the individual, and of the Church as a participant in world history, is lived out in the tension between these defining historical poles (*present*):

> The parousia of Christ . . . is conceived in the New Testament only in categories of expectation, so that it means not *praesentia Christi* but *adventus Christi*, and is not his eternal presence bringing time to a standstill, but his "coming," as our Advent hymns say, opening the road to life in time, for the life of time is hope.[19]

The temporal structure of commemoration and expectation is reflected in many liturgical formulae ("Christ *has* died, Christ *is* risen, Christ *will* come again").

Buddhism knows a certain equivalent of this in its conception of the Bodhisattva, the Great Being on the threshold of final liberation in *nirvāṇa* after coursing through countless rebirths in the karmic realm of *saṃsāra*. This reveals what one author calls the "karmic depth"[20] of the Buddha narrative. It is perhaps more appropriate to characterize this as cosmic rather than historical as scenarios unfold such as those throughout the *Lotus Sūtra*, which portray the Buddha as the personification of the eternal Dharma, illuminating the furthest recesses of countless universes through endless eons. But Buddhism also evolved structures of expectation. The final achievement of enlightenment, though it is never allowed to be the object of desire, is in a certain sense a hoped-for fulfillment, the culmination of not one but countless lifetimes of discipline and renunciation.

The Buddha Śākyamuni of the present world-age is one in a succession whose names are known, as is that of the coming Buddha Maitreya (from *maitrī*, "loving-kindness") after this eon has passed away. A whole new tradition in Mahāyāna Buddhism, by far the most numerous in East Asia though it is less known in the West, developed out of the quasi-mythical account of the forty-eighth vow of the Bodhisattva Dharmākara, whereby he undertook not to attain final liberation in Nirvāṇa until he had saved all beings from ignorance and suffering, by virtue of which he became the transcendent Buddha Amitābha, "Bringer of Life," or Amitāyus, "Bringer of Light," in Japanese Amida. This surely entails nothing less than an expectation of salvation for all beings, couched in terms of rebirth in a Buddha-realm or Pure Land in which the liberated could attain the bliss of Nirvāṇa. Making a vow, like promising, is a paradigmatic performative speech act, whose utterance in good faith commits the promiser to carry out the course of action proposed. Given this deep structure, to which hope is the correlate, it may well be that there is a Buddhist equivalent to hope as the *Existential* or fundamental condition of existence for Christian life and eschatology. But in order to establish this we need to explore further dimensions of their respective attitudes of expectation.

Hope and narrativity

In Buddhism and Christianity, as indeed in Judaism and Islam and many other religious traditions, there is an element of story-telling: one listens to a story and accepts it on faith. "But how are men to call upon him in whom they have not believed?," exclaims St Paul: "And how are they to believe in him of whom they have never heard? And how are they to hear without a preacher?" (Rom. 10.14). Such story-telling would recount the narrative of Jesus as it later came to be handed down, in markedly different forms, in the Gospels, and Jesus's own parables as recorded therein. The Buddhist *sūtras* typically begin with an assertion that is meant to guarantee their authenticity by indicating their provenance from original witnesses, for example: "Thus have I heard: At one time the Blessed One was living among the Kurus, at Kammāsadamma, a market town of the Kuru people. There the Blessed One addressed the monks thus . . ." (*Dīgha-Nikāya*, 22).

In neither case does this imply verifying the historical accuracy of the story in the modern sense. While it has now become possible to do this to a limited extent, thanks to the techniques developed by *modern* scholarship, this is not the main point of responding to a story of religious salvation. The "historicity" of such stories can have a different bearing on the "truth" of what is contained in them. The Gospel of Luke opens with an account of a Roman census of Palestine (2.1–3); the Christian creed mentions the obscure provincial governor Pontius Pilate. It is crucially important to Christian faith *that* Jesus of Nazareth lived and died; the *meaning* of his life and death for us, however, is conveyed in the variations on the *story* of his birth, his teaching, his arrest and crucifixion, and—beyond the boundaries of the historically verifiable— his resurrection and ascension to await his second coming at the end of time. The historicity of the Buddha-legend is much less accessible and does not have the same central importance as the Dharma he revealed, though much of what he said and did and his subsequent impact on the history of India and the world can be reconstructed.

But the stories of Gautama and Jesus have their meaning and authority *in themselves*, as narratives, and it is the significance of this intrinsic "narrativity" that we must now investigate.

The particular linguistic structuring of texts that links events occurring over time into a meaningful succession is known as "emplotment." This concept of plot or *muthos* derives from Aristotle's *mimēsis*, yielding not only the idea of narrative as a textually constructed world but also that of "narrated time" as a structuring of the life-world of the reader.[21] Emplotment, indeed, according to Paul Ricoeur, is the key to the relationship between time and narrative:

> . . . my basic hypothesis is that between the activity of narrating a story and the temporal character of human experience there exists a correlation that is not merely accidental but that presents a transcultural form of necessity. To put it another way, *time becomes human to the extent that it is articulated through a narrative mode and narrative attains its full meaning when it becomes a condition of temporal existence.*[22]

Ricoeur explains this as a "refiguration of our temporal experience by this constructed time. *We are following therefore the destiny of a prefigured time that becomes a refigured time through the mediation of a configured time.*"[23]

These are the three dimensions of *mimēsis* that allow the meaning of stories to engage with the meaning of existence. The first, the prefiguration of meaning in the text, might be called a semantics of action, for as its inner entelechy is disclosed through the second dimension, emplotment, it becomes the symbolic mediation of action, and according to the ordering of its temporal elements, it reveals goals and motives that raise questions about who is acting and why. "In passing from the paradigmatic order of action to the syntagmatic order of narrative, the terms of the semantics of action acquire integration and actuality."[24] Narrative thus supplies symbolic resources for the practical field, making the private public and action "readable."[25] Narrativity, even as fiction, has its own kind of reference: arising *in* being, it sheds light *on* being, and its reception demands a fusion of horizons, the text's, and the reader's; if poetry redescribes the world, narrative resignifies the world.[26]

Whereas Christianity was conceived entirely within the medium of the "history-like" Biblical stories,[27] combining story-telling (*Bericht*) with the praise of God (*Anrede*) and yielding genres such as law, prophecy, wisdom sayings, and hymns,[28] Buddhism, from the very beginning, was couched in an already existing quasi-philosophical terminology, such as can be found in the *Upaniṣads*. This was the medium of intense debates among the Buddha's contemporaries, which call to mind the philosophical schools of ancient Greece. The Buddha, too, taught in parables and illustrative stories, but the main content of the *Sutta-Piṭaka* ("The Basket of the *Sūtras*," that is the collection of teaching discourses) is subtle psychological analysis of the human condition, empirically based and logically argued. Always presupposing the power of the Enlightened One's personality and the authenticity of his testimony, and mindful of his constant teaching that deductions from "theories" or "views" (*diṭṭhī*) are irrelevant to the work of purification, it is nevertheless the force of these arguments that again and again precipitates the insight in which the liberation of his listeners fundamentally consists. In Jesus's case, again allowing for his compelling personal presence, it is the paradoxes structurally encoded in his incomparable parables that "turn people's minds around" (*metanōia*). Instead, then, in Ricoeur's apt phrase, of "extracting anemic generalities"[29] from the biblical stories as the starting point of a speculative theology, a narrative theology would work with the narrative structures of the stories themselves. This should be possible in the Buddhist context as well.

In Buddhism as in Christianity, the initial narratives embodying the significance of the life, teaching, and legacy of Gautama and Jesus were amplified and reconfigured into powerful symbolic structures, which systematized the original revelations in forms that provided the basis of future doctrinal developments. This process gave Christians the creeds—which were called "Symbols" in the early centuries—and the decrees of the great Christological councils. Buddhists, in the course of a long and involved evolution in controversy and dialogue with their Brahmin opponents for over 1,000 years, developed a doctrinal edifice that contemporary Buddhists are beginning to call "Buddhist theology" in a conscious comparison with its Christian counterpart.[30] At its core stands the symbolic structure known as the *Trikāya* or "Three Bodies" of the Buddha. In texts such as the *Lotus Sūtra*, which may have been composed as early as the second- or third-century CE[31] and became immensely influential in Chinese and Japanese Buddhism, the Buddha is represented as a transcendent being illuminating the entire cosmos with the brilliance of his teaching (*dharma*) and the perfection of his nature (*dharmatā*).

The resulting systematization of these developments distinguished a "manifestation" or "transformation body" (*nirmāṇa-kāya*) of the historical Buddha, which if the norms of Christian orthodoxy were applied would have to be called docetic; a "body of communal enjoyment" (*saṃbhoga-kāya*), in which Buddhas appear in their full glory to delight the minds of Bodhisattvas and the eyes of the enlightened; and the formless "body of the transcendent Buddha-nature" (*dharma-kāya*), a conception that seems reminiscent of Hindu rather than Buddhist thought but which plays an important role in East Asian Buddhism.[32] This yields the following schema:

Buddhology	Christology
Dharma-kāya (eternal Buddha-nature)	Eternal Word
Saṃbhoga-kāya (body of communal bliss)	Risen Christ
Nirmāṇa-kāya (earthly manifestation body)	Historical Jesus

We may take the term "body" as a metaphor for something very like what "person" represents in Trinitarian theology. The *Trikāya* doctrine, which may be traced back to the Yogācāra or "meditation consciousness" school in the fourth century,[33] while not an exact equivalent of the Trinity, is yet an invitation to reflect with Buddhists on the levels of intelligibility involved in historical mediations of transcendence. In each tradition, the symbolic structure thus evolves becomes normative for the retelling of the original story and is thus a touchstone of orthodoxy. The extent to which the narrative element in each of these reformulations correlates with what Christians call hope is less easily recognized. The key to unraveling this problem, I should like to propose, lies in the relationship of each tradition's core convictions to time, and to this we must now turn.

Hope and temporality

For the Hebrews, as we have seen, a "cultic" and a "chronological" conception of time existed side by side: having learnt to grasp the present as the *outcome* of a past that *looks forward* to a future, they began to experience time as irreversible, rather than as the cyclical renewal of a sacral order, for: "This sacral understanding of the world is essentially ahistorical; or at least in it the very thing that Israel saw as constitutive for its faith, namely the uniqueness of God's saving deeds within history, had no place."[34]

In considering the eschatological, then, which the prophets introduced into the Hebrew conception of history, we cannot avoid the problem of time, which for St Augustine was *distentio animi*, a temporal succession in the mind.[35] The uniqueness of each individual human life and the particularity of historical events are especially intense for Christians because they are bounded by time. *Hapax*—once only—is the *Leitmotif* of Christian existence (see Heb. 7.27, 9.12, 10.10). Both the responsibility accruing to each moral act and the uniqueness of the Christ event as the turning point of history, on this understanding, are intimately bound up with our situatedness in time. The entire structure of Christian faith is determined by its continuity with the story of creation, which implies that history and the cosmos itself had a *beginning* (protology); its reference to the story of Jesus's life, death, and resurrection as prefigured by the prophets in their interpretation of the history of Israel, in the belief that this is the *turning point* of history (soteriology); and the outcome toward which this historical and indeed cosmic drama is heading, which assumes that history and cosmos will have an *end* (eschatology). A corollary of this, and a difficulty for our present enterprise, is that without a beginning there is no story; and the fundamental Buddhist philosophy of interconnectedness or "co-dependent origination" of all things emphatically rejects an absolute beginning of the world as it rejects an absolute end, for these would entail a first cause and a final goal outside the world.[36]

Von Brück and Lai, questioning the assumption that there is an insuperable difference between Christian historicity and Buddhist timelessness, nevertheless propose that a structure of expectation is an integral part of the Buddhist logic of salvation.[37] Buddhists, as they rightly point out, manifest at least as much moral responsibility in history and society as Christians, "inspired by faith (in what is past), hope (for the future) and love (in the present)"; indeed, "the reconstruction of the Buddhist sense of history includes a critique of the Christian tendency to absolutize historicity."[38] The Hebrew scheme of things, which became paradigmatic for Christian faith, might be represented thus:

Patriarchs	→	Exodus	→	Messiah
Past	→	*Central event*	→	*Future*

The Christian temporal structure deriving from this would be:

Prophets	→	Christ-event	→	Parousia
Past	→	*Central event*	→	*Future*

There are major streams within Buddhism, however, which have a not dissimilar temporal structure. One is the Buddha-legend itself:

Previous Buddhas	→	Enlightenment	→	Maitreya
Past	→	*Central event*	→	*Future*

Another, though quasi-mythical, shapes a dramatic narrative:

Bodhisattvas	→	Dharmākara's vow	→	Pure Land
Past	→	*Central event*	→	*Future*

In the Christian scheme, it is God, conceived as the Creator Spirit who intervenes in history, who is centrally involved in the unfolding soteriological process; in the Buddhist scheme, the eternal Dharma is the transcendent dimension of persons and events whose existence in time is empty of independent subsistence. The emergence of a Buddha—Gautama in the quasi-historical reality of his "manifestation body" (*nirmāṇa-kāya*), Amitābha in the quasi-mythical realm of his Pure Land—marks the end of an age of ignorance and the beginning of a time of promise.[39]

At the root of the Buddhist insight that life consists of "unsatisfactoriness" or "incompleteness" (*dukkha*, often translated "suffering") is "impermanence" or "transitoriness" (*anicca*), which is a temporal category. The fundamental doctrinal development of Mahāyāna Buddhism, though in continuity with its origins in the *Abhidhamma* or analytical tradition of what is now called the Theravāda, was that this existence governed by ignorance (*avijjā*) and delusion (*moha*) in the endless cycle of rebirth (*saṃsāra*) is one and the same as the liberated existence "beyond telling" (*nibbāna, nirvāṇa*). In other words, nonduality (*a-dvaita*) is the touchstone of all authentically Buddhist existential analysis. This is apparent in the meditation tradition (*dhyāna*, Chin. *Ch'an*, Jap. *Zen*), which for its intellectual framework relied on the great Madhyamaka thinker Nāgārjuna (ca. 200 CE), who declared:

There is not the slightest difference

Between cyclic existence [*saṃsāra*] and nirvāṇa.

There is not the slightest difference

Between nirvāṇa and cyclic existence. (*MMK*, 25.19)[40]

This nondualism extends without compromise to the relationship of language to conceptual thought and of both to what is falsely taken to be a separate "reality";

concepts have meaning only in relation to each other.[41] It goes without saying that any dualism between past and present or present and future is rigorously eliminated. According to the *Platform Sūtra*, thinking, rightly understood, is not-thinking, because any admission that thinking grasped anything distinct from itself would mean attachment to its object, and the eradication of attachment is the very essence of Buddhist liberation: "What is no-thought? The Dharma of no-thought means: even though you see all things, you do not attach to them . . . being free and having achieved release is known as the practice of no-thought"; further, "No-thought is not to think even when involved in thought."[42] This is a striking way of expressing the fundamental insight that "emptiness" (*śūnyatā*) is not a metaphysical *concept* designating some transcendent reality, but the culmination of the *practice* of nonattachment, the utter elimination of "clinging" (*upādāna*). To achieve this is to awaken the "mind of enlightenment" (*bodhicitta*), which has been described as "the manifestation, even the irruption, within us of something transcendental," comparable perhaps to the Holy Spirit in Christian theology. This is not something merely individual, pertaining to a particular person; it is "supra-individual but not collective," the realization of emptiness and compassion as absolutes, though refracted through conditioned existence as the individual acts of compassion-in-emptiness that the enlightened can practice. A Bodhisattva is one of whom *bodhicitta* has taken complete possession; it is simply the undiluted manifestation of something we already are.[43] To achieve *bodhicitta* is to realize in oneself the Buddha-mind or Buddha-nature:

> In our mind itself a Buddha exists.
>
> Our own Buddha is the true Buddha.
>
> If we do not have in ourselves the Buddha mind,
>
> Then where are we to seek the Buddha?[44]

It may be possible to set this in relation with Rahner's conception of the "supernatural existential," which corresponds to the indwelling love of the Trinity.[45]

In order to illustrate this, we turn briefly to the Pure Land tradition of Amida Buddhism as exemplified in the thought of the great Japanese mystic and thinker Shinran Shōnin (1173–1262), pupil of Hōnen Shōnin (1133–1212) and founder of the *Jōdo-Shin* school. Far from being a mere popularizer who made the difficult doctrines of Zen accessible to ordinary people in a watered-down form, Shinran was not only a rebel (he married a Buddhist nun) but a profound thinker for whom Amida represented the possibility of liberation for all beings through his primordial vow, the manifestation of his limitless love:

> If, when I attain Buddhahood, the sentient beings of the ten quarters, with sincere mind entrusting themselves, aspiring to be born in my land, and saying my Name perhaps even ten times, should not be born there, may I not attain the supreme enlightenment. Excluded are those who commit the five grave offenses and those who slander the right dharma.[46]

For Shinran this was "the highest expression of the very core of Buddhist teaching."[47] The formless Dharma-body can only perform its liberating function if it becomes manifest in the form of Amida; in him the complementary movements from formlessness to form and from form to formlessness intersect.[48] The response demanded by the great compassion (*mahā-karuṇā*) of Amida is *shinjin*, "faith," or the trusting attitude of a pure heart, but this is not attained by our "own-power" (*jiriki*), rather it is solely attributable to the "other-power" (*tariki*) of Amida's compassion, which at the same time is its object. Only through the exercise of *shinjin* can Nirvāṇa be realized.[49] It follows that *shinjin* means transcending all temporal categories, because birth into the Pure Land is integral to the practice of *shinjin* itself and is not bound to any point in time such as the hour of death or the end of the world.[50] Exactly as in Zen, then—though differently symbolized— there is no hint of dualism between the compassion of Amida and the mind of those liberated by his will to save all beings, between the Pure Land and the practice of those striving to attain it. Sharing Amida's mind of compassion *is* liberation, right here in the midst of life in time: "*karuṇā* becomes manifest *as* Amitābha."[51] For Shinran, "the Pure Land is not something to attain, for we are already in the Pure Land; our practice does not help to take us there, but expresses gratitude," a stance that overcomes the "duality of practice *leading to* awakening."[52]

This confronts us anew with the problem of understanding the temporal structure of Buddhist historicity as the context of hope in Buddhism. The Bodhisattva Dharmākara might be termed the "mythical pre-existence" of the transcendent Buddha Amitābha; but Amitābha manifests in history not as *Dharmākara*, but as Gautama Śākyamuni. The "three bodies" doctrine is meant to explain how this is possible: Śākyamuni is the *nirmāṇa-kāya* or bodily manifestation in space–time of the *saṃbhoga-kāya* or Amitābha's body of bliss. This perspective amounts to an interpretation of the whole of history by establishing a temporal framework within which we may grasp its significance, in somewhat the same way as the world-transcending reality of the risen Christ provides the horizon for our interpretation of the historical Jesus. Amitābha is the fullness of what first became manifest in the Enlightenment of Gautama. This perspective becomes truly historical when we realize that Maitreya, the Buddha of the coming age, is expected to be not only an Enlightened One but a world-ruler who will make real the Dharma in world-history, a kind of Buddhist Messiah. His advent will change the course of history. One is inevitably reminded of the promised second coming of Christ to establish God's dominion over the whole of reality.[53]

Enough has been said to indicate that it is perhaps not necessarily contradictory to say that a structure of hope devoid of all attachment and reference to self is present in, indeed central to, all Buddhism. What the Japanese called "original enlightenment" (*hongaku*), the state of being enlightened, which constitutes our True Self, our Original Face, our intrinsic Buddha-nature, but of which we remain ignorant, may seem to remove those who realize it from any involvement in historical or social processes, but the opposite is the case—and this is the whole point and power of nondualism: precisely in Amida Buddhism, those who have attained their transcendent Buddha-nature "return" (*gensō*) to the world of moral dilemmas and ethical commitments to live out the Great Compassion of the Bodhisattvas in the struggles of everyday existence, their own, and others'. This is perhaps easier to recognize in practice than to account for in terms of doctrine, but it amounts to no less than the working out of the Dharma in historical existence in expectation of the coming of Maitreya to usher in a new age of enlightenment after the terminal decline of this era of evil and ignorance.[54] One way of conceptualizing this is a variation on the "two truths" (absolute, *paramārtha-satya*, and conventional, *samvṛti-satya*), a fundamental doctrine of later Buddhism: the Dharma itself represents a "vertical" dimension of existence, which transcends historical vicissitudes; the other is the "horizontal" dimension in which things can get better, delusion can be overcome, and we can look toward the future.[55] The key Buddhist insight, from which Christians can profit, is that these two dimensions are nondual, just as form and emptiness are in classical Madhyamaka. The question that remains is how hope in the horizontal dimension relates to the transcendence that characterizes the vertical dimension.

The tenor of this essay has been that Christianity has much to learn from the rigor of Buddhist nondualism as it applies to historical existence and the exercise of hope, particularly in its refusal to acquiesce in any dichotomy between good and evil, "us" and "them."[56] A striking example of this is David Loy's reaction as an American Buddhist to the atrocities of September 11, 2001.[57] He pointed out that the standpoints of Osama bin Laden and President Bush were mirror opposites, in that they unhesitatingly attributed evil to the "other." For Loy this is a dualistic reflex, whereas Buddhists would think in terms of our shared "karmic responsibility" for *all* evil, which in turn derives from the delusion that we are somehow separate from the world we are "in," including other people. "Paradoxically, then, one of the main causes of evil in this world has been human attempts to eradicate evil,"[58] so long, that is, as they remain within this dualistic framework.

For Paul Knitter, after Buddhist discipline had purified his Christian faith, the "not yet" of eschatology is *already in* the "already" of historical existence. The "now" and the future are nondual; there is no future "out there," only "being peace" in the here and now. He concludes that we don't need hope; it can even be an obstacle, distracting us from the immediate task. History, infused by the Spirit who connects all things, is part of the universal "interbeing" (Thich Nhat Hanh) that transcends Christian conceptions of creation and salvation.[59] At the same time it must be said—and one finds Buddhists who admit this—that Buddhist transcendence, however immanent the teachings on nonduality declare it to be, can have, and historically has had, the effect of detaching the moral subject from responsibility in history and society; Buddhists themselves have pointed to the deplorable record of parts of the Saṅgha in Sri Lanka and certain Zen masters under Japanese imperialism. Though there is no equivalent of hope in Buddhist terminology, Buddhist transcendence does have a temporal dimension, which serves to keep alive, in much the same way as the virtue of hope does for Christian faith, the realization that history could have a better outcome, that justice should be done, that compassion must be expressed in deeds. Though Buddhism is rightly associated with meditation (*dhyāna*), contemplation (*samādhi*), and wisdom (*prajñā*), at its very core, in all traditions, are loving-kindness and compassion (*metta-karuṇā*). If "faith, hope, love abide, these three; but the greatest of these is love" (1 Cor. 13.13), then love, like faith, is to be exercised in hope: "For in this hope we were saved" (Rom. 8.24). Is it too much to suggest that Buddhists, too, transcend selfish attachment and the delusions of ignorance in an attitude akin to hope?

Suffering and Loss within Shiʻi and Catholic Traditions in Dialogue

Kieran Flynn

Introduction

In both the Christian and Muslim traditions, there is little attention to human suffering and loss as central thematics in theological reflection within interreligious dialogue, though these themes are present separately in each. This chapter seeks to explicate the possibilities for dialogue and mutual learning in linking reflection on human loss and suffering in both Shiʻi and Catholic traditions. In this regard, I will focus on Catholic political theology and the narrative theology in Shiʻa Islam expressed by the understanding of *Ashura. Ashura* is the recalling and celebrating of the martyrdom of Imam Hussein, the grandson of the Prophet Muhammad, who was murdered in 670 CE by Umayyad troops.

Similarities in Shiʻi and Catholic traditions

John Allen, while writing about the future of the Catholic Church, identifies Shiʻi Islam as one of the most "dynamic worldwide religious movements"[1] today. He speaks of a "Shiʻa revival" and a "Shiʻa surge"[2] whereby Shiʻi Islam is experiencing a rapid rise and expansion worldwide and particularly across the Middle East. He indicates that there has been a growth of interest in dialogue between Shiʻi Islam and Catholicism and that the Catholic Church is well situated to promote this dialogue in the twentieth century.[3] He sees these developments rooted in the many shared parallels between Shiʻi Islam and Catholicism, including: a tradition of clerical authority; devotion to a holy family and saints; a theology of sacrifice and atonement; belief in free will; holy days, pilgrimages, and healing shrines; intercessory prayer; and emotional forms of popular piety.[4]

Both Catholic liberation theology and Shiʻism[5] continue to reject the alternatives of Western liberalism and eastern socialism. Each attempts its own delicate balance between centralization and participation, authority and liberty. However, both traditions have leaned in the direction of central control. Despite this, the Roman Catholic and Twelver Shi'i traditions have maintained a sensitivity to the needs of the individual and of the poor and to the importance of human rights and social justice.

Notwithstanding their resources in providing meaning, dignity, and justice to humankind, the challenges of modernity—while preserving a valued heritage— remain demanding to both these faith traditions as they face the twenty-first century. Among the Shi'i in Iraq, there has been an enormous revival of the *Ashura* tradition. Once banned under Saddam, now each year millions gather in Karbala to recall the martyrdom of their beloved Imam Hussein.

The *Ashura* narrative as a foundation for dialogue

Like Islam, Catholicism is as much a tradition as a community and a way of being in the world. It has its own universe of meaning, which, following O'Mahony,[6] we see as including sacramentality, mediation, communion, rationality, regard for authority and order, and openness to truth.

There have been significant encounters between Catholicism and Shi'ism over the centuries,[7] which have identified several parallels and areas of convergence. O'Mahony identifies three that are most significant: "mediation upon the significance of the passion of an innocent victim who took upon himself the sins of the community and atoned for them; belief that God's grace is mediated through earthly and heavenly hierarchies; and faith in intercessors."[8]

Suffering and martyrdom are essential marks in the history of both Shi'i Islam and Catholicism. The early Christian community witnessed the growth of a cult of martyrs. The blood of martyrs was regarded as the seeds of the Church, its resilience, its fidelity, and its forbearance. The central redemptive mystery at the heart of Christianity is the Pascal Mystery, the suffering, death, and resurrection of Jesus, a "free act of moral solidarity"[9] with suffering humanity. This redemptive event has been interpreted as an act of substitution, an act of atonement, an act of reparation, an act of liberation from death, and an act of deliverance.[10] With these interpretations, one can identify parallels with liberation theology and political theology that inform the Shi'i understanding and practice of *Ashura* among Shi'i communities in exile.

Within Islam and particularly Shi'i Islam, suffering and martyrdom have central significance. The suffering of the *Ahul Bayt* (the Holy Family)[11] in Islam and the suffering of the Prophet Muhammad are emphasized in Shi'i ritual and preaching. In the tradition reporting a dialogue between God and the Prophet, on the night of the Prophet's heavenly journey (*mi'raj*), the Prophet was told by God of his trials.[12] He was to live a life of poverty, he was to suffer persecution and exile, and his family would suffer persecution and martyrdom after his death. Such an interpretation is in sharp contrast to militant and domineering interpretations of the life of the Prophet, proposed by opponents of Islam and modern, radical Islamist movements. However, suffering is particularly associated with the Shi'i Imams and, especially, the third

Imam, Imam Hussein. These are regarded as the proofs of God, the *Hujaj Allah*, and they form a golden line of descendants who suffer oppression, injustice, tyranny, and eventually martyrdom.

In Shi'i Islam, the Imams constitute the cream of humanity, the best of creatures, earthly as well as celestial beings. Shi'i tradition, moreover, equates rejection of the *Imams* with the most unforgiveable sin of association, or *shirk*. For the Shi'a the doctrine of the Imamate is an integral part of the doctrine of prophethood. In early Islamic history, each Imam suffered injustice at the hands of Umayyad and Abbasid Caliphs despite their noble lineage. The martyrdom of Hussein is regarded as an event of "cosmic significance."[13] It is the central and defining event of Shi'i Islam. It provides for the Shi'i community the focal point from which all subsequent history must be viewed and in this it parallels Jesus's redemptive death on the cross. For Muslims it is as definitive in religious history as the Battle of Badr.[14] The martyrdom of Hussein is the central event and sacrifice in the struggle (jihad) against injustice, wrongdoing, and falsehood. In this way it is regarded as a redemptive act. Through recalling and reenacting this memory, Shi'i Muslims participate in the sacrifice of Imam Hussein, they identify with the tragedy of his family and receive his intercession. Through mourning and the shedding of tears, they win a participation in the heavenly rewards and paradise on the Day of Resurrection.[15] Through the recital of lamentation poetry (*marathi*), through participation in the ritual of *matam*,[16] through the remembrance of the *Ashura* narrative (*ta'ziyah majlis*), the Shi'i faithful relive an event in their spiritual history and renew their relationship with it. The past becomes a present to the religious community that is extended back into history and forward into the future, and is analogous to the Christian community as it gathers around the communion table to celebrate the Last Supper. The Christian understanding of *epiclesis* is that of linking past, present, and future in an eschatological mystery. In the same way those who visit the shrines of the Imams and grieve there for the family of the Prophet (*Ahul Bayt*) will cement their bonds with their past Imam and have their sins forgiven.

Anglican Bishop and Islamic scholar Kenneth Cragg has reflected upon the tragic in Islam and particularly within Shi'ism. According to Cragg the Shi'a are acutely aware "that there is more to being human than unpitying pursuit of success. The keenest theology is the one most alert to the tragic."[17] Recalling the tragic is of vital importance to the Shi'a. It is both a central religious theme and a point of convergence and dialogue with Christians.

Thus, in both Catholic Christianity and Shi'i Islam, there are significant events that recall believers to believe, pray, act, and live in similar identity-forming ways. And there are in both faiths significant intercessors who link the divine and human spheres: both faiths accept a mediator between God and humanity who plays a determining role in the divine plan for creation, in revelation, and in salvation. According to Henri Corbin, Shi'i imamology is a kind of "Islamic Christology."[18] As Ayoub identifies, Christ the eternal Logos, the divine Word, is the agent of creation, intercession, and redemption.[19] Similarly, the Imams are the pivot of creation, the link between the divine intercession and Islamic piety.

Islamic liberation theology

Identifying the reality at the heart of Islam is virtually impossible in a world religion that is globally poly-vocal and diverse.[20] Throughout history various narratives have emerged and assumed a dominant status in Islamic ideology. According to Hamid Dabashi,[21] militant Islamism emerged in the early nineteenth century in response to European colonialism and American imperialism in much the same way as liberation movements emerged throughout the colonial world at that time. This ideological resistance to empire transformed Islam into an Islamic ideology that came to a head and a conclusion with the Islamic revolution in Iran. Nevertheless, the true revolutionary disposition is found in the charismatic moment of Muhammad's prophetic mission and is most clearly expressed in Shi'i Islam.

What is called Shi'ism is nothing other than the very soul of Islam as a religion of protest. But Shi'ism has succeeded precisely because, as the very soul of the Islamic message, it is a paradox. It can never, and should never succeed. It should always speak the truth to power. It can never be in power.[22]

Shi'ism and particularly its *Ashura* narrative maintain, narrate, and display the central tension in Islamic doctrine and history between the Meccan and the Medinian paradigm. Following the death of the prophet, his charismatic authority became routinized into the Islamic caliphate. The charismatic figures of the Imam in Shi'i Islam personified the speaking to power, the Meccan spontaneity, the alterity that contrasts with the Medinian propensity to institution-building and consolidation. Thus, Shi'ism encapsulates the insurrectionary moment of the nascent Islam as a religion of protest. For Dabashi, this is the dream of Islam as well as the historical Other of Islam: Shi'ism must remain always the Other and yet dream of the Same.[23] The *Ashura* narrative speaks of the universality of protest, the universality or resistance to oppression, and the manipulation of political power. It thereby provided and provides revolutionaries and theologians alike with a paradigm of liberation.

What the world has witnessed anew in the Middle East during the emergence of the Arab Spring is a rising Islamic tragedy.[24] We are at the threshold of a new mode of Islamic consciousness. Many Islamic ideologues have been instrumental in the gradual mutation of Islam into militant Islamism—from Muhammad Abduh, Jamal al-Din al-Afghani, and Rashid Rida to 'Ali Shari'ati. But, the phenomenon that is Osama bin Laden (d. 2011) and al-Qaeda has denigrated militant Islamism into the criminal, the terrorist, and the ideologically corrupt. In Iraq, Muslims see innocent fellow-Muslims being murdered without cause or justification yet in the name of Islam and Allah. The exposure of violent hatred, vitriolic intolerance, and brutal criminality within Islam shocks the world and Muslims most of all. Among those most affected are Shi'i Muslims, and many of these have fled and become migrants. The results have been suffering, loss, and grief. The only consolation, but a powerful one for the Shi'a, is that the family of the Prophet suffered at the hands of militant Muslims in the early history of Islam, so who can be exempt from the tyrannies of radical Islam?

This is the rise of an entirely different set of circumstances to colonial invasion and American imperialism. The perpetrators are Muslim and essentially though not exclusively Sunni. This theodicy has deep historical roots in early Islam. The defining moment of Islam and particularly Shi'ism is the doctrinal sanctity of *mazlumiyyat*, of having been wronged, as is clearly outlined by Dabashi in *Authority in Islam*.[25] Dabashi distinguishes between the charismatic and the institutional, in the context of the emerging Imamate under the establishment of the Umayyads (661–750 CE). The instant Islam succeeds to power it negates itself. Thus Islam is determined to be in perpetual insurrection or negation. The present crisis in Islam is not due exclusively to its colonial history. The binaries of the past are breaking down under the influence of globalization. The sites of conflict and the sites of support are no longer situated along the fault-lines of history. The premodern and precolonial binaries of *Dar al Islam* (the Abode of Isalm) and *Dar al-Harb* (the Abode of Warfare) are no longer the geographical binaries of the West and the East. More modern designations are needed to describe the reality of Muslims living in the West today. Tariq Ramadan suggests the use of *Dar al Dawa* (the Abode of Proclamation) to describe these realities.[26] There are currently Muslims dispersed and displaced throughout the entire world and those in Europe and America have been more vocal and influential than most. Civil society is no longer the territorial possession of any particular state or category, uniting the unlikely and the unthinkable in common values and praxis. Dabashi says,

> *The difference between a liberation theology and a liberation theodicy is, very simply put, the difference between an emancipatory movement in categorical isolation from the rest of the world and one integral to the collapse of all binary oppositions.*[27]

According to Alastair Crooke, we stand at another key moment in history.[28] Islamic ideology has in the last century passed through the shadows. Sunni Islam was shocked and disorientated, dealt a psychological blow to a narrative that was already defensive. Muslims in the Middle East have seen their social and political continuities severed, their societies individualized and anaesthetized. The colonial project and the impact of neoliberalism have left citizens in the throes of great secularization and modernization, weakened society, broken capacity, eroded self-regulation, destroyed community, and increased ethnic tension. Significant and growing proportions of Muslim populations now live in absolute poverty, while their elitist overlords become richer and more powerful. Many societies in the Middle East are police states with little civil society and little civil freedom. Yet, this experience has not been one of entire isolation. New thinking is emerging, and resistance is occurring that places the suffering Muslim population at the center of its theodicy. There are green shoots of Islamic liberation theodicy, resistant to oppression and attentive to grief, best expressed in the political movement referred to as the Arab Spring.

The human desire for justice has been at the heart of Shi'i theology. More recent developments in the Middle East and atrocities in the Muslim world have emphasized the need for justice and the need for Islamic thinkers to highlight the yearning for justice within their respective traditions. Sayyid Hossein Nasr has been at the heart of Shi'i thought for many years. He describes in detail the innate human search for human justice and the search for justice within Shi'ism.[29] He says of Ali ibn Abi Talib: "Justice puts everything in its place." This follows the Quranic injunction, "Give full measure and full weight in justice" (6.152) in which Muslims are reminded to "establish weight with justice and fall not short in the balance" (55.9). Nasr reminds us that there can be no peace without justice and that justice implies a constant struggle to establish balance and equilibrium in the world, for one of the cardinal meanings of *shahadah* is: "There is no justice but the Divine Justice."

For Abdolkarim Soroush, moreover, there can be no external freedom without internal freedom, that is no freedom from potentates, despots, charlatans, and exploiters without the freedom from passion and anger.[30] This is not an avoidance of responsibility and activity but a call to interiority in the struggle for justice. In order to achieve freedom, we have to work toward truth, and truth is not the slave of any ideology. The movement toward wisdom is not a battle of the external will alone but the activity of the heart. Soroush quotes the poet and mystic Rumi:

> As much as I enlarge on love,
> I am ashamed when I come to Love.
> Renditions of the tongue reveal the core,
> But Silent love reveals more.

Here we recognize that the struggle for liberation and a liberation theology in Islam is also the movement of the heart toward internal freedom and not the work of political activism alone. We are reminded of the deep spiritual heritage at the heart of Islam and in Shi'ism in particular that is predicated on freedom and not blind submission. There is much to learn from Islam in the pursuit of liberty and justice that cannot be articulated by the West alone, and there is much to work toward in Islam that requires intelligibility and articulation by others.

Iraqi women in exile

Iraqi men and women have suffered a great deal in recent history. Al-'Ali[31] tells in a narrative style the realities of Iraqi women's lives within Iraq and among the Diaspora from 1948 until the present. Although there were times of state economic development and feminist emancipation, in recent years the realities of war, sanctions, and occupation have transformed the everyday lives of women into one of oppression, poverty, violence, and victimization. Al-Jawaheir[32] draws attention to the period of sanctions in post–Gulf War Iraq and its impact upon gender relations. This period was a humanitarian failure of unprecedented calamity, "hyperinflationary rates, high unemployment rates, excessive pressure on wages, a slump in labour productivity, and social tension and uncertainty."[33] Following the occupation in 2003, the humanitarian and political situation in Iraq changed for the worse. Despite putting an end to a brutal regime of dictatorship, a new era of "devastation, violence, hardship, and uncertainty for the Iraqi people"[34] ensued. Iraqi women were the unwitting victims, in a war situation where the most vulnerable suffer the greatest hardship. It is a tragic irony that, following the destruction of the myth of Iraq's weapons of mass destruction, the rhetoric promoting the continued occupation included the liberation of Iraqi women and sought to align the liberation of women with war and military occupation.

Within Islamic countries, women exercise the roles of homebuilder, family-bond-creators, and social-scene-creators. For exiled women, Mosque activities and the accompanying social interaction helped to replicate the intense social support and visiting that existed with extended family in their home societies. The Hussania or Mosque in the West became a "mosque-centred substitute family."[35] Religious activities and rituals took on a greater meaning and purpose as Shi'i Muslims attempted to maintain and impart to their children a particular identity amidst the variety of influences in a secular society. Al-'Ali maintains that recently arrived Iraqi Shi'i women in the West "have a strong sense of their roots and identity, both as Iraqi and Shi'as"[36] and that this involved a strong sense of entitlement in terms of rights and privileges in the new Iraq. They seized the opportunities offered to them and their children to promote themselves in society, to seek employment, education, and emancipation. Yet, in contrast with their Iranian counterparts, maintaining a strong conservative Islamic dimension to their lives remained important, but often carried with it a sectarian bias.

In light of their experience of grief, victimhood, and the loss of family members through warfare and sectarian violence, women and men find comfort in Shi'i *rowzehs*, *Moharram* rituals, and the *Ashura* Narrative. The experience of exile amplifies the importance of belonging and identifying with a spiritual community. Iraqi feminists living in the West seek to combine their Islamic faith with the experience of living in a society that promotes tolerance, pluralism, diversity, and mutuality. There are rich and potent narratives of liberation and emancipation that can be accessed within the Shi'i tradition; elements that favor the emancipation of women, the political participation of women in society at all levels, the education of girls and women, and the breaking down of gender barriers of discrimination and male privilege. Kadijha, Fatima, and Zaynab are presented as examples of powerful women who were at the center of their communities politically, religiously, and socially.

Many Muslims experience in Europe for the first time the liberation of their gender, freedom from intimidation, the accessibility of local government, the functioning of a health and education system that is empowering and respectful, a critical media, a transparent security service, and religious freedom. This dialogue of experience and faith happens while remaining faithful to a rooted Islamic identity, drawing together a rich symbolic field that extends beyond the polarities of East and West, Islam and Christianity, colonial and postcolonial. There is a linking of Islamic values such as "love of knowledge, egalitarianism and tolerance"[37] and the values of the individual, personal choice, and personal responsibility often only associated with the West. There is a "double difficult commitment"[38] taking place among Iraqi Shi'i women in the West as they reconcile their experience of sanctuary in the West with the rhetoric of radical Islam, as well as the resources expressed within the interpretation of *Ashura* as emancipating and the reality of sectarian violence, murder, and displacement. The dialogue is placed directly within the heart of Islam, and what is emerging challenges the easy and popular rhetoric of an Islamism that is all too often critical of the West and feminism. Many Islamic Shi'i feminists in the West see their feminism as emerging organically out of their faith commitment and particularly their interpretation of *Ashura*.[39]

Furthermore, this development of faith commitment and feminism together is not dominated by postcolonial discourse alone, rather it affirms the gift of sexual and psychological maturity as a dialogue open to God.[40] Faith development takes place as men and women share their experience of the transcendent and the numinous in a context of trust, openness, and love. Within the experience of a loving relationship and a faithful community, a dialogue takes place as men and women seek to situate their love and their future for each other in "liberating memory."[41]

Shi'i self-understanding and Catholic political theology

In this section, we will first turn to the rise of political theology from the ashes of liberal theology and the thought of Metz; then, we look at the dangerous memory that is the *Ashura* narrative. Shi'i thought could be greatly deepened and expanded through dialogue with political theology. There are many parallels within elements of reflection on *Ashura* and the dangerous memories of political theology. Political theology provides a framework from which to understand the centrality of *Ashura* within Shi'ism and its liberative and transformative effects in the lives of countless Shi'a.

If political theology investigates the ways in which theological concepts and ways of thinking underlie political, social, economic, and cultural discourses,[42] then the Christian religion has long been thoroughly political, and the political and the social have always been at the heart of theological reflection. In the aftermath of Vatican II and the Uppsala Assembly of the World Council of Churches (1968), the churches began to reflect strenuously on the challenge of the secular world. The euphoria of the 1960s gave way to sobriety when the horrors of the war on Vietnam and the failure of governments to curb corruption became known. There was increased disenchantment with the secular world and the positive developmental approaches in science and technology. A recognition that the Christian West had been elevated on the suffering of colonized masses helped to form a political theology that relocated the human subject in the mass of those who are marginalized, alienated, dispossessed, and poor— the "suffering"—and that reinterpreted human existence through a praxis of freedom. As Rebecca Chopp comments: *Political theology continues the Christian tradition only through its insistence that Christianity is the continual transformation of suffering and hope in the dangerous memory of Christ.*[43]

Political theology carries forward modern theology's critique of the secular; however, transformation and rupture, as the task of mediating tradition in a violent and changing world, are at the heart of this theology and they, too, come under close scrutiny. Without compressing the developments of twentieth-century theology, it is possible to identify significant moments along this complex and multifaceted journey that situate political theology. If liberal theologians such as Schleiermacher and Troeltsch sought to make Christian theology relevant to history, experience, and identity by reconciling modernity with religion, they did so by locating faith in the individual's encounter with God.[44] This contrasts with the "modern masters of suspicion."[45] These include Karl Marx, who accused the upper classes of hiding behind an ideology that supports their greedy interests while others are impoverished; Sigmund Freud, who revealed the power of the unconscious in influencing meaning, motivation, and behavior; and Friedrich Nietzsche, who warned that our conscious reflections of freedom disguise our unconscious drive for power. Critiques of modernity also emerge from the underside of history. The victims of history accuse modernity of building its progress upon their suffering. In postwar Europe, the Jews recall the memories of the Holocaust and their virtual extermination. Women accuse patriarchal modernity of maintaining and promoting misogyny by representing women as inferior. Blacks, though free from slavery, recognize that their liberation often led to poverty, homelessness, and social and racial discrimination. Latin America and the Middle East denounce their history as the colony of the first world. Yet, political theology responds by saying that meaning, value, and truth are always constituted in concrete historical particularity. Individual suffering, then, is what interrupts this constitution, and theology becomes reconstituted by its identification or solidarity with those who suffer. Memories of solidarity with the poor become the basis of critique, transformation, and hope.

The political theology of Johann Baptist Metz

Johann Baptist Metz specialized in interrogating these memories; for him, these were "dangerous memories." Catholic and German, he was born into and grew up in the world of Nazi Germany. He experienced first-hand Germany's march into fundamentalism, violence, war, and destruction. For Metz, as with many Germans, the question was how did the Germany of Goethe, Kant, and Beethoven become the Germany of Hitler, Himmler, and finally Auschwitz? This was a tremendous interruption in his life and his theology. How was theology to continue on and to address itself after the horror of Auschwitz?[46] In sum, the new paradigm of political theology understands theology in the twentieth century as being faced with three crises, three challenges, or three "end phenomena."[47]

Metz considered privatization to be the most important aspect of the crisis caused by the Enlightenment.[48] He pleads for a conversion of middle class and bourgeois consciousness. He uncovers the consciousness of the bourgeois subject as distorted, private, and comfortable. He finds our time to be one of postmodern Godless Christianity. Here he means that Christianity is practiced without recourse to the unsettling "history of catastrophe and consolation that comprises the narrative of Judeo Christian tradition."[49] This is recognized in people turning more and more to new and ahistorical forms of religious myth and ritual, symbolized by the concept of New Age religion. The rise in capitalism and technological and scientific achievement have ushered in an evolutionary worldview of progress and development. Yet, this has proved to be groundless, lacking in meaning and only producing fatalism and apathy. People find themselves reduced to being consumers, small parts of an anonymous, inevitable, so-called timeless, technological, and economic progress.

The interruption of suffering and the definite memory of suffering are dangerous and transformative in their ability to render a critique of this evolutionary worldview and to stimulate the human imagination for social–political action. Metz discovers that the freedom to be a human subject is the freedom to suffer. It is the memory of suffering and the ability to remember suffering that provide the possibility for the concrete identity of the human subject. In the freedom to experience and allow for suffering is the freedom to hope, to transform, and to become. Memory, narrative, and solidarity in suffering constitute human identity, community, and belonging. This is not an anonymous or a universal experience of the divine but grounded in specific memories, narratives, and events. Such an experience of suffering and solidarity in suffering is a foundational experience of the divine. God is the One who interrupts history on behalf of the suffering and provides the full freedom to human emancipation through suffering by providing hope and meaning in compassionate solidarity.

According to Metz the function of theology[50] is to protect the narrating memory of salvation in our scientific world by helping Christians understand their own life stories in light of the memory of the passion, death, and resurrection[51] of Jesus and in this way to pass on this dangerous memory in narrative form. Suffering unto God[51] is the authentic mystical stance in modernity and also the stance that can save the ideals of the Enlightenment from its own destruction. Christianity tries to keep alive the dangerous memory of the crucified Lord as a memory of freedom. It provides hope in the face of violent oppression and anticipation of a better future. Precisely because it is inspirational, it is dangerous, unsettling, and a shocking interruption.

One contribution of Metz to theology is the compelling case for how the modern subject of religion needs to be deconstructed by an awareness of suffering in history and reconstructed through a praxis of solidarity with those who now suffer or who have died violently, through cruelty, poverty, or neglect. This is in part the theodicy problem—the question of God in the face of human suffering and also the question of human empowerment and meaning in the face of the suffering of others. According to Metz it is only because we believe in a definite eschatological meaning of history that we can face negativities and catastrophes with hope.[52] There is a danger in being too pious and too mystical, though discipleship and imitation of the Crucified One always contain a mystical and a situational–political element.

Ashura Ritual in Shi'i Islam

The ritual of *Ashura* provides a rich metaphor in bringing together religious memory, suffering, and identity. This has been underutilized by Shi'i scholars[53] who in recent years have focused almost entirely in Shi'ite political thought on the developments in political rule (particularly *Wilayat al-Faqih*) and not on the rich theological vein of popular ritual and faith. There is the possibility of developing a Shi'ite political theology that is sensitive to memory, suffering, and ritual. Such a theology is deeply attentive to the religious faith and practice of the grassroots that situates itself within the narrative of *Ashura* and could draw strength and insight from Christian political theology and the challenge of suffering and memory to religious faith. Such developments would be transformative for Shi'ite political thought and Islamic theology as a whole, providing a new and fruitful basis for dialogue with other religions and the secular West that is rooted in experience, especially the experience of suffering. This theological focus on suffering and loss would also provide a key starting point for Christians who in the developing world also experience oppressive government, tyranny, and violence. Thus, both traditions have much to learn from each other in striving toward greater freedom and justice.

Memory and identity

We remember Auschwitz and all that it symbolizes because we believe that, in spite of all the past and its horrors, the world is worthy of salvation; and salvation, like redemption, can be found only in memory.[54]

Elie Wiesel spoke these words in an address delivered on November 10, 1987, recalling the infamous Kristallnacht in 1938, which propelled Germany closer to the horrors of the Holocaust. For Wiesel, the central theme of his work is the saving power of remembering suffered wrongs. He is concerned with all significant wrongdoing, redemption, and the fostering of human flourishing. Wiesel suggests that salvation lies in memory and right remembering. We are our memories, and healing emerges when we interpret our memories and inscribe them into the larger meaning-making of our lives. In order to do this, we need solidarity, companionship, and the witness of others. Memory-making toward salvation is an exercise in empathy. According to Miroslav Volf giving meaning to suffering is "borne on the wings of hope."[55] This is a hope for full disclosure and for ultimate redemption from others in the face of their apparent meaninglessness; hope that the future belongs to those who give themselves in love, not to those who nail others to a cross.

Transformed memories of wrongs suffered can become catalysts for doing justice. They can lead to solidarity, empathy, and compassion. Victims don't remain victims forever but can rewrite the moral narrative in ways that are transformative and redemptive for victimizers. It is from the memory of a wrong suffered that a principled opposition to injustice emerges. This does not need to be destructive but life-giving, healing, and mutually flourishing though clearly not without pain and solidarity. Dangerous memories disturb, sacred memories heal, and some dangerous memories are sacred memories but are deemed dangerous by the powerful. In the Exodus and the Passion of the Crucified One, God is remembered as having been at work in faithfulness to God's people.[56] God hears the cries of the Hebrews and God in Christ was reconciling the world to himself. These are dangerous memories for all victimizers, all who exercise political power and all systems that support oppression.

The journey of the human subject is that of remembering truthfully, condemning wrong deeds, healing inner wounds, and reconciling wrongdoers. It ends with letting the memory of violence go. As Roger Errera writes: "Memory is the ultimate form of justice."[57] This work is done therapeutically through providing new meaning to victimization, intimidation, and suffering. Even suffering can have a place in God's plan for the cosmos.

An essential part of politics in societies emerging from dictatorship and oppression is the flourishing of group memories as they seek to recover and win recognition by an overarching national collective memory. It is necessary for plural memories to emerge to critique the all-absorbing official story of the past.[58] That is the necessity of bearing witness, the responsibility of a community over time, to effect meaning, integrity, and ethical wholeness.

The *Ashura* narrative as a "Dangerous Memory"

The *Ashura* narrative is the attempt to recover the dangerous memory of Karbala and apply it to the social, religious, and political context of Iraqi Shi'i communities. This narrative, more than any other religious metaphor, provides meaning, healing, and integrity to this religious community. In the context of war and occupation, it becomes the narrative of resistance. In the context of exile, it becomes the narrative of loss, dislocation, emerging realities, and new religious articulations. In the context of state building, it becomes the narrative of accommodation, democratic participation, transparency, and leadership with integrity.

Political theology provides the *Ashura* narrative with a rich and fertile theological context for dialogue and appropriation. Those communities in the West who are aware of liberation theology and political theology employ these concepts in their preaching and within their narrations. The dangerous memory of Karbala not only enlivens, inspires, and transforms the Shi'i community each year in its narration during *Ashura* but also provides the context for political participation in a new emerging state. Shi'i politicians are aware of the demand of their religious communities for political participation and truthful representation.

The recent developments in Iraq for the Shi'a constitute an atrocity moment. Under Saddam people routinely disappeared, were imprisoned, and murdered. Following the American invasion, hundreds of thousands were killed, displaced, and suffered under occupation. Iraqi Shi'a are well acquainted with suffering, oppression, and violence. The memory of the *Ashura* narrative provides them with hope and consolation throughout difficult and trying years. In the modern state, the *Ashura* narrative is used to promote democratic values and emancipatiory leadership. Religion and politics are intertwined. The memory of past suffering provides the context for the formation of a future state, where all are cherished and the flourishing of all is respected.

As Shi'a remember the suffering, martyrdom, and victory of Imam Hussein in their mournful *majlis,* they connect with the memory of their own suffering, oppression, exile, loss, and grief. As they grieve for their beloved Imam, they are healed, transformed, and united in religious identity and motivated to implement their dream of a justice-filled democratic state. As Shi'a mourn those who died and suffered at the hands of terrorists and violent and fundamental radicals, they are encouraged to articulate an Islam free of radical rhetoric, in solidarity with victims of violence and oppression while open, tolerant, and faithful to the prophetic mission of foundational Islam.

As Shi'a dream the dream of prophetic Islam, they implement their own particular Islamic liberation theology and their own particular Islamic political theology deeply influenced by their dialogue with and experience of political theology in the West.

Conclusion

There are numerous resources in Western thought and political theology that can support Shi'i scholars and communities to seek the liberation and emancipation of their people, without becoming aggressors in turn. European political theology in the West has embraced the painful history of violence, dislocation, and trauma since World War II. It can provide valuable resources to Shi'i communities as they reflect on their experience and make sense of their faith in a world where violence and hatred have been dominant for many years. *Ashura* as a metaphor for liberation and political emancipation is symbol-rich in meaning for Shi'a. It can become a root symbol for an emancipated Shi'i political theology that takes account of suffering and the transformative power of memory and, at the same time, provides a solid basis for future interreligious and inter-theological dialogue. The debates within political theology resonate with Shi'i scholars. J. B. Metz in particular can offer a fruitful contribution to Shi'i self-understanding by elucidating and extending the conceptual framing of debate on grief, loss, suffering, and redemption. In a story that has risked being lost in recriminations and bitter divide, this chapter thus ends with a message of hope.

The Pedophile Scandal and Its (Hoped-for) Impact on Catholic Intra- and Interreligious Dialogue

Peter Admirand

Introduction: Disgraced

"When arrogance appears, disgrace follows, but wisdom is with those who are unassuming." (Prv. 11.2)

This chapter, replete with a crushing sense of loss, still seeks hope. But because such hope is phrased in the context of the child abuse scandal in the Catholic Church, it must especially be tempered, pastoral, and ethically sensitive. In seeking hope, one cannot hide or diminish the reality of loss. Hope is false when loss is not honestly faced and measured. Any hope facing loss sows the ground with the possibility of hopelessness. It is a risk that must be taken if hope is to bear any fruit.

In March 2013, seven out of ten Catholics in a poll conducted by The Pew Center's Forum on Religion and Public Life said that the child abuse scandal should be a top priority of the then newly elected Pope Francis.[1] Perhaps, this is a hopeful sign. While Francis has made various comments calling for "decisive action" or "zero tolerance" against those convicted of abuse, responses (as of December 2013) by child abuse advocates remain generally unimpressed.[2]

Amidst the ongoing or still underreported revelations and impact of systemic child abuse committed or poorly addressed within all levels of the Catholic Church, healing and aiding those who were abused and ensuring such crimes do not happen again remain priorities.[3] Secondarily, however, is a call to reexamine Church life, structure, and praxis in the process of repentance that Benedict XVI promoted and which his successor Francis I has echoed.[4] To further such reexamination, in this chapter, I will argue that the reality of these scandals challenges the Church's predominant view of inter- and intrareligious dialogue, in which Church teaching claims (or implies) predominant ownership of Truth. Highlighting the Church's often-pervasive failure to listen to, support, and love the Other—most recently the abused child-victims within the Catholic fold—demands a deeper turning to and engaging with so-called nontraditional sources and a deeper commitment to interreligious dialogue. Such a commitment also entails a responsibility to continue reexamining a range of issues that have been deemed closed or are not adequately addressed within intra-Catholic dialogue: 12 areas I will list toward the end of this chapter.

In building up to these areas, I will uphold seven virtues or traits that are indispensable if the Church—and its more recent apologies—can be sustained with any credibility.[5] In moving from (being) disgraced to (living in) grace, I will trace a parallel movement from a Church colonized by power to a liberation that demands a greater responsibility to the Other.

Colonized

"My name is Legion for we are many." (Mk. 5.9)

In the next three sections, I will examine how blindness, insincerity, and amnesia have led to a "colonized" Church culture that refused to see, evaluate, and remember the horrors that were committed against the "heretic," foreigner, Jew, or any so-called Other. Instead, I am advocating the need for awareness, truthfulness, and retentiveness as a means to help liberate the Church and Christianity from its current failures.

Blindness

"Though seeing, they do not see; though hearing, they do not hear or understand." (Mt. 13.14)

In What We Knew: Terror, Mass Murder, and Everyday Life in Nazi Germany, historian Eric Johnson and sociologist Karl-Heinz Reuband include and analyze the material gleaned from the surveys and oral interviews they conducted of a "large cross section of the German population, both Jewish and non-Jewish, about their everyday lives in Nazi Germany and about their brushes with Nazi terror, as well as their knowledge about the mass murder of the Jews."[6] In one oral interview, Hannelore Mahler describes her deportation in broad daylight from her native German city of Krefeld. Here is a small piece of her testimony:

> . . . After the war, (the Germans) all said, "We didn't know about it." (But in September 1944), when we were arrested, we were marched right past the main (Catholic) church, the Dionysiuskirche, with our Jewish stars and backpacks, and I was pushing the baby carriage with my little son in it. And, exactly then, the mass let out, and yes, they saw (us) . . . Indeed, they had to have seen us.[7]

The condemned group walked toward the train station. Theresienstadt was their destination.

Such refusal to see the suffering of others has also been a salient failure within the pedophile scandal. To be clear: while the title of this chapter rings with optimism and hope, the systemic, world-wide tragedy of pedophile abuse and cover-up within the Catholic Church is a topic that sends chills as one writes. It numbs and wretches. Curses seem called for, often as desperately as prayers.

This is especially so if one hears the testimony of a child-abuse survivor,[8] or a convicted priest explaining his actions,[9] or a Vatican official fumbling through a defensive, lawyerly response—in one infamous case even suggesting that the Church is being attacked by the media in this scandal in a similar way to the Jews during the Holocaust.[10] While the usual distancing and explanations were eventually offered, the fundamental issues at stake remain unaddressed. The genocide attempted against the Jews in so-called Christian Europe during the Shoah (or for the Roma, the Porajmos) was feebly resisted by all levels of the Church, who generally failed, or poorly lived up to, its calling and mission at that time. To then link the suffering of the Jews with any mudslinging leveled against the Church by the press is of course inappropriate and shameful.

Benedict XVI was generally very vocal in minimizing the Church as a victim and accentuating its failures. In his September 2010 visit to the United Kingdom, he said: "It is a great sadness . . . that Church leadership was not sufficiently vigilant and sufficiently swift and decisive in taking the necessary measures. On account of this we are living in a time of penance, humility, renewed sincerity, as I wrote to the Irish Bishops."[11] These were certainly welcoming comments. As Maimonides writes in his *Laws of Repentance*: "What is repentance? It is when a person abandons his sin and casts it from his mind, and decides not to repeat it."[12] Maimonides also stresses that contrition is only proven when one finds oneself in the same situation but refrains from committing the same transgression. Until the Church embodies such repentance, her words remain shallow and questionable.

From my work with testimonies of mass atrocity, four aphorisms come to mind:

1. Past actions never properly atoned for indeed do resurrect themselves.
2. There will always be a reckoning, eventually.
3. All graves, at some point, become full.
4. Concealment is rarely eternally possible.

To have to apply these phrases to the twenty-first-century Church is, simply, disgraceful. Building upon Benedict's words earlier, this chapter contends that one clear step toward embodying these virtues is in the realm of interreligious dialogue, where the official view of the Church often seems muddled, and the line between dialogue and mission (as conversion) is ambiguous. So, too, from documents such as *Dominus Iesus* to the CDF's "Note on the Expression 'Sister Churches'" to the "Doctrinal Note: On Some Aspects of Evangelization," it is evident where the fullness of salvation subsists and where it is absent or partial. While the Catholic Church professes desire for intra- and interreligious cooperation and partnership, exclusivist statements or ones that maintain religious superiority inevitably inflict lasting damage to such dialogue. They also blind Catholics from seeing the pain inflicted on the non-Catholic Other through often unnecessary, soteriological exclusivist propositions. While exceptions can be located, the gist of major Vatican documents often fails to address the Other and his or her views in a sacred, dignified way. At times, these exclusivist views have bordered on the slanderous, one obvious example being supersessionism, which still lingers post-*Nostra Aetate*, even if in what Eugene Korn calls "soft supersessionism."[13]

In Jewish tradition, desecrating another's honor is indeed a serious crime as the Talmudic Sages deemed slander (*lashon hara*/evil speech) worse than murder in some instances.[14] In fact, according to Normon Solomon: "The rabbis understood the biblical term tzara'at as referring to a special affliction sent by God to punish slanderers. . ."[15] It is a crime that should never be taken lightly. Tragically, many victims of the child abuse scandal were slandered even after they sought to tell their stories. So, too, a propensity to maintain one's so-called superior or exclusivist views is also likely to slander the Other. Like my general feeling after reading the Qur'an's clear condemnation of Christian Incarnational and Trinitarian views, what Jew does not feel this sense of slander when reading the gospels?[16] It should be incumbent that Catholic theological studies and catechesis promote a more sustained, spiritual prayerfulness and theological framework to be aware and see the Other and her beliefs, needs, and hopes on her terms and frameworks.

Insincerity

"For I do not know how to flatter—or my Maker would put an end to me!" (Jb. 32.22)

Earlier I stressed the need for seeing, even as what one sees challenges, numbs, and raises severe doubts. Such awareness also demands a courageous position that tries to protect the truth and the dignity of the Other. To be insincere is to be mired in hypocrisy, untruthfulness, and hollowness: attributes any living faith must obviously avoid. Consider, then, the words above from Elihu in the Book of Job as we will momentarily look upon Elihu as a potential guide toward how to respond to this abuse scandal with a sincere and open heart.

Bear in mind that commentators are often torn on how to judge Elihu: Gustavo Gutiérrez, for example, writes that: "Though conceited, Elihu has a good grasp of what has been said in the debate (between Job and his friends) and thus is able to focus on important points (like) . . . the greatness of God."[17] In commenting on Elihu's "jejune pronouncements," David Burrell pens that Elihu's role "prepares us to recognize that voice in the dramatic closure of this inner journey."[18] Some sages of the Talmud even include Elihu among the seven prophets who prophesied to the nations of the world: namely, Balaam and his father, Job, Eliphaz the Temanite, Bildad the Shuhite, (and) Zophar the Naamathite. The Talmudic passage from Bava Batra (the Last Gate) asks: "Are you suggesting that Elihu the Son of Barachel was not Israelite? Surely (he was for) it is written, 'Elihu the Son of Barachel the Buzite, of the family of Ram (Jb. 32.2)." Just as Job is later defended to be an Israelite, the attempt seems mainly to contain Elihu's recognized wisdom among Israelites. In *The Guide for the Perplexed*, moreover, Maimonides generally praises the words of Elihu, commenting: ". . . Later on a new theory was set forth, namely that ascribed to Elihu. For this reason he is placed above the others, and described as younger in years, but greater in wisdom."[19]

Of the Book of Job, a text certainly relevant to a discussion seeking God's presence despite evil, abuse, and suffering, one may have limitless opinions.[20] As James Kugel writes: "In the end—as with many a book of dialogues—the author of Job is playing both sides with his whole heart. His answer is neither Job's nor the comforters' nor, for that matter, even God's, but all three together, which is to say, his answer is the back-and-forth-of the book itself."[21] Can Elihu, then, be a type of flawed, but admiringly persevering guide in responding to the child abuse scandal? Ultimately, much of Elihu's actual views (and the Book of Job, in general) are not fully relevant or applicable for our context as we are overly burdened by an awareness of "useless suffering" and "useless knowledge."[22] Indeed, there are no justifications for the abuse so many children were forced to endure. They were evils that must be addressed by listening to and healing the victims, seeking justice, and striving to prevent the reoccurrence of such abuse. Elihu, however, can be admired for not concealing his views and for his bravery to insist upon them despite the likelihood of censure and rebuke. Interestingly, Elihu, unlike Job's "friends," is not censured by God. His words, in fact, are quite similar to what God says to Job, namely, who are you to question God? Still, God states that Job "has spoken of me what is right" (Jb. 42.7) and Elihu's final words are seemingly ignored as God addresses Job from the whirlwind.

In the context of abused children, moreover, it is difficult to remain dispassionate, neutral, placid—especially as (in my case) one still hopes for the Church's reform while aware of how a lack of flattery in these matters can sometimes be misinterpreted as questions about one's orthodoxy. Thus, who has the right to criticize the Church? In the extant (but minor) Jewish tradition of questioning God, for example, Zachary Braiterman writes: "The author of one midrash clearly makes his point when he asks: 'Do you know who can protest against His decree and say to him Why do you do such a thing? He who observes the commandments.'"[23] As one must tread lightly when questioning God, so Catholics are told to tread lightly when criticizing the Church. But in the scandals unfolding throughout the world, it is too painful to be silent: and it is no time to flatter, no matter the consequences. As Archbishop of Dublin Diarmuid Martin spoke during the 2011 Liturgy of Lament and Repentance for Survivors: "I appeal to you to continue to speak out. There is still a long path to journey in honesty before we can truly merit forgiveness."[24]

Amnesia

> "Write this down in a document as something to be remembered, and recite it in the ears of Joshua. I will completely blot out the memory of Amalek from under the heavens." (Ex. 17.14)

In the context of abuse victims, Christians have too often forgotten the cries and victims of the past and so have failed to dialogue and partner with such individuals and their stories when formulating or upholding theological decrees. Such dialogue and learning with the victims and their stories help to ensure that their voices are prevalent and heard. Here we enter the well-trod realm of an ethics of memory or the obligation to remember justly balanced by a certain reasonableness (or necessity) of ethical forgetting.[25] The call to blot out Amalek (Ex. 17.14) above is an example of a biblical injunction that should be forgotten with its overtones of "cultural genocide."[26] Instead, we forget what we should remember but can recall what should be forgotten.

Remembering, therefore, is crucially linked with an awareness of the contexts and the cries of the victims and with the intention of portraying and interpreting such scenes as objectively as possible. In the obligation to remember, one incorporates and portrays such memories truthfully and justly.

Making a commitment to remember victims of suffering and atrocity, moreover, is one potential way to develop and sustain such a conversion or purification of one's faith. The demand, obligation, and expectation—not only to remember, but to stave off the "attrition of memory"[27]—is indelibly linked to what it means, for example, to be a Jew, a Muslim, or a Christian. In the Qur'an, we read: "Remember God's blessing on you and the pledge with which you were bound when you said, 'We hear and we obey.'"[28]

Despite the need for clarification regarding some problematic biblical passages, biblical stories were composed in part to address and accommodate the role that remembering and forgetting constitute for a people's religious and moral identity.[29] Such memory is betrayed, however, when the stories and voices of the oppressed and victims of our world are forgotten, misrepresented, or silenced. The memory of the abused children and of their loved ones who have also suffered, must be remembered, ritualized, and channeled.

In the case of clerical child abuse within the Church, recall these words of Jesus: "If any of you put a stumbling block before one of these little ones who believe in me, it would be better for you if a great millstone were hung around your neck and you were thrown into the depths of the sea" (Mk. 9.42). Jesus's words hint at some of the rage most people feel when confronting such horrors. And yet, even here the language is metaphorical, entwined in the hyperbolic. It is ascribed to a Galilean peasant who before eventually succumbing to unjust charges, torture, and ignominious death, still could say: "Father, forgive them, for they know not what they do" (Lk. 23.34).

Of course, ignorance is one thing; willful pride or malfeasance is another. Sadly, Catholic Christians have often been plagued by a willingness to forget or overlook words and actions that have injured others. As Nietzsche writes: "'I have done that,' says my memory. 'I cannot have done that'—says my pride, and remains adamant. At last— memory yields."[30] It is time for an ethic of memory that refuses to yield to pride.[31]

As noted above, Benedict called for "penance, humility, (and) renewed sincerity." If these are not to be mere sentiments, we need to develop an ethic of theological memory and praxis, guided by the option for the poor and marginalized, to remember and hear the cries of the oppressed. Abused Catholic children, who have been battered and violated, silenced and dehumanized, are sadly not unique. They are not the first of the powerless and subaltern to be, ironically, battered by the Cross, joining those Others for whom the Church has repeatedly failed. Again, remember the historical relation of Judaism within Christianity.

Since the Church's inception, the Jewish people and Judaism have been one of her first and dominant victims. For centuries, spurred on by the *adversus Judeos* tradition, Catholics derided Jews through a pernicious deicide charge, promulgated a supercessionist theology, accused Jews of outrageously immoral behavior to then justify violent actions against them, and generally refused to listen to why Jews could not accept Christ as the hoped-for Messiah. What seemed such a clear truth to Christians could only be configured to a people deemed obdurate, blind, and wayward. As Christians have finally begun to listen to Jewish voices—especially when reflecting upon the majority of Jesus's fellow contemporaneous Jews who did not recognize him as the Christ—they are in a better position to accept some difficult, but salient interpretations.[32] Turning to the victims of the child abuse scandals will also reveal painful, but necessary revelations and truths.

Such theological retentiveness tries to support the victims despite the cost to one's faith and one's beliefs. Again, questions, doubt, and anger will increase but if one's faith truly seeks to be liberating, such consequences are the least one can bear in light of the horrors others have endured.

Liberation

"Let my people go!" (Ex. 5.1)

In the obligation to search for, see, remember, and act toward healing another's suffering, the need for a courageous language—without flattery to those in power—was outlined earlier. Thus I highlighted the virtues of awareness, truthfulness, and retentiveness. As a 2010 editorial in *The National Catholic Reporter* articulated: "We now face the largest institutional crisis in centuries, possibly in church history . . . It is time to tell the truth."[33] Indeed, how does one interpret and try to explain the methods, approach, and philosophy employed by the Vatican and a range of Church officials? What viable conclusion can one draw from these facts?

As noted, clarity and a lack of flattery—no matter the cost—are indispensable. My conclusion? Much of the structural, institutional Church is colonized by pride, patriarchy, and (static) certitude. Thankfully, there are vibrant voices within the Church that resist and have always resisted this take-over, emphasized by Francis in his rebuke of clericalism and careerism in the Church.[34]

But the problems are insidious, drenched in Christian history: from the burning of early heretics; the slaying and dehumanizing of the indigenous, colonized people of the Americas, Australia, Africa, and Asia; the attempted genocide against the Jews; the genocide in Rwanda (a predominantly Catholic country); to the abuse and raping of thousands of Catholic boys and girls by priests and other religious. As noxious is the systemic cover-up that plagues the Church and blinds it to the face of these innocent victims, for whom the Church has encircled with stumbling blocks. While Tertullian could once boast: "The blood of the *martyrs* is the *seed* of the church," we must now say that the blood of the victims is the blight of the Church.

As noted above, there have been limited, but encouraging signs that the Church is responding to the scandal more appropriately. Great hope was placed in Pope Francis to build upon some of Benedict's words, like Benedict's important statement in May 2010:

> The greatest persecution of the church doesn't come from enemies on the outside, but is born in sin within the church. The church thus has a deep need to relearn penance, to accept purification, to learn on one hand forgiveness but also the necessity of justice. Forgiveness does not exclude justice. We have to relearn the essentials: conversion, prayer, penance, and the theological virtues.[35]

While Benedict's words still suffer from a general us–them dichotomy, they are a potentially fruitful source to build a meaningful response. To do so, and to combat pride, apathy, patriarchy, and (static) certitude, I want to focus on four more fruitful virtues: humility, perseverance, fellowship, and (a fractured) faith. As humility is the keystone or foundation for any hope to sustain a movement from disgraced (colonization) to grace (liberation), I will inspect that virtue now.

Humility

"Blessed are the meek: for they shall inherit the earth." (Mt. 5.5)

At the official, Vatican level so much interreligious or ecumenical dialogue is stalled, regressing, or not proceeding as it should because of a lack of true humility, a humility that should be suffused with embarrassment in the midst of these pedophile atrocities. If these failures do not spur on such radical change, then one can hear Abraham in Jesus's parable say to the rich man: "If they do not listen to Moses and the prophets, neither will they be convinced even if someone rises from the dead" (Lk. 16.31).[36] If the cries of abused children by Church leaders do not spur a need for change, nothing it seems will.

The humility I am elevating, therefore, is necessarily scrappy, rugged, and obdurate, one that does not whimper or silence itself in the midst of oppression and injustice. Humility upholds a mirror to the self and the Other, illuminated by the Spirit of God. As Simone Weil provocatively pens:

> Humility is the root of love.
>
> Humility exerts an irresistible power upon God.
>
> If God had not been humiliated, in the person of Christ, he would be inferior to us.[37]

While I would hesitate fully to support Weil's last statement, the paradox of a humble pride or a prideful humility is one way to maintain this often abused and co-opted term. Humility is not abject silence, impotence, and degradation. Humility, indeed, can clamor and keen—it may even dance, if not strut, if the context is suitable. One may think of David's naked dance before the Ark (2 Sm. 6.1–23), though I also think of poor Mi'chal and the unjust road she was forced to trod, and even of her piteous, former husband Pal'tiel, coerced to abandon his wife because King David demanded her return. While Abner seizes Mi̇̄chal, the narrator describes how Pal'tiel "went with her, weeping as he walked all the way to Bahurim. Then Abner (formerly Saul's general) said to him, 'Go back home.' So he went back" (2 Sm. 16). There was no dialogue or debate: power and military might bellowed.

However, in light of Abner's subsequent murder (2 Sm. 3.27) and David's inconsistently egotistical and self-deprecating response to Mi̇̄chal about his naked dance, in which he is either proud of abasing himself before the Lord or for his being honored by the blushing maids (2 Sm. 6.21–3), it is crucial to distinguish pride and humility where necessary. Aristotle chides the person who is "unduly humble," a term that is useful for our discussion even if the criteria and context Aristotle employs would not be.[38]

Contra humility, pride is always rendered the deadliest of sins in common Christian parlance. One may recall Satan in Milton's epic, who addresses the Sun: "O sun, to tell thee how I hate thy beams, / That bring to my remembrance from what state I fell, / how glorious once above thy sphere, / Till pride and worse ambition threw me down. / Warring in Heaven against Heaven's Matchless King . . ."[39]

Notice how these lines are far from pride-ful, echoing more nostalgia and regret—and if not inward contrition, then one must call it duplicitous contrition. Its analysis is further complicated if read as a soliloquy. In *The History of Troilus and Cressida*, moreover, Shakespeare's Agamemnon says to Ajax: "He that is proud eats up himself. Pride is his own glass, his own trumpet, his own chronicle; and whatever praises itself but in the deed, devours the deed in the praise."[40] Paraphrasing Shakespeare's Marcus Antonius: "(Humility) should be made of sterner stuff."[41]

Perseverance

"Wait on the Lord: be of good courage, and he shall strengthen thine heart: wait, I say, on the Lord." (Ps. 27.14)

So much of our role in this world demands persevering. For billions of people, life is a daily struggle for survival. For the more fortunate, it is enduring different kinds of losses, especially when apathy reigns and the world's problems dominate. Like the rugged humility advocated above, however, this perseverance is not passive and resigned to the oppressive status quo, but is complemented by the fortitude to work for change.

In writing about courage, Aristotle remarks: "It is for facing what is painful, then . . . that men are called brave." Such courage is crucial for enduring various pains and fears, "for it is harder to face what is painful than to abstain from what is pleasant."[42] In the gospels, Jesus in Gethsemane is one apt illustration, and similar examples can be cited from other faith traditions. In recognizing the painful truth of a colonized Church, one knows any notion of dissent, rebellion, or challenging is rarely left uncontested. The enmeshed web of pride, apathy, patriarchy, and (static) certitude can seem omnipotent. Perseverance and courage are required to acknowledge these failures and to seek healing and a cure.

Fellowship

"Love one another as I have loved you." (Jn. 13.34)

Faith-seeking is only meaningful within community. It is characterized by a fellowship that transcends any borders and identity-based walls and divisions that seek to separate us from one another. What should unite is a pervasive responsibility for the Other, a recognition that the face of the Other obligates us and demands us to respond and bear the responsibility for this Other within us—to embrace this Other as one hopes to embrace oneself and one's God (or Ultimate Reality). This awareness also entails moral fortitude for there are many whom we loathe and shun.

Such individuals, like the abusive priests usually labeled perpetrator (or more venomous terms), must also be included: "Since I am responsible even for the Other's responsibility," as Levinas states. Such is to say that we are even responsible toward those who injure us. Such a remark does not curtail the role that juridical justice should play, as "Justice," for Levinas, "only has meaning if it retains the spirit of dis-interestedness which animates the idea of responsibility for the other man."[43] That is why the claims of the Church being slandered must be taken seriously. So too, must care be shown in the way individual priests and religious members are charged with any crime.

Charged individuals must refrain from Church activity (especially with children) until the full truth is disclosed. If guilty, they must be punished by the secular authorities as the penal or civil law (in accordance with the Moral Law) demands. Justice should also be applied to those who did not lawfully and morally act to ensure that such violations would not happen again. Claiming ignorance or arguing that times were different then are merely excuses to avoid public shame and loss of power. Great care, however, must be shown to uphold the honor of those who were falsely accused.

Contra the antiquated and troglodyte-notion of patriarchy, fellowship is at the heart of interreligious dialogue and so the possibility for renewal. Inter- and intrareligious dialogue is crucial because it is a process of mutual giving and sharing (and questioning and rethinking) whose ultimate aim is to seek a truth (or truths) that honors the dignity of the human person, the integrity of the cosmos and biosphere, and the deepest yearnings for existential meaning and purpose. True fellowship means a shedding of the pride and power of religious superiority that promulgates that the Truth only or supremely resides within one's own camp or jurisdiction. One should not even hope that this is the case, for to do so is to deny billions of people the resources of faith, hope, and love that inspire and fulfill their deepest longings and have sustained them amidst joy, horrific loss, absence, and affliction. That the life, actions, and words of Christ remain the fulcrum upon which my life and hopes turn does not mean that I cannot find deep truths within other faith (or secular) positions. Nor must I smuggle in a Christological or Trinitarian formula to account for any good and meaning I am lucky to perceive in non-Christian lives, texts, or devotions. Such a colonialist mindset is incompatible with the One who said: "Whoever is not against us is for us" (Mk. 9.40).

(A fractured) faith

"Immediately Jesus reached out his hand and caught him. 'You of little faith,' he said, 'why did you doubt?'" (Mt. 14.31)

In the biblical quote above, Christ chastises Peter for a dearth of faith as Peter began to sink into the Sea of Galilee. Doubt is rebuked and yet what really matters is how one employs doubt and faith as means for healing. Peter's doubt accelerated his sinking. But some doubt and questioning can open a space to listen to other voices and share one's concerns, fears, and anger. Such uncertainty can help one seek the truth openly and in solidarity with the poor and victims of injustice and oppression in our world. As I have written elsewhere, Christians can deeply learn in this area from the Jewish tradition of theological protest.[44]

Thus, living faith needs elements of doubt, protest, questioning, and plurality. For, one can also have a surfeit of faith: a lazy prideful belief that one will be saved and all will eventually work out, while millions of people suffer and live and die in agony and obscurity. Faith can become an oppressive word, being demanded of the abused to trust that all will resolve itself, to endure, and wait. Doubt, however, is only debilitating if it leads to inaction and hopelessness. If it spurs ethical action and a desire to right the wrongs of this world, then such doubt is not disgraceful, but empowered by grace.

Thus, a humbled, fractured faith, persevering with courage and mercy and desiring the pluralized, democratic table fellowship exhibited by Christ, is a Christian's best means to seek justice. Such virtues can also temper our seemingly universal need and obsession with power that few of us can avoid when tempted. Commenting upon the work of Edward Said's *Orientalism*, R. S. Sugirtharajah cogently writes: "The key to power is knowledge, and true power is held with the conviction that the ruler knows better than the ruled, and must convince the ruled that whatever the colonial master does is for the benefit of the ruled."[45] To be clear: Christ's power does not reside in the vengeance of bloodbath that Revelation seems to imagine. The power of Christ is in his humbling at the words of the Syrophoenician woman (Mk. 7.28); the parental corrections of his mother at the Wedding at Cana (Jn. 2.5); the woman with the hemorrhage whose faith and touch drew forth power from Jesus (Mk. 5.30); and the woman from Luke's gospel who anointed Jesus in the house of Simon the Pharisee (7.36–50). As Kenneth Bailey writes of this last example: "Jesus is willing to get hurt to publicly reach out in costly love to this unknown, immoral woman."[46] Jesus's faith in the Other is attested to repeatedly in the gospels and needs no further elaboration here.

Responsibility

"Salt is good; but if salt has lost its taste, how can its saltiness be restored?" (Mk. 9.50)

Interreligious dialogue and dialogue with the victims who have been abused in these atrocities are a potent means toward embracing humility and transformation.

In this section, therefore, I will offer areas that must be readdressed, restudied, and reformulated by the Catholic Church and which should be given preeminence in intra- and interreligious dialogue. It is too soon for me to say that the Church "has lost its taste"—or has eaten herself as the Shakespearean quote noted above—though for many she has rendered herself bitter and insubstantial.

Regardless, in speaking of a Church liberated, we need to stress the Church's responsibility toward the Other. Such responsibility includes reevaluating theological, ethical, and doctrinal issues that have tended to obscure, dehumanize, or silence the Other. Again, the child-victims we are focused on here are not the first victims of a Church deemed beyond reproach, enlightenment, or liberation. Steeped in closed or superior-obsessed claims that gainsay the potentially salvific beliefs and ways of other faiths, such tendencies create a culture where questioning, reexamining, and challenging various "truths" are severely censured.

If indeed the Catholic Church has been colonized, then one can see why reexamining key theological and doctrinal issues alongside sincere, open dialogue are desperately demanded. Below I list 12 areas, obviously a symbolic number. The aim here is to restore the taste of salt, as it were. Such may seem like a hopeless task, but then that is why Christians' faith and belief in the guidance of the Holy Spirit remains their (and my) fragile hope amidst all this legitimate doubt.

The 12 areas are:

1. The priesthood of all believers and the *sensus fidelium*. Who exactly are the people of God and what role should and do they play from outside and within all levels of the Church? Here, as in so many of these cases, the conciliar documents of Vatican II are helpful but no longer sufficient. In addition: can there be a clearer, pragmatic interpretation of the meaning of the Church, which can maintain its Christological foundation without the unhelpful language that the Church does not sin but only Christians do? Such "clarification" often unduly insults non-Catholic Christians, does not address some potential systemic problems within the Church, and is particularly inadequate for Jewish-Catholic dialogue and the attempt to address the Shoah. Ecumenical dialogue will also benefit.

2. Interreligious Dialogue. The need and purpose of interreligious dialogue must be highlighted—and debated. In our pluralist, postmodern world, it is needed more than ever for renewal, guidance, and growth.[47]

3. The role and status of the eternal Jewish covenant in light of the Church's Trinitarian belief. The status of the Jewish covenant (or covenants) seems answered by the adjective eternal, but the Magisterium needs to provide a lucid, clear, unequivocal statement that goes beyond merely quoting Romans 11.

4. Religious Pluralism. How does one maintain Christian identity in a sea of changing beliefs and other possibly viable alternatives?[48] At the least, the specter (and bogeyman) of relativism must also be interred (and exposed) once and for all.

5. Morally and spiritually problematic biblical passages. There is a reason that biblical texts can be used to support a range of immoral actions and ideas.

Passages that promote gender hierarchy, anti-Judaism, genocidal actions, ecological irresponsibility, and so on, need to be clearly condemned by the Church. Such passages should not be read in any Church liturgy, for example. If the Vatican II Church restored the practice of Catholics reading the Bible, the Pre-Vatican III Church needs to read the Bible with the Face of the Other in our midst.

6. Secularity. Is it a threat to religious belief or a partner that can help ensure respect to all paths and faiths in the public square and within one's more private spheres?

7. Sexual ethics. Try as one might, there is no avoiding the muddled ethics of sexuality, which encompasses so many issues that continue to mire the Church in an area that need not be so generally mucky, complicated, and negative. The mistaken link of homosexuality and pedophilia must also be continually clarified.[49] Moral courage is desperately desired here.

8. The Primacy of Rome. What happened to the debate that seemed to be encouraged after John Paul II's *Ut Unim Sint*?

9. The role and frequency of Church Councils.[50]

10. Mission and evangelization. What are the limits to mission as seeking conversion of another? How is dialogue distinct from evangelization? How does one maintain one's religious identity while respecting other possible truths and ways?

11. Jesus as the sole mediator for salvation. In addition, atonement theories have always been varied within the Church, but theologically one needs a renewal of the purpose of Jesus's life, death, and resurrection that does not emasculate the reality and power of sin and evil but avoids talk of God requiring sacrifice and death.[51]

12. The Cosmos, nonhuman life forms, and creation. It may usually begin with the abuse of the Other, but if left unopposed, the same means and methods of abuse and desecration will be inflicted against the so-called chosen or in-group (like Catholic children). Promoting the sanctity of all of creation needs to be revitalized and become a cornerstone of Catholic Social Teaching.

Conclusion: Grace

"But it is like yeast that a woman took and mixed in with three measures of wheat flour until the whole batch of dough was leavened." (Lk. 13.21)

Intra- and interreligious dialogues are a privilege and a sacred opportunity to listen to and learn from those who see, articulate, envision, and act in ways unfamiliar or distinct from us. They should not be taken for granted. To do so is to dismiss the value of the people for whom the ideas presented may be deemed sacred and integral to their identity. It may also unduly close a path that can guide and heal one's own journey. Just as the kingdom of God is likened to dough that needed three measures of wheat flour mixed in, so too our faith journeys will benefit from this mixing and stirring.[52] Entering such a dialogue with concealed or conflicted agendas or a prestated unyielding notion of the superiority of one's beliefs, doctrines, and means of revelation not only dooms such a dialogue to failure but inhibits true transformation and growth. But there is always hope: the blind disciples eventually see and the chained and possessed Legion soon proclaims the good news in the Decapolis. Of the saltless salt, I know little, only praying that despite these scandals, the Church has not lost its taste.

In this regard, recognizing the great potential within inter- and intrareligious dialogue is an important step in this process of growth and gracefulness. Until there are signs of a pervasive and cathartic humbling within the institutional Catholic Church, the face of the Other (and so oneself and Christ) will continue to be denied, sullied, and defiled. The din of the victims' pleas will only grow in intensity. As one survivor of clerical child abuse has uttered:

> I cannot change the fact that I was sexually molested by a Catholic priest. Believe me, I have tried for the past 15 years to do just that. I spent those years in denial—I am just now discovering the harm, pain and embarrassment this molestation has caused to my body and mind.[53]

These are the types of words and experiences that must be borne in mind whenever the Church seeks to respond to this crisis and seeks to uphold what magisterial documents refer to as the Truth or claims the fullness of salvation subsists in the Catholic Church.

The 12 areas for further dialogue above, moreover, are concrete ways to examine some salient issues that have caused great pain to many, bearing in mind the virtues promoted and the forces that need to be de-colonized within the Church. A corresponding, entwined approach is to combat blindness, insincerity, amnesia, pride, apathy, patriarchy, and (static) certitude with the virtues of awareness, truthfulness, retentiveness, humility, perseverance, fellowship, and (a fractured) faith. The road ahead is necessarily treacherous and uncertain, but these highlighted virtues are a means to help eyes to see, for memory no longer to yield to pride, and for the dough to rise to glorious heights within us and amidst us. They offer meaningful hope despite the crushing reality of unredeemed loss.

Part Three

Ethical and Interdisciplinary Perspectives on Loss and Hope

Intercultural Resources for Reconciliation and Peace: Drinking from Our Own Wells

Felix Wilfred

I would like to start this chapter by distinguishing between a *culture of peace* and *cultural resources for reconciliation and peace*. Much is discussed and written about a culture of peace today. What I am going to present here has another focus. It concerns the various resources in the cultures of peoples to overcome conflicts, to mend interhuman relationships, and to build peace. These resources are crucial for peoples and communities to overcome the sense of loss and be anchored in hope. When people grieve and mourn over loss, how can they be consoled if they do not hear the language of their own culture that brings closeness and intimacy? When lost in the sea of gloom and despair, will not people naturally tend to hold on to the plank of their culture with the hope of being saved? There are enough reasons why these cultural resources need to be discovered and harnessed so that they serve at the time of loss to awaken the sense of hope.

Barring some laudable exceptions such as Roman Lull (1235–1315), Nicholas of Cusa (1401–1464), Erasmus of Rotterdam (1466–1536), and Thomas More (1478–1535), theologians in the mainline Christian tradition rarely dwelt on peace.[1] Rather, spiritual warfare on heathens, crusades against Saracens, and just war for defense made rounds and found greater justification than the cause of peace. Today, peace has become an issue of utmost gravity and urgency for the life of the world, of nations, and societies. Hence, theology needs to turn its attention with greater determination and commitment to this public concern. In the process, it may need to play down and relativize certain issues, questions, and debates in which it has been engrossed in the past, which, however, may have scant significance for the life of the world in the present-day circumstances.

In modern times, it was Pope John XXIII who brought peace to the fore as a common issue of humanity that the Church needs to address for all people. The encyclical of Pope John XXIII *Pacem in Terris* (1963) set a new direction for opening up Church and theology to this concern. It was the first time that the world was to hear from the Church something addressed to the entire human family. Highlighting the significance of this encyclical, Joseph Gremillion notes:

> It was *Pacem in Terris* (Peace on Earth) which won for John and his aggiornamento a universal hearing. Millions who had never paid the least attention to popes and

their jaw-breaker encyclicals suddenly sat up and listened. Here for the first time, a pope was addressing himself "to all men of good will." And his message responded to a deep longing shared by all.[2]

The significance of Vatican II is that it went beyond an understanding of peace in relation to *war*, and viewed it, drawing from the Patristic tradition, as inextricably related to the practice of *justice*: "Peace cannot be limited to a mere absence of war, and the result of an ever precarious balance of forces. No, peace is something that is built up day after day, in the pursuit of an order intended by God, which implies a more perfect form of justice among people."[3]

Vatican II's view of culture and its implications for peace

One way for theology to contribute to peace is to take forward the important teaching of Vatican II on culture and draw out its implications for the promotion of peace. The colonial period was characterized by an evolutionary and hierarchical understanding of culture. Accordingly, some cultures were viewed as superior and developed, whereas others—those of the colonized peoples—were looked down upon as inferior and needing development. Thanks to the contribution of ethnology and anthropology, Vatican II refused to entertain any such evolutionary and hierarchical understanding of culture. Rather, it saw culture as an evident and essential human reality present among every people, requiring autonomy and freedom for its development.

What we have, then, are a plurality of cultures, each one of them different, but none of them superior or inferior to others. The plurality of cultures so clearly acknowledged and affirmed by the Council cannot be deployed only to contextualize Christianity. But then, it looks to me that Vatican II, after having presented a larger and humanistic view of culture, turned it in fact to the advantage of the Church for its program of inculturation. It saw in inculturation a testimony to the fact that the Church is not tied to any particular culture. Culture was viewed also as a means and object of evangelization. For example *Gaudium et Spes* says, "the Church has existed through the centuries in varying circumstances and has utilized the resources of different cultures in preaching to spread and explain the message of Christ."[4] But the point is that culture has a larger and active role to play in humanizing the world and society, and in fostering mutual understanding among peoples. It offers, among other things, ways and means to resolve differences in human and societal relationships. Peace at the local level nourishes itself by these sources and latches on to the concrete strategies each culture has devised to overcome conflicts.

Cultures are not bounded and self-contained units or closed systems as a static and ethno-centric view of them may suggest. Rather, every cultural formation is the fruit of many encounters and negotiations. Cultural differences are not constituted by their isolation from one another. Rather, cultures offer difference in ways of life, patterns of behavior, and engagement with realities common to all humanity. This dynamic and universalistic aspect of culture helps us view it as a force for continuous dialogue and means to reach out to the other in peace and harmony. The local culture may also have important lessons for the construction of peace in other societies and at the global level. To be able to appreciate and affirm these aspects of culture, we need to turn to a theology of creation.

Culture and theology of creation

If the project of inculturation and evangelization tends to view culture from a Church-centered perspective, we have a theology from above which also does not recognize culture as a value in itself. Postliberal or neo-orthodox theology from above, for example, would argue that culture should conform to God's Word, instead of God's Word coming in encounter with culture. John Milbank and others would go to the point of claiming that Christians form an alternative society all by themselves, and as a distinct social organization have a culture and practices of their own.[5] Here, the cultures of peoples and nations would have no place, unless they are brought into the Church community. On the other hand, a theology of creation would view culture as a reality of human collective life and having value in itself. Faith needs to relate to cultures of peoples. Since culture is a result and an integral part of collective human activity, "Christians ought to be convinced that the achievements of the human race are a sign of God's greatness and the fulfillment of his mysterious design."[6] This Conciliar perspective on culture needs to be rediscovered.

If God acts through the medium of human agency in different areas of life, this applies as well to the issue of peace. The evil of violence is caused by human beings, and God brings about peace through the same human beings by letting them use positive means and ways at their disposal in their cultures. If violence and conflicts have existed from the beginning of humanity, the same humanity has also found the means to resolve conflicts and bring to an end hatred and violence. Human interrelationships and encounters are shaped by culture, and the ways in which people relate are culturally embedded. On the other hand, a culture is not the result of any coercion; it is formed through a constant process of implicit consensus-building and creation of shared symbols in particular human groups. It is easy then to understand, why, when ruptures take place in these relationships and manifest themselves in conflicts and violence, the same culture is crucial in bringing about healing touch, reconciliation, and peace. Thus it makes sense to investigate the cultural potential among every people for overcoming hostilities and entering into a process of peace and reconciliation. There is no pretension that culture is only positive. Like all human realities, culture too carries its own ambiguity. It is also a realm of "sin," violence, and contradictions. But that is no reason why we should not look for creative means and sources for reconciliation and peace in them.

Mystical approach to culture—way to peace

I already referred to Nicholas of Cusa. In his work *De Pace Fidei* (Peace of Faith), he tells us that his conviction about the harmony of religions was the fruit of a vision. It is remarkable that in a provocative situation such as the fall of Constantinople (1453)—a cultural earthquake that shook the very foundations of Europe's identity—he was able to relate the warring religions from a mystical perspective and see their ultimate unity, proposing reconciliation, harmony, dialogue, and peace rather than aggression and revenge.

> It came to pass that after a number of days—perhaps because of his prolonged, incessant meditation—a vision was shown to this same zealous man. Therefrom he educed the following: the few wise men who are rich in the experiential knowledge of all such differences as are observed throughout the world in the (different) religions can find a single readily available harmony; and through this harmony there can be constituted, by a suitable and true means, perpetual peace within (the domain of) religion.[7]

Today, even as we try to deepen the mystical dimension called for in interreligious understanding, we also need to see the mystical dimension in the plurality of cultures, and in the harmony of cultures. Mysticism has the power to break all barriers and borders and make us see greater unity. It also has the power to make us see things in a different light. That applies to different cultures. They do not become rivals but are bonded together as manifold expressions of a single humanity united with the divine mystery. The sense of unity and harmony helps us also discover in each culture, though circumscribed by particularities of geography and history, something that surpasses these, something that relates it at a different plane with other cultures.

Searching internal solutions to conflicts

One thing history and experience have unmistakably shown is that solutions to conflicts that are not rooted in culture, but imposed from outside, do not serve the cause of sustaining peace. Numerous examples at macro and micro levels could be adduced in support. To cite some of the glaring ones, the process of sustaining peace in Afghanistan, in Iraq, or Libya seems still far removed. What external factors and forces are able to bring cannot but be a fragile peace that breaks up in no time. The project of peace needs to sprout from the soil and engage the people themselves, especially as our world contains such a wide diversity of societies with unique situations of conflict, transgression, and violence. For example, the understanding and the practice of reconciliation and peace are different in a society whose basic social structure is the ascriptive identity of caste, as in India. The mode of reconciliation in this society is not the same as in a liberal society created through social contract and with individuals as its basic units. This is yet another reason to fall back on cultural resources. The potential inherent in culture needs to be brought out into the open and deployed for the purpose of promoting peace. Peace may not dawn were one to depend on reasoning and arguments to resolve conflicts and create reconciliation. This is all too evident. Reconciliation and peace require that issues are addressed at the emotional level, and precisely here symbols and other cultural means deeply matter.

We have, from the African continent, examples in deployment of cultural means and institutions for reconciliation after conflicts. A case in point is Rwanda. In the post-genocide period, there was an urgent need for trials. After much cruelty and brutal mutual killings of Hutu and Tutsi, if the country is today on the path of recovery and peace-building, this owes in no small measure to the indigenous cultural means of trials. The traditional institution of *gacaca* courts has been functioning in the country, and it has taken up thousands of cases. *Gacaca* in the local language means "neat and well-kept grass." The lush green grass-fields are where the local community meets and sorts out differences, and they are a symbol of dialogue and participation. How successful have these courts been? Certainly they are far from perfect; there are many flaws and loopholes, and still many things are wanting. Yet, they proved to be slightly more effective than all the means and initiatives from outside trying to generate reconciliation and peace in the postconflict period. How could even a modicum of justice and peace come to this society when in 2001, more than 100,000 accused of genocide were lodged in prisons? It would have taken several decades to mete out justice and come to reconciliation—and that too at a very large financial cost—were one to depend upon modern court processes.

What the Rwandan experiment further proves is how local and culturally embedded means such as *gacaca* courts can create greater transparency in dispensing justice. Local and community-centered conflict resolution involves people so close to each other that they usually cannot pretend or hide facts and get away with impunity. Trials can be sped up. Moreover, they help people to be accountable. The chances of a durable peace are greater because reconciliation processes strengthen the ties among peoples and communities. The impact of the *gacaca* courts has been captured vividly by the documentary film *My Neighbour, My Killer*, directed by Anne Aghion.

An illustration from the field of economics

I would like to illustrate the community and culture-based peace-construction by drawing a parallel from some insights in the field of economics. In 1968 Garrett Hardin wrote a celebrated article titled "The Tragedy of the Commons" in the journal *Science*.[8] He said that common resources such as pasture land, forests, air, water, and fisheries, which served the community for millennia, have entered into a situation of crisis due to greed and exploitation. Destruction of the commons results, ultimately to nobody's advantage. For Hardin, what caused this tragedy was the absence of well-defined property-rights. Decades later, Elinor Ostrom, who was awarded the Nobel Prize for Economics in 2009, returned to the question. She showed that the real tragedy is in the destruction of the *community-based systems* of *conserving the commons*.[9] These systems had the advantage of turning the people into active participants using common resources responsibly. It allowed identifying easily the violators and dealing with them—something that created greater accountability for and control over the commons.

There is no need to reinvent the wheel. People themselves have structures and means for peace, which require activation and deployment. Placing the community as the important player and most effective manager of its common resources challenges the role of primacy given to individual actors in neoliberal economies. Community management of what is common itself is an expression of culture and it helps overcome the violence, competition, and conflicts between individuals. In neoliberal economies, the state and the market are viewed as the ones who protect natural resources from overuse and destruction. The community management of commons comes as an alternative to these two traditional actors.

Peace and justice in cultural soil

It is obvious today that any lasting peace involves the recognition of human dignity and the practice of equity and justice. Achieving conflict resolution, restorative justice, and forgiveness must occupy an important place. While recognizing key values for the promotion of peace, we also need to be aware of the fact that these universal conditions for peace are bound up with culture. The way social justice is practiced has its own history and tradition among the different cultures. We need to identify culturally rooted and community-centered practices of justice to be able to build bridges of peace and reconciliation.

The definition of peace by St Augustine as "*tranquillitas ordinis*" (tranquility of order) is not to be understood as an exhortation to conform to the existing order. His definition needs to be viewed as a process of right relationship of part to the whole and the harmony resulting thereof. Now, as a continuous process of building up right relationships, the construction of peace remains a community project with all its historical and cultural resources. The reconstruction of peace after creating violent disorder also calls for community resources.

In the discussion on peace after conflict, one of the central issues is the restoration of justice before reconciliation can take place and peace be established. Though right in itself, this disjunction of justice and peace would appear foreign to many cultures that have developed ways to relate one to the other in such a manner that both justice and peace are attained simultaneously without having to dichotomize or sacrifice one for the other. Even if we assume that complete justice can be restored, we are not sure that the relationship between the perpetrator of the evil and the victim can be set right. There is more to peace than what justice can offer. It is precisely here that cultural resources for reconciliation and peace could help to heal the wounds and to sustain communion. In other words, each cultural soil has its own potential resources so that justice and peace may bloom and flower in a particular context.

From a theological point of view, culture, as I noted earlier, is part of the economy of God's creation and is a site of God's grace too, in spite of the sinfulness it may manifest. By deploying cultural means for the noble goals of justice and peace, we are in the realm of every day grace. If, as Amartya Sen rightly noted, perfect justice eludes us and we are in a quest from less justice to more justice,[10] this applies as well for the journey toward peace.

Given our human condition, we can move only from a situation of less peace to more peace, and perfect peace may elude us. In this unending journey of peace, culture, and cultural resources could play important roles. Culture represents embedded interhuman relationships and in the quest for peace, these could offer the balm necessary for healing of wounds and for reconciliation.

Reconciliation versus compassion

Speaking of cultural resources we need to be aware of the fact that these resources keep evolving as the community grows. It may require harnessing new breakthroughs, insights, and strategies. Following the development of culture is important to understand its resources for reconciliation and peace in a dynamic sense. The Indian tradition[11] and culture, for example, was originally very strongly oriented to revenge. In fact, one of the two major epics of India—*The Mahabharata*—is a story of revenge, hatred, violence, and bloodletting.[12] It took a Gautama Buddha to break all this and give a new direction to the Indic civilization by introducing the crucial element of compassion (*karuna*).[13] Compassion is not based on the *I-Thou* relationship (Martin Buber), or on *alterity* or the face of the Other (Emmanuel Levinas). Compassion is a comprehensive attitude, which includes within itself all those aspects that we associate with the process of reconciliation—realization of truth, forgiveness, and repentance. Compassion does not spring from alterity but from identity. For ultimately the other is oneself—an intuition characteristic of classical Hindu *advaita* thought of nonduality. Buddha showed that we could move in the direction of peace only when we practice compassion. Compassion is truly grace, to use a Christian as well as Hindu term. It implies justice, but also beckons us to something beyond. It makes us realize that ultimately peace is not simply the fruit of human efforts, but a gift.

In this paradigm, the tool-kit for reconciliation and peace needs compassion, nonviolence, *syadvada*, and *anekatva*.[14] This is different from the process in the Christian tradition of confessing the truth or admission of guilt, penance, punishment, reconciliation, and peace. In the paradigm of compassion, penance is not very central as in the case of reconciliation where the Christian soteriology has a lot of influence. If we were to look for a homologous reality corresponding to penance in the Hindu or Buddhist traditions, it would be the *conquest of the self*. In the conquest of oneself, the impulse of hatred melts and evaporates. Compassion springs forth from enlightenment. The conquest of the self is the supreme expression of renunciation.

What we have said makes it clear that cultures and civilizations may not only have different resources for peace, but also different *paradigms* in relating the self and the other harmoniously. The Western practice of reconciliation is informed by the Christian theology and Catholic penitential tradition. The Hindu-Buddhist paradigm, on the other hand, derives from another world-view. Yet, a deeper conversation and dialogue between these two traditions seem to be very important for the practical task of reconciliation, peace-building, integration, and wholeness. In the Christian tradition of reconciliation, we have not sufficiently incorporated the element of *sunyata* (emptiness) or *kenosis*. The conversation with the Hindu-Buddhist tradition could help us weave within the Christian understanding of reconciliation the call to self-emptying or kenosis. The quality of reconciliation is proportionate to the degree of self-emptying.

Culture and peace initiatives

The Nobel Prize for Peace for the year 2012 was awarded to the European Union. A continent that fiercely fought two World Wars and witnessed violence, immense destruction, and deaths of millions in the twentieth century has emerged as a continent of dialogue, peace, and understanding. The cessation of hostilities and the promotion of dialogue are obviously facilitated by economic integration. However, without the support of a cultural dialogue and shared common values and history, this change would not have been possible. We may recall here the contribution of such personalities as Cardinal Suhard and Bernard Lalande who were all engaged in reconciliation among the European nations, especially for German and French reconciliation.

East Asia is one of the few regions of the world which is still in the era of the Cold War, especially what concerns the relationship between the two Koreas. Today, peace is further threatened in East Asia, with the escalation of tension among Japan, China, Taiwan, and Korea on the issue of some uninhabited islands.[15] National sentiments and passion run high in these countries. There are vehement anti-Japanese riots in China, evoking painful memories of Japanese militarism and imperialism during World War II. And yet, we note, there are a lot of prospects of peace if these countries look at their shared culture, history, way of life, and adherence to some traditional common values. The Church in these countries can play a very significant role in the construction of peace by having recourse to cultural means available among the peoples of this part of Asia. These initiatives could be at the macro- and micro-levels. In one example of a micro-level initiative, consider a Korean pastor (Hyun-Ju Kili) and a Japanese pastor (Katsuhiko Seino) at Tsuchiura Grace Church, Tokyo, involved in a movement called "Koinonia" that tries to bring the two peoples together in cultural dialogue. Similarly dramatic and forceful has been the initiative by a young priest Paul Mun Kuyhyun of the Priest's Association for Justice of Korea. Fired on by the ideal of a united Korea and relying on the common culture and history both Koreas share, he crossed the borders to North Korea on August 15, 1989 and got arrested. It was a great symbolic gesture of protest against the division of a people who are united by culture and history. His subsequent initiatives proved that culture can unite what politics divide.[16] Cultural exchanges, education, and honest textbooks of history could help overcome prejudices and move beyond ideological differences. Political initiatives and economic integration may not bring about peace, unless they are cemented by cultural dialogue and interaction at a broader level. Such culture-based peace initiatives would be very much in line with the affirmation of the value of culture in human life by Vatican II.

Conclusion

I have pointed out areas in which theology needs to engage itself actively, namely in the overcoming of hostilities and conflicts; in promoting reconciliation; and in the construction of enduring peace. For this to happen, theology needs to look at culture and its potentials beyond the program of inculturation. Exploring the mine of culture for reconciliation and peace will be one of the major tasks of theology in the future. By involving itself at the local level for the cause of peace, theology will become contextual and closer to the realities of everyday life. Public theology should help the Church in promoting cultural dialogue for the cause of peace and understanding.[17] This task is no less important than interreligious dialogue. Theology could play the role of leveraging the existing systems and procedures to prevent conflicts, and when these occur, help resolve them by drawing from contextual resources.

The process of reconciliation and peace is not a domain under the monopoly of religion. State, economic agents, and civil society also play key functions; hence, the need for theology to be in conversation with these actors. Such conversations can help theology play a more constructive, public role and can help the Church to strike its roots deeper in the cultural universe of peoples. The Federation of Asian Bishops' Conferences (FACBC), for example, at its very First Plenary Assembly spoke very clearly about the need of dialogue with cultures along with dialogue with religions and with the poor.[18] Today we begin to see the wider implications of this dialogue with cultures and its potential for the construction of peace at the service of a harmonious and shared future of humanity.

Loss and Hope in Levinas's *Otherwise than Being* and Vasily Grossman's *Life and Fate*

Steven Shankman

God is . . . transcendent to the point of absence.. . . His absolute remoteness, his transcendence, turns into my responsibility . . . for the other.[1]

Emmanuel Levinas

I begin this chapter on loss and hope with an acknowledgment of two momentous losses registered by Emmanuel Levinas in his second and last magnum opus, *Otherwise than Being, or Beyond Essence*. The first acknowledgment inaugurates the book, the second concludes it. The two are intimately connected. Let us begin with the dedication of the book:

> To the memory of those who were closest among the six million assassinated by the National Socialists, and of the millions on millions of all confessions and all nations, victims of the same hatred of the other man, the same anti-semitism.[2]

Levinas then names, in the discreet letters of the Hebrew language, those irreplaceable others closest to him who were victims of the Nazi horror: his father, mother, brothers, father-in-law, and mother-in-law.

Levinas concludes his great book with the following paragraph, consisting of a single, breathless sentence:

> In this work which does not seek to restore any ruined concept, the destitution and desituating of the subject do not remain without signification: after the death of a certain god inhabiting the world behind the scenes, the substitution of the hostage discovers the trace, the unpronounceable inscription, of what, always already past, always "he," does not enter into any present, to which are suited not the nouns designating beings, or the verbs in which their essence resounds, but that which, as a pronoun, marks with its seal all that a noun/name can convey.

What is acknowledged as lost here, and what hope might be engendered in the wake of that loss? And what is the relation, if any, between this concluding sentence/paragraph and the book's dedication?

What is lost is the belief "in a certain god (*un certain dieu*) inhabiting the world behind the scenes." The god declared dead by Nietzsche is indeed dead. This was both the particular god whom Nietzsche pronounced dead— a "certain" god in this sense— and also a god in whom one could believe with certainty: "un dieu certain" as well as "un certain dieu." An undeniable and untransferable sense of being held hostage by the other is precisely that which, for Levinas, replaces or substitutes for this now dead, certain god. As a subject, I sense this trace, impossible to write or even to enunciate, in the pronoun "he" or "it" (*il*), as the subversive force of "illeity," which Levinas describes earlier in *Otherwise than Being*.

Levinas gives the name "illeity" to the source of the ethical command, which, "beyond representation, affects me unbeknownst to myself, slipping into me like a thief" (150). The word "illeity" is derived from the Latin *ille*, meaning "that" or "he." As opposed to the Latin word *hic* ("this"), *ille* means "the Other, the more remote, person or thing."[3] The word "illeity" signifies that the command that I say "Here I am!" before the face of the Other is sensed by the "I" as a supervening "that-ness" or "he-ness,"[4] a "thirdness" (*OTB*, 150) that is separate from self and Other. It comes neither from the self nor from the Other, is neither "I" nor "you." One could refer to "illeity" by the word "God," but for Levinas that would be to "tame the subversiveness worked by illeity" (151) and would turn "God" into a being, while what Levinas wishes to convey is that the word God signifies a beyond being, an otherwise than being that "gets its meaning from the witness borne, which thematization certainly betrays in theology" (*OTB*, 151). Theo-logy names "God" as a being, turns "illeity" into a theme or a proposition.

The Shoah, for Levinas, signaled the definitive end of theodicy, of the attempt to explain evil as somehow part of a divine plan. The Shoah meant the end of happy endings, the end of a providential view of history. Six million innocents were murdered. The word "holocaust," which literally means "a burnt offering" and thus a sacrifice, regretfully suggests, when referring to the six million who perished at the hands of the National Socialists, that these deaths are part of a divine plan that is beyond our understanding. The word Shoah, meaning "catastrophe," in its bluntness, is far more respectful of the unique and irreplaceable specificity of those who were murdered. And here we have a link between the conclusion of *Otherwise than Being* and its dedication. The unspeakable loss of human lives that is the Shoah bears witness to the loss of a certain god inhabiting the world behind the scenes, of a providential God pulling the strings. But in the wake of this loss there is born, or revived, a hope in the continued manifestation of acts of human goodness.

And here we have a link between Levinas's last great philosophical work, *Otherwise than Being*, and the literary work that obsessed Levinas during the last 15 or so years of his life, Vasily Grossman's *Life and Fate*. My contention is that, in the wake of the devastation of the Shoah and World War II, it is precisely their shared hope in the possibility of a continuing manifestation of acts of human goodness that unites the observant, orthodox Jew Emmanuel Levinas and the secular, even atheist Jew, Vasily Grossman. Both Levinas and Grossman manage to think God on the basis of ethics.

Je dirai non, mio padre, je dirai non!

Vasily Grossman's massive novel *Life and Fate*, a Chekhovian epic modeled in many ways on Tolstoy's *War and Peace*, is often regarded as the greatest novel of the Soviet era. Grossman juxtaposes narrative accounts of the Battle of Stalingrad during World War II with scenes from everyday life in Soviet Russia, and he reflects on the relation between the two. In my remarks on Grossman's great novel and the moral hope it inspires in the wake of profound loss, I will focus on the characters Ikonnikov and Viktor Shtrum, the nuclear physicist who is the novel's protagonist, who discovers his Judaism in the course of the novel, and who is based on Grossman himself.

It is the character Ikonnikov, "the preacher of senseless kindness" (531), who, for Levinas, speaks the novel's essential truth. We first meet Ikonnikov early on in the novel. He comes from a long line of priests. Hence the significance of his name, which is suggestive of the Russian religious symbol par excellence, the icon. Ikonnikov became a disciple of Tolstoy. He believed in the promise of the Russian Revolution to "bring about the Kingdom of Heaven on earth," but after witnessing Stalin's brutal persecution and murder of the kulaks (the wealthier peasants), "he began preaching the Gospel and praying to God to take pity on the dying." He was first sent to prison and then, as a result of the traumas he had experienced, was sent for a year to the prison's psychiatric hospital. The traumas experienced by Ikonnikov included witnessing an emaciated peasant woman, starving as a result of Stalin's collectivization campaign, who "had just eaten her two children." After the war began and the Nazis invaded Bylorussia, Ikonnikov desperately entreated others to save the Jews and made efforts, despite the dangers to his personal safety, to save Jewish lives. After witnessing the murder of 20,000 Jews—"women, children, and old men—in a single day," Ikonnikov concludes "that God could not allow such a thing and that therefore he did not exist" (28). "The essential thing about *Life and Fate*," Levinas writes, "is simply what the character Ikonnikov says: 'There is neither God nor the Good, but there is goodness'—which is my thesis" (*IRB*, 89).

This remark, uttered by an observant Jew and a philosopher, is perhaps a bit less shocking than it might appear at first glance, especially when we recall the title of Levinas's last magnum opus, *Autrement qu'être ou au-delà de l'essence* (*Otherwise than Being, or Beyond Essence*). For Levinas, God does not appear and thus has nothing to do with the word "is," with ontology. God signifies in a manner "autrement qu'être," otherwise than being. I can say "'Here I am, in the name of God,' without referring myself directly to his (i.e., God's) presence. 'Here I am,' just that! The word God is still absent from the phrase in which it is for the first time involved in words." For Levinas, I am true to the meaning of the word God, as it first becomes involved in words in the Hebrew Bible, when I say "Here I am" before the face of the Other rather than by stating "I believe in God (*je crois en Dieu*)."[5] And it was no less a philosopher than Plato who insisted that the Good was "beyond being" (ejpevkeina th`~ oujsiva~, *Republic* 508e–509a), beyond essence. Indeed, the phrase "au-delà de l'essence" in the title of Levinas's last great book is a literal translation of Plato's "beyond being" (ejpevkeina th`~ oujsiva~). Hence, technically speaking, for Levinas there "is" neither God nor the Good, for both are beyond, or signify in a manner otherwise than, being.[6]

Let us return to our theme of loss and hope—the loss of a certain god inhabiting the world behind the scenes and a consequent hope in the miraculous appearance of acts of human kindness that may be said to bear witness to God through the ethical relation. I turn now to an extraordinary passage in *Life and Fate*, indeed to one of the most extraordinary passages in modern literature. We are with Ikonnikov at a critical moment in his own tortured but magnificent spiritual journey, as he has just realized that the work his Nazi captors have engaged him to do is to dig the foundations of what will be a gas chamber.

It will be necessary, before we turn to the passage itself, to identify the characters involved. We are introduced to a group of prisoners in a German concentration camp. Mikhail Sidorovich Mostovskoy is an Old Bolshevik. "Bolshevik" is derived from the Russian adjective meaning "large," referring here to the "majority" wing of the Russian Social Democratic Party led by Lenin. Chernetsov is a former member of the Mensheviks, the "minority"—as opposed to the "majority" or Bolshevik—wing of the party, which was the more liberal faction. Chernetsov has one eye. In conversation, Chernetsov tends to cover with his hand the gaping socket of his missing eye so as not to distract and disturb his interlocutor. Gardi is a Roman Catholic priest. Mostovskoy and Chernetsov have reached an impasse in a heated political discussion:

> Chernetsov's blind, bloody pit stared point-blank at Mostovskoy.
>
> Ikonnikov reached up and tugged at the bare foot of the priest sitting on the second tier of boards; in broken French, German, and Italian he began to ask:
>
> —"*Que dois-je faire, mio padre? Nous travaillons dans una*
> *Vernichtungslager.*"
>
> Gardi's coal-black eyes looked around and scrutinized people's faces.
>
> "*Tout le monde travaille là-bas. Et moi je travaille là-bas. Nous*
> *sommes des esclaves,*"—he said slowly—"*Dieu nous pardonnera.*"
>
> "*C'est son métier,*"—added Mostovskoy.
>
> "*Mais ce n'est pas votre métier,*"—Gardi said reproachfully.
>
> Ikonnikov-Morzh quickly retorted:
>
> —"That's just it, Mikhail Sidorovich; from your point of view, too,
> it's exactly the same, don't you see? But I don't want an absolution of sins. Don't tell me that the guilty ones are those who are compelling you, and that you are not guilty because you are not free. I *am* free! I am building a Vernichtungslager. I am answerable to the people who will be choked by gas here. I can say 'no'! What power can stop me, if I find in myself the power to be fearless in the face of my own destruction? I can say 'no!' *Je dirai non, mio padre, je dirai non!*"
>
> Gardi's hand touched the grey head of Ikonnikov.
>
> "*Donnez-moi votre main,*"—he said.
>
> "*All right, now here comes the admonishing by the shepherd of his wayward sheep's pride,*"—said Chernetsov, and Mostovskoy, with a knee-jerk reaction of ideological sympathy, nodded in agreement.

But Gardi did not admonish Ikonnikov. He took Ikonnikov's dirty hand to his lips and kissed it.[7]

Here we have an extraordinary instance of Grossman's thinking God on the basis of ethics in precisely Levinas' sense.

Ikonnikov, who is descended from a long line of priests, appears, at first, to want to make a kind of preemptive confession, in four different languages, to the Catholic priest named Gardi lying in the bed above him. He grasps the priest's bare foot and, in anguish, shares with him the shocking truth, which Ikonnikov has just discovered, that they are all working in an extermination camp—that the prisoners are in fact engaged in building a gas chamber for the Nazi authorities. Everybody is working on the same project, Gardi comments, including the priest himself. We are all slaves, Gardi insists, speaking these words slowly. God will pardon us. That's his job, Mostovskoy comments with the sarcasm of a true-believing Bolshevik and hence atheist for whom religion is the opiate of the people. People believe in God, for Mostovskoy, so that they can be forgiven for their sins rather than make the effort to roll up their sleeves and free the proletariat from exploitation. Gardi reproaches Mostovskoy for what he takes to be the communist's hubris. Don't put yourself in the place of God, Gardi implies, with your arrogance of imagining that you know perfectly well whom to pardon and whom to condemn.

It is here that the passage takes a turn toward a deeper moral and spiritual complexity. Ikonnikov tells Mostovskoy that he is no different from the allegedly poor benighted souls who seek the opium of forgiveness from the Christian church, for he, Mostovskoy, expects forgiveness. "That's just it," Ikonnikov says to Mostovskoy, "from your point of view, too, it's exactly the same, don't you see?" You, precisely like the priest, in other words, expect to be forgiven. But in what sense could a Bolshevik be said to be seeking forgiveness? Surely not from God! From whom, then? The answer returns us to the passage that immediately precedes the one we are now discussing, to a bitter point of disagreement between the Bolshevik Mostovskoy and the Menshevik Chernetsov. Chernetsov had castigated the Bolsheviks for trampling on human rights in order to achieve their goals of a classless society. Mostovskoy, in response, had minimized the importance of individual rights and freedom. As a supporter of Lenin and, later, of the even more horrific Stalinist regime, Mostovskoy imagines—as Ikonnikov sees it—that he, Mostovskoy, will be forgiven for his condoning of tyranny and murder by the trajectory of history itself, by the ultimate triumph of the working class, which, Ikonnikov is here suggesting, is the atheist's equivalent of God's will.

Is God a principle, an abstraction? If so, then we have betrayed the insight articulated by Levinas with which I began this essay, namely that the concrete human being must not be erased by—and assimilated into—the notion of his being a necessary sacrifice, a holocaust, for a greater "Good." God, for Levinas, leaves His trace, rather, in the face of the Other, who is naked and destitute and for whom I am responsible. God appears as the command to live up to my untransferable responsibility for the Other. No one can take my place. That is the meaning of my uniqueness, my freedom understood not in the negative sense as freedom from constraints but rather, in the positive sense, as an elevation to uniqueness. As Levinas writes in *Totality and Infinity*, published at roughly the same moment (1961) Grossman completed *Life and Fate*, "To be free is to have time to forestall one's own abdication under the threat of violence (Etre libre, c'est avoir du temps pour prévenir sa propre dechéance sous la menace de la violence.)"[8]

Hence Ikonnikov says that he does not want to be absolved of his sins, as the priest Gardi offers to do on God's behalf. I am reminded here of one of Levinas's Talmudic readings, composed at roughly the same time as Grossman's novel, that ponders the wisdom of the Oral Law (the Mishna, compiled toward the end of the second century of our era) stipulating that, on the Day of Atonement (Yom Kippur), God will not forgive transgressions committed against others if the transgressor has not first sought out the offended party and asked for forgiveness from him or her personally. One of the rabbis cited in the Gemara (the commentary, compiled in the fifth century, on the Mishna) wishes to absolve the transgressor of the necessity of seeking forgiveness from the offended party. This commentator argues that the transgressor may short-circuit this painful and unpredictable process in order to seek, and gain, forgiveness directly from God. According to Levinas, "the text of the Gemara rises (up) against this . . . overly virile proposition . . . which puts the universal order above the inter-individual order." Levinas continues:

> No, the offended individual must always be appeased, approached, and consoled individually. God's forgiveness—or the forgiveness of history—cannot be given if the individual has not been honored (*respecté*). God is perhaps precisely this permanent refusal of a history that would put up with our private tears. (*Dieu n'est peut-être que ce refus permanent d'une histoire qui s'arrangerait de nos larmes privées.*)[9]

God, for the Talmud, is not equivalent to the ineluctable march of history in the Hegelian sense. God is rather the permanent refusal, beyond and despite history, to put up with, or to come to any easy or comfortable arrangement with, my painful awareness of the harm I have done, or may be tempted to do, to a unique and irreplaceable other.

Hence Ikonnikov insists that, even as a prisoner in a Nazi concentration camp, he is responsible (or "guilty"/виноватъ/*vinovat'*) and that he is free. He must answer to—respond to—the people who will be gassed in the chambers he will have consented to build. "The I who am building an extermination camp (фернихтунслагеръ) is the very same I who am now answering (отвечаю/*otvechayu*) to those who will be gassed," Ikonnikov says. The Russian verb отвечатъ/*otvechat'* is the precise equivalent to the French *répondre*, which means "to respond to," "to answer to," "to be responsible for," and even "to answer for," the other. By suddenly writing the German word *Vernichtungslager* (extermination camp) in Cyrillic letters rather than in Roman, as he had just previously done, Grossman is emphasizing that the speaker of these words, whose native tongue is Russian, is now taking full responsibility for his actions, that he is owning up to them.

Ikonnikov realizes, as if this realization were a revelation from beyond, that he has the ability, the freedom, to say no. The priest Gardi has just told Ikonnikov, Mostovskoy, and Chernetsov that he and they are all slaves in a concentration camp and that God will therefore pardon them. Ikonnikov begs to differ. Don't tell me, he says, that the only guilty/responsible ones (виноваты/*vinovat'y*) are those who are compelling you to act in a shameful manner, that "you are a slave" (ты раб/*ty rab*) and that "you are not guilty/responsible (ты не виновен/*ty ne vinoven*) because you are not free" (ты свободен/*ty svoboden*). He declares that I, Ikonnikov, am free (Я свободен/*ya svoboden*). My oppressors have no power (сила/*sila*) to force me to build an extermination camp (*Vernichtungslager*/фернихтунслагерь) and thus to betray my responsibility to the other so long as I draw on my own moral power (сила/*sila*) to accept my own extermination (уничтожения/*unichtozheniya*) at the hands of the Nazis and say no: "I will say 'No!' *Je dirai non, mio padre, je dirai non.*" Difficult freedom!

Gardi places his hands on Ikonnikov's head. The priest then asks Ikonnikov— with all the politesse of addressing the Other with the formal version of the second-person in French—to give him his hand (*Donnez-moi votre main*), a command which contrasts with the more intimate *ty* of Ikonnikov's previous address, in Russian, to Gardi. Chernetsov caustically remarks that he fully expects the shepherd will now admonish his wayward sheep for the pride the sheep has shown in refusing the priest's generous offering, on God's behalf, of God's forgiveness. Mostovskoy nods in supercilious agreement. But Gardi hardly admonishes Ikonnikov. The priest rather honors Ikonnikov's deep spiritual wisdom by kissing Ikonnikov's dirty hand, a hand that has been dirtied by digging—at first in ignorance—the foundations of a gas chamber. Petitioners kiss the hand of a Roman Catholic priest immediately following the priest's inauguration as a priest. Here the tables are turned. The priest Gardi kisses the hands of the nonbeliever Ikonnikov who has now, in effect, just been inaugurated as a priest of the creed of senseless kindness, of responsibility for the Other, of answering for the Other even at the risk of certain death and with no reward, such as gaining immortal life for one's own soul in a world to come. Ikonnikov here critiques the priest's theology of a too hastily and prematurely offered notion of a kind of blanket forgiveness by, instead, thinking God on the basis of ethics. The Roman Catholic priest Gardi then blesses the nonbeliever Ikonnikov for his superior spiritual insight.

"He didn't believe in God, but somehow it was as if God were looking at him."

How and what does the word God signify in Vasily Grossman's novel *Life and Fate*? How does this correspond to what Emmanuel Levinas has to say, in his late work, about ethics and the word "God?" In the last 15 years of his life, Levinas, an observant Jew, turned almost obsessively, in the original Russian, to *Life and Fate,* the first Russian edition of which was published in 1980. Levinas believed that this novel, written by a secular Jew—indeed, by an atheist!—affirmed, in the aftermath of the Shoah and of Stalinism, Levinas's own radical rethinking of the word God solely through the ethical relation. The protagonist of Grossman's novel is a Jewish nuclear physicist named Viktor Shtrum. The novel, with its focus on Shtrum, tells the story of Shtrum's moral struggles. Shtrum is a thoroughly assimilated Jew, as was Grossman himself. In the course of the novel, as Shtrum embraces his identity as a Jew, he at the same time imagines himself not so much as believing in God but rather, through responding to the command of ethical responsibility, as bearing witness to God, to the word God, in a manner that accords with a radical though deeply Jewish understanding of the word God as embraced by Levinas.

When the word "God" appears in *Life and Fate* it sometimes signifies unquestioned authority, and in this sense—from a Jewish perspective—God would here mean its opposite, that is, idolatry. At other times the word is associated with the Greek, and more specifically with the Platonic and Aristotelian, understanding of reason or *noesis* as a divine force in man, as the way in which mortals can participate in divine immortality. And then there is the Hebraic understanding of God as a commanding ethical responsibility. All three meanings appear in the section of the novel in which Grossman portrays Shtrum's great moral struggle, but it is, in the end, the ethical understanding—that is, the Jewish understanding—that predominates.

As the massive novel draws to its conclusion, Grossman focuses on Viktor's struggle. The momentum of the great battle of Stalingrad, a battle that would decide the fate of the entire world, has now shifted decisively in favor of the Soviets. Fascism will be defeated. But now an even greater battle will be decided: the battle for men's souls in the totalitarian Soviet State. Viktor is the head of an institute dedicated to research on nuclear physics. The State is engaged in an anti-semitic campaign. Viktor has been targeted, as have other Jews in his institute. The State is requiring that Viktor confess to a political crime that he has not committed. Viktor has expressed some criticisms of the State in private conversations, it is true, but he is hardly a traitor. Viktor's wife, from whom he has become increasingly estranged emotionally, urges him, for the family's sake, to capitulate. It is a moment of great moral crisis for Viktor. He has a life-changing decision to make. Just before he makes that decision, he goes to visit his mentor, Dmitry Petrovich Chepyzhin, who has left the institute, apparently, precisely because he did not want his scientific research to be compromised by politics. Chepyzhin is a moral man, but in his conversation with Viktor, Grossman makes Chepyzhin the spokesman for what I have called the Greek or Platonic-Aristotelian, rather than the Hebraic-ethical, notion of the divine.

The reader is struck by how, in an officially atheist Soviet society, two nuclear physicists can make such easy reference to God. "One might think that only God was able to limit Infinity," Chepyzhin tells Viktor. Chepyzhin continues: "Beyond a cosmic boundary, we have to admit the presence of a divine power. Right?," to which Viktor responds, "Of course" (690). Viktor is completely preoccupied with the meeting, scheduled for the next day at the institute, at which he is expected to confess. Chepyzhin, who has distanced himself from politics, wants to talk about the joys of scientific discovery, of pure research, that will allow him not only to participate in the divine, but even to surpass God!

Chepyzhin, sounding very much like Grossman himself, argues passionately for freedom as "the fundamental principle of life" (690), as the essence of the transformation of inanimate matter into living matter. In a rapturous monologue, Chepyzhin imagines that "One day man will be endowed with all the attributes of the deity—omnipresence, omnipotence and omniscience. . . . Omnipresence—formerly an attribute of God, will have become one more conquest of reason. But man won't just stop there. After attaining equality with God, he will not stop. . . . The abyss of time and space will be overcome. Man will finally be able to look down on God" (691). Viktor does not doubt that science may well proceed with the extraordinary triumphs, straining credibility, as envisioned by Chepyzhin. But this brings Viktor "not joy, but utter despair" (692). "We think we're so wise," Viktor says,

> yet on this very day the Germans are slaughtering Jewish children and old women as though they were mad dogs. And we ourselves have endured 1937 (Viktor is referring to one of Stalin's purges) and the horrors of collectivization—famine, cannibalism, and the deportation of millions of unfortunate peasants. . . . You say man will be able to look down on God—but what if he also becomes able to look down on the Devil? What if he eventually surpasses *him*? You say life is freedom. Is that what people in the camps think? . . . Do you think this man of the future will surpass Christ in his goodness? . . . What I want to know is—do you believe in the evolution of kindness, morality, mercy? Is man capable of evolving in that way?

Viktor concludes that today's science—he is no doubt thinking here particularly of nuclear science—must "be entrusted only to men of spiritual understanding, to prophets and saints." Instead it is being left to apparatchiks like Sokolov in Viktor's own laboratory, who is clever but very timid, "who prostrates himself before the State and believes there is no power except that of God," as does Markov, also in Viktor's laboratory, who "hasn't the slightest inkling of questions of good and evil, of love and morality" (693). "God" here signifies an amoral force that commands our unquestioning obedience.

But is Viktor capable of bearing witness to God as a moral force? Viktor is very clear-sighted and honest, in this passage, about his own vanity and egoism. He observes that his colleague Savostyanov thinks of science "as another kind of sport," that "solving a particular problem is the same as setting a new athletic record. All he cares about is getting there first. And I'm no better" (693). Grossman named his protagonist "Viktor" for good reason! Viktor is obsessed with being victorious, with winning, with triumphalism. But Viktor is also self-aware. He wonders painfully if he can bear witness to God in the Jewish sense of the word. "Where can I find faith, strength, determination?" he asks Chepyzhin, now speaking "with a strong Jewish accent." "What can I say?" Viktor continues. "You know what's happened—and now I'm being persecuted just because. . . ." Viktor jumps up without finishing his sentence, drops his teaspoon to the floor, begins to tremble all over, thanks Chepyzhin, and leaves in tears, careful to avoid looking at Chepyzhin, his moral model, "in the face." Let us take the liberty of finishing Viktor's sentence. Viktor is being persecuted because . . . he is a Jew. As Viktor remarked earlier in this chapter, he has been accused of "dragging science into the swamp of Talmudic abstraction, cutting it off from reality" (687). Those who see the discussions in the Talmud as abstract exercises in splitting hairs, however, fail to take note of the kind of profound ethical engagement that we discovered in our earlier discussion of forgiveness in the Tractate *Yoma*. Will Viktor, at the meeting at the institute the following day, choose to assimilate, to capitulate, and thus to betray the very meaning of moral truth, truth that is persecuted precisely because it is true?

Viktor appears to be headed toward making a public confession of a political crime he never in fact committed. He then abruptly changes his mind and chooses not to repent. As soon as he arrives at this decision, Viktor says that he "felt calm and thoughtful. He didn't believe in God (Он не верил в Бога/ *On ne veril v Boga*), but somehow it was as though God were looking at him. Never in his life had he felt such happiness, such humility. Nothing on earth could take away his sense of rightness now." Grossman continues: "He thought of his mother. Perhaps she had been standing beside him when he had so unaccountably changed his mind. Only a minute before he had sincerely wanted to make a hysterical confession. Neither God nor his mother had been in his mind when he had to come to that last unshakeable decision. Nevertheless, they had been there beside him" (697–698).

By not confessing to crimes he never committed, Viktor stays true to his conscience. And for Viktor, as he remarks to his family after he makes his fateful decision not to engage in the charade of a pretended repentance in order to save his own skin, "Socialism is, first of all, the right to a conscience" (совесть/*sovest'* 655, 699). There is, however, perhaps a touch too much of virility and of heroism, of triumphalism, in Viktor's victorious struggle to maintain his integrity in the passage from *Life and Fate* in which he makes his "last unshakeable decision" not to repent. Viktor himself "had been conscious of something wooden in his voice as he made his speech about conscience" (701). His decision hardly costs him, in the end, his career or his life, as becomes vividly clear when, remarkably, he later receives an admiring telephone call from Stalin himself. The virile Man of Steel, the very embodiment of the totalitarian state, wants to make sure that Viktor has all the means necessary to pursue his important scientific research, which Stalin no doubt hopes, but does not explicitly mention, will help secure the atomic bomb for the Soviet state before its rivals reach that same goal. In the wake of the approving phone call from Stalin, Viktor's anxiety about some of the less than positive things he had said in the past about the regime dramatically lessens and then all but disappears, but with that vanished anxiety Viktor also begins to lose his empathy for those who suffer at the hands of the all-powerful Soviet state. When he was a pariah awaiting state arrest, "his head had been full of thoughts about life, truth and freedom, thoughts about God (о боже/*o bozhe*)" (828). Now, after being officially embraced by Stalin and thus morally compromised, Viktor's head is no longer "full of thoughts . . . about God."

Not long after his triumph, Viktor is pressured to sign a public letter denouncing two innocent men, two doctors—one of whom was certainly Jewish—absurdly accused of assassinating a famous Russian author. At first he responds with moral horror at the prospect that he could possibly sign such a letter, and in urging his colleagues to back off from pressuring him to sign, Viktor evokes God, whom he clearly associates with conscience, with ethics: "Oh my God (Ну Боже мой/ *Nu Bozhe moy*)!" Viktor exclaims. "Please understand that I have a conscience. . . . I'm under no obligation. . . . You must allow me the right to a clear conscience" (837). Viktor is convinced of the doctors' innocence, but his overweening desire to be regarded as a true "patriot," a real "Russian," and "a true Soviet citizen" (834)—that is, not as a Jewish misfit—is part of what persuades him to sign the letter. He signs the letter and is then immediately consumed with an overwhelming sense of remorse.

When Viktor made up his mind not to repent for his alleged and nonexistent crime(s), he had felt indescribably happy and imagined that God, along with his mother, was by his side. He now feels that he has committed a "terrible sin" (841). He has utterly lost his moral authority. Just after signing the document, one of his laboratory assistants, Anna Stepanovna, a Jew whom Viktor had defended when the State dismissed her because she was Jewish, tells Viktor that she wants him to know "how much you have done for me and for others (других/*drugikh*)"[10] and that his manifest responsibility for others "is more important than any great discovery." Those with no power or prestige in the Soviet hierarchy—"mechanics, cleaners and caretakers"—to a person all say, she remarks, that Viktor is "a righteous person (правильный человек/*pravil' nyy chelovek*)," the equivalent, in the Hebrew tradition, of a *tzadik*, a "righteous one." And righteous ones, in this tradition, are those who are especially favored by God. At the conclusion of the chapter in which he shamefully signs the letter, Viktor receives a telephone call from Chepyzhin, who tells Viktor that he, Chepyzhin, had been quarreling with some prominent officials over the letter, which he, Chepyzhin, clearly refuses to sign. "Have you heard about this letter?" he asks Viktor. Viktor manages to respond to Chepyzhin with a tepid half-truth. Grossman then vividly imagines Viktor's sense of shame at his betrayal of responsibility, as Viktor comments: "God, God (Боже, Боже/*Bozhe, Bozhe*), what had he done?"[11] Here the word God, stated twice, bears powerful witness to Viktor's commanding sense of responsibility to others that he has just shamefully betrayed.

Turned inside-out: God, transcendence, hope

The word God appears for the final two times in a brief chapter (58 in the Russian text)[12] toward the end of *Life and Fate*. This chapter is preceded by a slightly longer chapter in which the word God also appears, but with different associations. The juxtaposition is suggestive. In modernist fashion, Grossman often juxtaposes chapters of varying lengths with little or no explicit commentary explaining the artistic reasons for the juxtapositions. I mentioned earlier that Grossman is struggling with at least three associations that come to mind when we say the word God: God understood as a principle to which its believers owe total obedience; God as reason; and God as the word par excellence that bears witness to my inescapable and untransferable responsibility for a unique and irreplaceable Other. The juxtaposed endings of these two chapters guide the reader toward embracing as authoritative the third of these associations that come to mind when I say the word God.

These two chapters are set in a hut near the Lubyanka, the notorious prison in Moscow that held many political prisoners in the Stalin era. Chapter 57 ends with a passage that contains a chilling Soviet version of Dostoevsky's famous chapter, in *The Brothers Karamazov*, on the Grand Inquisitor. Both chapters 57 and 58 take place in the environs of the Lubyanka, and both feature Nikolay Grigorevitch Krymov, the dedicated, even fanatical, Bolshevik who is the husband of Zhenya, Viktor's sister-in-law.

Zhenya is a lively and free-spirited artist who early in the novel had left Krymov for the dashing and imposing tank-commander, Novikov. Krymov is devastated by Zhenya's leaving him, especially now that Krymov, a true-believing and rigid Communist, has himself been arrested and imprisoned for no apparent reason. Krymov has now become a victim of the very regime to which he is so devoted. He refuses to confess, despite repeated beatings and torture. And he continues to believe in the justice of the Communist party's cause. He trusts that, in the end, justice and equality—and even freedom—will ultimately prevail.

One of the major subplots of the novel is the love triangle between Zhenya, Novikov, and Krymov. Zhenya believes in the autonomy of the self, of the modern woman's right and ability to make her own choices, including the choice to leave her husband for another man. But a gnawing sense of obligation draws her to return to Krymov, especially after his arrest, despite her belief in her own autonomy. "I don't like saints," she remarks at one point in the novel. "There's usually some kind of hysteria underneath. . . . I'd rather have an outright bitch. . . . It's of her own free will that a woman . . . goes to bed with a man, lives with him, or decides to leave him" (705). Despite her belief in the complete autonomy of the self, Zhenya somehow feels compelled to leave Novikov and to return to Krymov. Zhenya's returning to Krymov bears witness to the very sanctity that Zhenya derides, but which *Life and Fate* continually extols. The novel tells of a number of remarkable examples of random, apparently senseless acts of human kindness in the midst of unfathomable human destruction. "Human history," for Grossman, "is not the battle of good struggling to overcome evil. It is a battle fought by a great evil struggling to overcome a kernel of human kindness. But if what is human in human beings has not been destroyed even now, then evil will never conquer" (410). So Levinas, in the penultimate paragraph of *Otherwise than Being* (185), speaks of the great hope that is inspired by even "the little humanity that adorns the earth" (*le peut d'humanité qui orne la terre*).

Let us return to the conclusion of chapter 57. Krymov is speaking to Katsenelenbogen, a fellow prisoner in the Lubyanka. The two are discussing another prisoner named Dreling. Katsenelenbogen is a dedicated Communist who was a Chekist, a member of the first Soviet security organization set up by Lenin that later became the infamous KGB. Dreling is a Menshevik who refuses to bow to authority. Krymov, like Katsenelenbogen, is a devoted Communist, but he—in contrast to Katsenelenbogen— looks forward to the day when social equality will be achieved and the repressive measures of the Soviet state will no longer be necessary. Katsenelenbogen refers to "personal freedom"—the very freedom that permitted Ikonnikov to rise to his full humanity and to say "no" to building a gas chamber—as a "cave-man principle" (846). Krymov accuses Katsenelenbogen of ascribing "to the security organs all the attributes of the deity." Katsenelenbogen agrees. "Yes, I believe in God," the avowed atheist paradoxically confesses to Krymov. He continues: "I'm an ignorant, credulous old man. Every age creates the deity in its own image. The security organs are wise and powerful; they are what holds sway over twentieth-century man. Once this power was held by earthquakes, forest-fires, thunder, and lightning—and they too were worshipped."

Krymov mentions the rebellious Dreling to Katsenelenbogen, who remarks that "that vile old man disturbs my faith." For Katsenelenbogen, God means an amoral power that commands my absolute obedience. This is a god, moreover—to recall Levinas's wording in *Otherwise than Being*—that is "un certain dieu," "a certain god" in the sense of a god in whom one can and must believe with certainty. Dreling's rebellious witness, for Katsenelenbogen, threateningly calls the existence of this god into question.

Grossman juxtaposes Katsenelenbogen's understanding of god with that which is signified by the last reference to God in the novel. This final reference to God appears at the conclusion of Chapter 58. Krymov's interrogators continue to insist that he sign the trumped-up confession they have prepared. Krymov refuses. Then another, very different kind of document, requires his signature. Krymov is asked to sign for a parcel of food items that was left for him by his estranged wife Zhenya. Krymov is stunned. "'Oh God, oh God (Боже, Боже/*Bozhe, Bozhe*).' He began to cry." The word God, uttered here twice by the atheist Krymov, bears witness to Zhenya's totally unexpected gift, to the responsibility she has miraculously assumed for the Other, with no expectation of a reward, for her estranged and suffering husband Nikolay Grigorevich Krymov.

A totally unexpected gift, an act of kindness and of sacrifice given with no expectation of a reward, to which Krymov responds with the words "Oh God, oh God!" This, for both Levinas and Grossman, is how God appears after his death announced by Nietzsche, after the death of a certain god inhabiting the world behind the scenes, after the Shoah, after the Gulag.

I would like to bear witness, in conclusion, to the context that has inspired many of the insights I have developed in this essay. For the past seven years, I have been teaching classes on literature and ethics in prison to a mix of undergraduates at the University of Oregon and inmates at two correctional institutions. In the spring quarters of 2010 and 2012, I taught a class on "Literature and Ethics: Levinas and Vasily Grossman's *Life and Fate*" at the Oregon State Penitentiary (2010) and the Oregon State Correctional Institution (2012). This context is relevant to the theme of this volume on loss and hope. The physical setting in which I taught these classes was grim, but hope sprang out of this grimness.

My classes are part of the national Inside-Out Prison Exchange program. One of the things that is unique about the Inside-Out model is that it consists of a mix of incarcerated students ("inside" students) and university students ("outside" students); hence the name "Inside-Out." Inside-Out classes proceed through real dialogue. There are no lectures. We sit in a circle, with inside students sitting next to outside students. The atmosphere is electric. No one ever yawns—or at least very rarely.

To me, the phrase "inside-out" suggests something that happens emotionally to those participating in the class. You are turned inside-out, emptied of your ego as you transcend labels and categories—"student," "teacher," "murderer," "prisoner," "criminal"—and respond to the other as fully human. The class becomes a community of learning based on the dignity of every individual. It is a transformative experience for those involved. We not only read about and discuss ethics in these classes, but the students enact the ethical encounter in which the ego (the "moi"), as Levinas describes this encounter in *Otherwise than Being*, is experienced as "a being divesting itself, emptying itself of its being, turning itself inside out (*à l'envers*)."[13] In precisely this sense, Ikonnikov was turned inside-out by his responsibility for, by his sense that he had to answer to, each of those human beings who would certainly perish in the gas chambers he was being ordered to build by his Nazi captors. Zhenya, similarly, was turned inside-out by her sense of obligation to Krymov, despite her belief in the autonomy of a self that believes it has a right to act in accordance with maximizing its own self-interest.

What does the prison context have to do with the theme of our volume, with the relation between loss and hope? I will end with the testimony of several of my Inside-Out students, whom I will identify by first names only (students are known only by the last names in Inside-Out classes). The first quotation, from an outside student named Leslie (spring 2009), testifies to the transcendence she experienced in the classroom, to her having been turned inside-out by the Other. Leslie associates this transcendence with God understood not in the sense of "a certain god inhabiting the world behind the scenes" but rather with human relationships:

> This wasn't a religion class, (but) it was a spiritual sanctuary for me. This class transformed my personal spirituality. I felt God, the spirit, the humbling force, or some higher power within human interaction. I no longer doubt a higher being because one was evoked in conversations in the class.[14]

In this second quotation, an inside student named Sam reflects on how, during the class meetings of our Inside-Out class in spring 2012 on Grossman and Levinas, he miraculously felt he was no longer in prison:

> I can without a doubt say that this class has changed me forever. . . . A huge reason why this class had such a powerful effect on me was the atmosphere in every class meeting. I came from a world full of stereotypes, prejudice, and "violence against the other." And walked into a sanctuary. I wasn't judged for my circumstances or my past. I was welcomed into a community where we respected, even admired, each other's differences. We encouraged participation and respected the right to just listen. After crossing the threshold into class, I felt free in every sense of the word.[15]

In this third and last quotation, an inside student named Cannon describes the sense of hope he experienced in that same Inside-Out class in the spring of 2012 on Grossman and Levinas:

> This class has been a wonderful and profoundly inspiring experience. See, over time I had begun to have fear and uncertainties about the capabilities between in here and out there. Time and experience had brought dread of the public stereotypically viewing us as Frankenstein-like abhorrences. To be viewed with fear and disdain, as those lost to humanity. I had even begun to fear the same for myself, that I might be losing the capability to reasonably and effectively interact with the "real people" of society. This class changed that. The way the professor and all the students treated us has reintroduced a long-lost sense of optimism.[16]

Practicing A-tonal Ethics: The Loss of Old Certainties as the Ground of Our Hope

Celia Kenny

Pluralism, as a political matrix, has ambiguous ramifications. On the one hand, it is associated with a generative negotiation of difference and increased openness to the cultural/religious other, in what William Connolly calls "the conventional pluralist celebration of diversity."[1] The up-beat side of cultural diversity is routinely celebrated and marketed from Aberdeen to Zanzibar as the ever-expanding range of visual complexity, eclectic music, and culinary fusion, which have come to be the familiar signs of the benign face of cosmopolitanism. Simultaneously, however, cultural diversity is manifest in religious and ethnic practices and beliefs, taboos, dress and bodily habits that symbolize, for many people, irreconcilable differences that threaten world peace. The pluralist milieu can be said to account for a range of fundamentalisms that include: "ethnic cleansing; enforced heterosexuality; racialization of crime and punishment; redogmatization of divinity, nature, and reason; and intensification of state border controls."[2] Contrasting and contested responses to pluralism raise issues of authority, and, in particular, the desire for "final" authority. Moreover, it has been suggested that the confluence of pluralization and fundamentalization is not accidental:

> . . . for each conditions the other: each drive to pluralization is countered by a fundamentalism that claims to be authorized by a god or by nature . . . [t]hese struggles, in turn, churn up old dyspeptic debates over the role of divinity, nature, tradition, and reason in moral and political life.[3]

As Zygmund Bauman pithily comments, "the problem of modern society is not how to eliminate strangers, but how to live in their constant company."[4] Thus, the contemporary reflexive subject, living in the company of strangers, is exposed to, and interacts with, a broad "menu" of norms. Far from having no foundations, there is widespread awareness, in pluralist democratic societies, of a new freedom to identify with a diverse range of social norms and multiple jurisdictions mediated through religious laws, civil law, and international human rights instruments.

One of the results of living with the complexity of late modern society is cognitive dissonance, reminiscent of Foucault's "epistemological ruptures . . . (which) suspend the continuous accumulation of knowledge, interrupt its slow development, and force it to enter a new time, cut it off from its empirical origin and its original motivations, cleanse it of its imaginary complicities."[5] Put differently, cognitive dissonance refers to the anxiety that can result from having to hold together a set of values and beliefs where the overlapping norms do not correlate, but cut across the familiar religious and cultural narrative lines associated with our identity.

Musical metaphors are central to the logic of this chapter; in particular, dissonance, a-tonality, and modulation. They are intended, in this context, as neologisms that carry overtones of both loss and hope. Dissonance, already mentioned, is suggestive of a break in harmony, but also of an energy that carries us forward toward the hope of a resolution. A-tonality is commonly applied to musical compositions that are not constructed on the tonal system most closely associated with classical music at one particular period in European culture. It does not signify the *absence* of tonality but the arrangements of sounds that may be less familiar to ears which have been acculturized into western, classical European musical styles.[6] A sequence of tones will be apprehended as being either harmonious or dissonant, resolved or pending, according to the milieu in which they are encountered. Importing the metaphor to ethics, my suggestion is that, in the pursuit of moral patterns that can hold up in the a-tonal context of contemporary pluralist societies, what is necessary is to acknowledge a type of modulated epistemology, in which the participants in the dialogical process learn to live with the dissonance of pending solutions in order to allow the conversation to continue, modulating their voices in response to the other.

In contemporary multicultural societies, the social actor who justifies values and beliefs by attempting to trace a single and continuous line through a cultural history or religious tradition is likely to find her reasoning deeply challenged by the range of competing claims to authority, which are operative in the contemporary construction of a plural "world." One of the most salient questions, therefore, concerns the nature of objectivity and the place of "truth" in the process through which we evaluate and construct patterns of morality.

Resisting ambiguity

In the process of moral deliberation, the family of words that relates to the idea of truth carries weight in terms of authority and the validation of our beliefs and actions. Since they are commonly used to imply that there is a way in which things "are in reality" to which our words and actions either correspond or do not correspond, this is a group of words that has implications at the level of epistemology, in terms of what we believe; at the level of practice, in terms of how we justify our actions; and for the way that authority is conferred upon those who set the norms for cultural and political ordering.

A number of reasons contribute to the current academic and popular skepticism around the idea and the application of words like true and truth. On the experiential level, the extent of the lies and corruption recently exposed within political, banking, and religious institutions has caused seismic shifts in the public's ability to trust.[7] The existential reality of living in a world that appears to run on the basis of institutionalized deception is further compromised by some of the current philosophical strands that inform education and popular literature, including certain versions of postmodern relativism and the salmagundi of religious and cultural snapshots, now marketed globally, where the appeal lies in the dissolution of borders, authoritative full-stops, and dogmatic restrictions on thought.

There are pressing political and social reasons to deflate the idea of a single truth, not least when the notion of final authority is touted through fundamentalism. Connolly defines fundamentalism as:

> a general imperative to assert an absolute, singular ground of authority; to ground your own identity and allegiances in this questionable source; to define political issues in a vocabulary of god, morality, or nature that invokes such a certain, authoritative source; to condemn tolerance, abortion, pluralism, radicalism, homosexuality, secular humanism, welfarism, and internationalism (among other things) by imputing moral weakness, selfishness, or corruption to them.[8]

He continues: "Fundamentalism . . . converts stresses and strains in (doctrine or identity) into evidence of deviation and immorality in the other (concealing) the political dynamic of this strategy of self-protection by enclosing it in a vocabulary . . . above the possibility of critical reflection."[9] Connolly's "stresses and strains in doctrine and identity," otherwise construed here as cognitive dissonance or epistemic ruptures, commonly result in the construction of opposing pairs (good/bad; truth/falsity; natural/unnatural), intended to short-circuit the necessity to sift all ethical, religious, or political positions through a diversity of viewpoints and to relieve the tension of trying to balance complexity and ambiguity.

A most influential and contested contemporary example of religious fundamentalism is manifest in the resurgence of "new natural law" as the basis for an exclusive type of Roman Catholic morality. New natural law is associated with the name of John Finnis, and was first promulgated by Germain Grisez's reading of Thomas Aquinas.[10] One of the distinctive characteristics of the Grisez school is the proponents' insistence that the conservative views that they hold have their foundations in secular, not doctrinal, reasoning. New natural lawyers have exercised their influence beyond the academy and the church by influencing, for instance, the outcome of important constitutional cases in the United States through *amicus* briefs.[11] Nicholas Bamforth and David Richards describe new natural law as a late modern defense of the patriarchal structure of Roman Catholic authority, in general, and the conservatism of the last two papacies in particular.

At a practical level, its proponents argue in favor of nuclear disarmament and against contraception, abortion, and any sexual activity outside of marriage (and many common practices within it)—including all lesbian and gay activities.[12]

Bamforth and Richards contend that "new natural law defends . . . a sectarian religious view that, because of internal and external flaws, constitutes neither a consistent nor an appealing approach to law and individual rights in a modern constitutional democracy."[13] The writers further argue that the new natural lawyers' basic principles of human flourishing, while being touted as intuitive and universal, are, in fact, only defensible within the framework of a prior commitment to religious belief as that is understood within current doctrinal papal statements. Importantly, they point out that these doctrinal positions, ". . . devalue the role of women and divide them into the idealized (and asexual) and denigrated (and sexual), and which are associated with and enforced by the patriarchal hierarchy of the celibate male priesthood, now seeming increasingly dubious or even willfully irrational."[14]

New natural law exhibits two of the central characteristics of fundamentalism, as indicated above, with reference to Connolly. The first is a tendency to be persuaded that deviation and immorality (notably sexual immorality) are embodied in others and disseminated through their convictions and their lifestyles. The second is the adoption of dogmatic religious, cultural, and moral political positions, which are then presented in vocabularies intended to confer, upon ancient narratives, an aura of originality and timelessness. The leitmotif of such narratives is often the idea that there exists a final truth: an all-embracing narrative of the meaning and purpose of human life, which transcends the immanent frame of historical intersubjectivity. Truth, in other words, as an instrument of power.

Modulated epistemology: The new agnosticism

If the assumption is that truth, or the really real, is "out there" in a realm external to the immanent frame of human existence, then it is quite consistent to envisage that the pressing epistemological task for humans is to strive hopefully (through rational understanding, intuition, or religious inspiration) to attain an objective view of things; the ethical implication being that, when we have reached the point at which we no longer see through a glass darkly, we might discern the difference between good and bad starkly and simply because the "eternal standards" will be revealed. That is one way to justify moral positions. I am interested in another, less definitive, less permanent way.

Paul Horwitz, writing about law, religion, and the constitution, defines what he calls a "new agnosticism."[15] Horwitz celebrates this far from wishy-washy middle ground: a religious, political, and ethical position ("an adamant position of its own"[16]) from which the new agnostic, who may desist from the habit of drawing final conclusions, may, nevertheless, exhibit essential qualities of good judgment and citizenship. The new agnosticism, according to Horwitz: "denotes the ability to occupy, as fully and empathetically as possible, the varied worldviews of our citizens, even at those moments when their worldviews come into the sharpest conflict with each other and with our own perspectives."[17]

The type of ethical engagement that would follow from an embrace of new agnosticism would not rest on a metaphysical epistemology, but on what I call a *modulated* way of knowing. That is, understanding and acting in full acknowledgment that all values are human constructs, contingent upon the historical, cultural, and religious context in which they are framed. Even moral judgments that do not claim transcendent authority, however, (whether religious, ideological, rational, or in the sense of an essentializing conception of human nature), need not eschew the belief that certain conceptions of the good can be practiced in ways that might resonate beyond the local and the historical; they may also claim to be normative.

I believe that there are values and beliefs that have epistemological significance and moral weight, although I am perfectly aware that such values require to be constantly reinvested with substantial content and reexpressed in terms of changing planetary circumstances. The doctrine of human rights, for example, rests on the idea that there are social goods that ought to be recognized universally, but the vision does not depend, for its normative authority, on metaphysical grounds. The vision, the modifications, and the implementation of human rights instruments arise from immanent fields of practice through reflection on the "clash" of human experiences (the plural being vital here). Many feminist political projects can also be interpreted thus, when they work out of a type of antifoundational normativity, taking, as their starting point, a strategic essentialism: a politically inspired solidarity intent on finding points of commonality in full acknowledgment that what binds us today may lose us tomorrow. In a modulated epistemological approach, the values that are espoused are not imagined to be solely the content of revelation, but in a reasoning process that is grounded in material effects.[18] That brings, in its wake, the awareness that our "knowing" needs to be modulated. Our judging, deciding, and evaluating, cut loose from traditional sources of authority, require to be tempered and retuned to the sound of other voices. Modulated epistemology signifies that understanding has moved into another register in response to modifying factors from the experience of living in a multicultural, democratic environment. A modulated epistemology still allows us to grasp the nettle of ethical evaluation while refraining from suggesting that the foundations on which we build our judgments are a-historical and a-cultural. Fabrizio Trifiro, for example, has articulated the distinction between the *universal grounds for* and the *universal scope of* normativity, further adding:

> anti-foundationalism is particularly suited for a liberal democratic culture . . . (in its denial that) any particular practice has an absolute privileged authority over all the others . . . reminding us of the contingency of our convictions and practices and that every consensus reached is only a temporary resting point prone to turn into an oppressive status quo.[19]

There are echoes, here, of the distinction between pluralism (when it refuses to go beyond the bounds of its internal differentiation) and pluralization (awareness of the contingency and, therefore, the incompleteness, of all epistemological stances). As Connolly puts it:

> The most fragile and indispensable element in a pluralizing democracy is an ethos of critical responsiveness to new social movements (applying) new pressures to existing constellations of identity/difference by shaking the cultural ground in which they are rooted.[20]

Crucially, Connolly goes on to suggest that, through such pressure for change, the effect upon hegemonic identities cannot simply be expressed in terms of "overcoming prejudice" or "promoting tolerance" because this very vocabulary takes its meaning from existing majority/minority power dynamics.

While it follows from this that there is no single way to pronounce, outside of specific cases, how the individual will, or should, engage with conflicting values, a modulated epistemological approach will most likely include the following procedural aspects. First, the acknowledgment that diversity is an ontological characteristic of human life will entail an acceptance of the fact that conflicts in beliefs, values, and practices should not be regarded as temporary aberrations to be flattened out or obliterated. The assumption that diversity is of the "essence" of social interaction will under-write policies for education, health, the "management" of religion, and the arrangement of public space. This is so because only within societal structures that allow for the expression of diverse ways of being human are individuals and groups able to risk articulating new ways of describing the relationships among all things, including: human relationships, hierarchical systems of power, and ecological sensibility. I would also note that a mark of pluralist societies is the freedom to imagine and articulate her ultimate concerns, which entails an understanding of the relationship between human and God.[21]

Pluralism is both a process and an intentional *mid-point* that will involve a multilevel process of public debate on matters of morals, the place of religion in public discourse, and a continual reworking of both the content of liberal values and the methods by which they might be put into practice. This is the distinction between the pluralist and the pluralizer. Connolly warns of the paradox that "the culture of pluralism also engenders obstacles to new drives to pluralization . . ."[22] Counterintuitive as this may seem, the point that Connolly is making here concerns the potential for the pluralist imagination to align itself with conservative forces that set limits to acceptable expressions of diversity, in a refusal to move beyond "the congealed results of past struggles as if they constituted the essential standard of reasonableness or justice itself."[23] Into this disjuncture, Connolly proposes the construction of an ethos of critical responsiveness, adding that "a pluralizing culture pluralizes *sources* of ethics as well as *models* of what is ethical: several parties to this ethical pluralism then engage each other across relations of agonistic respect and selective collaboration."[24] Judith Butler, acknowledging Connolly's use of the notion of pluralization, makes the crucial point that pluralization is not equivalent to universalization, since "equality is not a principle that homogenizes those to whom it applies."[25] As Butler reminds us, a political commitment to equality is meaningless without an accompanying affirmation of diversity. Pluralizing structures are, as she puts it, "universalizing and differentiating . . . at once and without contradiction."[26]

If politics is a learned activity, then the art of being politically inclusive must become part of the educational agenda, a process of life-long learning. The citizen in a multicultural and fluid environment needs to become cognizant of the mechanics of the political process; learning the different effects of procedural and deliberative democracy; knowing enough about the power of ideologies to distinguish among them and practice some resistance to them; and understanding the historical events as they have contributed to dominant cultural and religious modes of operation. All of these represent pedagogical steps toward effective political agency, as they also rest on a type of knowing that is open for revision, or, as I have put it, a modulated epistemology. In addition, contemporary patterns of morality in late modernity intersect at such a complex level that it is not helpful to proceed from theory to practice. What should be foregrounded are moral patterns in their particularity, in their historical roots and their present political expressions, paying attention to the social impact that specific beliefs and practices have on those most closely affected by them.

In 1972, Foucault wrote that ". . . in analyzing discourses themselves, one sees the loosening of the embrace, apparently so tight, of words and things, and the emergence of a group of rules proper to discursive practice."[27] Foucault invites us to acknowledge the danger of *classification*, through which human discourse, by setting things side-by-side, reduces the difference between them and creates categories that, although existing purely in the realm of imagination, take on the force of the "real." I intend, by the concept of modulated epistemology, a way of knowing that rests on the assumption that there is no necessary connection between words and things. There is nothing in our *understanding* of the thing apprehended, which can possibly stand outside of our *relationship* with the thing apprehended; nothing that would allow us to claim a correspondence between our way of predicating "reality" and a realm beyond the limitations of social interaction. When knowing is disassociated from notions of certainty and truth, we are freed up to make conscious choices among the diversity of authoritative sources, and to learn to live with the dissonance and tension of having to do so.

The justification for our choices is through a commitment to continue the conversation with those who do not share our views. Human beings are epistemological taxonomists, socialized to encounter all things through imaginative categories. Categories of the imagination, however, will always be circumscribed by the contextual parameters of a particular history and culture. A modulated epistemology, therefore, having sundered the necessary connection between words and things, will envisage human vocabulary as the attempt to signify the constant displacement of things. That is a definition of modulation. When it is acknowledged that human communication attempts to communicate the constant displacement of things, the knowing subject is wrested away from Cartesian notions of disinterested observation from a fixed point and is reimagined in terms of a web of power-relations, acknowledging instability in the experience of self. I would put it this way: post-Cartesian knowledge of the "other" is premised on contiguity, where the primary significance of contiguous is to be touched by something or someone; to be changed by the imprint of the other person or thing. That is another definition of modulation.

The loosening of the embrace of words and things, and the detachment from the traditional notion of the knowing subject can be interpreted to signify a move away from the idea of truth as a metaphysical end-point and as a disruption of the view that parochial patterns of morality necessarily bear universal ethical significance. Recent shifts in human sensibility are manifest in the culture of human rights, the ideology of multiculturalism, and feminist critique. Inextricably linked, each of these ethical trajectories constructs a mode of "hearing" that calls into question the mystique of single-sourced authority, including over-arching narratives of the meaning of human life and human nature. One of the results is that the contemporary subject, responding to the multiplicity of foundational roots/routes to knowledge, becomes aware of her responsibility to deconstruct and reconstruct patterns of morality through interaction with others.[28] This is close-up, ethical work in which the form of practice will vary from situation to situation. Crucially, the point is not to arrive at a new overarching theory but to situate whatever knowledge and understanding is generated by the process of dialogue, listening, and of consciousness-raising, within existing theories, in order to recontextualize old answers and generate new questions. Thus do we practice a-tonal ethics.

Conclusion

There is no doubt that the erosion of traditional certainties is experienced as a deep loss by many who fear a slide into relativism. The ground of our hope, however, lies in a commitment to communication, finding from within the plurality of human embodiment and experience, common strands upon which ethical and political solidarity can be built. Crossing the barriers of religious and cultural difference is risky. It is a kind of ethical loss of balance, inducing in most of us a dissonance that longs for resolution and the peace of a final cadence. Cadences, however, are better understood as interim points in a forward-moving chain of voices that temporarily halt the flow, but which, by the nature of art and of life, always prove, in retrospect, to be unfinished.

The idea of *practicing* is central to the ethic that I propose. Ethics is a doing word, intimately linked to language usage and community relations. As we predicate, so we relate; as we interpellate each other, so we contribute to the constitution of another person or a group, and in the process, we form our "selves." I work on the assumption that identities are constituted relationally, with the caveat that our apprehension of the "other" cannot be separated from an acknowledgment of our own shifting and unstable understanding of our "selves." Note that "practicing" is a verb in the continuous present. There is no end to the process through which we weigh up each other, or come to know ourselves. Historical attempts at rounding off the process have resulted in the objectification of those who are not in a position to keep the religious/political/ethical conversation going; either because they use the wrong vocabulary or because they are the wrong gender, or skin-color, or because they have been silenced in the *ultimate solution* to diversity. The temptation to round off the diversity of human narratives or to close down complex moral problems is a perennial danger in the story of human relations. Contemporary religious and political fundamentalist projects are examples of closure in their intentional disruption of international dialogue and diplomacy. This is a disenfranchizing strategy of substituting, for democratic exchange and the rule of law, the myth of an external authority in nature, God, or politics, wheeling out deus ex machina to obscure the tragic, but inescapable fact that the moral life of humans must be constantly negotiated.

The idea of a-tonality is at the center of the title, as a metaphor to indicate the loss of one single direction in an era in which epistemological foundations have been thoroughly shaken. I have already noted that contemporary moral patterns and the search for sources of authority are characterized, not by the loss of foundations, but by their multiplication. It is into this mixture of choice and uncertainty that I have posited the metaphor of dissonance. A-tonal ethics signifies the contemporary task of constructing patterns of morality based on multiple sources of authority; as it also entails evaluating the practice of others in whatever strange forms they are encountered. The multiplicity of norms (political, cultural, parochial, and international) and multiple jurisdictions (religious laws, civil law, and international human rights instruments) need to be negotiated and weighed up in relation to the construction of personal ethics and public morality.

In the absence of traditional, fixed points of reference, practicing a-tonal ethics is decidedly not a form of moral relativism. It is crucial to make the distinction between: on the one hand, being skeptical about the possibility of establishing ultimate foundations for our beliefs; and, on the other, the inability, or refusal, to offer any justification for the values that we hold dear. It is reasonable to ground a political movement or a social ethic on an explicitly stated value-system while simultaneously acknowledging that these values are contingent upon history and cultural specificity and open to revision should conditions change.

Finally, I have proposed an epistemological model, a modulated understanding of what it means "to know," which, in the context of the contemporary a-tonality of moral patterns, might be a better way to evaluate strangeness when that is what we encounter. It is crucial to remember that the practice of a-tonal ethics is not a process of discovery of something that already exists in a realm beyond social interaction. It is, rather, a route taken alongside others, in which worlds are made and unmade; a route, not to some authentic or preordained version of human identity but to a constant reinvention of the patterns of human interaction. In the words of Rowan Williams, "confronted with what seeks to close down exchange or conflict, we discover we can always say more."[29] The hope of justice in a pluralist society will entail the constant task of finding new vocabularies for the ongoing conversation that will be, simultaneously: religious, ethical, and jurisprudential. The loss of old certainties, I believe, may yet be the ground of our hope.

Losing Confidence in Free-market Economics and Free-market Religion: Recovering True Hope

Joerg Rieger

The so-called Great Recession that started in 2007 and its lasting effects have shattered much confidence in neoliberal free-market economics that was largely taken for granted for several decades. While large corporations and top investors have recovered and are doing better than ever before, small investors, small businesses, and workers are increasingly beginning to doubt whether the fantastic wealth that was promised to them will ever materialize. Many are losing hope in the American Dream, according to which anyone can strike it rich by their own efforts.

These doubts, I suspect, cannot be limited to matters of the economy. Among other matters, religion is increasingly affected as well. Examples of such widening doubts include the religious trappings of economics itself.[1] Belief in the workings of the invisible hand of the market, for instance, which will invariably balance the interests of all, is hard to sustain when the rich keep getting richer and the poor keep getting poorer. An example of growing doubt in the realm of religion is the so-called Gospel of Prosperity, which has an even harder time to deliver on its promises in difficult economic climates. Even mainline religion has to deal with increasing levels of doubt, as the numbers of church members and worship attendance are shrinking.

In my book *No Rising Tide*, I have discussed the lessons of large-scale economic downturn in terms of the "logic of downturn."[2] This logic helps us to gain a clearer sense for what is really going on, both in economics and in religion, as opposed to the widely promoted faith claims of both realms that are often tied to the proverbial mountaintop experiences, which are hardly sustainable long-term. The logic of downturn does not provide a pessimistic view of the world; just the opposite: it maintains that the bursting of economic and religious bubbles is ultimately good news, for only when we lose false hope can we gain true hope. As the hope for "pie-in-the-sky" is increasingly called into question both in economics and religion, true hope can shine through. This hope is no longer found at the top, with celebrity business and faith leaders, but at the bottom, where common people are forming new ways of working and living in solidarity.

In the Abrahamic faith traditions, there are many examples for such hope, including the Exodus, the Babylonian Exile, the Jesus traditions, and the traditions of the early Paul. In this chapter, I will explore some parallels between then and now.

The logic of downturn and the exodus

According to the Moses traditions that are shared by Judaism, Christianity, and Islam, Moses was raised at the court of the Egyptian pharaoh as an Egyptian prince. As a member of the Egyptian elites, he would therefore have been one of the primary beneficiaries of the Egyptian economy. The decisive turn in this story occurs when Moses begins to notice that the success of this economy is built on the back of the labor of slaves. The logic of downturn catches up with Moses when he notices the economic hardship that his kinsfolk have to endure (Ex. 2.11).

That Moses overreacts and kills one of the Egyptian slave masters is part of the story (Ex. 2.12), but this act does not need to be justified and it does not lead to the liberation of the slaves. Liberation becomes a possibility when Godself joins Moses in the logic of downturn, realizing what is going on. In the book of Exodus, Yahweh makes this statement:

> I have observed the misery of my people who are in Egypt; I have heard their cry on account of their taskmasters. Indeed, I know their sufferings, and I have come down to deliver them from the Egyptians, and to bring them up out of that land to a good and broad land, a land flowing with milk and honey. . . . The cry of the Israelites has now come to me; I have also seen how the Egyptians oppress them. So come, I will send you to Pharaoh to bring my people, the Israelites, out of Egypt. (Ex. 3.7–10)

It seems as if Godself is learning in the process, as God hears the cry of the people and their hopelessness and, as a result, becomes involved in acts of liberation.

It is not hard to see potential parallels to today. Although, like Moses and Yahweh, many people may not have experienced the most brutal consequences of economic downturn in their own bodies, these realities are presented to them by the fate of members of their communities such as relatives, loved ones, friends, and coworkers. Of course, it may take a while until deep-seated false hopes wear out, but the realities of long-term unemployment, of children moving back home due to their inability to find adequate employment, of lack of benefits and health care that lead to people dying before their time, cannot be deferred forever. Whenever the existence of people is threatened in sustained fashion, things are beginning to change.

What is perhaps most important in the story of the Exodus is that it runs counter to the false hopes of the status quo. As Moses and Yahweh begin to understand what is happening to their people, no effort is made to justify the situation or to encourage the Hebrew slaves to put up with their situation in the hope that things will be different in some distant future. Neither is there any effort made to integrate the Hebrew slaves into Egyptian society in order to improve their status.

This might lead us to wonder whether contemporary efforts at integration and inclusion, commonly promoted by socially engaged religious communities, provide true hope or peddle the false hopes of the status quo. Even when corporations seek to integrate workers into the status quo, for instance, often with cheap promises ("everybody is a leader") or threat that things could be much worse, workers do not necessarily benefit a great deal. And when diversity is celebrated in liberal society, those who are different from the dominant majority are often co-opted for the dominant interests rather than liberated to pursue their own concerns.

In the parts of the Exodus story that are shared by Muslims, Christians, and Jews, there is no question of what the outcome is. Despite the dire situation of the Hebrew slaves, seen in full force only by those who embrace the logic of downturn, liberation eventually takes place. This is the location of true hope, over against the false hope that puts up with the status quo and declares it ultimate and final. Moreover, in this story there is no question where God is found. God is neither the impartial judge in the middle, nor is God on the side of the status quo; rather, God is on the side of the slaves. Here, true hope shifts from those who feel secure in their hopes—the Egyptian elites represented by Pharaoh—to those who may feel that they have nothing to hope for—the Hebrew slaves.

In these ancient stories lay the deep and strong roots of a liberative religious tradition that is shared by different religious communities in different historical periods; in US history, the Exodus tradition manifested its power both in the liberative religion of the African American slaves and in the Civil Rights movement. Nevertheless, we must not forget that, almost from the beginning, there were efforts by dominant religion to subvert and assimilate these traditions. In addition, the slaves themselves, after the experience of liberation, at times lose heart and vision. Many of the interpretations of what happens when they reach the Promised Land are designed to cancel out the hope of the slaves and turn it into the hope of the powerful. Traditions that describe the arrival in the Promised Land as conquest (Jo. 1–12) are particularly relevant. According to one of these traditions, Jericho is destroyed and all its inhabitants and their livestock killed, saving only precious metal and the family of an informant (Jo. 6).

Traditions like these do not necessarily express the hopes of the liberated slaves, who would not have had the means or the power required for such acts of conquest, but the hopes of those in power who seek absolute control. Besides, whatever little historical evidence exists for what happened after the Exodus points to a very different process of immigration into the Promised Land, according to which the Hebrew slaves joined forces with the residential rural population in order to form liberation movements from the rule of oppressive city states. Even in the Bible, there are alternative traditions of how the Hebrew slaves settle in the Promised Land, in solidarity with the population, and the good news is that these alternative traditions, which guide us to a much more substantive hope, could never be completely repressed.[3]

The logic of downturn and the Babylonian Exile

The Babylonian Exile represents an important turning point in the Hebrew Bible, combining both a severe crisis and critical renewal. About 70 percent of the Hebrew

Bible deals with the question of how the Exile happened and what can be learned from it, even though it never acquired the same theological centrality as the Exodus.[4] Although there are few solid historical sources about the Babylonian Exile, it is estimated that 20,000 persons, about 25 percent of the population, were displaced.[5]

It is commonly acknowledged that most of the people exiled to Babylon as a result of the Babylonian Empire's agenda of conquest were members of the Judean elites. One of the important themes of the Exile is, therefore, the logic of downturn found in a loss of power and control, which is related to important transformations of the topic of hope. The experience of the Exile shattered the hope built on a dominant theology, which believed that David's monarchy would last forever. This dominant theology remembered the Exodus not as subversive hope but as hope for domination: "Who is like your people, like Israel? Is there another nation on earth whose God went to redeem it as a people, and to make a name for himself, doing great and awesome things for them, by driving out before his people nations and their gods?" (2 Sam. 7.23). In the United States, the myth of American exceptionalism is also built on theological themes of dominance; not surprisingly it, too, is being challenged during extended times of downturn.

While the false hope of dominance was shattered in the Exile, the exiled were treated relatively well and the expectation was that they would assimilate. Assimilation, in this context, would have meant the exchange of the false hope of the Judean Empire for the false hope of the Babylonian Empire. Nevertheless, despite a host of opportunities for Jews to assimilate and make it in the Babylonian Empire, the hope for liberation did not die out. To many, the hope of the Babylonian Empire seemed less real than the newly emerging hope in a God who would redeem the people.

What is perhaps most fascinating is that in the situation of the Exile, Jews developed new hope linked to a new set of earth-shaking theological insights. Many of the biblical writings on creation, for instance, were produced during the Exile, as the people began to understand that their God was not subject to the Babylonian Empire that controlled them, but the creator of a world that allowed for alternatives and a place where even the widows, the orphans, and the strangers could flourish.

The Judeo-Christian doctrine of creation has its origins in these experiences of an alternative and greater God: the God whom the people of Judah and Israel worshipped could no longer be envisioned merely as a personal or tribal deity, located exclusively on Mount Zion, but was now seen as the creator of the whole world, who was at work in the liberation of the whole world. Most important to the emergence of an alternative hope was that this faith in the creator was not a triumphalistic vision, but a vision that encouraged the endurance and resistance of the people in exile. Similar hope has been emerging in recent decades in various liberation theologies, which understand that the marginalized are not only surviving in mysterious ways but that they are acquiring new agency.

Key to this new hope is that, like in the Exodus, suffering is not only experienced by the people but by Godself. While the Exile is often attributed to God's anger and disappointment about God's people, God is also said to redeem in "love" and "pity" (Is. 63.9). According to the prophet Ezekiel, God is disappointed and God's anger is directed against the prophets of false hope, who say "peace" when there is no peace, and who "smear whitewash" on a bad situation (Ez. 13.10). As this false hope is actively broken down by God ("I will break down the wall that you have smeared with whitewash, and bring it to the ground, so that its foundation will be laid bare" (Ez. 13.14)), new hope emerges that is stronger and perhaps more hopeful than any hope of an elitist system could ever be.

The liberation that is promised here reflects a new understanding of God and of hope. Hope emerges where God associates with people who are beginning to organize: "Assemble yourselves and come together, draw near, you survivors of the nations!" (Is. 45.20a), and where the false gods of power are rejected: "They have no knowledge—those who carry about their wooden idols, and keep on praying to a god that cannot save" (Is. 45.20b). This emerging vision is broader than the hope of the elites, as it includes all of the downtrodden who are experiencing the pressures of the empire. As Pinchas E. Rosenblüth has pointed out, the various theological interpretations of the Exile helped Jewish people to make sense of their suffering and, thus, prevented them from annihilation. In this way they also maintained an ongoing sensitivity for the suffering of other people and the injustice they experienced.[6]

What has often been described as Deutero-Isaiah's monotheism is not an abstract theological development but rooted in the rejection of the gods of false hope. Like the false hope of the empire, the hope that emerges among the people in exile cannot be limited to one aspect alone: it is not only a religious hope, it is at the same time social, political, and economic. The images of God that emerge out of this alternative hope are holistic. This insight is crucial for contemporary religion as well, at a time when narrow modern definitions of religion that filter out social, political, and economic categories still rule supreme.

To be sure, the hope that grows out of a new vision of God as the creator of the earth, defeating the idols of the empire, has also been misused. In the first creation story in the book of Genesis, for instance, God creates the human being with the following directive: "Be fruitful and multiply, and fill the earth and subdue it; and have dominion over the fish of the sea and over the birds of the air and over every living thing that moves open the earth" (Gen. 1.28). While interpreters of this passage have often emphasized that dominion does not have to be structured according to the domination modeled by empires, there is a resonance of empire theology here that is ambiguous. Without close links to the resistance theology of the exiles, such passages were often misinterpreted and misused, even if only in the sense of dominion as a benevolent paternalism.

Visions of God that emphasize God's absolute power and superiority remind of the old domination theology of the Judean Empire, but they can be read as subversive if seen as part of the resistance traditions of the exiles that subvert the power of the empire and exchange false hope for true hope: "See the Lord's hand is not too short to save, nor his ear too dull to hear" (Is. 59.1). And while the Babylonian Empire eventually fell, the hope of the exiles is still alive and continues to inspire struggling people even today.

The Babylonian Exile marks the beginning of Israel's life in the Diaspora, which has continued ever since. Hope is tied to life as an ethnic minority, which requires rethinking one's identity, as Albertz has pointed out.[7] Yet more is at stake than ethnicity, if the universal hope proclaimed by Deutero-Isaiah is taken seriously: all those who are marginalized by the empire are provided new hope through the work of God. In the history of the United States, this is embodied in social movements that have been supported by religion, including abolitionism, suffragism, the labor movement, and the Civil Rights movement. Today, the Occupy movement reports similar experiences.[8]

The logic of downturn and the Jesus traditions

In the history of christology, the Greek term *kenosis*—emptying—has gained currency. According to an ancient Christian tradition that Paul picks up in Philippians 2, Jesus Christ, "who, though he was in the form of God, did not regard equality with God as something to be exploited, but emptied himself, taking the form of a slave, being born in human likeness. And being found in human form, he humbled himself and became obedient to the point of death—even death on a cross" (Phil. 2.6–8). While systematic theologians might feel tempted to conceptualize the theological terms of this passage and speculate about their meaning, the logic of downturn requires us to take a closer look at the history that is described here.

The *kenosis* of Jesus Christ is tied to the incarnation—God becoming fully human—yet this becoming-human is not a matter of generic humanity. Jesus is born into a family of day laborers in construction.[9] Perhaps this is the dangerous memory that is preserved when Philippians 2 talks about the form of a slave. The logic of downturn would not have been foreign to day laborers, as they were easily exploited by their masters, and their jobs were never secure. Unemployment was a prominent reality at the time of Jesus; when big building projects ended, workers were simply let go. It is likely that Jesus and Joseph experienced unemployment themselves, and they would have known many fellow workers who struggled with unemployment. In our own time, when unemployment rates are sky high and jobs are less secure than ever in the history of the United States, more and more of us can relate to these experiences as well.

In this context, false hope does not aid the survival of working people and their families. The promises of false messiahs, like the false hopes of the neoliberal economy that each generation will be better off than the one before, are, therefore, not only a theological problem; rather, they can be matters of life and death. Perhaps this is the reason why Jesus was so concerned: "Beware that no one leads you astray. Many will come in my name and say, 'I am he!' and they will lead many astray" (Mk. 13.5–6). True hope, in contrast, does not necessarily come in the form of big ideas, promises, or theological claims, nor does it take the shape of some vague optimism that everything will turn out all right.[10]

There were several persons by the name of Jesus in the first century, as Richard Horsley has noted, who preached radical messages. Some were harassed and beaten by the Romans, but only one of them was executed on a cross in the manner of a political revolutionary: Jesus of Nazareth was executed because he had become too dangerous or, expressed in terms of hope, because the hope that he preached to the "least of these" was a real hope that the world could be different and that their oppression would end. The message of the kingdom of God, which Jesus preached, was not just a pious idea, disconnected from reality; the kingdom of God was not a false hope, designed to keep the people docile, but it was at hand (Mt. 3.2: "Repent, for the kingdom of heaven has come near") in a real fashion. What differentiated Jesus of Nazareth from his contemporary radical preacher Jesus ben Hananiah was that he not only preached but also organized people as part of his ministry.[11] Organizing has taken on new importance again in religious communities today, from community organizing to a budding religion and labor movement.[12] True hope is found here.

In light of this history, the theological notion of *kenosis* takes on a very different shape. It is not an abstract metaphysical concept that talks about God and humanity in general—the stuff of too many sermons. *Kenosis* describes a historical process in which God in Christ divests Godself of the dominant power, represented by the Roman Empire and status-quo religion. This kind of *kenosis* is parallel to Jesus rejecting the devil's offer of top-down rule over all the kingdoms of the world (Mt. 4.8–10). Moreover, this divestment of dominant power is not a divestment of power in general, a notion that is fashionable with a romanticizing form of Christianity that represents another form of false hope. Survival for day laborers in construction or for slaves depends on maintaining some form of power. True hope also cannot be maintained without some power.

The alternative power that Jesus of Nazareth embodies is diametrically opposed to the top-down power of the status quo. It is the power of the last, which shall be the first (Mt .20.16). It is the power of the poor, whom Jesus calls blessed, and not the power of the rich, on whom he pronounces woe (Lk. 6.20, 24), a message that is also embraced by Mary, his mother (Lk. 1.48, 52). In other words, the *kenosis* of dominant power is not a rejection of all power but the reversal of dominant power manifest in humility (the everyday reality of a slave) and obedience. True hope is ultimately rooted in this alternative power, although it might seem for a while as if the dominant power has the corner on the market of hope. Yet dominant power invariably fails: the Roman Empire is no more, and the glory of the conquests and colonialisms that shaped the world from the sixteenth to the twentieth centuries has by and large ended. True hope reminds us that the dominant form of globalization that marks our age and promotes top-down power can be expected to meet a similar fate.[13]

Obedience, in the context of Jesus's history, is thus not a matter of seeking death, as theologians have often argued. The popular claim that "Jesus was born to die" might claim some reference to Philippians' "obedience to the point of death," but something else appears to be at stake here. Jesus's obedience to God takes on a particular form in his life and ministry, in his message of the kingdom of God and of good news to the poor, in his healings, and in his work of organizing the people ("follow me" (Mk. 1.17)). Jesus's obedience is not the moribund desire to die; obedience is an active way of life that is ready to face the consequences, including death. And the consequences for a life embodying an alternative hope that contradicts the dominant hope of the Roman Empire and the supporting establishment religion are not hard to envision: such alternative hope became so real and so dangerous that it had to be defeated, "to the point of death."

Parallel to the Moses traditions, there are many efforts to assimilate this budding hope as soon as it emerges. Some interpret the passage in Philippians 2 in terms of triumphalism. Jesus's *kenosis*, it is assumed, has a "happy ending," just like mainline Christianity in the United States considers Easter to be the "happy ending" of a temporarily lost battle on Good Friday. Philippians 2.9–11 concludes the *kenosis* passage quoted in the beginning in this way: "Therefore God also highly exalted him and gave him the name that is above every name, so that at the name of Jesus every knee should bend, in heaven and on earth and under the earth, and every tongue should confess that Jesus Christ is Lord, to the glory of God the Father." Might this mean that Jesus is Lord just like all the other lords, beginning with Caesar, whose official title was "lord?"

The exaltation, which follows the *kenosis* of the day laborer in construction, needs to be seen on the backdrop of the history of dominant lordship in the Roman Empire. Was God's incarnation in Jesus, the day laborer in construction, a mistake or a meaningless accident of history? Was this day laborer eventually exalted according to the model of the Roman emperor? If this is indeed the exaltation into the top floors of the empire or of the corporations, Philippians 2.9–11 amounts to the negation of the existence of the day laborer. But the logic of Jesus's incarnation, life, ministry, death, and resurrection points in a different direction: the last who will be the first embody a different power and a different hope. If the greatest in the kingdom of God are those who serve (9.33–37), power and glory need to be redefined. Here lies the real hope for day laborers and their friends; everything else is pie in the sky, as the position of the emperor or the CEO must always remain the position of the few, never of the many.

The logic of downturn and Paul

In the world of the Roman Empire, hope is defined by the success of the emperor, who is confessed as Lord and Son of God. This hope has been mistakenly linked to the hope of the apostle Paul, who is described as a Roman citizen in the book of Acts and whose mission is often said to have been supported by the infrastructure of the Roman Empire, including the opportunities it afforded for travel.

Nevertheless, it is hard to deny that Paul found himself in ongoing conflict with the Roman Empire, constantly in and out of its prisons (2 Cor. 11.23), brutally beaten (2 Cor. 11.23), and probably executed by it. According to Marcus Borg and John Dominic Crossan, Paul's recollection that he was beaten with rods (2 Cor. 11.25) calls into question whether he held Roman citizenship, as Roman citizens were not to be subjected to this particular punishment.[14] Whether he was a citizen or not, Paul was painfully aware of the abuses of the Roman Empire and the fate of those who did not comply with it. There is little doubt that he experienced the logic of downturn in his own body.

In a world where the emperor claimed the title lord, calling Christ lord must have been dangerous. Why would Paul maintain this practice, if he could have used alternative titles? There is growing agreement among scholars that when Paul proclaims the lordship of Christ, he rejects the lordship of the Roman emperor in the same breath.[15] The separation of religion and politics, according to which Christ might have been lord over matters of religion and the emperor might have been lord over matters of politics, was not an option in the ancient world. Rome did not allow for the separation of religion and politics, as it sought to rule over religion just as much as over politics, and neither did Jewish-Christian theological thought, because God was seen as ruler over the whole world and not just over matters of religion.[16]

No matter what privileges Paul might have enjoyed at some points in his life, with his conversion to Christianity he took the side of the God of the crucified Jesus Christ, whom he understood to have called those who were not wise, not powerful, and not of noble birth: "But God chose what is foolish in the world to shame the wise; God chose what is weak in the world to shame the strong; God chose what is low and despised in the world, things that are not, to reduce to nothing things that are" (1 Cor. 1.27–28). This is no abstract theological claim. In Paul's ministry, this theology amounts to an act of solidarity that contradicts the logic of the empire. No wonder that the empire struck back, an experience that continues to be made even today by those who keep taking the side of the underdogs.[17]

Key theological notions in Paul's theology provide us with a fresh understanding of the alternative hope that he proclaimed in opposition to what he understood to be the false hope of the Roman Empire. His theology of justification is a case in point. Whereas the justice of the Roman Empire supported those in positions of privilege and wealth—a form of justice that is quite common in neoliberal capitalism where the lawyers of the corporations tend to maintain the upper hand—the justice of God supported those who were not able to support themselves: "For we hold that a person is justified by faith apart from works prescribed by the law" (Rom. 3.28). What is at stake here is not just a religious transaction but a way of life that includes everything; like Roman justice, God's justice comprises matters of religion, politics, economics, etc. If Paul wanted to talk about an exclusive religious transaction, he might have chosen other theological terms that were not as loaded politically and economically as the terms of justice and justification.

Hope is built, therefore, not on the privilege of the Roman Empire but on the solidarity of God in Christ: "Therefore, since we are justified by faith, we have peace with God through our Lord Jesus Christ, through whom we have obtained access to this grace in which we stand; and we boast in our hope of sharing the glory of God" (Rom. 5.1–2). While the full implications of this often-debated aspect of Paul's theology are commonly overlooked when theology is done in a context of privilege, theologians working on the margins have taken note, particularly in Latin America.[18] The subject matter at hand—hope that moves from the bottom-up rather than from the top-down—is experienced today by many others who do not have access to such interpretations of Paul.

Paul knows that the glory of God is manifest in suffering for the reign of God: "We also boast in our sufferings, knowing that suffering produces endurance, and endurance produces character, and character produces hope, and hope does not disappoint us, because God's love has been poured into our hearts through the Holy Spirit that has been given to us" (Rom. 5.3–5). Hope, according to this passage, is not a matter of the emotional high that people experience in so-called mountain-top experiences; rather, it grows out of the character that is developed in situations of downturn. For Paul, this was experienced in the communities of the early Christian churches that were not narrowly religious but provided a new way of life. For good reasons, the book of Acts calls Christians the "people of the way" (9.2, 19.9, and several other places) and gives reports of early Christian solidarity (2, 4).

Today, the hope that Paul talks about, growing out of suffering, is at work in communities who embrace suffering and struggle against it. The Christian base communities in Latin America have often been cited as examples, and it is inspiring to know that many of them are alive and well despite the fact that they had to endure great adversity, not least of all from the churches themselves; but there are similar communities around the world, found in Pentecostal and Evangelical traditions as well as in some mainline denominations. The liberation theologies that are rooted in these groups are transformed as the movements are transformed, but they are alive and well, even in the United States.[19] This may well be the greatest miracle of all.

Conclusions

For true hope to emerge, the unsustainable hopes of the status quo need to shatter. Both free-market economics and free-market religion have built some successful organizations that have done some good and have benefited some people, but they are increasingly failing to benefit the majority. In the current economic climate, the one percent's shares continue to grow, while the 99 percent are left behind.[20] The same is true for the religious climate, where the preachers of prosperity have benefited and built huge enterprises. To be sure, some of the followers of the Gospel of Prosperity also struck it rich, but the Gospel of Prosperity is unlikely to lift the masses out of poverty. In the process, mainline Christianity is losing credibility as well. Although it does not proclaim the message of prosperity as blatantly, by not providing alternatives to a system that benefits the few rather than the many, it becomes complicit with it.

If the false hope promoted here were merely not producing results, we might move on to the next thing. Unfortunately, the promotion of false hope results in the victims being blamed for their misfortune. In economics, the belief that anyone can make it results in the dismissal of those who fail to make it and who have fallen on hard times. This mechanism is internalized to such a degree that the unemployed often blame themselves for losing their jobs rather than looking at the deeper roots of the problem. Those unfortunate souls do not even seem worthy of support from the community, as unemployment benefits end fairly quickly and continue to be cut. In religion, those who are not successful, healthy, and wealthy are likely to be seen as the ones who are less faithful and committed. Here, too, the fault is found with those for whom the dominant hope does not materialize, and no alternative empowerment is provided.

True hope, by contrast, never blames the victims. Just the opposite: true hope is tested where people fall through the cracks in terms of what difference it makes in the lives of those who need it the most. As a result, true hope can never be a grand concept pronounced by those who are better off. Telling the person who is struggling that things will be better in the future (whether in a couple of years or decades, as economists claim, or after death, as religionists have so often asserted) only makes things worse. True hope in this context is what encourages people to keep fighting and to organize, as they realize that hope emerges from the struggle and that this is the place where they are most likely to find God at work. Is this not also the message of the Exodus, the Exile, of Jesus, and of Paul?

Journey from Optimism to Hope

David Burrell, C.S.C.

Timothy Radcliffe has called optimism the "bastard stepchild" of hope. Yet, does not that presume we know what authentic hope would be like? I have come to realize that when we Americans use "hope" we regularly mean "optimism." There are cultural reasons for this, and in exploring some of them, we may catch a glimpse of the genuine article. But no more than a glimpse, as Augustine noted in the end of Book 7 of the *Confessions*, when he spied the path ahead but had yet to traverse it, painfully aware of its treacherous pitfalls. I shall attempt to show how the passage from optimism to hope will involve suffering, and what makes it a journey is that we are as confused about the meaning of "suffering" as we are about that of hope. Yet it also seems that unless such a journey will become part of one's life, we risk losing hope altogether.

The letter to the Romans speaks of Abraham "hoping against hope" (4.18), first for the birth of a son, and then for that same son's life when Abraham felt constrained, as his father, to fulfill the Lord's command to sacrifice him on an altar on Mount Moriah. Yet "hoping against hope" accentuates perfectly the ambiguities in the term that I have tried to temper by distinguishing "optimism" from "hope," as French distinguishes between *espérance* and *éspoir*. That it will prove impossible to legislate linguistic proprieties, however, is significant in itself, suggesting that the shift from optimism to hope, profound as it is, may often be invisible. Yet Aristotle distinguished "natural" from "acquired" virtues, innate character traits from those that require effort and training, intimating that spontaneous ones should not really be called "virtues" at all. That may help us trace a line between optimism and hope, once experience brings us to feel the difference.

Years resident in Tantur, a Christian ecumenical institute on the seam between Jerusalem and Bethlehem, between Israel and Palestine, brought me into daily contact with the oppression inherent in administering an occupation, and the way Palestinians endure it patiently. Something I did not feel I could, for I would bristle at the humiliations meted out to my friends, yearning to find ways to remedy the injustice involved. Yet my attitude was on a par with the reactions I regularly heard from Americans on returning home: "When are they going to solve that problem over there?" Notice how we Americans will try to turn everything into a problem we can solve! So I tried to focus my interlocutors on the key expression: "problem." What if it is not a "problem" that can be solved, but something more intractable: something that involves our common humanity so we cannot neatly detach it and solve it? What if each of the peoples involved are confronting *suffering*, which they cannot escape and which is enduring or undergoing? Problems can be confronted and inspected, whereas we need to live through intractable situations. In a similar way, I would ask myself how I could possibly "cope with" what my Palestinian friends endure daily? But "cope with" elicits a similar strategy: keep whatever it is at arm's length so we can "deal with" it. Neither of these commonplace expressions leaves room for "suffering," yet they are the forms of speech ready to hand in western society. What is going on? What does our language reveal about us?

Heidegger called it "instrumental reason," and it works much of the time, yet interestingly enough, not when we ourselves are involved; hence, the term "instrumental." Think of marriage or any intimate relationship: it has to be self-involving for both parties or it is not a relationship at all. And of course, for one or the other to come to realize they are not in fact "involved" signals the end of the marriage. So the way to genuine hope will have to be self-involving; detached calculation is of another order. Yet since hope inevitably involves "the future," that is, what may or may not come to be, we may approach it as a form of prediction, assessing probabilities, exhibiting yet another type of instrumental reason, usually illustrated by "linear projections." Yet the entire enterprise of linear projecting readily reveals its inherent weakness for "dealing with the future," as we naively put it. One or two variables are isolated for scrutiny over a previous stretch of time, and then used to extrapolate what could happen, given what has happened. As fragile as this procedure patently is, it should be equally clear that the entire enterprise is questionable, for the central presumption has to be that all the other variables remain fixed. Yet the one thing we can know a priori is that anything can happen with the remaining variables; contingency reigns. Yet we are willing to suppress this common-sense observation in the interest of "planning," so linear projects offer the best tools we have.

At this point, we may be ready to follow the psalmist's injunction to "trust in the Lord" (Ps. 37.3). Yet accustomed as we are to instrumental reason, we may be tempted to substitute formulas for a trusting relationship to the Lord, like "the Lord will reward those faithful to Him." Yet the book of Job nullifies any impersonal calculation regarding the ways of God. So invoking the psalmist's injunction to trust will inevitably fail without a profound shift in perspective. How might that take place? Let us reflect for a moment on all that goes into trusting another person, which has to be the most salient form of trust we know. First of all, there is a studied perspicacity regarding persons, and notably this person. Socrates reminds us that trusting blindly cannot but lead to despising others, since we cannot but feel "taken." Yet who is to blame, he asks? Had we used our common sense, we would have realized that the one we trusted was not trustworthy. In his terms, "misology" cannot but lead to misanthropy: failure to use our reason can put us at odds with all human beings, yet the fault is not theirs but ours. So there is no substitute for perspicacity, yet that too has to be learned, and usually learned the hard way.

So we need to learn whom to trust, and then cultivate the relationships we can test, to learn how to live in that trust. Could it also be that way with "the Lord?" That is, learning to discriminate between a fruitful and an ersatz relationship with the transcendent. And that is precisely what the celebrated "spiritual exercises" of Ignatius seek to accomplish, usually and paradigmatically with another who can help us to negotiate the sinuous ways of discernment. So we cannot even imagine trusting without friends, and friends appropriate to each stage of trust. One is reminded of Dante's journey of discovery out of crippling perplexity, negotiated most of the way with the discerning guide, Virgil, yet at the very end none would do except his virginal loved one, Beatrice. Yet here the ladder allowing us to mount from human trust to trust in God cannot be anchored in Beatrice herself, but in a Beatrice whose gaze has been diverted from Dante to the living God. So the only persons we can really trust will themselves have to be rooted in God; there can be no other way once we are able to acknowledge that all is grace, gift. If that seems circular, it is, for trust, like faith, can only be received, yet once received it can become the air we breathe. That explains why faith and hope are considered to be theological virtues, given to us rather than something we can induce or work up ourselves. So there will be no "self-help" manuals to teach us how to trust; the grammar will be quite different.

Yet we must still ask: how can one be inducted into that grammar? Try René Girard: by imitating those whom we admire for having made the switch, though they may not have needed to switch at all; their culture may have never been distracted with optimism. Learning, as best we can, how to "go with the flow," letting the edge one has acquired from years of knowing how things ought to be ceded to the way they are. For the persistent corollary of a pervasive optimism must be zest for improving what is, for optimism is endemically tied to a better world in the offing; indeed, one that we can forge. Yet while the optimist will be tempted to regard "going with the flow" as an irresponsible form of "fatalism," some practice—usually in the company with others—may open doors leading to marvelous discoveries that augur a more realistic relating to what is.

I am suggesting that a cultural shift can more effectively open us to ways of grace than pious exhortation or theological reflection. That proved to be the case for me in moving to Rome to study, to become forcibly aware how Protestant my sensibilities had been. Not all bad, of course, nor will much of it ever leave me, but to become aware that there can be other ways of relating to the world, and to name these ways "catholic" proved immensely liberating—like discovering who I truly was, and now wanted to become. I am reminded of a Danish friend who freely translated herself into a Palestinian family, where the mother became her second mother well before the son became her spouse. She came to welcome a new world, savoring its richness, yet never ceased to embody tidy Scandinavian virtues. All this suggests that "identity" is often multiple, belying what that unnaturally fixed term—"identity"—connotes. We may be manager to our employees, friend or lover to those close to us, or absentee parent to our children. We can be all of those things at once, certainly, yet awakening to feeling the gaps between them can allow novelty into our lives, a convenient aperture for grace. The most obvious example of this can be found in American students spending time in another culture, forcing them to move from a comfortable position in "the most powerful nation on earth" to share the lives of others never so afflicted. Before long they may come to prefer their new culture and seek to appropriate it as best they can.

As already noted, for me the change began, and is still going on—instrumental reason is always on tap!—thanks to a combined intercultural and interfaith stimulus. Palestinians taught me suffering as a way of life, as Muslims there and in east Bengal taught me *tawakkul*: trust in God, moving me to translate al-Ghazali's axial treatise (from his "Summa Theologiae"—*Ihya' Ulum ad-Din, Kitab at-Tawhid wa Tawakkul*, as *Al-Ghazali on Faith in Divine Unity and Trust in Divine* (Louisville, KY: Fons Vitae, 2000). Jean-Pierre de Caussade had explored "abandonment to divine providence" in the eighteenth century, delivered to us in an engaging translation by Kitty Muggeridge: *Sacrament of the Present Moment* (San Francisco: Harper and Row, 1989). But it was the ubiquity of "*in sh'Allah!*" in ordinary Muslim discourse, inspired by the Qur'anic injunction to always use "God willing" when speaking of the future: what might or might not happen; much as can be found in the west of Ireland. I explore the affinity between these two spiritual writers in *Towards a Jewish-Christian-Muslim Theology* (Oxford: Wiley-Blackwell, 2011), but the references simply gesture to the worlds that can open as we are drawn into unfamiliar ways, yet find there the One, the God, if you will, that has been drawing us all along.

Put more generally, intercultural exchange can produce a salutary "cognitive dissonance," through which new worlds may begin to appear. Recall how translation to Rome opened me to a Catholic culture that led me to affirm myself as Catholic in a completely new way—precisely by realizing how Protestant my American Catholicism had been. Anyone who had asked me before if I were Catholic would have received an affirmative response, but now I knew better what it was like really to be "Catholic," if you will. Indeed, religious traditions are inescapably imbedded in culture; in fact, some prominent Americans have become Catholic in Italy, as the culture they encountered opened them to a fresh sense of that reality. And, one might also say, some cultures seem more attuned to the riches of the Christian tradition than others. In fact, that is the precise way *mission* contributes to the growth of a tradition: once we realize that it is pointless to think of bringing our Christ to a strange culture, when that very culture has the potential of directing us to a fresh appreciation of Jesus! It should be clear by now that I am stuttering: trying to convey—with intercultural parallels—what it is to allow oneself to become de-centered: to shift one's *modus operandi* from calculation to reception, from planning to gift. How can we describe the way learning to relying on gifts rather than on one's own ingenuity turns things upside down? Much like falling in love, of course, which is how the eminently cerebral Catholic theologian, Bernard Lonergan, came to describe the onslaught of grace in one's life: "falling in love with God." Things will never be the same afterward. Trust will accompany one like a buoyant jet stream, facilitating what used to require assiduous planning.

So as optimism shows itself to be empty, the accidental issue of a series of contingencies that can easily collapse, as we can feel as the United States unravels from the "land of opportunity" to a lightly masked oligarchy whose actual face showed itself in the financial meltdown, space opens for an expressly theological hope. No one can predict whether they will enter that space, of course, for we are in a new field of grace, yet it does happen, it has happened, so it can happen. That is the most we can say of the critical transition from optimism to hope. May it happen to each of us, for otherwise it seems impossible to negotiate the times in which we live while remaining conscious and responsible. No one wants to live in denial, but without the grace of authentic hope, there seems no alternative today.

Afterword: What Shape Does Hope Take When Loss Is Embodied in Death?

Fulata L. Moyo

Narrative of loss

When my husband, Solomon Jon Moyo, died on the evening of Thursday, April 22, 1999, I could not believe that life could still go on as if nothing tragic had happened. It felt as if a heavy dark cloud of loss and hopelessness had enveloped my whole life and cut me off from any hope for continued living. For the first time, I had an epiphany into Miss Havisham, a character from Charles Dickens's *The Great Expectations*.[1] As many will remember, Miss Havisham allowed Compeyson's betrayal of her to mark the rest of her life: she stopped all the clocks at 20 minutes to 9, the moment when she learned that her betrothed had left. I wanted to stop everything surrounding my life at 19 hours when Solomon breathed his last and "condemned" me to widowhood and its reproach. Why were people still being heard laughing; cars still buzzing past my alienated house; and people still planning holidays and having fun? Didn't they know that my husband and intimate friend for 13 years was no more and that my life had suddenly come to a standstill? Or was there anything that could reverse this hopeless loss to something more positive?

In this afterword, loss is perceived in terms of the death of an intimate companion and it is shared through narrative discourse. I share from my heart the experience that deeply and painfully epitomized loss to me. I will reflect on how the death of a beloved one can be a hopeless loss despite the African religious understanding of the living-dead where death is just a transition from one state of living to another with a sense that the "dead" are actually still presently alive among their communities of the physically living. In my case, my husband Solomon's death felt like he had been completely cut off from me. I am using narrative discourse because narrative itself becomes part of the process of building hope, since:

> Telling our stories helps us (start) engaging in dialogue with others . . . relat(ing) personal hurt and (the) search for healing . . . provid(ing) other perspectives that . . . enrich our own; . . . reflecting on them in dialogue with . . . others . . . help(ing) us shift from positions of helplessness as victims to being agents who make a contribution to theologies of life and wholeness; and the act of narration

(moreover) is in itself therapeutic. In other words, the telling of painful stories helps us embark on the process of "narrative therapy" for health (and hope).[2]

These reflections flow into three sections. The first section deals briefly with the understanding of hope within the religious context in which my loss happened. The next section takes the reader back to the struggle of accepting loss as part of the struggle toward hope. This is deliberate because at this first level, in the first section, hope can be conceived in terms of an unmerited and gratuitous gift, which is embodied in the sense of a divine presence that accompanied me in my state of shock, denial, and anger as part of grieving—an inevitable response when loss happens.

The second section deals with the second and third stages of grieving death as loss. It captures the transition from the unquestioning faith in a divine whose presence can be said to have been sensed experientially, to the spiritual crisis characterized by spiritual dryness. Such dryness occurs when the process of grieving moves on to a combination of anger and depression before the journey toward acceptance of loss. Such loss, as part of a spiritual journey, can be conceived in terms of reaching a sense of wholeness or a kind of "union with God." Using the language of mystics like St John of the Cross, fruition from the purification of the soul comes through the "dark night of the soul."[3]

During my grief from the loss of my husband—while I cannot identify with Elisabeth Kübler-Ross's myth of the five stages of grieving in the order that they are listed[4]—I can identify each of the five being part of my grieving, especially the first year after my husband died. After experiencing shock, denial, and anger in a recurring spiral, I was later in that same first year, thrown into a dry spell of doubt. This period was characterized by many unanswered and unasked questions especially in the face of my community who had surrounded me during the first weeks of my loss but moved on because their lives had to return to its own rhythm and demands.

This reality of walking through the desert of my life is also compared to the Jungian[5] psychological analysis of "owning the shadow" as the possibility of accepting my loss as an epitome of hope. Finally, there will be short, tying-in remarks exploring the added tension and suspense of living in this paradox as hope: for how long? Can such hope last? Is there room for a possibility of loving again for a widow that is told that God has become her husband?

Hope: Trusting in someone greater than you

In "A Narrative Theology of Eschatological Hope as Healing,"[6] I used the Christian teaching of eschatology as it seemed to bring an initial sense of healing after the death of my husband. This sense was immensely elevated by the encouraging words that I seemed to hold tightly to at a time when my grief manifested itself in a roller coaster of disbelieving shock, denial, and anger. As I wrote:

> ... this hope consists not only in the *parousia* (future event) nor "as something which has already taken place in the confrontation of the believers with *kerygma*

(proclamation)" (McGrath 2001, 632), it consists rather in our calling and mission to transform the world. This hope encourages us to find new meanings and expressions in life even after bereavement . . . another aspect of that hope might be our ability to create a safe space for the expression of emotional frustrations, whether to God or to those who are therapeutically journeying with us.[7]

This was especially possible because this hope was mainly embodied by the presence of friends, family members, and community who surrounded me. This was the first indicator that life had to go on. Being an African Christian within the context where the Christian faith coexists with my African Traditional Religion and Culture, and in which my African worldview holistically embraces the sacred and secular, I received comforting counsel from all those around me. These comforting words were mainly expressed through the media of song, chanted prayers, and reflective interpretation of written and oral sacred texts giving me reasons why I was not expected to respond to death as if I was without hope. I was even told that with the death of Solomon, God had become my husband; the ever loving, present, powerful, and faithful God was my intimate companion, a father to my otherwise fatherless children. What widowhood needs were they envisioning when imaging God as my husband? At that point of fresh, sizzling pain of loss, I had no capacity to engage my critical analysis further. I desperately imbibed their encouraging words as an intoxicating healing drink offered by the caring community that was reaching out to help remove my pain. They meant to give me hope so that I could allow the image of God to embody the basis of my trust and as the foundation of hope for the future.

After I came back from the village where Solomon's remains were laid to rest, friends and family's accompaniment was still very important to me, even as they had to focus on their own rhythm of life and therefore could not spend as much time as I would have loved. In *Why Me?*, Erika Schuchardt shows through her analysis of more than 2,000 life stories, biographies of persons in crisis from many different social and geographical contexts. Her narratives and analysis show how important support and accompaniment are for healing and wholeness. She uses "Theology of Life Stories" and demonstrates how persons in a crisis through professional accompaniment enriched by spirituality, religion, and culture can journey toward healing and become part of a free and truly human community of hope.

According to Schuchardt, this journeying together with the suffering can be positively supported by family and friends as in the case of my story. The basis of whether their accompaniment is a source of care in a major way depends on whether they are prepared to actively listen to the afflicted and be of practical help in everyday life, assuring the sufferer that they are not alone. Taking time to listen also bears the important assuring and dignity-enhancing message that they are still a complete and valuable person. In my case, such accompaniment could also mean that they are able to bear with my fears, questions, deficiencies, and helplessness without judging me or trying to superficially console me out of my suffering.

Mutual vulnerability as stepping stones to hope

The solidarity of my friends and family became even more meaningful as hope-building, when those accompanying me dared to embark on mutual vulnerability. As a relational resource, it made clear to me, as the accompanied, that my doubts and fears were actually also their doubts and fears. It was the admitting of their own helpless vulnerability that made their accompaniment more real, authentic, and credible to me. It was like they were giving me permission to wrestle with my questions, doubts, and fears. I felt that it was not abnormal to ask God questions and even seem to accuse God in all honesty, as my own return to the same God (through those accompanying me) did not reject me or judge me. Rather I was cared for and accompanied on this journey of loss back to hope for a better future.

For hope in the context of religion can be understood in terms of having *something or someone* to trust in. It was not the image of God as husband that gave me hope because that would have been problematic with the sexual implication of some husbandly duties. It was rather the understanding that my trust in a relational and vulnerable God who allowed to be embodied in those who physically accompanied me was always present and was reaching out to me even with their own vulnerabilities, even weeping with me sometimes. This God was not some unapproachable King that confined ("his")self to the inaccessible thrones pathetically trying to control everyone else. This compassionate God was always there holding my hand and allowing my tears to soak God's own heart. When I was bawling my eyes out in so much pain and anguish, this Divine presence had a way of warming the coldness of my tears and soothing the heat of my pain with such a gentle touch and a deep understanding whisper that seemed to say: "I love and understand you. Trust me to journey with you to your wholeness." What a soothing presence of hope!

In Dickens's Miss Havisham, it is not the above religious perspective of hope as trusting in something or someone but rather her appetite for vengeance what gave her hope in a context where otherwise she was surrounded by dilapidation. Through Estella's beauty and enticement, Miss Havisham hoped to gain a sense of reparation for the pain she experienced. How can vengeance be hope? In her case it could be the sense of paying back, a reversal that restorative justice discourse espouses. Unlike the above understanding of reparation that is meant to contribute to healing and reconciliation, to Miss Havisham, Compeyson the jilter was embodied in all male humanity whatever their affluence or lack of. She looked forward with great expectation to those moments when Estella, her protégée, would break the heart of a man. Even when she knew what the outcome would be, she advised Pip coldly: "Love her, love her, love her! If she favours you, love her. If she wounds you, love her. If she tears your heart to pieces—and as it gets older and stronger, it will tear deeper—love her, love her, love her!" (29.85).

Can real hope be manifested through the cold shackles of revenge? If it does not liberate, bring rays of a better tomorrow, or promise wholeness, can it still parade as hope?

Living in the paradox as hope

As time went on, the sense of my loss grew deeper and with life having turned to normal for the rest of my community, I felt like I was in the wilderness of my own heart-rending thoughts and unanswered and unasked questions. I seemed to lose the sense of presence of the basis of my trust. The ever faithful and powerful presence of God could not be sensed anymore. God was silent; my soul was passing through the dark night with no light to illuminate the way. I did not know what or whom to trust in anymore. Death and loss were the only continuous companions I had. I could not suppress the reality of my loss nor the fact that death had physically taken my husband and best friend away and therefore nothing could rectify that. Even when I tried to put up a brave public face about this, the emotional outbursts had no warning as to when and where they would manifest. I needed to find a way of making conscious this painful reality and use it for my enhancement of hope. I had to find a way of embracing this loss in a way that it could bring out hope in the tension of light and shadow: loss for my healing and a way of healing others in similar situations. I had to find a way of "knowing" and accepting loss through death so as to be able to coexist with it positively. Such immense presences seemed to speak to me of the possibility that I could only reach God by finding a way to embrace the two that had become my shadow as my husband would not come back to this life. Rather it was the possibility that in the face of such painful loss, I could still find strength to invest positively into my work and life of those around me. Jungian psychologists like Robert A. Johnson talk of embracing or owning the shadow. My pain of my loss brought a level of vulnerability that I embraced as part of my relational resource to reach out to others in pain for our healing together. It helped enhance the other qualities in my personality so that I could dare to have strength in pain, beauty in the ashes of loss, and the possibility of light embracing the shadow, as evidence of its substantial visibility. Going further, I could strive to reach the ability to live within the tension of the pain of loss and still trust God's presence and light even when my soul was so much in the dark and totally overwhelmed with the reality of pain and loss.

How then, to allow faith to be the assurance of things hoped for even when I could not see beyond loss and pain? In the language of grieving, how does one transcend depression to reach acceptance of this loss through death so as to work toward healing as wholeness? I needed to come to a point where I could embrace this "dark night" my soul was enveloped in as actually God's gift that purifies me and makes me ready for intimate union with my God. This is not a progression that can be seen in a linear motion from loss to hope but rather a journey of discernment into the possibility of existing in the paradox of loss and hope, sometimes painfully knowing that you cannot have one without the other. Loss and hope have to overlap into each other so as to provide a space of coexistence—the only space where wholeness is possible. In mystic spirituality, this dark night of the soul is not like a temporal tunnel that one hopes to bypass or rush through, but is a necessary purification for the soul. It is an undeserved and rare favor, which if the soul gets, should take as long as necessary to indwell, leading to the yearned for union with the holy God.

To prevent any confusion here, I should clarify that the death of my husband was not strictly a gift from God because I would never want to believe in such a cruel God whose idea of a gift is to inflict pain. The divine gift is rather the successful process of and ability to accept such pain as an inevitable happening, which necessarily dragged my life's journey through a reflective purification process. Unlike the continuous, echoed misconceptions in the name of encouragement that I kept on receiving: "accept it as God's will," my process of accepting this painful loss was not because "God gives and God takes, blessed be God's name-Amen!" Rather, it was the ability to overcome depression and move toward acceptance in my grieving process. The gift was being able to embrace this loss as a shadow that can contribute to my wholeness and not the occurrence of death itself.

Loss and hope: Two sides of the same coin?

While loss can take so many other expressions apart from death, my story shows that whatever manifestation hope bears, it has to lead to healing and wholeness. It cannot be negatively about revenge and therefore a threat to life and wholeness. So while in Miss Havisham's case her desire to cause pain to men through Estella cannot in essence be hope, her dying realization of the pain she had been part of and Pip's growth into a better person could qualify as hope. Hope is more sustainable when it is born as a coexistent ally to loss because life's reality occurs in the tension of light and darkness, the shadow and the ego. When someone experiences loss through the death of a beloved, the vehicle to lasting and growing hope could be the mutual vulnerable accompaniment of family and friends. Somehow hope seems to be reached when life is lived holistically in the paradox or tension with loss.

This publication speaks to the tension of loss and hope in deeper ways than my story alone can sufficiently articulate. One clear connecting thread is how loss has to either coexist with, or be preceded by, genuine—and not cheap—hope for life to be livable in a meaningful way in the face of pain and violence. In a similar regard, each piece is a daring gem that speaks to this struggle in individual experiences as well as collective national struggles. Together the volume brings a holistic discourse that charts loss and hope within its various nuances and complexities. Amidst loss' tendency to talk more about deprivation and hope about looking forward to a better life, the work highlights the tension of both coexisting in life, thus making their explorations particularly vital.

Notes

Introduction

1 Katherine Boo, *Behind the Beautiful Forevers: Life, Death, and Hope in a Mumbai Undercity* (New York: Random House, 2012), 244.
2 Christian Meier, *A Culture of Freedom: Ancient Greece and the Origins of Europe*, trans. Jefferson Chase (Oxford: Oxford University, 2011), 102.
3 Thucydides, *History of the Peloponnesian War*, trans. Rex Warner (London: Penguin, 1972), II.42 (149).
4 Eugenia Semyonovna Ginzburg, *Journey into the Whirlwind*, trans. Paul Stevenson and Max Hayward (San Diego: Harvest, 1995), 100.
5 Dalai Lama, *Beyond Religion: Ethics for a Whole World* (Boston: Houghton Mifflin Hardcourt, 2011), 31.
6 Fyodor Dostoevsky, *Memoirs from the House of the Dead*, trans. Jessie Coulson (Oxford: Oxford University, 2008), 18.
7 Halim Bashir, with Damien Lewis, *Tears of the Desert: A Memoir of Survival in Darfur* (New York: Oneworld, 2008), 216.
8 See Irving Greenberg, "Dialectic Living and Thinking: Wiesel as Storyteller and Interpreter of the Shoah," in *Elie Wiesel: Jewish, Literary, and Moral Perspectives*, edited by Steven T. Katz and Alan Rosen (Bloomington and Indianapolis: Indiana University, 2013), 173–189.
9 Emmanuel Ringelblum, *Notes from the Warsaw Ghetto*, ed. and trans. Jacob Sloan (New York: Schocken, 1958), 296.
10 See, for example, Yehuda Bauer, *Rethinking the Holocaust* (New Haven and London: Yale University, 2001), 214.
11 Jürgen Matthäus, ed., *Approaching an Auschwitz Survivor: Holocaust Testimony and Its Transformations* (Oxford: Oxford University, 2009), 110.
12 Jonathan Lear, *Radical Hope: Ethics in the Face of Cultural Devastation* (Cambridge, MA: Harvard University, 2006), 103.

Chapter 1

1 Asociación Civil El Periscopio, *Del otro lado de la mirilla: Olvidos y Memorias de ex Presos Políticos de Coronda 1974–1979* (Santa Fé: El Periscopio, 2003), 26: "Creo que lo más difícil de la tarea que nos propusimos reside en que la escritura es fundamentalmente un hecho individual, y nosotros pretendemos escribir un libro en forma colectiva." This and all other English translations of the quoted texts are mine.
2 Jorge Semprun, *Literature or Life*, trans. Linda Coverdale (New York: Viking, 1997), 13.
3 *Del otro lado*, 244: "Porque a decir verdad, ellos querían volvernos locos, calculada y sistemáticamente." His name is not disclosed in the book, but for reasons to be discussed later in this chapter, former prisoner and editorial team member José

Luis Hisi Páez revealed to me that those pages were written by Destéfanis. Personal communication. June 19, 2010.

4　Personal communication. July 24, 2010: "¡Allí, en la mutual Torquato Tasso, en 1999, fue la primera gran convocatoria! Esperábamos 60, llegaron como 600."

5　Argentina's most recent dictatorship (1976–1983) disappeared about 30,000 people, mostly political dissidents, their families, and friends. Survivors were rarely released. After our time in secret detention centers, the regime usually sent us to maximum security prisons.

6　John Beverly's term alludes to a testimonio "made up of accounts by different participants in the same event" ["The Margin at the Center: On Testimonio (Testimonial Narrative)]," in *The Real Thing. Testimonial Discourse and Latin America*, ed. Georg Gugelberger (Durham: Duke University, 1996), 28 [23–41].

7　Before the actual 1976 military coup, political power had shifted to sectors who facilitated it. Therefore in 1974, after the death of democratically elected Juan Domingo Perón, his wife—Vice-president María Estela Martínez de Perón (Isabelita)—supported the detention and torture of political dissidents at the hands for the armed forces, the police, and the paramilitary group Argentine Anticommunist Alliance (AAA).

8　For an extensive analysis of *Nosotras*, please see my article "Concealing God: How Argentine Women Political Prisoners Performed a Collective Identity," *Biography* 36.1 (Winter 2013): 214–242.

9　For an extended discussion of the role Liberation Theology, the Movement of Third World Priests (*Sacerdotes para el tercer mundo*), and the Base Communities (*Comunidades cristianas de base*), played in fighting for social justice and resisting dictatorships in Argentina, see Michael Burdick, *For God and Fatherland: Religion and Politics in Argentina* (Albany, NY: SUNY, 1995).

10　Personal communication. August 8, 2012. "Más o menos en el año 1998, desde antropólogos, Darío Olmo, convocó a algunas de nosotras . . . para que le narráramos nuestra vivencia en la cárcel ya que por los testimonios que habían tomado se evidenciaba una experiencia colectiva que tenía una gran importancia para ellos . . . Mariana venía de Europa y se había entrevistado con un sobreviviente de los campos de concentración nazis que le manifestó la importancia de la memoria, de escribir de contar . . . Ella tomó la propuesta y nos convocó para escribir el libro."

11　*Nosotras*, 8. For copious information in Spanish about these books, reviews, activities, and original documentation about Coronda, Villa Devoto, and other detention centers during the dictatorship, please visit the site created by the former political prisoners, Presos Políticos Argentinos.

12　Daniel Gorosito, sick and deprived of medical attention, was brutally murdered by the police after his transfer to another facility (*Del otro lado*, 193–198); Luis Alberto Hormaeche (ibid., 209–214) and Juan Carlos Voisard (ibid., 165–171) died due to lack of medical attention and medication for their high blood pressure, and Raúl Manuel San Martín died as a result of malpractice, after contracting meningitis (ibid., 239–241).

13　Translation published under the title *Steps under Water: A Novel*.

14　María del Carmen Sillato, author of *Diálogos de amor contra el silencio: Memorias de prisión, sueños de libertad*, suffered the cruel separation from her son, born in captivity, when she was transferred to the Buenos Aires prison. Others, like Carmen Cornes, who told her story to Beatriz López in *Hasta la victoria siempre . . . Testimonio de Carmen Cornes, emigrante gallega y militante de la vida*, had learned in captivity about the disappearance of their own child. Kozameh, Drago, and Lo Prete had been arrested and tortured under the rule of President María Estela Martínez de Perón while the military coup was in gestation. Drago published *Fragmentos de la Memoria: Recuerdos de una experiencia carcelaria (1975–1980)/Memory Tracks: Fragments from Prison (1975–1980)*; and Lo Prete's *Memorias de una presa política* was published posthumously under her prison alias La Lopre, after her suicide.

15 Other testimonial and literary texts produced by male former political prisoners have appeared in anthologies like María del Carmen Sillato's *Huellas*, the book *Eslabones*, concentrating on the experience of survivors from the Córdoba province, and most recently, *La risa no se rinde*, that includes excerpts from the Coronda narrative.

16 Personal communication. June 19, 2010: "En Buenos Aires, el compañero Bas y Mansilla consiguió un libro que fue casi el totem inspirador de los redactores: *La escritura o la vida*, del gran escritor y guionista español Jorge Semprún. Ese libro nos ayudó a comprender por qué era que nos juntábamos tantos años después a escribir el libro de Coronda! Y nos confirmó en el camino de la versión literaria."

17 Semprún, *Literature or Life*, 13.

18 I have further discussed these issues in "Cuando vienen matando: On Prepositional Shifts and the Struggle of Testimonial Subjects for Agency." *PMLA* 121.5 (October 2006): 1665–1669.

19 Personal communication. June 19, 2010: "Estoy recordando algo triste de los entretelones de la escritura del libro de Coronda. El que escribió las páginas mas brillantes del libro fue el compañero Corcho Destefanis . . . redactó con tal hermosura . . . que fue el único capítulo que entró directo al libro, sin correccion alguna, por consenso y decisión unánime de los que estábamos en la comision redactora! . . . y es uno de los textos con mas vuelo literario que se haya logrado. Y el Corcho era alguien que no se dedicaba a la literatura . . . Ese cumpa era el esposo de Silvia Suppo, la compañera. que fue asesinada hace poco en Rafaela. En ese momento me enteré que él ya había fallecido pocos meses antes de una enfermedad muy fea . . . El crimen de Silvia Suppo se 'aclaró' como un delito de robo, pero nadie cree en las coincidencias: ella era un testigo importante en los juicios por la verdad."

20 After her killing, security measures for all witnesses and survivors testifying in the trials were increased. When I went to testify on the case of the killings at The Little School, where I had been held captive, tortured, and disappeared, I was very aware of the risks and sought the protection of the Ministry of Justice.

21 *Del otro lado*, 53: "Sí, estoy de acuerdo con que hay que darle carnadura al sujeto, pero cuando le damos carnadura a este sujeto colectivo, se supone que estamos en acción, que somos militantes populares: estudiantes, campesinos, trabajadores, intelectuales . . . Un poco todo esto que vos planteabas. ¿Quiénes son estos tipos?. . . ¿por qué están en estas situaciones? Y ¿qué hicieron para que el plan de aniquilamiento de la dictadura en la cárcel de Coronda no diera tanto resultado?. . . Estos tipos ganaron la batalla, aunque perdieron la guerra . . ."

22 Ibid., 28: "Yo no sé si les conté o no, pero este escrito, del cuaderno mío . . . que es lo que recuerdo de mi experiencia, lo empecé a escribir cuando mis hijos eran chicos, pensando en mostrárselos, o contarles . . . lo que viví como parte de mi militancia en aquellos años. Ahora son adolescentes, y creo que va a ser muy lindo mostrarles en lugar de mi cuaderno, un libro que escribamos entre todos."

23 Personal communication. June 19, 2010: "Lo hicimos de la manera más entretenida posible: ¡la hermana de una alumna mía, una jovencita de 18 años, se lo leyó en un fin de semana, ni bien salió el libro! ¡Por supuesto que nosotros también nos divertimos un montón!"

24 Adolfo Pérez Esquivel, Prologue to *Del otro lado*, 11: "Este libro de ex prisioneros de Coronda, quienes decidieron después de varios años, reunirse y hacer memoria, aporta a la conciencia colectiva, rescata los valores humanos y la capacidad de resistencia frente a la opresión."

25 On each anniversary of this massacre, massive demonstrations take place to demand the closing of WHINSEC (Western Hemisphere Institute for Security Cooperation). This is the morphed version of the US military facility known as the School of the Americas (SOA), where some of the perpetrators, members of the Atlacatl Battalion, had been trained.

26 Ignacio Martín-Baró, *Writings for a Liberation Psychology*, trans. Tod Sloan (Cambridge: Harvard University, 1994), 26.

27 Peter Admirand, *Amidst Mass Atrocity and the Rubble of Theology: Searching for a Viable Theodicy* (Eugene, OR: Cascade, 2012), 63.

28 Martín-Baró, *Writings*, 143.

29 Personal communication. June 19, 2010: "Las autoridades querían imponer el aislamiento, la incomunicación y la ruptura de toda estructura organizativa."

30 Personal communication. June 29, 2010: ". . . me gustaría contarte . . . de mi experiencia en Coronda con la Iglesia, mas que nada con Zazpe, en ese entonces arzobispo de Santa Fe, muy jugado y muy apreciado por todos nosotros, a pesar de que muchos de nosotros no somos creyentes."

31 *Del otro lado*, 121: "Habló cuando todos callaban, incluídos tantos que tenían la obligación de hacerlo."

32 Ibid., 121: "Es justo también recordar a otros luchadores por los derechos humanos como los obispos Metodistas Carlos Gattinoni y Federico Pagura, y el rabino Marshal Meyer, quienes también presionaron y se jugaron por nosotros aunque sólo les permitieron visitas individuales. Y quizás algún que otro humilde cura o pastor, cuya memoria, injustamente, no hemos retenido."

33 Horacio Verbitsky, "Buenos Oficios," *Página* 12, July 22, 2012.

34 See Uki Goni, "Jorge Rafael Videla Convicted of Baby Thefts." *The Guardian*. July 5, 2012. http://www.guardian.co.uk/world/2012/jul/05/jorge-rafael-videla-convicted-baby-thefts.

35 ". . . le solicita la apertura de 'los archivos del Vaticano, de la iglesia argentina y de comunidades como el Movimiento Familiar Cristiano, donde monjas recibían niños de la dictadura militar y los daban en adopción'" ["El Papa a Estela de Carlotto: 'Cuenten conmigo.'" *Crónica*, April 24, 2013. http://www.cronica.com.ar/diario/2013/04/24/46064-el-papa-a-estela-de-carlotto-cuenten-conmigo.html].

36 Verbitsky's extensive research includes Mignone's sources and elaborates on Pope Francis's role. Of particular importance are his book *El Silencio* and his recent article "Cambio de piel."

37 Msgr. Angelelli's death in 1976 was promptly dismissed as a car accident. See Burdick, *For God and Fatherland*, 205, for a list of other priests assassinated in those days. Recently, the investigation was reopened and General Videla is one of the accused. At the time of his death, Angelelli was carrying evidence of the recent assassination of two priests from his diocese. See "Videla a juicio por el asesinato del obispo Angelelli," *El Nuevo Herald*, July 28, 2012.

38 *Del otro lado*, 177: "Llevo 97 días sin salir al recreo y no sé cuándo pisaré la tierra del patio. Son tantas las faltas cometidas—la última: tirar migas de pan a las palomas, que si no viene una amnistía del Papa, no sé cuándo saldré. Pero esas circunstancias a uno le agudizan la capacidad de observación, el tiempo disponible es un factor determinante para desarrollarla."

39 Personal communication. September 13, 2010: "Lo que es seguro es la correlación directa entre la entrada en la militancia 'Subversiva' con la participación previa en comunidades de base o experiencias en grupos ligados a la iglesia postconciliar en muchos de nosotros. Lo segundo, alianza milicos—sectores fachos eclesiásticos se cae de maduro y es ampliamente conocido . . ."

40 *Del otro lado,* 126: "Más preocupado por el presente que por el pasado, activo a pesar de sus años y muy compenetrado de la realidad . . . las desdichas de su gente . . ."

41 Ibid., 127: "Una de las cosas que realmente admiré de muchos es eso, por ejemplo los que sufrieron mucho en la cárcel, saben con quién hablar y hablan con aquellos, y son gente normal . . . Y justamente hacer memoria para que no se repita la historia, estamos viviendo la historia de salvación . . ."

42 Gottfired R. Bloch, *Unfree Associations: A Psychoanalyst Recollects the Holocaust* (Los Angeles: Red Hen, 2004), 3.

43 Ibid., 4.

44 *Del otro lado*, 262: "La trama de Steinbeck, jugó . . . un papel decisivo en la conservación de mi salud mental."

45 Ibid., 263: "Indudablemente todos elegimos todos los días ser o no ser Caín. Oprimir o asesinar o no al hermano."

46 Admirand, *Mass Atrocity*, 284.

47 "El periscopio . . . fue nuestra gran arma de combate . . . O sea, ante una realidad muy dura, de aislamiento, de mucha perversión, de tratar a la persona de llevarla a sus rincones más íntimos, digamos, para acercarlo a la locura, teníamos que confrontarlo con lo que teníamos, y eso significaba poder hacer algo en la celda, poder cantar, poder hablar con el compañero de la otra celda de al lado, hacer algo de gimnasia, comentar algún libro, una película. Entonces para eso necesitábamos algún instrumento que nos permitiera controlar el ingreso de los guardias al pabellón." Miguel Espinaco, "El periscopio fue nuestra gran arma de combate."

48 Ibid.: "que fue un aparatito que era un pequeño espejito . . . sostenido con miga de pan . . . que se sostenía con una pajita . . . se sacaba por los agujeritos que hay abajo de la celda y se miraba el ingreso del personal penitenciario al pabellón."

49 María Eva Cangiani and Martina Noailles, Foreword, 5: "La risa es liberación porque tiene la capacidad de hacer que el poder pierda, aunque sólo sea por un breve instante, su función de administrador del miedo."

50 "La risa fue una de las principales herramientas de resistencia de miles de presos políticos 'legales'y secuestrados, de perseguidos, de exiliados y de militantes populares durante la última dictadura militar" (Contratapa). (Back cover).

51 *Del otro lado*, 291: "Los muros lloran y nosotros reímos . . ., simplemente porque seguimos caminando. Viajando por la estrecha franja de la ruta, transitando entre esos dos mundos, como un símbolo que quisiera recordarnos que nuestro camino transcurre en el frágil límite entre la vida y la muerte, entre Coronda y la libertad."

52 Semprún, *Literature or Life*, 10.

Chapter 3

This chapter is based on the paper that was presented at the 9th Biennial Conference of the International Network of Genocide Scholars (INGS) which was held in Universidad Nacional de Tres de Febrero in Buenos Aires, Argentina on July 19–22, 2011.

1 The war between the Sinhala-majority-dominated GoSL and the LTTE continued nearly for 30 years with several unsuccessful ceasefire agreements and peace

processes (1987–1989, 1994, 2002–2007). The GoSL unilaterally withdrew from the 2002 CFA and launched massive military operations (2006–May 2009) against the Tamil population in the North and East of the country—which is considered to be the Tamil homeland—where the LTTE had created a de facto state during the 30 years of war. By the 2002 CFA, the boundaries of this de facto state were recognized as the line of control between the GoSL and the LTTE.

2   Mannar is a district in the northwest of the Tamil region.

3   The ban was imposed while the ceasefire agreement was in place and the respective parties were still making attempts to restart negotiations. In fact, even after the ban, there were two rounds of talks between the two parties in Switzerland.

4   International Crisis Group: "Sri Lanka: Sinhala Nationalism and the Elusive Southern Consensus," www.crisisgroup.org, Asia Report No. 141, 2007.

5   The PTSL was conducted by the Permanent People's Tribunal (PPT), which is renowned for conducting opinion tribunals on violations of human rights by governments throughout the world. The origin of PPT is in the Bertrand Russell/Satre Tribunal on Vietnam, which investigated the crimes committed by the American government against the Vietnamese people. See http://www.ptsrilanka.org/, downloaded: September 10, 2013.

6   Michaela Frulli. "Are Crimes against Humanity More Serious Than War Crimes?" *European Journal of International Law* 21.2 (2001): 333.

7   Permanent People's Tribunal: *People's Tribunal on Sri Lanka* (Dublin: PPT and IFPSL, 2010), 20.

8   The word, "reconciliation" is being used by the GoSL to establish a sociopolitical mechanism of amnesia where justice to the victims is denied. In that context the word "justice" has become more meaningful for the victims than the word "reconciliation."

9   The Tribunal acknowledged that the LTTE also violated human rights. However, the Tribunal states that "neither war crimes, nor crimes against humanity would be justified by any act committed by the victims" (People's Tribunal on Sri Lanka, 2010), 19.

10 This myth also influenced Nazism against Jews and others, and Hindutva ideology in India against Muslims and others.

11 "Fifty Years of Violent War Deaths from Vietnam to Bosnia: Analysis of Data from the World Health Survey Programme," http://www.bmj.com/content/336/7659/1482?tab=full, downloaded on February 20, 2013.

12 See Ananda Guruge, *Return to Righteousness: A Collection of Speeches, Essays and Letters of Anagarika Dharmapala* (Colombo: Ministry of Cultural Affairs and Information, 1991), 541.

13 Kumari Jayawardena, *Ethnic and Class Conflict in Sri Lanka: The Emergence of Sinhala-Buddhist Consciousness, 1883–1983* (Colombo: Sanjiva Books, 2003), 30–40.

14 Rajan Hoole, *Sri Lanka: The Arrogance of Power: Myths, Decadence and Murder* (Colombo: University Teachers for Human Rights [Jaffna], 2001), 5.

15 Ibid., 5.

16 Ibid., 471.

17 Ibid.

18 J. R. Jayawardene, *Daily Telegraph*, July 1983. Jaffna in this statement is the northern peninsula of the Tamil region.

19 Marisa Agnell, "Understanding Aryan Theory," in *Culture and Politics of Identity in Sri Lanka*, ed. Mithran Tiruchelvam and C. S. Dattathreya (Colombo: International Centre for Ethnic Studies, 1998), 44–48.

20 Pradeep Jeganathan, "Authorizing History, Ordering Land: The Conquest of Anuradhapura," in *Unmaking the Nation: The Politics of Identity and History in Modern Sri Lanka*, ed. Pradeep Jeganathan and Qadri Ismail (Colombo: Social Scientists' Association, 1995), 110–113.

21 Pradeep Jeganathan outlines three levels of "transformative operation" of the text: from oral to textual, from text to positivist history and from claim to acceptance, and calls this process a "violent transformation" of knowledge. The text was seen as a chronological history of the island of Lanka, which also illuminates the history of Indian Buddhism. Undermining the reality of precolonial politics, the reading of the text began to treat the history of Lanka as "a separate analytic field" from the history of India. A choice of the "pasts" was made and the knowledge about the past was filtered through the lenses of the present (ibid.).

22 Ibid.

23 International Crisis Group: "Sri Lanka."

24 Owing to the strategic location of Sri Lanka in the Indian Subcontinent and the Indian Ocean, its political/military control is of paramount importance for the global powers who use main sea lines of communication that run through the Indian Ocean. As a result, major powers such as the United States, United Kingdom, European Union, China, Japan, and India were involved in supporting the GoSL in its war against the LTTE.

25 See http://www.ptsrilanka.org/, downloaded on February 20, 2012.

26 Alexander K. A. Greenwalt, "Rethinking Genocidal Intent: The Case for a Knowledge-based Interpretation," *Pace Law Faculty Publications*, Paper 338 (1999): 2259–2294.

27 Greg Grandin, "History, Motive, Intent, Law: Combining Historical and Legal Methods in Understanding in Guatemala's 1981–1983 Genocide," in *The Specter of Genocide: Mass Murder in Historical Perspective*, ed. Robert Gallately and Ben Kiernan (Cambridge: Cambridge University, 2003), 339–352.

28 This is the zone that was declared safe by the GoSL. The civilians were asked to move this zone by the GoSL.

Chapter 4

1 Mario I. Aguilar, *Theology, Liberation, Genocide* (London: SCM, 2009b), 24.

2 Boubacar Boris Diop, Murambi, *The Book of Bones: A Novel* (Bloomington and Indianapolis: Indiana University, 2006), 176–177.

3 Paz Rojas Baeza, "Torturas: Romper el silencio" in *De la tortura no se habla: Agüero versus Meneses*, ed. Patricia Verdugo (Santiago: Catalonia, 2004), 175.

4 Mario I. Aguilar, *A las puertas de la Villa Grimadi: Poemas* (Santiago: Caliope Ediciones, 2008); and *Retorno a la Villa Grimaldi: Poemas* (Santiago: Caliope Ediciones, 2009).

5 Mario I. Aguilar, "Public Theology from the Periphery: Victims and Theologians," *International Journal of Public Theology* 1 (2007b): 321–337.

6 Peter Admirand, *Amidst Mass Atrocity and the Rubble of Theology: Searching for a Viable Theodicy* (Eugene, OR: Cascade, 2012), xxiii.

7 This figure keeps changing as human remains are found and identified. Thus in November 1996 the list of those who disappeared or were executed at the Villa Grimaldi included 223 names, see Corporación Parque por la Paz Villa Grimaldi,

"Nómina de detenidos desapararecidos y ejecutados que permanecieron en Villa Grimaldi," November 1996; and see Mario I. Aguilar, "El Muro de los Nombres de Villa Grimaldi (Chile): Exploraciones sobre la Memoria, el Silencio y la Voz de la Historia," *European Review of Latin American and Caribbean Studies* 69 (October 2000): 81–88.

8   Mario I. Aguilar, *Current Issues on Theology and Religion in Latin America and Africa* (Lewiston, NY and Lampeter, UK: Edwin Mellen, 2002), 143–144.

9   Victor Y. Turner, *The Forest of Symbols: Aspects of Ndembu Ritual* (Ithaca, NY: Cornell, University, 1967).

10 Javier Rebolledo, *La danza de los cuervos: El destino final de los detenidos desaparecidos* (Santiago: Ceibo Ediciones, 2012).

11 My translation from ibid., 10.

12 My translation from ibid., 14.

13 The text is available at http://www.hrweb.org/legal/cat.html. On February 4, 1985, the Convention was opened for signatures at the United Nations Headquarters in New York. At that time, representatives of the following countries signed it: Afghanistan, Argentina, Belgium, Bolivia, Costa Rica, Denmark, Dominican Republic, Finland, France, Greece, Iceland, Italy, Netherlands, Norway, Portugal, Senegal, Spain, Sweden, Switzerland, and Uruguay. Subsequently, signatures were received from Venezuela on February 15, from Luxembourg and Panama on February 22, from Austria on March 14, and from the United Kingdom on March 15, 1985.

14 *Convention against Torture* Part I, article 1.1.

15 Question developed in a new contextual biblical light by Leonardo Boff, *Jesus Christ Liberator: A Critical Christology of Our Time* (London: SPCK, 1980), 114–117.

16 Gustavo Gutiérrez, *On Job: God-Talk and the Suffering of the Innocent*, trans. Matthew J. O'Connell (New York: Orbis, 2002), 102.

17 Gustavo Gutiérrez, "God's Revelation and Proclamation in History," in *The Power of the Poor in History: Selected Writings* (London: SCM, 1983), 3–22 at 4.

18 Ibid.

19 Ibid., 20.

20 For some of the cultural critiques and the ideological reading of the collapse of the Berlin Wall see, among others, David Wetzell, ed., *From the Berlin Museum to the Berlin Wall: Essays on the Cultural and Political History of Modern Germany* (Westport, CT and London: Praeger, 1996); Sunil Manghani, *Image Critique & the Fall of the Berlin Wall* (Bristol and Chicago: Intellect, 2008); and Peter Schneider, *The German Comedy: Scenes of Life after the Wall* (London: Tauris, 1992).

21 Eight Chilean bishops applied penalties of excommunication to torturers and those aiding them after a concerted public declaration against torture on December 12, 1980. See Eugenio Ahumada, Javier Luis Egaña, Augusto Góngora, Carmen Quesney, Gustavo Saball, and Gustavo Villalobos, *Chile: La memoria prohibida—Las violaciones a los derechos humanos 1973–1983*, Vol. III (Santiago: Pehuén, 1989), 334–336.

22 Paul VI, "Address to the United Nations," Church of the Sacred Family, New York, October 4, 1965.

23 Archbishop Oscar Romero, "Georgetown Address: Address of Archbishop Romero on the Occasion of His Academic Investiture as a Doctor of Humanities, Honoris Causa, in the Cathedral of San Salvador, 14 February 1978," in *Archbishop Oscar Romero: Voice of the Voiceless—The Four Pastoral Letters and Other Statements* (Maryknoll: Orbis, 1985), 162–167 at 165.

24 In terms of European theology, a theologian is somebody who has acquired a doctorate in theology; in terms of Latin American theology and the understanding of

theology as a "second step," Romero was a theologian because he critically acted and reflected on God's presence in El Salvador. Following this rationale I have included him among Latin American theologians in Mario I. Aguilar, *The History and Politics of Latin American Theology*, Vol. 1 (London: SCM, 2007a), 105–118.

25 "Testimonio del reo político Reynaldo Cruz Menjívar," *Estudios Centroamericanos* 360 (1978), 850–858.

26 Patricia Verdugo, "Los protagonistas," in *De la tortura no se habla: Agüero versus Meneses,* ed. Patricia Verdugo (Santiago: Catalonia, 2004), 33.

27 Luis Muñoz passed through several detention centers after being arrested by the DINA in December 1974. See *Report of the Chilean National Commission on Truth and Reconciliation* II: 540; eventually he came to the United Kingdom as a political refugee and he still lives in the United Kingdom. María Cristina Stewart was arrested by the DINA on September 22, 1974 and after passing through secret detention centers remains among the disappeared (AFDD 1986), 45–48, *Report of the Chilean National Commission on Truth and Reconciliation* II: 537.

28 Diana Frida Aron Svigiliski was arrested by the DINA on November 18, 1974; *Report of the Chilean National Commission on Truth and Reconciliation* II: 540.

29 Luis Muñoz, *Being Luis: A Chilean Life* (Exeter: Impress, 2005), 108.

30 Jon Sobrino, "Redeeming Globalization through Its Victims," in *Globalization and Its Victims*, ed. Jon Sobrino and Felix Wilfred (London: SCM, 2001), 105–114.

31 A full analysis of this concept developed by Ellacuría was presented by Jon Sobrino at the Second International Congress on Xavier Zubiri at the José Simeón Cañas Universidad de Central America, and published in *Revista Latinoamericana de Teología* 66 (2005): 209–210.

32 I previously developed some of these ideas in Aguilar, "Public Theology from the Periphery," 321–337.

33 Ronaldo Muñoz, *The God of Christians* (Turnbridge Wells: Burns & Oates, 1991), 81.

34 Ibid., 90–91.

35 William T. Cavanaugh, *Torture and Eucharist: Theology, Politics, and the Body of Christ* (Malden, MA: Blackwell, 1998), 22.

36 At the start of the twenty-first century, the Catholic Church in Chile faced several accusations of improper behavior and sexual abuse by Chilean clergy with the central case being that of Fr Fernando Karadima, parish priest of the church of El Bosque in the archdiocese of Santiago. Karadima was condemned to a life of prayer and penance by the Vatican after a canonical investigation that condemned him and a civil litigation by his victims, a process that publicly disclosed many of the pastoral failures of the Catholic Church in Chile within the elite circles that were accessed by Karadima. See Juan Andrés Guzmán, Gustavo Villarrubia, and Mónica González, *Los secretos del imperio de Karadima: La investigación definitiva sobre el escándalo que remeció a la Iglesia chilena* (Santiago: Ediciones Universidad Diego Portales, Catalonia and Escuela de Periodismo—Universidad Diego Portales, 2011).

Chapter 5

1 Noting that women's movement in Islamic countries is not homogenous "or been shaped by the same forces"; Loubna H. Skalli, "Communicating Gender in the Public Sphere: Women and Information Technologies in the Mena," *Journal of Middle East Women's Studies* 2.2 (Spring 2006): 39.

2   See, for example, the works of: Leila Ahmad, *Women and Gender in Islam: Historical
    Roots of a Modern Debate* (New Haven: Yale University, 1993); Haifa Jawad, *The
    Rights of Women in Islam: An Authentic Approach* (Basingstoke: St Martin's, 1998);
    Ann Elizabeth Mayer, *Islam and Human Rights: Tradition and Politics* (Boulder, CO:
    Westview, 1999); Yvonne Y. Haddad and John L. Esposito, *Islam, Gender, and Social
    Change* (New York: Oxford University, 1998); Fatima Mernissi, *The Veil and the Male
    Elite: A Feminist Interpretation of Women's Rights*, trans. Mary Jo. Lakeland (New
    York: Addison-Wesley, 1991); Ziba Mir-Hosseini, *Islam and Gender, the Religious
    Debate in Contemporary Islam* (Princeton: Princeton University, 1999); Haleh Afshar,
    Islam and Feminism, An Iranian Case-study (London: MacMillan, 1998).

3   See, for example, the works of: Anne Sofie Roald, *Women in Islam: The Western
    Experience* (New York: Routledge, 2001); David S. Landes and Richard A. Landes,
    "Do Fundamentalists Fear Our Women?" *New Republic*, September 29, 2001, 20–23.
    See also Samuel P. Huntington, "The Age of Muslim Wars," *Newsweek*, January 2002.
    See also: Francis Fukuyama, "Their Target: The Modern World," *Newsweek*, January
    2002, 6–13.

4   Deniz Kandiyoti, *Women, Islam, and the State* (Philadelphia: Temple University,
    1991); Valentine M. Moghadam, *Modernizing Women: Gender and Social Change in
    the Middle-East*, 2nd edn (Boulder, CO: Lynne Reinner, 2003).

5   Janet Afary, *The Iranian Constitutional Revolution, 1906–1911: Grassroot Democracy,
    Social Democracy, & the Origins of Feminism* (New York: Columbia University, 1996),
    176.

6   Noushin Ahmadi Khorasani and Parvin Ardalan, *Senator: Faliyathaye Mehrangiz
    Manouchehrian ba bastar mobarezat hughughi zanan dar Iran* (*Senator: The Works of
    Senator Mehrangiz Manouchehrian for Legal Rights for Women* (Tehran: Nashr Tose-e,
    2003), 1382.

7   Afshar, *Islam and Feminism*; Haideh Moghissi, *Feminism and Islamic
    Fundamentalism, the Limits of Postmodern Analysis* (London: Zed Books, 1999);
    Moghadam, *Modernizing Women*; Mir-Hosseini, *Islam and Gender*; Janet Afary,
    "Seeking a Feminist Politics for the Middle East after September 11," *Frontier Journal
    of Women's Studies* 25.1 (Winter 2004): 128–137; Azadeh Kian, "Women and Politics
    in Post-Islamist Iran: The Gender Conscious Drive to Change," *British Journal of
    Middle Eastern Studies* 24.1 (1997): 75–96; Mehrangiz Kar, *Raf-e Tabeez Az Zanan,
    Moghayesey-e Convension-e Raf-e Tabeez Az Zanan ba Qavaneen-e Dakheliy-e Iran*
    (*End Discrimination against Women: A Comparison between the Convention on All
    Forms of Discrimination against Women and Iranian Laws*) (Tehran, Iran: Nashr-e
    Qatr-e Publications, 2000).

8   For more on the Tobacco boycott, see Asghar Fathi, "Role of the Traditional Leader in
    the Modernization of Iran, 1890–1910," *International Journal of Middle East Studies*
    11.1 (February 1980): 87–98; Nikki Keddie, "Iranian Revolution in Comparative
    Perspective," *The American Historical Review* 88.3 (June 1983): 579–598.

9   See Afary, *Iranian Constitutional Revolution*; see also Homa Katouzian, *State and
    Society in Iran, The Eclipse of the Qajars and the Emergence of the Pahlavis* (London:
    I.B. Tauris, 2000), 25–214. See also Nikki R. Keddie, *Modern Iran, Roots and Results
    of Revolution* (New Haven: Yale University, 2006), 37–73.

10 Note that scholars such as Haleh Afshar in her paper, "Behind the Veil, The Public
    faces of Khomeini's Policies on Iranian Women," in *Structures of Patriarchy: State,
    Community and Household in Modernising Asia*, ed. Bina Agarwal (New Delhi:
    Kali for Women, 1988), 228–247 and Akram Mirhosseini in her paper "After the

Revolution: Violations of Women's Human Rights in Iran," in *Women's Rights Human Rights, International Feminist Perspectives*, ed. Julie Peters and Adrea Wolper (London: Routledge, 1995), 72, regard the forced de-veiling as female emancipation, forgetting to note that emancipation or a gain of rights should be accompanied by choice.

11 See Doreen Hinchcliff, "The Iranian Family Protection Act," *The International and Comparative Law Quarterly* 17.2 (April 1968): 516–521. The 1967 FPA gave women more rights in the areas of law concerned with custody, polygamy, and divorce among others. See former (pre-1979) Iranian Civil Code articles: 1133, 1121, 1092, 1123, 1101, 1122, 1129.

12 The Laws Governing the Appointment of Judges ratified in 1982.

13 In the year 2002, the sixth parliament proposed that the age of marriage for boys and girls be increased to 18, however, this met fierce opposition from the Guardian and Expediency Councils.

14 Moghissi, *Feminism and Islamic Fundamentalism*, 100.

15 Ziba Mir-Hosseini, "Stretching the Limits: A Feminist Reading of the Shari'a in Post-Khomeini Iran," in *Feminism and Islam, Legal and Literary Perspectives*, ed. Mai Yamani (Reading: Ithaca, 1996), 292.

16 *Mahr* is a nominal sum (it could also be property), which is traditionally negotiated by the parents of the bride and groom but is intended as a gift to the bride for the marriage.

17 According to most interpretations of Islamic law, when a woman is divorced or widowed she has to wait a certain period of time, usually three to four months, before she is allowed to remarry. This waiting period is known as the period of *idda*.

18 Mir-Hosseini, "Stretching the Limits," 292.

19 Ibid.

20 Also refer to Roja Fazaeli, "Contemporary Iranian Feminism: Identity, Rights and Interpretations," *Muslim World Journal of Human Rights* 4.1 (2007): 1–24.

21 Nayerah Tohidi, "Iran's Women's Rights Movement and the One Million Signatures Campaign," *Change for Equality*, November 2006. http://www.we-change.org/spip.php?article208.

22 This entailed the reform of the Family Law or the Code of Personal Status *Mudawana*, which was based on *Maliki* jurisprudence and instituted a year after Morocco's independence in 1957. For a detailed study of recent law reform in Morocco, see Fatima Sadiqi and Moha Ennaji, "The Feminization of Public Space: Women's Activism, the Family Law and Social Change in Morocco," *Journal of Middle East Women's Studies* 2.2 (Spring 2006): 86–115.

23 Ibid.

24 Ibid.

25 Ibid.

26 About "One Million Signatures Demanding Changes to Discriminatory Laws," *Change for Equality*, August 28, 2006.

27 Ibid.

28 Ibid. On June 12, 2006 about 2,000 Iranian women participated in a sit-in, to protest discriminatory laws against women. In particular, they demanded change to the clauses in the Constitution that deny women's rights. See also, Mahsa Shekarloo, "Iran: Iranian Women Take on the Constitution," *Women Living under Muslim Laws*, July 21, 2005.

29 "One Million Signatures Demanding Changes."

30   Ibid.

31   Conducted by phone on August 11, 2013. The activist now lives in London.

32   Ibid.

33   Ibid.

34   Ibid.

35   Ibid.

36   For more on the actual Velvet Revolution in Czechoslovakia see Bernard Wheaton and Zdenek Kavan, *The Velvet Revolution: Czechoslovakia, 1988–1991* (Boulder, CO: Westview, 1992). See also Robin H. E. Shepherd, *The Velvet Revolution and Beyond* (London: Macmillan, 2000).

37   Parvin Ardalan, "Who Is Accused of Being a 'Threat to Civil Security?'" trans. Sussan Thamasebi, *Change for Equality*, May 6, 2007.

38   Sadiqi and Ennaji, "Feminization of Public Space," 87–88.

39   For more on the changing nature of public space in MENA refer to Valentine Moghadam and Fatima, Sadiqi "Women's Activism and the Public Sphere: An Introduction and Overview," *Journal of Middle East Women's Studies* 2.2 (Spring 2006): 1–7.

40   Ibid., 1.

41   Ibid.

42   Noushin Ahmadi Khorasani, "The Two Storytellers of the Women's Prison and the Imaginary Literature of the One Million Signatures Campaign," *Change for Equality*, April 28, 2007.

43   Sadiqi and Ennaji, "Feminization of Public Space," 86–114.

44   Ibid.

45   Noushin Ahmadi Khorasani, "Signed with an X," *New Internationalist*, NI 398, March 2007, 8.

46   Noushin Ahmadi Khorasani, "Treating Us like Criminals! Pressures Increase on Activists Involved in the One Million Signatures Campaign," trans. Sussan Tahmasebi, *Change for Equality*, February 19, 2007.

47   Moghadam and Sadiqi, "Women's Activism and the Public Sphere," 1–7.

48   Iranian Constitution, Article 10.

49   Moghadam, 118.

50   Khorasani, "Treating Us like Criminals!"

51   Ibid.

52   I am not of the opinion that men have or should have any claim over women's honor, however as reality prevails, in patriarchal societies such ownership is claimed as such.

53   Nahla Abdu, "Globalization, 'Culture Talk', and Palestinian Women Resistance," Draft paper presented at Trinity College Dublin, March 2007, 15.

54   Although I was able to leave the house, I would be openly followed by the agents either in plain clothes or in uniforms.

55   For more on the arrest of bloggers see Elizabeth Bucar and Roja Fazaeli, "Free Speech in Weblogistan? The Off-Line Consequences of On-Line Discourse," *International Journal of Middle-Eastern Studies* 40 (July 2008): 403–419. See also Roja Fazaeli, "Contemporary Iranian Feminisms: Definitions, Narratives, and Identity, in *Self-determination and Women's Rights in Muslim Societies*, ed. Chitra Raghavan and James P. Levine (Lebanon, NH: University of New England, 2012), 273–303; and Fazaeli, "Contemporary Iranian Feminism," 1–24.

56 Ardalan, "Who Is Accused of Being a 'Threat to Civil Security?'"

57 Ibid.

58 Khorasani, "Treating us like Criminals!"

59 Abdo, "Globalization 'Culture Talk', and Palestinian Women Resistance," 15.

60 Illicit sexual act refers to sex or sexual acts outside the confines of marriage. Those in this category may include girls who were caught with their boyfriends, run away girls, prostitutes, and adulterers, as well as others.

61 Maryam Hosseinkhah, "Evin Az Negah-e Zendanian (Evin through the Lens of Prisoners)," *Etemad Meli*, March 29, 2007. See also Maryam Hosseinkhah and Solmaz Sharif, "Gozareshi Az Band Zana Zendan Evin: Jayee Shabih Khodesh (A Report from Women's Prison: A Place like No Other)," *Etemad Meli*, 2006. Translations are my own.

62 Maryam Hosseinkhah, "Campein Yek Million Emza Dar Band Umoomiye Evin (The One Million Signature Campaign in Evin Women's Prison)," *Hawwa*, March 2007. Translations are my own.

63 Kobra Rahmanpour is a 26-year-old woman, sentenced to death and awaiting execution in Evin Prison. She "was sentenced to death for the premeditated murder of her mother-in-law in 2000"; for more see: Amnesty International, "Iran: Fear of Imminent Execution, Kobra Rahmanpur," *Public AI Index*: MDE 13/041/2003, December 15, 2003. See also Sohaila Sharifi, "Kobra Rahmanpour: Four Years on Death Row in Iran," *Worker-Communist Party of Iran*, May 22, 2005.

64 Ashraf Kalhori, a 37-year-old mother of four, was sentenced to death by stoning, charged with *zina* (adultery).

65 Another death-row convict.

66 Ibid.

67 See also Maryam Hosseinkhah, "Sakenine Band Nesvan Evin; Zanani ke Hich az Ghanun Nemidand (The Inhabitants of Women's Prison in Evin; Women Who Know Nothing of Laws)," *Hawwa*, March 20, 2006.

68 Ibid.

69 Ibid.

70 Ibid.

71 Mahboubeh Hossein Zadeh, "All Women Are Victims, Not Just Those in Prison," trans. Sussan Tahmasebi, *WLUML*, February 17, 2007.

72 Ibid.

Chapter 6

1 See *Dominus Iesus* (August 6, 2000): "For this reason, the distinction between *theological faith* and *belief* in the other religions, must be firmly held. If faith is the acceptance in grace of revealed truth, which 'makes it possible to penetrate the mystery in a way that allows us to understand it coherently,' then belief, in the other religions, is that sum of experience and thought that constitutes the human treasury of wisdom and religious aspiration, which man in his search for truth has conceived and acted upon in his relationship to God and the Absolute" (n. 7).

2   *Spe Salvi*, November 30, 2007. Number references are to those given in the text.

3   My emphasis.

4   For a fuller exposition of these points, see Francis X. Clooney, SJ, *Beyond Compare: St. Francis de Sales and Sri Vedanta Desika on Loving Surrender to God* (Georgetown: Georgetown University), chapter 4.

5   *The Essence of the Three Mysteries*, chapter 13, pp. 136–137 in the translation of Vedanta Deshika's *Srimad Rahasyatrayasara* by M. R. Rajagopala Ayyangar (Kumbakonam, India: Agnihotram Ramanuja Thathachariar, 1956); but translations are my own from the Sanskrit/Tamil original.

6   Chapter 13, p. 139. As an injunction, it indicates an objective reality, not merely a whim or personal experience.

7   Chapter 11, p. 121.

8   In fact, Benedict dramatizes the situation by turning to the Gospel story of the Magi and, with a Patristic slant, seeing this as the moment that ends astrology: "Paul illustrates the essential problem of the religion of that time quite accurately when he contrasts life 'according to Christ' with life under the dominion of the 'elemental spirits of the universe' (Col 2.8). In this regard a text by Saint Gregory Nazianzen is enlightening. He says that at the very moment when the Magi, guided by the star, adored Christ the new king, astrology came to an end, because the stars were now moving in the orbit determined by Christ." In turn, this reading of the Magi stands in for a version of modernity that is hopeless before conversion and the casting off of old beliefs: "This scene, in fact, overturns the world-view of that time, which in a different way has become fashionable once again today. It is not the elemental spirits of the universe, the laws of matter, which ultimately govern the world and mankind, but a personal God governs the stars, that is, the universe; it is not the laws of matter and of evolution that have the final say, but reason, will, love—a Person. And if we know this Person and he knows us, then truly the inexorable power of material elements no longer has the last word; we are not slaves of the universe and of its laws, we are free" (n. 5). In his homily for the Epiphany, January 6, 2009, Benedict adds: "St Gregory of Nazianzen states that the birth of Christ gave the stars new orbits; see *Dogmatic Poems*, V, 53–64: *PG* 37, 428–429. This is clearly to be understood in a symbolic and theological sense. In effect, while pagan theology divinized the elements and forces of the cosmos, the Christian faith, in bringing the biblical Revelation to fulfillment, contemplates only one God, Creator and Lord of the whole universe." Which pagan theology? Neither Benedict nor Gregory gives a clear answer. In "that time"—but what of religions today, which surely ought not to be confused with a spiritual materialism still more common in the Christian West? No detail is given, but one can suspect that even regarding religions today Benedict saves "hope" for a Christian worldview, and allocates the other to the "elemental spirits" and "the power of the material elements," etc.

9   On despair and presumption, see Thomas Aquinas, *Summa Theologiae* II.II.20–21.

10 *Dominus Iesus*, nn. 2–3; my emphasis.

11 Ibid., n. 21.

12 Consider, for instance, the dour claim made later in the document: "If it is true that the followers of other religions can receive divine grace, it is also certain that objectively speaking they are in a gravely deficient situation in comparison with those who, in the Church, have the fullness of the means of salvation" (n. 22). This is a faith statement, to be sure, but I would suggest that it is not sufficiently leavened by a substantive hope about God's work in the world.

Chapter 7

1   Space prohibits a more complete listing. For example, Hindus and Buddhists consider life's experiences—suffering and pleasure, joy and sadness—to be illusory. Their spiritual task is to attempt to comprehend the reality behind the illusion. Suffering and joy are one and the same, like dreams, while the object of life is enlightenment, the transcendence of all passions and attachments.

2   Hindus and Buddhists don't usually have to deal with this problem. In the Hindu-Buddhist traditions, life is a series of reincarnations, and what happens in one life is partially the result of actions in previous lives. This is the process of *karmaphala*. As an example, the death of a child may be seen as accumulated bad *karma* from a previous life. Suffering uses up this bad *karma* and therefore can help on one's way to liberation from the bonds of this illusory world. (However, if bad things do happen in this life, it follows that one *must* have done wrong in a previous life and I have seen accounts of people being treated as past-life sinners.) Following the various Hindu ways toward enlightenment can greatly speed this liberation process, as does following the Buddha's teaching of the Four Noble Truths and the Noble Eightfold Path. In both cases, enlightenment ends *karma* and makes of suffering the illusion it is.

3   For more on God as an abuser, see David R. Blumenthal, *Facing the Abusing God: A Theology of Protest* (Louisville, KY: Westminster John Knox, 1993).

4   This perspective is shared by dualistic religions such as Zoroastrianism and polytheistic religions such as Wicca.

5   This is my version of my teacher, Yitz Greenberg's "working principle," a kind of moral plumb line by which post-Holocaust theological claims should be measured: that no statement, theological or otherwise, should be made about the Holocaust that would not be credible in the presence of burning children; "Cloud of Smoke, Pillar of Fire: Judaism, Christianity and Modernity after the Holocaust," in *Auschwitz: Beginning of a New Era? Reflections on the Holocaust,* ed. Eva Fleischner (New York: Ktav, 1977), 7–55.

6   Father James Eblen of Seattle University raises two significant questions to this dichotomy. First, what about the mystery of a divine integrity beyond our knowing and the freedom of God to act within this context? Second, who says God created "best"—the Torah only says "good"—so why can't our world be imperfect, a creation that includes the persistence of evil?

7   See Anson Laytner, *Arguing with God: A Jewish Tradition* (Northvale, NJ: Jason Aronson, 1998).

8   Midrash Tehillim 44:1, ed. Solomon Buber (Vilna: Rom, 1891; reprint, New York: Om Publishing, 1947).

9   Talmud Bavli, Ta'anit 24b.

10 Menachem b. Yaakov (d. 1203), "Woe unto me"; *Sefer HaDema'ot (The Book of Tears),* ed. Simon Bernfeld, 3 vols. (Berlin: Eschkol Publishers, 1924–1926), 1: 239–240. See also the poem by Yitzhak b. Shalom in the same, 1: 217.

11 Gavriel b. Yehoshua Strassberg of Raisha (seventeenth century), "How Can I Lift My Face?"; Bernfeld, *Sefer HaDema'ot,* 3: 179–184.

12 I. Ashkenazy, ed., *Otzroth Idisher Humor* (1929), quoted in Louis I. Newman, *Hasidic Anthology* (New York: Schocken, 1963), 57.

13 Friedrich Torberg, "Seder, 1944," in *Voices within the Ark: The Modern Jewish Poets,* ed. Howard Schwartz and Anthony Rudolf (New York: Avon, 1980), 980–981. Torberg fled Vienna in 1938 for Switzerland and settled in the United States in 1940.

14   William S. Morrow, *Protest against God: The Eclipse of a Biblical Tradition* (Sheffield, UK: Sheffield Phoenix, 2007), 3, n. 8–10, points to Claus Westermann's and Walter Brueggermann's pioneering work in this field in the Christian world in the 1970s—precisely when I also began my research into this subject as a young rabbinical student.

15   See Blumenthal, *Facing the Abusing God*.

16   Kathleen Billman and Daniel Migliore, *Rachel's Cry: Prayer of Lament and Rebirth of Hope* (Cleveland: United Church, 1999); Morrow, *Protest against God*, 214, n. 32, references a number of Christian works dealing with the pastoral possibilities for addressing individual suffering through psalms of individual lament.

17   Morrow, *Protest against God*. Unique in Christian tradition, African-American spirituality apparently also protested against God. Morrow cites David E. Goatley's *Were You There? Godforsakeness in Slave Religion* for the tradition of complaint against God among Afro-American slaves (210, n. 20).

18   Peter Admirand, *Amidst Mass Atrocity and the Rubble of Theology: Searching for a Viable Theodicy* (Eugene, OR: Cascade, 2012).

19   AIDS is the first plague—a so-called natural evil—since the Black Death that has challenged belief in a divine plan and a beneficent God in the Western world.

20   I am referring here to the grand miracles of the Bible, but still allow for "mystery" in our world and the presence of many small apparent miracles: healings, avoidance of tragedies, serendipitous encounters, etc.

21   When Jews see the letters "YHVH," we say "Adonai" meaning "Lord" and most Bible translations follow this convention. Christians later took the vowels of "Adonai," placed them under the Tetragrammaton, switched the "Y" for a "J" and got Jehovah. Thus God acquired another name.

22   This makes the Divine Name almost meditative, akin to what Sri Tirumalai Krishnamacharya (November 18, 1888–February 28, 1989) once said about breathing: "Inhale, and God approaches you. Hold the inhalation, and God remains with you. Exhale, and you approach God. Hold the exhalation, and surrender to God." The Buddhist teacher Thich Nhat Hanh said similar things: "Breathing in, I calm body and mind. Breathing out, I smile. Dwelling in the present moment I know this is the only moment"; *Being Peace* (Berkeley, CA: Parallax), 7. See also http://www.goodreads.com/work/quotes/321908-being-peace.

23   Supremely pragmatic *for a religion*, Judaism basically says: "We can't really say anything concrete about God, but we know how we are supposed to act because The Name told us what to do" (see Deut 29.28 and 30.11–14, for example).

24   Since we are talking about human perceptions of the divine, I cannot exclude aggressive or vengeful concepts of God, much as I would like to. I can however, reject them based on how they propose to treat God's creatures and Creation.

25   The need to transform protest/lamentation into hope through the act of testimony is a theme common to both Jewish and Christian "arguing with God" traditions. Perhaps hope for the future is at the core of faith in YHVH/God.

26   The rabbis of the classical period greatly developed the concept of an anthropopathetic and empathetic god, conjecturing that God, or His Shekhinah, suffered when Israel suffered, was enslaved when Israel was enslaved, and will be redeemed when Israel is redeemed. God is said to feel pain when Israel feels pain and God weeps and mourns for the destroyed Jerusalem and its Temple just like a king of flesh and blood. See Laytner, *Arguing with God*, 83 and texts referenced in notes 41–49, 268.

27 Pirkei Avot 1.2 and Talmud Bavli, Avodah Zarah 17b.
28 See Leviticus 19.2. The rabbis taught (playfully) that God personally performed deeds of lovingkindness for us to emulate: God clothed the naked (Adam and Eve), visited the infirm (Abraham, after his circumcision), and buried the dead (Moses), among other things. Talmud Bavli, Sotah 14a.

Chapter 8

1 See Jürgen Moltmann, *Theology of Hope: On the Ground and the Implications of a Christian Eschatology* (London: SCM, 1967), 26–32.
2 The American Zen Buddhist David Loy has thematized this fundamental existential condition as "lack," which we continually seek to mask by recurring to the unreality of a constructed ego and the blandishments of equally artificial social and cultural worlds. See David Loy, *Lack and Transcendence: The Problem of Death and Life in Psychotherapy, Existentialism, and Buddhism* (Amherst, MA: Humanity Books, 1999). Commenting on an earlier draft of this chapter, Loy said: "Hope is not a concept I ever heard from my Zen teachers, and I'm not sure how well it fits Buddhism, if it does" (email communication, February 24, 2011). Robert Magliola, on the other hand, who meditated for many years with monks and nuns in Taiwan and Thailand, found that for both groups "'hope' was very alive and extremely important" because of their inability to know "what bad karma they had 'made' in past lives," which could bring about "a horrifying retribution for a serious misdeed in a previous life"; thus they would say, "I hope I have a good death" (email communication, April 13, 2011). I would like to thank Robert Magliola, David Loy, and John O'Grady for a number of helpful comments on this chapter, though responsibility for the final version remains mine.
3 Jean Calvin, *Institutes of the Christian Religion*, Vol. I, ed. John T. McNeill, trans. and ed. Ford Lewis Battles (Louisville and London: Westminster John Knox, 1960), 590.
4 See Arvind Sharma, *Hinduism and Its Sense of History* (Oxford: Oxford University, 2003).
5 See Gerhard von Rad, *Theologie des alten Testaments, Band II. Die Theologie der prophetischen Überlieferungen Israels* (München: Chr. Kaiser Verlag, 1980), 108–121.
6 Ibid., 111–118.
7 Michael von Brück and Whalen Lai, *Buddhismus und Christentum. Geschichte, Konfrontation, Dialog* (München: Beck, 1997), 294, where they helpfully interrelate the faith community's *verbum interpretationis* with the *verbum internum* of individual faith experience and the *verbum externum* of data about the historical Jesus.
8 See Elizabeth J. Harris, *Theravada Buddhism and the British Encounter: Religious, Missionary and Colonial Experience in Nineteenth Century Sri Lanka* (London: Routledge, 2006).
9 An example is the eminently reasonable exposition by K. N. Jayatilleke, *The Message of the Buddha*, ed. Ninian Smart (London: Allen & Unwin, 1975); a considerably more polemical, though sharply argued, approach is that of Jayatilleke's student Gunapala Dharmasiri, *A Buddhist Critique of the Christian Concept of God* (Colombo: Lake House, 1974).
10 See the insightful work of L. A. Jude Lal Fernando, "Dynamics of Essentialist Representations of Nationhood and the Politics of Interpretation: The Role of Religion in the Making and Unmaking of the Sri Lankan Nation-State" (PhD diss., Irish School of Ecumenics, Trinity College Dublin, 2008).

11 See Rita M. Gross, "The Crisis of Authority: Buddhist History for Buddhist Practitioners," *Buddhist-Christian Studies* 30 (2010): 59–72. See also Peter Harvey, "Between Controversy and Ecumenism: Intra-Buddhist Relationships," in *Buddhist Attitudes to Other Religions*, ed. Perry Schmidt-Leukel (St Ottilien: EOS Verlag, 2008), 114–142.

12 See von Brück and Lai, *Buddhismus und Christentum*, 298–301.

13 See, for instance, Hans Wolfgang Schumann, *Der historische Buddha. Leben und Lehre des Gautama* (Kreuzlingen und München: Hugendubbel, 2004, rev. edn); Hans-Joachim Klimkeit, *Der Buddha. Leben und Lehre* (Stuttgart-Berlin-Köln: Kohlhammer, 1990); Trevor Ling, *The Buddha: Buddhist Civilization in India and Ceylon* (Harmondsworth: Penguin, 1976); and many others, right back to classics such as Hermann Oldenberg, *Buddha. Sein Leben, seine Lehre, seine Gemeinde* (Stuttgart und Berlin: Cotta, 1920).

14 Von Rad, *Theologie des alten Testaments*, 122; see 120.

15 See ibid., 124–127.

16 See Rudolf Otto, *Reich Gottes und Menschensohn. Ein religionsgeschichtlicher Versuch* (München: Beck, 1940, 2nd rev. edn). Otto derives the Iranian terminology from the Sanskrit: "kingdom" or "dominion" = *kṣatra*; "lord" = *asura*, that is the Vedic god Varuṇa; "king" = *rājā*, 7–20. The story of interreligious relationships in central Asia is far too complex to be summarized here, but it is told superbly by Richard Foltz, *Religions of the Silk Road: Premodern Patterns of Globalization* (New York: Palgrave Macmillan, 2010, 2nd edn).

17 On this see Otto, *Reich Gottes*, 132–154, where he shows how Henoch draws on the Iranian notion of a wise judge and his good spirits in a final struggle against Ahriman and his evil spirits to portray the coming end, even identifying himself with the "Son of Man," 155–170.

18 Moltmann, *Theology of Hope*, 120.

19 Ibid., 31.

20 John S. Strong, *The Buddha: A Short Biography* (Oxford: OneWorld, 2001), 16–19. Strong provides not so much a biography as the structural framework around which the widely varying accounts of the Buddha's life are constructed.

21 See Paul Ricoeur, *Time and Narrative*, Vol.1, trans. Kathleen Mclaughlin and David Pellauer (Chicago and London: University of Chicago, 1984), chapter 2. Ricoeur distinguishes *mimēsis* 1 (prefiguration), 2 (configuration), and 3 (refiguration). In the following I draw on my "Time and Narrative in Buddhism and Christianity," in *Religion and Culture: A Multicultural Discussion: Festschrift in Honour of Francis X. D'Sa, SJ*, ed. Clemens Mendonca and Bernd Jochen Hilberath (Pune: Institute for the Study of Religion, 2011), 290–299.

22 Ricoeur, *Time and Narrative*, 1, 52.

23 Ibid., 54.

24 Ibid., 56.

25 Ibid., 56–58.

26 Ibid., 78, 81.

27 Paul Ricoeur, *Figuring the Sacred: Religion, Narrative, and Imagination*, trans. Donald Pellauer (Minneapolis: Fortress, 1995), 244.

28 Ibid., 246.

29 Ibid., 237.

30 Other variants are "Buddhalogy" and "Dharmalogy." See John Makransky, *Buddhahood Embodied* (Albany: State University of New York, 1997); Roger Jackson

and John Makransky, eds, *Buddhist Theology: Critical Reflections by Contemporary Buddhist Scholars* (London: RoutledgeCurzon, 2003), especially the introductory essay by José Cabezón; from the Christian side see Paul J. Griffiths, *On Being Buddha: Maximal Greatness and the Doctrine of Buddhahood in Classical India* (Albany: State University of New York, 1994). In the following I draw on my "Creator Spirit: A Narrative Theology of the Trinity in Interreligious Relations," in *Trinity and Salvation: Theological, Spiritual and Aesthetic Perspectives*, ed. Declan Marmion and Gesa Thiessen (Oxford: Peter Lang, 2009), 161–180, 170–177.

31   Though the original Sanskrit manuscripts have not been preserved, copies have been found going back to the fifth or sixth century; by this time there had been numerous Chinese translations. See Kōgen Mizuno, *Buddhist Sūtras: Origin, Development, Transmission* (Tokyo: Kosei, 1982).

32   For a succinct presentation, using slightly different translations from those employed here, see Perry Schmidt-Leukel, *Understanding Buddhism* (Edinburgh: Dunedin Academic, 2006), 108–112.

33   See von Brück and Lai, *Buddhismus und Christentum*, 461–466.

34   Von Rad, *Theologie des alten Testaments*, 120; see 117–118.

35   Augustine's conception of time, together with Aristotle's account of emplotment, forms the starting point of Ricoeur's analysis; see *Time and Narrative*, Vol. 1, chapter 1.

36   This question plays a crucial part in the fascinating discussions between scientists and the Dalai Lama recorded by Pier Luigi Luisi with Zara Houshmand, *Mind and Life: Discussions with the Dalai Lama on the Nature of Reality* (New York: Columbia University, 2009).

37   See von Brück and Lai, *Buddhismus und Christentum*, 328. My schematizations in what follows are loosely based on theirs, 330–343. The Christian schema is not intended to imply that Christianity supersedes Judaism, but merely that the "past" in this case is the history of Israel.

38   Ibid., 329.

39   Ibid., 337.

40   *The Fundamental Wisdom of the Middle Way: Nāgārjuna's* Mūla-Madhyamaka-Kārikā, translation and commentary by Jay L. Garfield (New York and Oxford: Oxford University, 1995), 75, also 331–333.

41   See Schmidt-Leukel, *Understanding Buddhism*, 119.

42   *Avataṃsaka-Sūtra*, trans Yampolsky, cit. Perry Schmidt-Leukel, *"Den Löwen brüllen hören." Zur Hermeneutik eines christlichen Verständnisses der buddhistischen Heilsbotschaft* (Paderborn-München-Wien-Zürich: Schöningh, 1992), 587, 588. In what follows I can only refer briefly to Schmidt-Leukel's superb exposition of the continuity at the core of all genuinely Buddhist traditions.

43   Sangharakshita, *The Bodhisattva Ideal: Wisdom and Compassion in Buddhism* (Birmingham: Windhorse Publications, 1999), 31–38.

44   *Avataṃsaka-Sūtra*, tr. Yampolsky, cit. Schmidt-Leukel, *"Den Löwen,"* 581.

45   See John D'Arcy May, "Sympathy and Empathy: The Compassionate Bodhisattva and the Love of Christ," in *Crossroad Discourses between Christianity and Culture*, ed. Jerald D. Gort, Henry Jansen, and Wessel Stoker (Amsterdam and New York: Rodopi, 2010), 395–411, 400–401.

46   From *The Larger Sukhāvatīvyūha-sūtra* as cited by Shinran in his "Notes on the Inscriptions on Sacred Scrolls (*Songō shinzō meimon*)," *The Collected Works of Shinran* Vol. 1, ed. Dennis Hirota, Hisao Inagaki, Michio Tokunaga, and Ryushin Uryuzu (Kyoto: Jōdo Shinshū Hongwanji-ha, 1997), 493.

47 Schmidt-Leukel, *"Den Löwen,"* 607.

48 See ibid., 611.

49 See the brief presentation in Schmidt-Leukel, *Understanding Buddhism*, 149–152, and the much fuller development of the theme in Schmidt-Leukel, *"Den Löwen,"* 605–632. See also the ground-breaking doctoral thesis of John O'Grady, *Beyond Immanence: A Buddhological Observing of Grace* (Irish School of Ecumenics: Trinity College Dublin, 2010).

50 See Schmidt-Leukel, *"Den Löwen,"* 627.

51 Von Brück and Lai, *Buddhismus und Christentum*, 344.

52 David Loy, email communication, February 24, 2011; the emphasis is mine.

53 See von Brück and Lai, *Buddhismus und Christentum*, 343–347.

54 See ibid., 342–347.

55 I owe this clarification to an email communication from David Loy, February 24, 2010. For a number of different perspectives on this, see the recently published papers from the ninth conference of the European Network of Buddhist-Christian Studies, Elizabeth J. Harris ed., *Hope: A Form of Delusion? Buddhist and Christian Perspectives* (St Ottilien: EOS Verlag, 2013).

56 Paul Knitter's gripping account of how painful he found it as a Christian committed to peace and justice to become "one with the death squads" he was opposing in Latin America can be found in his autobiographical and profoundly theological book *Without Buddha I Could Not be a Christian* (Oxford: OneWorld, 2009), chapter 7, esp. 173–174.

57 See David Loy, *The Great Awakening: A Buddhist Social Theory* (Boston: Wisdom Publications, 2003), chapter 5, "The Nonduality of Good and Evil: Buddhist Reflections on the New Holy War." His chapter originated as an email circulated to friends immediately after 9/11, which led to some sharp rejoinders from those who found Loy's perspective unpalatable.

58 Loy, *The Great Awakening*, 103.

59 See Knitter, *Without Buddha*, 181–182, 187, 190–194.

Chapter 9

1 John Allen, *The Future Church* (New York: Doubleday, 2009), 75.

2 Ibid., 107.

3 Ibid., 422.

4 Ibid., 125–126.

5 James A. Bill and John Alden Williams, *Roman Catholics and Shiʻi Muslims* (Chapel Hill: University of North Carolina, 2002), 134–141. Martin McDermott, "Liberation Theology and Imam Khomeini's Jihad, A Comparison," *Faith Power and Violence, Orientalia Christiana Analecta*, ed. John J. Donohue and Christian W. Troll. Vol. 258 (Rome: Ponticicio Instituto Orientale, 1998), 75–85.

6 Anthony O'Mahony, "Interreligious Dialogue, Muslim-Christian Relation and Catholic Shiʻa Engagment," in *Catholics and Shiʻa in Dialogue, Studies in Theology and Spirituality*, ed. Anthony O'Mahony, Walstan Peterburs, and Muhammad ʻAli Shomali (Trowbridge: Fox Publications, 2004), 98.

7 Ibid., 99.

8 Ibid.

9 Bill and Williams, *Roman Catholics and Shiʻi Muslims*, 64.

10   Adrian Hastings, Alistair Mason, and Hugh Pypers, eds., *The Oxford Companion to Christian Thought* (Oxford: Oxford University, 2000). See especially the headings: "Redemption," "Atonement," and "Liberation Theology."

11   The Ahul Bayt (Holy Family in Islam) refers to Muhammad, Kadijha, Ali, Fatima, Hasan, and Hussein.

12   Mahmoud Ayoub, *Redemptive Suffering in Islam* (New York: Mouton Publishers, 1978), 199.

13   Ibid., 55.

14   The Battle of Badr took place in 624. It was the first battle between the early Muslim community of Medina and the leaders of the city of Mecca. In this battle the Muslim community was victorious despite the strength of the opposition.

15   Ayoub, *Redemptive Suffering*, 143. Ayoub quotes the following hadith: "There is no servant ('*abd*) whose eyes shed one drop of tears for us, but that God will grant him for it the reward of the countless ages in paradise."

16   During the ritual of *matan*, adult men beat their chests with the palm of their hands. In some occasions *matan* can refer to flagellation.

17   Kenneth Cragg, *The Tragic in Islam* (London: Melisende, 2004), 94.

18   Ayoub, *Redemptive Suffering*, 199.

19   Ibid.

20   Kieran Flynn, "At the Heart of Islam," in *Ecumenics from the Rim*, ed. John O'Grady and Peter Scherle (Berlin: Lit Verlag, 2007), 229–235.

21   Hamid Dabashi, *Islamic Liberation Theology, Resisting the Empire* (New York: Routledge, 2008), 38.

22   Ibid., 142.

23   Andrew Davison and Himadeep Muppidi, eds, *The World is my Home, A Hamid Dabashi Reader* (Piscataway, NJ: Transaction Publishers, 2011), 57–66. Hamid Dabashi, *Shi'ism, A Religion of Protest* (Cambridge: Harvard University, 2011).

24   We see currently in Syria the displacement of millions of mostly Muslim citizens by Muslims. The internal divisions within Islam are becoming more pronounced. There is a growing polarization between Islamic sects, between the radicalized and the moderate, the center and the periphery.

25   Hamid Dabashi, *Authority in Islam* (Piscataway, NJ: Transaction Publishers, 2006).

26   Tariq Ramadan, *Western Muslims and the Future of Islam* (New York: Oxford University, 2004), 72, 239. Ramadan suggests the formation of Dar al Dawa as that space which Muslims occupy in the West, between *Dar as Islam* and *Dar al Harb*. He sees Muslims in the West as occupying a fruitful place of witness and encounter that goes beyond the binaries of the past. This space is open to dialogue and interpenetration.

27   Dabashi, *Islamic Liberation Theology*, 216.

28   Alastair Crooke, *Resistance: The Essence of the Islamist Revolution* (London: Pluto, 2009), 277.

29   Seyyid Hossein Nasr, *The Heart of Islam, Enduring Values for Humanity* (New York: Harper Collins, 2002), 239–272.

30   Mahmoud Sadri and Ahmad Sadri, eds., *Reason, Freedom and Democracy in Islam, Essential Writings of Abdolkarim Soroush* (Oxford: Oxford University, 2000); and Mehran Kamrava, ed., *The New Voices of Islam, Reforming Politics and Modernity—A Reader* (London: I.B. Tauris, 2006).

31   Nadje Sadid Al-'Ali, *Iraqi Women, Untold Stories from 1948 to the Present* (London: Zen, 2007).

32 Yasmin Husein Al-Jawaheir, *Women in Iraq, The Gender Impact of International Sanctions* (London: I.B. Tauris, 2008).

33 Ibid., 133.

34 Ibid., 141.

35 Mary Elaine Hegland, "Women of Karbala, Moving to America," in *The Women of Karbala*, ed. Kamran Scot Aghaie (Austin: University of Texas, 2005), 219.

36 Al-'Ali, *Iraqi Women*, 38.

37 Akbar Ahmed, *Postmodernism and Islam, Predicament and Promise* (London: Routledge, 1992).

38 Sa'diyya Shaikh, "Transforming Feminisms: Islam, Women and Gender Justice," in *Progressive Muslims, On Justice, Gender and Pluralism*, ed. Omid Safi (Oxford: OneWorld, 2003), 155.

39 Kamran Scot Aghaie, ed., *The Women of Karbala* (Austin: University of Texas, 2005).

40 Abdelwahab Bouhdiba, *Sexuality in Islam* (London: Saqi, 2004), 247.

41 Fatima Mernissi, *The Veil and the Male Elite, A Feminist Interpretation of Women's Rights in Islam* (New York: Basic, 1991), 195.

42 Michael Kirwan, *Political Theology, A New Introduction* (London: Darton, Longman, and Todd, 2008), x.

43 Rebecca S. Chopp, *The Praxis of Suffering* (Eugene, OR: Wipf and Stock, 2007), 28.

44 Neo-orthodoxy followed a similar trajectory.

45 Chopp, *Praxis of Suffering*, 34.

46 James Matthew Ashley, *Interruptions, Mysticism, Politics and Theology in the Work of Johann Baptist Metz* (South Bend: University of Notre Dame, 2002), 32. Metz saw that Rahner never mentioned Auschwitz; this was critical for Metz, for whom theology could not be the same after Nazi Germany.

47 John K. Downey, ed., *Love's Strategy: The Political Theology of Johann Baptist Metz* (Harrisburg: Trinity, 1999), 135.

48 Bruce T. Morrill, *Anamnesis as Dangerous Memory* (Collegeville: The Liturgical Press, 2000), 21–26.

49 Ibid., 25.

50 Ashley, *Interruptions, Mysticism, Politics, and Theology*, 132–133.

51 *Leiden an Gott*, is translated by Ashley as *Suffering Unto God*. This is a stance toward God, which is full of complaint, lament, but also of passionate expectation and hope that God will respond. It is closely related to following Jesus, the Crucified One and with biblical Israel's poverty of spirit. It allows the suffering and the oppressors to become and remain authentic subjects.

52 Downey, *Love's Strategy*, 139.

53 Ahmad al Katib, *The Development of Shi'ite Political Thought, From Shura to Wilayat al-Faqih*, self-published by Ahmad al Katib, London, 2008.

54 Elie Wiesel, *From the Kingdom of Memory: Reminiscences* (New York: Summit, 1990), 201.

55 Miroslav Volf, *The End of Memory, Remembering Rightly in a Violent World* (Grand Rapids: Eerdmans, 2006), 78.

56 Ibid., 101.

57 Quoted in James Booth, *Communities of Memory: On Witness, Identity, and Justice* (Ithaca: Cornell University, 2006), 117.

58 Ibid., 175.

Chapter 10

1 The poll was conducted in March 2013. http://www.pewforum.org/Christian/
   Catholic/US-Catholics-Happy-with-Selection-of-Pope-Francis.aspx#priorities.
2 Thomas Reese, "Pope Francis Supports Zero Tolerance of Child Abuse." *National
   Catholic Reporter*, March 19, 2013. http://ncronline.org/blogs/ncr-today/pope-francis-
   supports-zero-tolerance-child-abuse. For criticism from Survivor Groups, see Nick
   Squires, "Victims' Groups Cool to Pope Francis's First Comments on Abuse Scandal,"
   The Christian Science Monitor, April 5, 2013. In December 2013, Francis announced
   plans to establish a new commission to examine the rape and abuse of children by clergy,
   but survivor groups remained skeptical, at best. See Elisabeta Povoledo, Alan Cowell,
   and Rick Gladstone, "Pope Setting Up Commission on the Sexual Abuse of Children
   by Priests." *New York Times*, December 5, 2013. http://www.nytimes.com/2013/12/06/
   world/europe/pope-setting-up-commission-on-clerical-child-abuse.html.
3 Unless stated otherwise, I will use the words "Church" and "Catholic Church"
   interchangeably in this chapter. For my examination of the way hope within interfaith
   dialogue has changed and developed in the Catholic Church (and hope's links with
   love and faith), see my "No Dialogue without Hope: Interfaith Dialogue and the
   Transformation of a Virtue," in *Hope in All Directions*, ed. Geoffrey Karabin (Oxford:
   Inter-Disciplinary, 2014), 3–15.
4 See, for example, his comments in the volume co-written with Rabbi Abraham Skorka
   in 2010 and published in English as *On Heaven and Earth: Pope Francis on Faith,
   Family, and the Church in the Twenty-First Century* (New York: Image, 2013), 50–51.
   See also Peter Admirand and Yazid Said, "The Pope and the Archbishop: Ecumenical
   Reflections," *SEARCH: A Church of Ireland Journal* 36.3 (Autumn 2013): 163–178.
5 Steve Scherer, "Pope Francis Says Hypocrisy Undermines Church's Credibility,"
   Reuters, April 14, 2013. http://www.reuters.com/article/2013/04/14/us-pope-
   idUSBRE93D09A20130414.
6 Eric Johnson and Karl-Heinz Reuband, *What We Knew: Terror, Mass Murder, and
   Everyday Life in Nazi Germany* (Cambridge: Basic, 2006), xiv–xv.
7 Ibid., 307.
8 Listen, for example, to the NPR religion podcast from May 2, 2010, which includes
   the following related audio stories: (1) "Dutch Church Promises Full Abuse
   Investigation" and (2) "Vatican Set to Rule on Legionaries of Christ." http://www.npr.
   org/rss/podcast.php?id=1016. See also Partick McCafferty, "'A Cry from the Depths':
   Entering into the Mystery of Christ Forsaken," in *Broken Faith: Why Hope Matters*,
   ed. Patrick Claffey, Joe Egan, and Marie Keenan (Oxford: Peter Lang, 2013), 25–30.
9 See Ali Bracken, "Inside the Mind of a Paedophile," *Sunday Tribune*, May 2, 2010,
   14; and Barry Roche, "Former Priest Speaks of Shame of Being among 'The Most
   Despised,'" *The Irish Times*, June 25, 2013. http://www.irishtimes.com/news/former-
   priest-speaks-of-shame-of-being-among-the-most-despised-1.1441391.
10 Daniel J. Wakin and Rachel Donadio, "Vatican Priest Likens Criticism over Abuse to
   Anti-Semitism," *New York Times*, April 2, 2010. http://www.nytimes.com/2010/04/03/
   world/europe/03church.html. As is well known, the priest who was the preacher to
   Pope Benedict claimed that he was reading segments from a letter given to him by a
   Jewish friend.
11 "Interview of the Holy Father Benedict XVI with the Journalists on the Flight to the
   United Kingdom," September 16, 2010. http://www.vatican.va/holy_father/benedict_

xvi/speeches/2010/september/documents/hf_ben-xvi_spe_20100916_interv-regno-unito_en.html.

12 Maimonides, "Laws of Repentance," in *Maimonides—Essential Teachings on Jewish Faith and Ethics: The Book of Knowledge and the Thirteen Principles of Faith*, ed. and trans. Marc D. Angel (Woodstock, VT: SkyLight Paths, 2012), 109 (2.2). For my evaluation of the child abuse scandal and the legacy of John Paul II, see my "Rifts, Trust, and Openness: John Paul II's Legacy in Catholic Intra- and Inter-religious Dialogue," *Journal of Ecumenical Studies* 47.4 (Fall 2012): 555–575.

13 Eugene B. Korn, "The People Israel, Christianity, and the Covenantal Responsibility to History," in *Covenant and Hope: Christian and Jewish Reflections*, ed. Robert W. Jenson and Eugene B. Korn (Grand Rapids: Eerdmans, 2013), 165 (145–172).

14 George Robinson, *Essential Judaism: A Complete Guide to Beliefs, Customs, and Rituals* (New York: Pocket, 2001), 235–236.

15 See also Normon Solomon, *The Talmud: A Selection* (Penguin: London, 2009), 677.

16 See, for example, Rabbi Michael J. Cook, *Modern Jews Engage the New Testament* (Woodstock, VT: Jewish Lights, 2008).

17 Gustavo Gutiérrez, *On Job: God-Talk and the Suffering of the Innocent*, trans. Matthew J. O'Connell (Maryknoll: Orbis, 1992), 44.

18 David Burrell, *Deconstructing Theodicy: Why Job Has Nothing to Say to the Puzzle of Suffering* (Grand Rapids: Brazos, 2008), 47.

19 Maimonides, *The Guide for the Perplexed*, trans. M. Friedlander (New York: Dover, 1956), 302.

20 See, especially the final chapter of Harold S. Kushner, *The Book of Job: When Bad Things Happened to a Good Person* (New York: Schocken, 2012).

21 James L. Kugel, *How to Read the Bible: A Guide to Scripture Then and Now* (New York: Free Press, 2007), 641.

22 See Emmanuel Levinas, "Useless Suffering," in *The Problem of Evil: A Reader*, ed. Mark Larrimore (Malden, MA: Blackwell, 2004), 371–380; and Charlotte Delbo, *Auschwitz and After*, trans. Rosette C. Lamont (New Haven: Yale University, 1995), respectively.

23 Zachary Braiterman, *(God) After Auschwitz: Tradition and Change in Post-Holocaust Jewish Thought* (Princeton: Princeton University, 1998), 54.

24 Archbishop Diarmuid Martin, "Liturgy of Lament and Repentance for the Sexual Abuse of Children by Priests and Religious in St. Mary's Pro-Cathedral, Dublin," *Irish Catholic Bishops Conference* website. February 20, 2011. http://www.catholicbishops. ie/2011/02/20/20-february-2011-liturgy-of-lament-and-repentance-for-the-sexual-abuse-of-children-by-priests-and-religious-in-st-marys-pro-cathedral-dublin. For my article on theological dissent, see "'My Children Have Defeated Me!': Finding and Nurturing Theological Dissent," *Irish Theological Quarterly* 77.3 (2012): 286–304.

25 See, for example, Avishai Margalit, *The Ethics of Memory* (Cambridge: Harvard University, 2001); and Miroslav Volf, *The End of Memory: Remembering Rightly in a Violent World* (Grand Rapid: Eerdmaans, 2006).

26 Ben Kiernan, *Blood and Soil: A World History of Genocide and Extermination from Sparta to Darfur* (New Haven: Yale University, 2007), 13.

27 Jeffrey Blustein, *The Moral Demands of Memory* (Cambridge: Cambridge University, 2008), 245.

28 Surat Al-Mã'idah 5:7, *The Qur'an*, trans. M. A. S. Abdel Haleem (Oxford: Oxford University, 2010), 68.

29 Yosef Hayim Yerushalmi, *Zakhor: Jewish History and Jewish Memory* (Seattle: University of Washington, 1996), 9.

30   Friedrich Nietzsche, *Beyond Good and Evil: Prelude to a Philosophy of the Future*, trans. R. J. Hollingdale (London: Penguin, 1990), 91 (68).

31   See my *Amidst Mass Atrocity and the Rubble of Theology: Searching for a Viable Theodicy* (Eugene, OR: Cascade, 2012), 285–294.

32   See Irving Greenberg, *For the Sake of Heaven and Earth: The New Encounter between Judaism and Christianity* (Philadelphia: The Jewish Publication Society, 2004), 194; Michael Kogan, *Opening the Covenant: A Jewish Theology of Christianity* (Oxford: Oxford University, 2008); Edward Kessler, *An Introduction to Jewish-Christian Relations* (Cambridge: Cambridge University, 2010); and *The Jewish Annotated New Testament*, ed. Amy-Jill Levine and Marc Zvi Brettler (Oxford: Oxford University, 2011).

33   Editorial, "Credibility Gap: Pope Needs to Answer Question," *National Catholic Reporter*, March 26, 2010. http://ncronline.org/news/accountability/credibility-gap-pope-needs-answer-questions; and Hans Kung, "Open Letter to the Catholic Bishops," *The Irish Times*, April 16, 2010. http://www.irishtimes.com/newspaper/opinion/2010/0416/1224268443283.html.

34   Paige Hochschild, "Pope Francis on the Priesthood," *First Things*, April 29, 2013. http://www.firstthings.com/onthesquare/2013/04/pope-francis-on-the-priesthood. See also Antonio Spadaro's interview of Francis, "A Big Heart Open to God," *America*, September 30, 2013; http://americamagazine.org/pope-interview.

35   John Allen, Jr., "On the Crisis, Benedict XVI Changes the Tone," *The National Catholic Reporter*, May 11, 2010. http://ncronline.org/blogs/examining-crisis/crisis-benedict-xvi-changes-tone.

36   For an excellent reading of this parable, see Kenneth E. Bailey, *Jesus through Middle Eastern Eyes: Cultural Studies in the Gospels* (London: SPCK, 2008), 378–396. One may also think of the woman who anointed Jesus in Bethany in the house of Simon the Leper (Mt. 26.6–13). For my examination of the Syrophoenician Woman, see "Traversing towards the Other (Mk. 7.24–30): The Syrophoenician Woman amidst Voicelessness and Loss," in *The Bible: Culture, Community, and Society*, ed. Angus Paddison and Neil Messer (London: T&T Clark, 2013), 157–170.

37   Simone Weil, *The Simone Weil Reader*, ed. George Panichas (New York: David McKay, 1977), 436.

38   Aristotle, *Nicomachean Ethics*, in *Introduction to Aristotle*, trans. and ed. Richard McKeon (New York: McGraw Hill, 1947), 1125b (388).

39   John Milton, *Paradise Lost*, ed. Stephen Orgel and Jonathan Goldberg (Oxford: Oxford University, 2008), 85 (4.37–41).

40   William Shakespeare, *The History of Troilus and Cressida* in *The Riverside Shakespeare* (Boston: Houghton Mifflin, 1974), 465 (III.iii.155).

41   William Shakespeare, *Julius Caesar* in *The Riverside Shakespeare* (Boston: Houghton Mifflin, 1974), 1121 (III.2.92).

42   Aristotle, *Nicomachean Ethics*, 367–368 (III.9).

43   Emmanuel Levinas, *Ethics and Infinity: Conversations with Phillipe Nemo*, trans. Richard A. Cohen (Pittsburgh: Duquesne University, 2009), 99.

44   See my *Amidst Mass Atrocity*, 169–219.

45   R. S. Sugirtharajah, "Charting the Aftermath: A Review of Postcolonial Criticism," in *The Postcolonial Biblical Reader*, ed. R. S. Sugirtharajah (Oxford: Blackwell, 2006), 10. Contra my statements that follow, see Frank Kermode's *The Genesis of Secrecy: On the Interpretation of Narrative* (Cambridge: Harvard University, 1979).

46   Bailey, *Jesus through Middle Eastern Eyes*, 259.

47 See my "Mission in Remission: Inter-religious Dialogue in a Post-modern, Post-colonial Age," *Concilium* 1 (2011): 95–104; and my "The Other as Oneself within Judaism: A Catholic Interpretation," *Journal of Inter-Religious Dialogue* 3 (2010): 113–124. http://irdialogue.org/wp-content/uploads/2010/03/JIRD-3-Admirand.pdf.

48 See my "'All lost! To prayers, to prayers! All lost': Why Postmodernity, Religious Pluralism, and Interreligious Dialogue Need to be Embraced," in *Redefining Modernism and Postmodernism*, ed. Sebnem Toplu and Hubert Zapf, 79–98. (Cambridge: Cambridge Scholar's Press, 2010).

49 Kathleen McChesney, "What Caused the Crisis? Key Findings of the John Jay College Study on Clergy Sexual Abuse." *America*, June 6, 2011. http://www.americamagazine.org/content/article.cfm?article_id=12884. My list was written before Francis's apostolic exhortation *Evangelii Gaudium*, but some of these issues are addressed or mentioned in that exhortation and share a generally similar tone of professed faith and the call for renewal and dialogue.

50 In his *For Christ's Sake: End Sexual Abuse in the Catholic Church . . . for Good* (2013), Australian Bishop Geoffrey Robinson calls for a Church council to address the sex abuse scandal. See Jamie Manson, "Australian Bishop Launches Petition for Council on Sex Abuse," *National Catholic Reporter*, June 5, 2013. http://ncronline.org/blogs/grace-margins/australian-bishop-launches-petition-council-sex-abuse.

51 See my "Healing the Distorted Face: Doctrinal Reinterpretation(s) and the Christian Response to the Other," *One in Christ* 42 (2008): 302–317.

52 See the commentary on this passage in Ernesto Cardenal, *The Gospel in Solentiname*, trans. Donald D. Walsh (Maryknoll: Orbis, 2010), 167–174.

53 Speech given by Mark Furnish, Diocese of Rochester, NY, to the United Nations Committee on the Rights of the Child. Geneva, Switzerland, October 12, 2002. SNAP website. http://www.snapnetwork.org/survivors_voice/survivors_voice_home.htm.

Chapter 11

1 It is interesting to note that historically, it is the so-called sects such as the Mennonites and the Quakers who directly concerned themselves with issue of peace.

2 Joseph Gremillion, *The Gospel of Peace and Justice. Catholic Social Teaching since Pope John* (Maryknoll: Orbis, 1976), 68.

3 Pope Paul VI, *Populorum Progressio* 76 (echoing *GS* 78).

4 *Gaudium et Spes* 58.

5 See John Milbank, *Theology and Social Theory. Beyond Secular Reason*, 2nd edn (Oxford: Blackwell, 2006); Kathryn Tanner, *Theories of Culture: A New Agenda for Theology* (Minneapolis: Fortress, 1997), 96 ff; and Georges De Schrijver, *Recent Theologial Debates in Europe: Their Impact on Interreligious Dialogue* (Bangalore: Dharmaram, 2004), 37 ff.

6 *Gaudium et Spes* 34.

7 Nicholas of Cusa, *De Pace Fidei*, trans. Jasper Hopkins (Minneapolis: Arthur J. Banning, 1994), chapter 1. See also Inigo Bocken, ed., *Conflict and Reconciliation: Perspectives on Nicholas of Cusa* (Leiden and Boston: Brill, 2004).

8 Garrett Hardin, "The Tragedy of the Commons," *Science* 162 (1968): 1243–1248.

9 See Elinor Ostrom, *Governing the Commons. The Evolution of Institutions for Collective Action* (Cambridge: Cambridge University, 1990).

10   See Amartya Sen, *The Idea of Justice* (London: Allen Lane, 2009).
11   By Indian Tradition is not meant a tradition belonging to a particular nation-state. "Indian" here is to be understood in a civilizational sense, and sometimes it is referred to as "Indic."
12   See Rajmohan Gandhi, *Revenge and Reconciliation* (London: Penguin, 1999).
13   In India today persists the mixture of both these traditions—the pre-Buddhist tradition of revenge, and the Buddhist tradition of compassion. The former could be seen in the continuing "honor-killings" that take place and it is a practice of violent revenge.
14   The *syadvada* is a characteristic mark of Jainism. It holds that "every proposition gives us only a perhaps, a maybe or a syad . . . It emphasizes the extremely complex nature of reality and its indefiniteness . . . The dynamic character of reality can consist only with relative or conditional predication. Every proposition is true, but only under certain conditions, i.e. hypothetically"; Sarvepalli Radhakrishnan, *Indian Philosophy*, 7th edn (Delhi: Oxford University, 1994), 302. *Anekatva* is a doctrine that affirms diversity and plurality.
15   This is different from South East Asia. How shared culture, history, and civilization could contribute to the promotion of peace is exemplified by the creation of the Association of South East Asian Nations (ASEAN). Ever since the creation of this body, there have been hardly any serious conflicts among the South East Asian nations.
16   For details see the work of Paul Mun Kyuhyun, *The Korean People and the Catholic Church: A History* (Seoul: Dulsum Nalsum, 2012).
17   See Felix Wilfred, *Asian Public Theology. Critical Concerns in Challenging Times* (Delhi: ISPCK, 2010).
18   See Gaudencio Rosales and C. G. Arevalo, eds, *For All the Peoples of Asia: Federation of Asian Bishops' Conferences Documents from 1970 to 1991* (Maryknoll: Orbis, 1992).

Chapter 12

1   Emmanuel Levinas, "God and Philosophy," *Of God Who Comes to Mind*, trans. Bettina Bergo (Stanford, California: Stanford University, 1998), 69.
2   Levinas, *Autrement qu'être ou au-delà de l'essence* (Dordrecht, Netherlands: Nijhoff, 1974); the French is cited from the Livre de poche edition (Paris, 2001), v. The English translation of this work is cited from *Otherwise than Being, or, Beyond Essence*, trans. Alphonso Lingis (Pittsburgh: Duquesne University, 1981).
3   *Oxford Latin Dictionary*, ed. P. G. W. Glare (Oxford: Clarendon, 1996), 827.
4   See Michael L. Morgan, *Discovering Levinas* (Cambridge: Cambridge University, 2007), 189, who refers the reader to Levinas's essay "Meaning and Sense," in *Basic Philosophical Writings*, ed. Adrian T. Peperzak, Simon Critchley, and Robert Bernasconi (Bloomington and Indianapolis: Indiana University, 1996), 61 and 64.
5   Levinas, *Autrement qu'être*, 233.
6   Grossman similarly believes that Raphael's inspiring Sistine Madonna "is a purely atheistic expression of life and humanity, without divine participation"; "The Sistine Madonna," in *The Road: Stories, Journalism, and Essays*, trans. Robert and Elizabeth

Chandler, with Olga Mukovnikova (New York: New York Review of Books, 2010), 166. In Levinas's terms, God is not present, does not appear, does not participate in Being, but the Madonna's maternal devotion may be said to *bear witness to God* in the sense that, when Viktor refuses to repent to the Stalinist authorities for a crime he did not commit, he imagines that God—along with his mother—was standing beside him.

7   My own translation of the Russian text cited from *Zhisn' i sud'ba* (Moscow: Eksmo, 2011), 310–311.

8   *Totality and Infinity: An Essay on Exteriority* (1961), trans. Alphonso Lingis (Pittsburgh: Duquesne University), 237. The French edition, originally published by Martinus Nijhoff, The Hague, is cited from the Livre de Poche edition (Paris, 1990), 265.

9   Emmanuel Levinas, *Nine Talmudic Readings*, trans. with an introduction by Annette Aronowicz (Bloomington and Indianapolis: Indiana University, 1994), 20. I have slightly altered this translation. The French is cited from *Quatre lectures talmudiques* (Paris: Les Éditions de minuit, 1968), 44. The Talmudic passage on which Levinas comments is from the Tractate *Yoma*, 85a–85b.

10   The word for "the Other," in Levinas' sense, in Russian would be другой/*drugoy*.

11   Chandler's translation ("Heavens, What Had He Done?") omits Grossman's and Viktor's direct, and repeated, reference to the word God (Боже).

12   Chapter 57 in the Chandler translation.

13   Levinas, *Autrement qu'être*, 185; *Otherwise than Being*, 117.

14   Madeline, James, and Katie, eds, *Turned inside-out: Literature, Art, and Testimony from the Inside-Out Prison Exchange Program*, Vol. 1, Clark Honors College (Summer 2010), 50.

15   *Zhizn' i Sud'ba* (*Life and Fate*), an anthology of student writings from my spring 2012 Inside-Out class on "Literature and Ethics: Levinas and Vasily Grossman's *Life and Fate*," ed. Pepe, Abs, Seth, Talon, Steve, Carolina, Robyn, and Anna (Salem, Oregon: Oregon Corrections Enterprises, Oregon State Correctional Institution, 2012), 7.

16   Ibid.

Chapter 13

1   William E. Connolly, *The Ethos of Pluralization* (Minneapolis and London: University of Minnesota, 2004), xii.

2   Ibid.

3   Ibid.

4   Zygmund Bauman, *Postmodern Ethics* (Oxford: Blackwell, 1993), 159.

5   Michel Foucault, *The Archaeology of Knowledge* (London: Routledge, 1972), 4.

6   See Max Weber, *The Rational and Social Foundations of Music* (Carbondale: South Illinois University, 1958); and E. M. Forster, *A Passage to India* (Canada: Penguin, 1979), where the authors write about the link between cultural imperialism in India and the naturalization of the European musical system of tonality.

7   It is noteworthy that, in the English language, the words "true" and "trust" share etymological roots.

8   Connolly, *Ethos of Pluralization*, 105.

9   Ibid., 106.

10 John Finnis, *Natural Law and Natural Rights* (Oxford: Clarendon, 1980); Germain Grisez, *The Way of the Lord Jesus: Volume One, Christian Moral Principles* (Quincy, IL: Franciscan, 1987).

11 It is important to note that, while the original meaning of the term *amicus*, was intended to signify a "friend of the court," whose role was to instruct or to clarify, it is now often applied to the provision of a highly partisan account of the facts. For example, In *Lawrence v Texas* (2003) 123 S CT 2472, the "new natural law" *amicus* brief was submitted by Robert George and Gerard Bradley on behalf of the pressure group, *Focus on the Family* (2002), US Briefs, 102.

12 Nicholas C. Bamforth and David A. J. Richards, *Patriarchal Religion, Sexuality and Gender: A Critique of New Natural Law* (Cambridge: Cambridge University, 2008), 1.

13 Ibid., 3, 4.

14 Ibid., 332.

15 Paul Horwitz, *The Agnostic Age: Law, Religion and the Constitution* (Oxford: Oxford University, 2011), xxi.

16 Ibid.

17 Ibid., xxii.

18 Note that I have not dismissed the possibility that, for many people, the content of revelation or of a deductive reasoning process will be consonant with, and strengthened by, their experience. This, as far as I am concerned, is fully consonant with the idea of modulated epistemology because it implies that religious experience, scientific methodology, or any other route to understanding remains reflectively open to experience and reflection.

19 Fabrizio Trifiro, Institute of International Integration Studies, Trinity College Dublin. Discussion Paper no. 47 (January 2005).

20 Connolly, *Ethos of Pluralization*, 180.

21 By this phrase, I intend to signify: human relationships, hierarchical systems of power, and ecological sensibility, which is also a kind of relationship. In addition, I would add that a mark of pluralist societies is the freedom of each person to imagine and articulate her ultimate concerns, which entails an understanding of the relationship between human and God.

22 Connolly, *Ethos of Pluralization*, xiv.

23 Ibid., xv.

24 Ibid., note 13, 203.

25 Judith Butler, "Is Judaism Zionism?" in *The Power of Religion in the Public Sphere*, ed. Judith Butler, Jurgen Habermas, Charles Taylor, and Cornel West (New York: Columbia, 2011), 85.

26 Ibid.

27 Foucault, *The Archaeology of Knowledge*, 49.

28 As Robert Brandom concludes, "Discursive practice is understood in terms of reasoning and representing, but above all in terms of *expressing*—the activity of making it explicit ... (and) this expressive account of language, mind, and logic is an account of who *we* are." Brandom points out that the theoretical attempt to track the normative dimension of human discourse always leads us back to the commitments that can be inferred from our practices and from the conversational exchange of reasons that accompany practice. See Robert B. Brandom, *Making It Explicit: Reasoning, Representing, and Discursive Commitment* (Cambridge, MA: Harvard University, 1998), 649, 650.

29 Rowan Williams, *Dostoevsky: Language, Faith and Fiction* (London: Baylor University, 2008), 11.

Chapter 14

1   For good reasons, economists have talked about economics as religion. See, for instance, Robert H. Nelson, *Economics as Religion: From Samuelson to Chicago and Beyond* (University Park, PA: Pennsylvania State University, 2001).

2   Joerg Rieger, *No Rising Tide: Theology, Economics, and the Future* (Minneapolis: Fortress, 2009), chapter 2.

3   See, for instance, the account in Norman Gottwald, *The Hebrew Bible: A Brief Socio-literary Introduction* (Minneapolis: Fortress, 2009), 150–157.

4   See Rainer Albertz, "More and Less than a Myth: Reality and Significance of Exile for the Political, Social, and Religious History of Judah," in *By the Irrigation Canals of Babylon: Approaches to the Study of the Exile*, ed. John J. Ahn and Jill Middlemas, *Library of Hebrew Bible/Old Testament Studies* 526 (New York: T&T Clark International, 2012), 27. "The exilic period represents the most profound caesura of all eras in Israel's history. Here, the religion of Israel underwent its most severe crisis, but here, too, the foundation was laid for its most sweeping renewal" (33).

5   Albertz, "More and Less than a Myth," 23.

6   Pinchas E. Rosenblüth, "Exil II," *Theologische Realenzyklopädie*, Vol. 10, ed. Gerhard Krause and Gerhard Müller (Berlin: Walter de Gruyter, 1982), 714.

7   Albertz, "More and Less than a Myth," 31.

8   See Joerg Rieger and Kwok Pui-lan, *Occupy Religion: Theology of the Multitude* (Lanham, MD: Rowman and Littlefield, 2012).

9   Mk. 6.3a: "Is not this the carpenter, the son of Mary?" The Greek term "*tektōn*," which is often translated as carpenter, would be more adequately translated as construction worker, which was a day laborer's job.

10 See the critique that the role of optimism has been misleading generations of Americans as developed by Barbara Ehrenreich, *Bright-Sided: How Positive Thinking is Undermining America* (New York: Metropolitan, 2009).

11 Richard Horsley, *Jesus and Empire: The Kingdom of God and the New World Disorder* (Minneapolis: Fortress, 2002), 51, 129.

12 See, for instance, the work of the following organizations: Industrial Areas Foundation (IAF), Interfaith Worker Justice (IWJ), and Clergy and Laity United for Economic Justice (CLUE).

13 For an in-depth argument on globalization see Joerg Rieger, *Globalization and Theology, Horizons in Theology* (Nashville: Abingdon, 2010).

14 Marcus Borg and John Dominic Crossan, *The First Paul: Reclaiming the Radical Visionary behind the Church's Conservative Icon* (New York: HarperOne, 2009), 68.

15 For an extended theological assessment of this topic see Joerg Rieger, *Christ and Empire: From Paul to Postcolonial Times* (Minneapolis: Fortress, 2007), chapter 1.

16 This was the point of Jesus's request to give Caesar the things that belong to Caesar and to God the things that belong to God (Mk. 12.17). Every Jew would have known what belongs to God: everything.

17 In the United States, countless labor leaders have been killed, for instance, without receiving much recognition. The events of the Haymarket massacre in Chicago in May 1886, for instance, are remembered in May Day celebrations around the world as the international day of labor, while May is not officially observed in the United States.

18   See, for instance, Elsa Tamez, *Amnesty of Grace: Justification by Faith from a Latin American Perspective*, trans. Sharon H. Ringe (Nashville: Abingdon, 1993).

19   See, for instance, the work of Latin American theologians Jung Mo Sung and Néstor Míguez, as well as many North American theologies that address the matters of class, race, ethnicity, sexuality, and gender.

20   See Harry Bradford, "U.S. Income Inequality Worse Now than in 1774: Study," *Huffington Post*, September 12, 2012. http://www.huffingtonpost.com/2012/09/20/us-income-inequality_n_1898539.html. See also Nathaniel Popper, "U.S. Is among Developed Economies with Highest Income Inequality," *Los Angeles Times*, December 6, 2011. http://articles.latimes.com/2011/dec/06/business/la-fi-1206-oecd-income-20111206. According to Popper, the nonpartisan Congressional Budget Office reported that the income of the richest 1 percent of American households rose 275 percent between 1979 and 2007, while during the same time the income of the poorest 20 percent grew only 18 percent.

Afterword

1   While Pip is the main character of Charles Dickens's *Great Expectations*, it is the response of Miss Havisham's to loss that is of interest to this discussion and how she decides that revenge will be her message of "hope." She learns on the morning of her wedding that her soon-to-be-husband has escaped (as a convict) leaving her heart broken. Her response is deep depression and hatred for all men. She refuses to neither take off her decaying, tattered wedding gown nor clean up the rotten, set-up wedding banquet table. She raises her adopted daughter, Estella, as her weapon for revenge on men to cruelly and heartlessly break the hearts of others especially those she "bewitches" into love with her beauty. One of the victims of her scheme is Pip, the main character, who falls madly in love with Estella only to have his heart crushed. As time goes on, Miss Havisham's own reality of dying finally opens her eyes to the realization of how much she was to blame for the suffering of others, and how wrong she was in doing so. Meanwhile Pip becomes a better man after going through all the frustration and pain of being heartbroken by Estella (Charles Dickens, *Great Expectations*, London: Chapman & Hall, 1860).

2   Fulata L. Moyo, "Navigating Experiences of Healing: A Narrative Theology of Eschatological Hope as Healing," in *African Women, Religion, and Health: Essays in Honor of Mercy Amba Ewudziwa Oduyoye*, ed. Isabel A. Phiri and Sarojini Nadar (Maryknoll: Orbis, 2006), 244.

3   St John of the Cross, *The Dark Night of The Soul* (New York: Barnes and Noble, 2005).

4   Elisabeth Kübler-Ross identifies denial and isolation as the first stage of grieving, followed by anger, then bargaining, then depression, and, finally, accepting. For details, see her *Death and Dying* (London: Collier, 1969).

5   C. G. Jung and Jungian psychologists talk of the shadow in terms of the personality traits that one grows up suppressing as unacceptable as compared to one's ego. This process of "sidelining" such traits is mainly through the socialization process where the "positive" characteristics are often upheld as acceptable while the "others" are suppressed. Yet according to Jung and the Jungians, the suppressed traits, if allowed to be known and owned, have high potential of making the person very uniquely and

holistically personal. For the purpose of the discussion on loss and hope, engaging further into what this shadow represents in the development of personality traits falls outside the realm of this discussion, but the use of the shadow depicts a more general understanding of an experience that can be considered as a deprivation of the ideal situation: in this case, the death of my husband as deprivation, and therefore the temptation to categorize it the same way unacceptable traits are, as a shadow. For more discussion on this, read Robert A. Johnson, *Owning Your Shadow: Understanding the Dark Side of the Psyche* (San Francisco: HarperSanFrancisco, 1991); Connie Zweig and Jeremiah Abrams, eds, *Meeting the Shadow: The Hidden Power of the Dark Side of Human Nature* (New York: Penguin, 1991); and Peter A. Levine with Ann Frederick, *Waking the Tiger: Healing Trauma* (Berkeley: North Atlanta, 1997).

6   The conception of hope was based mainly on the teaching of "life after death" in the eschatology teaching of the Christian faith. It was mainly made alive by the physical presence of friends and family that kept on reminding this teaching to me through prayers, songs, and continued narrative in response to my grieving. When this presence was not easily accessible, I started experiencing the dry spell of doubt at whether God was present anymore. Within that reality of the silence of God, it was the possibility of embracing this loss of death partly through the practice of spiritual discipline as espoused by Ignatius of Loyola that I learned to live in the tension or embracing my shadow. See Fulata L. Moyo, "A Narrative Theology of Eschatological Hope as Healing," 243–257.

7   Ibid., 252.

Bibliography

Admirand, Peter. "'All lost! To prayers, to prayers! All lost': Why Postmodernity, Religious Pluralism, and Interreligious Dialogue Need to be Embraced." In *Redefining Modernism and Postmodernism*, edited by Sebnem Toplu and Hubert Zapf, 79–98. Cambridge: Cambridge Scholar's Press, 2010.

—. *Amidst Mass Atrocity and the Rubble of Theology: Searching for a Viable Theodicy*. Eugene, OR: Cascade Books, 2012.

—. "Healing the Distorted Face: Doctrinal Reinterpretation(s) and the Christian Response to the Other." *One in Christ* 42 (2008): 302–317.

—. "Mission in Remission: Inter-religious Dialogue in a Post-modern, Post-colonial Age." *Concilium* 1 (2011): 95–104.

—. "'My Children Have Defeated Me!': Finding and Nurturing Theological Dissent." *Irish Theological Quarterly* 77.3 (2012): 286–304.

—. "No Dialogue without Hope: Interfaith Dialogue and the Transformation of a Virtue." In *Hope in All Directions*, edited by Geoffrey Karabin, 3–15. Oxford: Inter-Disciplinary Press, 2014.

—. "The Other as Oneself within Judaism: A Catholic Interpretation." *Journal of Inter-Religious Dialogue* 3 (2010): 113–124.

—. "Rifts, Trust, and Openness: John Paul II's Legacy in Catholic Intra- and Interreligious Dialogue." *Journal of Ecumenical Studies* 47.4 (Fall 2012): 555–575.

—. "Traversing towards the Other (Mark 7.24–30): The Syrophoenician Woman amidst Voicelessness and Loss." In *The Bible: Culture, Community, and Society*, edited by Angus Paddison and Neil Messer, 157–170. London: T&T Clark International, 2013.

Admirand, Peter and Yazid Said. "The Pope and the Archbishop: Ecumenical Reflections." *SEARCH: Church of Ireland Journal* 36.3 (Autumn 2013): 163–178.

Afary, Janet. *The Iranian Constitutional Revolution, 1906–1911: Grassroot Democracy, Social Democracy, and the Origins of Feminism*. New York: Columbia University Press, 1996.

—. "Seeking a Feminist Politics for the Middle East after September 11." *Frontier Journal of Women's Studies* 25.1 (Winter 2004): 128–137.

Afshar, Haleh. "Behind the Veil: The Public Faces of Khomeini's Policies on Iranian Women." In *Structures of Patriarchy: State, Community and Household in Modernising Asia*, edited by Bina Agarwal, 228–247. New Delhi: Kali for Women, 1988.

—. *Islam and Feminism, An Iranian Case-study*. London: Macmillan, 1998.

Aghaie, Kamran Scot, ed. *The Women of Karbala*. Austin: University Press of Texas, 2005.

Agnell, Marisa. "Understanding the Aryan Theory." In *Culture and Politics of Identity in Sri Lanka*, edited by Mithran Tiruchelvam and C. S. Dattathreya, 41–71. Colombo: International Centre for Ethnic Studies, 1998.

Aguilar, Mario I. *A las puertas de la Villa Grimadi: Poemas*. Santiago: Caliope Ediciones, 2008.

—. *Current Issues on Theology and Religion in Latin America and Africa*. Lewiston, NY and Lampeter, UK: Edwin Mellen Press, 2002.

—. "El Muro de los Nombres de Villa Grimaldi (Chile): Exploraciones sobre la Memoria, el Silencio y la Voz de la Historia." *European Review of Latin American and Caribbean Studies* 69 (October 2000): 81–88.

—. *The History and Politics of Latin American Theology*, Vol. 1. London: SCM Press, 2007a.

—. "Public Theology from the Periphery: Victims and Theologians." *International Journal of Public Theology* 1 (2007b): 321–337.

—. *Retorno a la Villa Grimaldi: Poemas*. Santiago: Caliope Ediciones, 2009a.

—. *Theology, Liberation, Genocide*. London: SCM Press, 2009b.

Ahmad, Leila. *Women and Gender in Islam: Historical Roots of a Modern Debate*. New Haven: Yale University Press, 1993.

Ahmed, Akbar. *Postmodernism and Islam, Predicament and Promise*. London: Routledge, 1992.

Ahumada, Eugenio, Javier Luis Egaña, Augusto Góngora, Carmen Quesney, Gustavo Saball, and Gustavo Villalobos. *Chile: La memoria prohibida—Las violaciones a los derechos humanos 1973–1983*, Vol. III. Santiago: Pehuén, 1989.

Albertz, Rainer. "More and Less than a Myth: Reality and Significance of Exile for the Political, Social, and Religious History of Judah." In *By the Irrigation Canals of Babylon: Approaches to the Study of the Exile*, edited by John J. Ahn and Jill Middlemas, 20–33. *Library of Hebrew Bible/Old Testament Studies* 526, New York: T&T Clark International, 2012.

Ali, Nadje Sadid al. *Iraqi Women, Untold Stories from 1948 to the Present*. London: Zen Books, 2007.

Allen, John. *The Future Church*. New York: Doubleday, 2009.

Aquinas, Thomas. *Summa Theologiae*. Translated by Thomas Gilby, et al. 60 vols. London: Eyre and Spottiswoode, and New York: McGraw–Hill, 1964–1973.

Aristotle. *Introduction to Aristotle*. Translated and edited by Richard McKeon. New York: McGraw Hill, 1947.

Ashley, James Matthew. *Interruptions, Mysticism, Politics and Theology in the Work of Johann Baptist Metz*. South Bend: University Press of Notre Dame, 2002.

Asociación Civil El Periscopio. *Del otro lado de la mirilla. Olvidos y Memorias de ex Presos Políticos de Coronda 1974–1979*. Santa Fé: El Periscopio, 2003.

Asociación Ex-Presos Políticos de Córdoba. *Eslabones: Crónicas, relatos, poesías, cuentos, ilustraciones*. Córdoba: AEPP, 2009.

Ayoub, Mahmoud. *Redemptive Suffering in Islam*. New York: Mouton Publishers, 1978.

Baeza, Paz Rojas. "Torturas: Romper el silencio." In *De la tortura no se habla: Agüero versus Meneses*, edited by Patricia Verdugo, 163–180. Santiago: Catalonia, 2004.

Bailey, Kenneth E. *Jesus through Middle Eastern Eyes: Cultural Studies in the Gospels*. London: SPCK, 2008.

Bamforth, Nicholas C. and David A. J. Richards. *Patriarchal Religion, Sexuality and Gender: A Critique of New Natural Law*. Cambridge: Cambridge University Press, 2008.

Bashir, Halim with Damien Lewis. *Tears of the Desert: A Memoir of Survival in Darfur*. New York: Oneworld, 2008.

Bauer, Yehuda. *Rethinking the Holocaust*. New Haven and London: Yale University Press, 2001.

Bauman, Zygmund. *Postmodern Ethics*. Oxford: Blackwell, 1993.

Benedict XVI. *Spe Salvi*. Online: http://www.vatican.va/holy_father/benedict_xvi/encyclicals/documents/hf_ben-xvi-enc_20071130_spe-salvi_en.html.

Bergoglio, Jorge Mario and Abraham Skorka. *On Heaven and Earth: Pope Francis on Faith, Family, and the Church in the Twenty-first Century*. New York: Image Books, 2013.

Beverley, John. "The Margin at the Center. On Testimonio (Testimonial Narrative)." In *The Real Thing. Testimonial Discourse and Latin America*, edited by Georg Gugelberger, 23–41. Durham: Duke University Press, 1996.

Bill, James A. and John Alden Williams. *Roman Catholics and Shi'i Muslims*. Chapel Hill: University of North Carolina Press, 2002.

Billman, Kathleen and Daniel Migliore. *Rachel's Cry: Prayer of Lament and Rebirth of Hope.* Cleveland: United Church Press, 1999.

Bloch, Gottfired R. *Unfree Associations. A Psychoanalyst Recollects the Holocaust.* Los Angeles: Red Hen Press, 2004.

Blumenthal, David R. *Facing the Abusing God: A Theology of Protest.* Louisville, KY: Westminster John Knox Press, 1993.

Blustein, Jeffrey. *The Moral Demands of Memory.* Cambridge: Cambridge University Press, 2008.

Bocken, Inigo, ed. *Conflict and Reconciliation: Perspectives on Nicholas of Cusa.* Leiden and Boston: Brill, 2004.

Boff, Leonardo. *Jesus Christ Liberator: A Critical Christology of Our Time.* London: SPCK Publishing, 1980.

Bohoslavsky, Pablo. *Cierta fortuna.* Buenos Aires: Libros del Zorzal, 2010.

Boo, Katherine. *Behind the Beautiful Forevers: Life, Death, and Hope in a Mumbai Undercity.* New York: Random House, 2012.

Booth, James. *Communities of Memory: On Witness, Identity, and Justice.* Ithaca: Cornell University Press, 2006.

Borg, Marcus and John Dominic Crossan. *The First Paul: Reclaiming the Radical Visionary behind the Church's Conservative Icon.* New York: HarperOne, 2009.

Bouhdiba, Abdelwahab. *Sexuality in Islam.* London: Saqi Books, 2004.

Braiterman, Zachary. *(God) after Auschwitz: Tradition and Change in Post-Holocaust Jewish Thought.* Princeton: Princeton University Press, 1998.

Brandom, Robert B. *Making It Explicit: Reasoning, Representing, and Discursive Commitment.* Cambridge, MA: Harvard University Press, 1998.

Brück, Michael von and Whalen Lai. *Buddhismus und Christentum. Geschichte, Konfrontation, Dialog.* München: Beck, 1997.

Bucar, Elizabeth and Roja Fazaeli. "Free Speech in Weblogistan? The Off-line Consequences of On-line Discourse." *International Journal of Middle-Eastern Studies* 40 (July 2008): 403–419.

Burdick, Michael A. *For God and Fatherland: Religion and Politics in Argentina.* Albany: SUNY Press, 1995.

Burrell, David, trans. *Al-Ghazali. Faith in Divine Unity and Trust in Divine Providence.* Louisville, KY: Fons Vitae, 2000.

Burrell, David. *Deconstructing Theodicy: Why Job Has Nothing to Say to the Puzzle of Suffering.* Grand Rapids: Brazos Press, 2008.

—. *Towards a Jewish-Christian-Muslim Theology.* Oxford: Wiley-Blackwell, 2011.

Butler, Judith. "Is Judaism Zionism?" In *The Power of Religion in the Public Sphere*, edited by Judith Butler, Jurgen Habermas, Charles Taylor, and Cornel West, 70–91. New York: Columbia University Press, 2011.

Calvin, Jean. *Institutes of the Christian Religion*, Vol. I. Edited by John T. McNeill and translated and edited by Ford Lewis Battles. Louisville and London: Westminster John Knox Press, 1960.

Cardenal, Ernesto. *The Gospel in Solentiname.* Translated by Donald D. Walsh. Maryknoll: Orbis Books, 2010.

Caussade, Jean-Pierre de. *Sacrament of the Present Moment.* Translated by Kitty Muggeridge. San Francisco: Harper and Row, 1989.

Cavanaugh, William T. *Torture and Eucharist: Theology, Politics, and the Body of Christ.* Malden, MA: Blackwell, 1998.

Chopp, Rebecca S. *The Praxis of Suffering.* Eugene, OR: Wipf and Stock, 2007.

Clooney, Francis X. *Beyond Compare: St. Francis de Sales and Sri Vedanta Desika on Loving Surrender to God*. Georgetown: Georgetown University Press, 2008.

—. *His Hiding Place Is Darkness: A Hindu-Catholic Theopoetics of Divine Absence*. Stanford: Stanford University Press, 2013.

Connolly, William E. *The Ethos of Pluralization*. Minneapolis and London: University of Minnesota Press, 2004.

Cook, Michael J. *Modern Jews Engage the New Testament*. Woodstock, VT: Jewish Lights, 2008.

Cragg, Kenneth. *The Tragic in Islam*. London: Melisende, 2004.

Crooke, Alastair. *Resistance: The Essence of the Islamist Revolution*. London: Pluto Press, 2009.

Dabashi, Hamid. *Authority in Islam*. Piscataway, NJ: Transaction Publishers, 2006.

—. *Islamic Liberation Theology, Resisting the Empire*. New York: Routledge, 2008.

—. *Shi'ism, A Religion of Protest*. Cambridge: Harvard University Press, 2011.

Dalai Lama. *Beyond Religion: Ethics for a Whole World*. Boston: Houghton Mifflin Hardcourt, 2011.

Davison, Andrew and Himadeep Muppidi, eds. *The World Is My Home: A Hamid Dabashi Reader*. Piscataway, NJ: Transaction Publishers, 2011.

Delbo, Charlotte. *Auschwitz and after*. Translated by Rosette C. Lamont. New Haven: Yale University Press, 1995.

De Schrijver, Georges. *Recent Theologial Debates in Europe: Their Impact on Interreligious Dialogue*. Bangalore: Dharmaram, 2004.

Deshika, Vedanta. *The Essence of the Three Mysteries*. Translated by M. R. Rajagopala Ayyangar. Kumbakonam, India: Agnihotram Ramanuja Thathachariar, 1956.

Dharmasiri, Gunapala. *A Buddhist Critique of the Christian Concept of God*. Colombo: Lake House, 1974.

Dickens, Charles. *Great Expectations*. London: Chapman & Hall, 1860.

Diop, Boubacar Boris. *Murambi, The Book of Bones: A Novel*. Bloomington and Indianapolis: Indiana University Press, 2006.

Dostoevsky, Fyodor. *Memoirs from the House of the Dead*. Translated by Jessie Coulson. Oxford: Oxford University Press, 2008.

Downey, John K., ed. *Love's Strategy: The Political Theology of Johann Baptist Metz*. Harrisburg: Trinity Press, 1999.

Drago, Margarita. *Fragmentos de la Memoria: Recuerdos de una experiencia carcelaria (1975–1980)*. Nueva York: La Campana, 2007.

—. *Memory Tracks: Fragments from Prison (1975–1980)*. Translated by Margaret Ballantyne. New York: Editorial Campana, 2007.

Ehrenreich, Barbara. *Bright-Sided: How Positive Thinking Is Undermining America*. New York: Metropolitan Books, 2009.

Espinaco, Miguel. "El periscopio fue nuestra gran arma de combate." In Suchergebnisse. Cárceles Clandestinas, pdf book. 2011–2012. Online: http://jorgedanielpedraza. lacoctelera.net/post/2006/07/19/-detras-la-mirilla-libro-la-asociacion-periscopio.

Fathi, Asghar. "Role of the Traditional Leader in the Modernization of Iran, 1890–1910." *International Journal of Middle East Studies* 11.1 (February 1980): 87–98.

Fazaeli, Roja. "Contemporary Iranian Feminism: Identity, Rights and Interpretations." *Muslim World Journal of Human Rights* 4.1 (2007): 1–24.

—. "Contemporary Iranian Feminisms: Definitions, Narratives, and Identity." In *Self-determination and Women's Rights in Muslim Societies*, edited by Chitra Raghavan and James P. Levine, 273–303. Lebanon, NH: University of New England Press, 2012.

Fernando, Jude Lal. "Dynamics of Essentialist Representations of Nationhood and the Politics of Interpretation: The Role of Religion in the Making and Unmaking of the Sri Lankan Nation-State," PhD diss., Irish School of Ecumenics, Trinity College Dublin, 2008.

Finnis, John. *Natural Law and Natural Rights*. Oxford: Clarendon Press, 1980.

Flynn, Kieran. "At the Heart of Islam." In *Ecumenics from the Rim*, edited by John O'Grady and Peter Scherle, 229–235. Berlin: Lit Verlag, 2007.

Foltz, Richard. *Religions of the Silk Road: Premodern Patterns of Globalization*, 2nd edn. New York: Palgrave Macmillan, 2010.

Forster, E. M. *A Passage to India*. Canada: Penguin, 1979.

Foucault, Michel. *The Archaeology of Knowledge*. London: Routledge, 1972.

Frulli, Michaela. "Are Crimes against Humanity More Serious than War Crimes?" *European Journal of International Law* 21.2 (2001): 329–350.

Gandhi, Rajmohan. *Revenge and Reconciliation*. London: Penguin, 1999.

Ginzburg, Eugenia Semyonovna. *Journey into the Whirlwind*. Translated by Paul Stevenson and Max Hayward. San Diego: Harvest, 1995.

Goatley, David Emmanuel. *Were You There? Godforsakeness in Slave Religion*. Maryknoll: Orbis Books, 1996.

Gottwald, Norman. *The Hebrew Bible: A Brief Socio-literary Introduction*. Minneapolis: Fortress Press, 2009.

Grandin, Greg. "History, Motive, Intent. Law: Combining Historical and Legal Methods in Understanding in Guatemala's 1981–1983 Genocide." In *The Specter of Genocide: Mass Murder in Historical Perspective*, edited by Robert Gallately and Ben Kiernan, 339–352. Cambridge: Cambridge University Press, 2003.

Greenberg, Irving ("Yitz"). "Cloud of Smoke, Pillar of Fire: Judaism, Christianity and Modernity after the Holocaust." In *Auschwitz: Beginning of a New Era? Reflections on the Holocaust*, edited by Eva Fleischner, 7–55. New York: Ktav, 1977.

—. "Dialectic Living and Thinking: Wiesel as Storyteller and Interpreter of the Shoah." In *Elie Wiesel: Jewish, Literary, and Moral Perspectives*, edited by Steven T. Katz and Alan Rosen, 173–189. Bloomington and Indianapolis: Indiana University Press, 2013.

—. *For the Sake of Heaven and Earth: The New Encounter between Judaism and Christianity*. Philadelphia: The Jewish Publication Society, 2004.

Greenwalt, Alexander K. A. "Rethinking Genocidal Intent: The Case for a Knowledge-based Interpretation." *Pace Law Faculty Publications*, Paper 338 (1999): 2259–2294.

Gremillion, Joseph. *The Gospel of Peace and Justice. Catholic Social Teaching since Pope John*. Maryknoll: Orbis Books, 1976.

Griffiths, Paul J. *On Being Buddha: Maximal Greatness and the Doctrine of Buddhahood in Classical India*. Albany: SUNY Press, 1994.

Grisez, Germain. *The Way of the Lord Jesus: Volume One, Christian Moral Principles*. Quincy, IL: Franciscan Press, 1989.

Gross, Rita M. "The Crisis of Authority: Buddhist History for Buddhist Practitioners." *Buddhist-Christian Studies* 30 (2010): 59–72.

Grossman, Vasily. *Life and Fate*. Translated by Robert Chandler. New York: New York Review of Books, 1985; rpt. 2006.

—. "The Sistine Madonna." In *The Road: Stories, Journalism, and Essays*, translated by Robert and Elizabeth Chandler, with Olga Mukovnikova, 163–174. New York: New York Review of Books, 2010.

—. *Zhisn' i sud'ba*. Moscow: Eksmo, 2011.

Guruge, Ananda, ed. *Return to Righteousness: A Collection of Speeches, Essays and Letters of Anagarika Dharmapala*. Colombo: Ministry of Cultural Affairs and Information, 1991.

Gutiérrez, Gustavo. "God's Revelation and Proclamation in History." In *The Power of the Poor in History: Selected Writings*, 3–22. London: SCM Press, 1983.

—. *On Job: God-Talk and the Suffering of the Innocent*. Translated by Matthew J. O'Connell. New York: Orbis Books, 2002.

Guzmán, Juan Andrés, Gustavo Villarrubia, and Mónica González. *Los secretos del imperio de Karadima: La investigación definitiva sobre el escándalo que remeció a la Iglesia chilena*. Santiago: Ediciones Universidad Diego Portales, Catalonia and Escuela de Periodismo—Universidad Diego Portales, 2011.

Haddad, Yvonne Y. and John L. Esposito. *Islam, Gender, and Social Change*. New York: Oxford University Press, 1998.

Hanh, Thich Nhat. *Being Peace*. Berkeley, CA: Parallax Press, 2005.

Hardin, Garrett. "The Tragedy of the Commons." *Science* 162 (1968): 1243–1248.

Harlow, Barbara. *Barred. Women, Writing, and Political Detention*. Hanover: Wesleyan University Press, 1992.

Harris, Elizabeth J. *Theravada Buddhism and the British Encounter: Religious, Missionary and Colonial Experience in Nineteenth Century Sri Lanka*. London: Routledge, 2006.

Harris, Elizabeth J., ed. *Hope: A Form of Delusion? Buddhist and Christian Perspectives*. St Ottilien: EOS Verlag, 2013.

Harvey, Peter. "Between Controversy and Ecumenism: Intra-Buddhist Relationships." In *Buddhist Attitudes to Other Religions*, edited by Perry Schmidt-Leukel, 114–142. St Ottilien: EOS Verlag, 2008.

Hastings, Adrian, Alistair Mason, and Hugh Pypers, eds. *The Oxford Companion to Christian Thought*. Oxford: Oxford University Press, 2000.

Hegland, Mary Elaine. "Women of Karbala, Moving to America." In *The Women of Karbala*, edited by Kamran Scot Aghaie, 199–228. Austin: University Press of Texas, 2005.

Hinchcliff, Doreen. "The Iranian Family Protection Act." *The International and Comparative Law Quarterly* 17.2 (April 1968): 516–521.

Hochschild, Paige. "Pope Francis on the Priesthood." *First Things*. April 29, 2013.

Hoole, Rajan. *Sri Lanka: The Arrogance of Power: Myths, Decadence and Murder*. Colombo: University Teachers for Human Rights (Jaffna), 2001.

Horsley, Richard. *Jesus and Empire: The Kingdom of God and the New World Disorder*. Minneapolis: Fortress Press, 2002.

Horwitz, Paul. *The Agnostic Age: Law, Religion and the Constitution*. Oxford: Oxford University Press, 2011.

Humor como Resistencia. *La risa no se rinde*. Paraná: Entre Ríos, 2011.

Jackson, Roger and John Makransky, ed. *Buddhist Theology: Critical Reflections by Contemporary Buddhist Scholars*. London: RoutledgeCurzon, 2003.

Jawad, Haifa. *The Rights of Women in Islam: An Authentic Approach*. Basingstoke: St. Martin's Press, 1998.

Jawaheir, Yasmin Husein al. *Women in Iraq, The Gender Impact of International Sanctions*. London: I.B. Tauris, 2008.

Jayatilleke, K. N. *The Message of the Buddha*. Edited by Ninian Smart. London: Allen & Unwin, 1975.

Jayawardena, Kumari. *Ethnic and Class Conflict in Sri Lanka: The Emergence of Sinhala-Buddhist Consciousness, 1883–1983*. Colombo: Sanjiva Books, 2003.

Jeganathan, Pradeep. "Authorizing History, Ordering Land: The Conquest of Anuradhapura." In *Unmaking the Nation: The Politics of Identity and History in Modern Sri Lanka*, edited by Pradeep Jeganathan and Qadri Ismail, 110–113. Colombo: Social Scientists' Association, 1995.

Johnson, Eric and Karl-Heinz Reuband. *What We Knew: Terror, Mass Murder, and Everyday Life in Nazi Germany*. Cambridge: Basic Books, 2006.

Johnson, Robert A. *Owning Your Shadow: Understanding the Dark Side of the Psyche*. San Francisco: HarperSanFrancisco, 1991.

Kamrava, Mehran, ed. *The New Voices of Islam, Reforming Politics and Modernity—A Reader*. London: I.B. Tauris, 2006.

Kandiyoti, Deniz. *Women, Islam, and the State*. Philadelphia: Temple University Press, 1991.

Kar, Mehrangiz, *Raf-e Tabeez Az Zanan, Moghayesey-e Convension-e Raf-e Tabeez Az Zanan ba Qavaneen-e Dakheliy-e Iran*. Tehran, Iran: Nashr-e Qatr-e, 2000.

Katib, Ahmad al. *The Development of Shiite Political Thought, From Shura to Wilayat al-Faqih*. Self-published by Ahmad al Katib, London, 2008.

Katouzian, Homa. *State and Society in Iran, The Eclipse of the Qajars and the Emergence of the Pahlavis*. London: I.B. Tauris, 2000.

Keddie, Nikki R. "Iranian Revolution in Comparative Perspective." *The American Historical Review* 88.3 (June 1983): 579–598.

—. *Modern Iran, Roots and Results of Revolution*. New Haven: Yale University Press, 2006.

Kermode, Frank. *The Genesis of Secrecy: On the Interpretation of Narrative*. Cambridge: Harvard University Press, 1979.

Kessler, Edward. *An Introduction to Jewish-Christian Relations*. Cambridge: Cambridge University Press, 2010.

Khorasani, Noushin Ahmadi and Parvin Ardalan. *Senator: Faliyathaye Mehrangiz Manouchehrian ba bastar mobarezat hughughi zanan dar Iran*. Tehran, Iran: Nashr Tose-e, 2003.

Kian, Azadeh. "Women and Politics in Post-Islamist Iran: The Gender Conscious Drive to Change." *British Journal of Middle Eastern Studies* 24.1 (1997): 75–96.

Kiernan, Ben. *Blood and Soil: A World History of Genocide and Extermination from Sparta to Darfur*. New Haven: Yale University Press, 2007.

Kirwan, Michael. *Political Theology, A New Introduction*. London: Darton, Longman, and Todd, 2008.

Klimkeit, Hans-Joachim. *Der Buddha. Leben und Lehre*. Stuttgart-Berlin-Köln: Kohlhammer, 1990.

Knitter, Paul. *Without Buddha I Could Not Be a Christian*. Oxford: OneWorld, 2009.

Kogan, Michael. *Opening the Covenant: A Jewish Theology of Christianity*. Oxford: Oxford University Press, 2008.

Korn, Eugene B. "The People Israel, Christianity, and the Covenantal Responsibility to History." In *Covenant and Hope: Christian and Jewish Reflections*, edited by Robert W. Jenson and Eugene B. Korn, 145–172. Grand Rapids: Eerdmans, 2013.

Kozameh, Alicia. *Pasos bajo el agua*. Buenos Aires: Contrapunto, 1987.

—. *Steps under Water. A Novel*. Berkeley: University of California Press, 1996.

Kübler-Ross, Elisabeth. *Death and Dying*. London: Collier Books, 1969.

Kugel, James L. *How to Read the Bible: A Guide to Scripture Then and Now*. New York: Free Press, 2007.

Kushner, Harold S. *The Book of Job: When Bad Things Happened to a Good Person*. New York: Schocken Books, 2012.

Kyuhyun, Paul Mun. *The Korean People and the Catholic Church: A History*. Seoul: Dulsum Nalsum, 2012.

Landes, David S. and Richard A. Landes. "Do Fundamentalists Fear Our Women?" *New Republic*. September 29, 2001, 20–23.

Laytner, Anson. *Arguing with God: A Jewish Tradition*. Northvale, NJ: Jason Aronson, 1998.

Lear, Jonathan. *Radical Hope: Ethics in the Face of Cultural Devastation*. Cambridge, MA: Harvard University Press, 2006.

Levinas, Emmanuel. *Autrement qu'être ou au-delà de l'essence*. Dordrecht, Netherlands: Nijhoff, 1974.

—. *Autrement qu'être ou au-delà de l'essence*. Paris: Livre de poche edition, 2001.

—. *Ethics and Infinity: Conversations with Phillipe Nemo*. Translated by Richard A. Cohen. Pittsburgh: Duquesne University Press, 2009.

—. "Meaning and Sense." In *Emmanuel Levinas: Basic Philosophical Writings*, edited by Adrian T. Peperzak, Simon Critchley, and Robert Bernasconi, 33–64. Bloomington and Indianapolis: Indiana University Press, 1996.

—. *Nine Talmudic Readings*. Translated by Annette Aronowicz. Bloomington and Indianapolis: Indiana University Press, 1994.

—. *Otherwise than Being, or, Beyond Essence*. Translated by Alphonso Lingis. Pittsburgh: Duquesne University Press, 1981.

—. *Quatre lectures talmudiques*. Paris: Les Éditions de minuit, 1968.

—. *Totalité et Infini*. Paris: Livre de Poche, 1990.

—. *Totality and Infinity: An Essay on Exteriority*. Translated by Alphonso Lingis. Pittsburgh: Duquesne University Press, 1961.

—. "Useless Suffering." In *The Problem of Evil: A Reader*, edited by Mark Larrimore, 371–380. Malden, MA: Blackwell, 2004.

Levine, Amy-Jill and Marc Zvi, eds. *The Jewish Annotated New Testament*. Oxford: Oxford University Press, 2011.

Levine, Peter A. with Ann Frederick. *Waking the Tiger: Healing Trauma*. Berkeley: North Atlanta Books, 1997.

Ling, Trevor. *The Buddha: Buddhist Civilization in India and Ceylon*. Harmondsworth: Penguin, 1976.

López, Beatriz. *Hasta la victoria siempre . . . Testimonio de Carmen Cornes, emigrante gallega y militante de la vida*. Galicia: Ediciós do Castro, 1992.

Lopre, La. *Memorias de una presa política. 1975–1979*. Buenos Aires: Grupo Editorial Norma, 2006.

Loy, David. *The Great Awakening: A Buddhist Social Theory*. Boston: Wisdom Publications, 2003.

—. *Lack and Transcendence: The Problem of Death and Life in Psychotherapy, Existentialism, and Buddhism*. Amherst, MA: Humanity Books, 1999.

Luisi, Pier Luigi with Zara Houshmand. *Mind and Life: Discussions with the Dalai Lama on the Nature of Reality*. New York: Columbia University Press, 2009.

Madeline, James, and Katie, eds. *Turned Inside-Out: Literature, Art, and Testimony from the Inside-Out Prison Exchange Program*, Vol. 1. Clark Honors College, Summer 2010.

Maimonides. *The Guide for the Perplexed*. Translated by M. Friedlander. New York: Dover, 1956.

—. "Laws of Repentance." In *Maimonides—Essential Teachings on Jewish Faith and Ethics: The Book of Knowledge and the Thirteen Principles of Faith*, edited and translated by Marc D. Angel, 105–149. Woodstock, VT: SkyLight Paths, 2012.

Makransky, John. *Buddhahood Embodied*. Albany: SUNY Press, 1997.

Manghani, Sunil. *Image Critique and the Fall of the Berlin Wall*. Bristol and Chicago: Intellect Books, 2008.

Margalit, Avishai. *The Ethics of Memory*. Cambridge: Harvard University Press, 2001.

Martín-Baró, Ignacio. *Writings for a Liberation Psychology*. Translated by Tod Sloan. Cambridge: Harvard University Press, 1994.

Matthäus, Jürgen, ed. *Approaching an Auschwitz Survivor: Holocaust Testimony and Its Transformations*. Oxford: Oxford University Press, 2009.

May, John D'Arcy. "Creator Spirit: A Narrative Theology of the Trinity in Interreligious Relations." In *Trinity and Salvation: Theological, Spiritual and Aesthetic Perspectives*, edited by Declan Marmion and Gesa Thiessen, 161–180. Oxford: Peter Lang, 2009.

—. "Sympathy and Empathy: The Compassionate Bodhisattva and the Love of Christ." In *Crossroad Discourses between Christianity and Culture*, edited by Jerald D. Gort, Henry Jansen, and Wessel Stoker, 395–411. Amsterdam and New York: Rodopi, 2010.

—. "Time and Narrative in Buddhism and Christianity." In *Religion and Culture: A Multicultural Discussion: Festschrift in Honour of Francis X. D'Sa, SJ*, edited by Clemens Mendonca and Bernd Jochen Hilberath, 290–299. Pune: Institute for the Study of Religion, 2011.

Mayer, Ann Elizabeth. *Islam and Human Rights: Tradition and Politics*. Boulder, CO: Westview, 1999.

McCafferty, Partick. "'A Cry from the Depths': Entering into the Mystery of Christ Forsaken." In *Broken Faith: Why Hope Matters*, edited by Patrick Claffey, Joe Egan, and Marie Keenan, 25–30. Oxford: Peter Lang, 2013.

McDermott, Martin. "Liberation Theology and Imam Khomeini's Jihad, A Comparison." In *Faith, Power and Violence, Orientalia Christiana Analecta*, Vol. 258, edited by John J. Donohue and Christian W. Troll, 75–85. Rome: Ponticicio Instituto Orientale, 1998.

Meier, Christian. *A Culture of Freedom: Ancient Greece and the Origins of Europe*. Translated by Jefferson Chase. Oxford: Oxford University Press, 2011.

Mernissi, Fatima. *The Veil and the Male Elite: A Feminist Interpretation of Women's Rights*. Translated by Mary Jo Lakeland. New York: Addison-Wesley, 1991.

Midrash Tehillim. Edited by Solomon Buber. Vilna: Rom, 1891; reprint, New York: Om Publishing, 1947.

Mignone, Emilio. *Witness to the Truth. The Complicity of Church and Dictatorship in Argentina, 1976–1983*. Translated by Phillip Berryman. Maryknoll: Orbis Books, 1988.

Milbank, John. *Theology and Social Theory. Beyond Secular Reason*, 2nd edn. Oxford: Blackwell, 2006.

Milton, John. *Paradise Lost*. Edited by Stephen Orgel and Jonathan Goldberg. Oxford: Oxford University Press, 2008.

Mirhosseini, Akram. "After the Revolution: Violations of Women's Human Rights in Iran." In *Women's Rights Human Rights, International Feminist Perspectives*, edited by Julie Peters and Adrea Wolper, 72–77. London: Routledge, 1995.

Mir-Hosseini, Ziba. *Islam and Gender: The Religious Debate in Contemporary Islam*. Princeton: Princeton University Press, 1999.

—. "Stretching the Limits: A Feminist Reading of the Shari'a in Post-Khomeini Iran." In *Feminism and Islam, Legal and Literary Perspectives*, edited by Mai Yamani, 285–319. Reading: Ithaca Press, 1996.

Mizuno, Kōgen. *Buddhist Sūtras: Origin, Development, Transmission*. Tokyo: Kosei, 1982.

Moghadam, Valentine M. *Modernizing Women: Gender and Social Change in the Middle-East*, 2nd edn. Boulder, CO: Lynne Reinner Publishers, 2003.

Moghadam, Valentine and Sadiqi Fatima. "Women's Activism and the Public Sphere: An Introduction and Overview." *Journal of Middle East Women's Studies* 2.2 (Spring 2006): 1–7.

Moghissi, Haideh. *Feminism and Islamic Fundamentalism: The Limits of Postmodern Analysis*. London: Zed Books, 1999.

Moltmann, Jürgen. *Theology of Hope: On the Ground and the Implications of a Christian Eschatology*. London: SCM Press, 1967.

Morgan, Michael L. *Discovering Levinas*. Cambridge: Cambridge University Press, 2007.

Mori, Miguel Angel. *Las rondas y los sueños*. Rosario: Ediciones de la Sexta, 1998.

Morrill, Bruce T. *Anamnesis as Dangerous Memory*. Collegeville: The Liturgical Press, 2000.

Morrow, William S. *Protest against God: The Eclipse of a Biblical Tradition*. Sheffield, UK: Sheffield Phoenix Press, 2007.

Moyo, Fulata L. "A Narrative Theology of Eschatological Hope as Healing." In *African Women, Religion, and Health: Essays in Honor of Mercy Amba Ewudziwa Oduyoye*, edited by Isabel A. Phiri and Sarojini Nadar, 243–257. Maryknoll: Orbis Books, 2006.

—. "Religion, Spirituality and Being a Woman in Africa: Gender Construction within the African Religio-cultural Experience." *Agenda* 61 (2004): 72–78.

—. "Singing and Dancing Women's Liberation: My Story of Faith." In *Her-Stories: Hidden Histories of Women of Faith in Africa*, edited by Isabel A. Phiri, Deverakshanam, Betty Govinden, and Sarojini Nadar, 389–408. Pietermaritzburg: Cluster Publications, 2002.

Muñoz, Luis. *Being Luis: A Chilean Life*. Exeter: Impress Books, 2005.

Muñoz, Ronaldo. *The God of Christians*. Turnbridge Wells: Burns & Oates, 1991.

Nāgārjuna. *The Fundamental Wisdom of the Middle Way: Nāgārjuna's Mūla-Madhyamaka-Kārikā*. Translated by Jay L. Garfield. New York and Oxford: Oxford University Press, 1995.

Nasr, Seyyid Hossein. *The Heart of Islam: Enduring Values for Humanity*. New York: Harper Collins, 2002.

Nelson, Robert H. *Economics as Religion: From Samuelson to Chicago and Beyond*. University Park, PA: Pennsylvania State University Press, 2001.

Newman, Louis I. *Hasidic Anthology*. New York: Schocken Books, 1963.

Nicholas of Cusa. *De Pace Fidei*. Translated by Jasper Hopkins. Minneapolis: Arthur J. Banning, 1994.

Nietzsche, Friedrich. *Beyond Good and Evil: Prelude to a Philosophy of the Future*. Translated by R. J. Hollingdale. London: Penguin, 1990.

Nosotras, Presas Políticas. 1974–1983. Obra Colectiva de 112 prisioneras políticas entre 1974 y 1983. Edited by Viviana Beguán, Blanca Becher, Mirta Clara, Silvia Echarte, and Alicia Kozameh. Buenos Aires: Nuestra América, 2006. Print, with CD.

Oduyoye, Mercy Amba. *Daughters of Anowa: African Women and Patriarchy*. Maryknoll: Orbis Books, 1995.

Oduyoye, Mercy Amba and Musimbi Kanyoro, eds. *The Will to Arise: Women, Tradition and the Church in Africa*. Pietermaritzburg: Cluster Publications, 2006.

O'Grady, John. *Beyond Immanence: A Buddhological Observing of Grace*. Irish School of Ecumenics: Trinity College Dublin, 2010.

Oldenberg, Hermann. *Buddha. Sein Leben, seine Lehre, seine Gemeinde*. Stuttgart und Berlin: Cotta, 1920.

O'Mahony, Anthony. "Interreligious Dialogue, Muslim-Christian Relation and Catholic Shi'a Engagment." In *Catholics and Shi'a in Dialogue, Studies in Theology and Spirituality*, edited by Anthony O'Mahony, Walstan Peterburs, and Muhammad 'Ali Shomali, 291–315. Trowbridge: Fox Publications, 2004.

Ostrom, Elinor. *Governing the Commons. The Evolution of Institutions for Collective Action.* Cambridge: Cambridge University Press, 1990.

Otto, Rudolf. *Reich Gottes und Menschensohn. Ein religionsgeschichtlicher Versuch*, 2nd rev. edn. München: Beck, 1940.

Oxford Latin Dictionary. Edited by P. G. W. Glare. Oxford: Clarendon Press, 1996.

Partnoy, Alicia. "Concealing God: How Argentine Women Political Prisoners Performed a Collective Identity." *Biography* 36.1 (Winter 2013): 214–242.

—. "Cuando Vienen Matando: On Prepositional Shifts and the Struggle of Testimonial Subjects for Agency." *PMLA* 121.5 (October 2006): 1665–1669.

—. *The Little School. Tales of Disappearance and Survival.* Translated by Lois Athey and Sandra Blaustein. San Francisco: Cleis Press, 1986.

Pepe, Abs, Seth, Talon, Steve, Carolina, Robyn, and Anna, eds. *Zhizn' i Sud'ba* [*Life and Fate*]. Salem, Oregon: Oregon Corrections Enterprises, Oregon State Correctional Institution, 2012.

Permanent People's Tribunal: *People's Tribunal on Sri Lanka.* Dublin: PPT and IFPSL, 2010.

Presos Políticos Argentinos. *Memoria y resistencia de los presos políticos durante el terrorismo de estado en Argentina.* "Cárcel de Villa Devoto." Online: http://www.pparg.org/pparg/carceles/buenos_aires/capital/carcel_villa_devoto/.

The Qur'an. Translated by M. A. S. Abdel Haleem. Oxford: Oxford University Press, 2010.

Rad, Gerhard von. *Theologie des alten Testaments, Band II. Die Theologie der prophetischen Überlieferungen Israels.* München: Chr. Kaiser Verlag, 1980.

Radhakrishnan, Sarvepalli. *Indian Philosophy*, 7th edn. Delhi: Oxford University Press, 1994.

Ramadan, Tariq. *Western Muslims and the Future of Islam.* New York: Oxford University Press, 2004.

Rebolledo, Javier. *La danza de los cuervos: El destino final de los detenidos desaparecidos.* Santiago: Ceibo Ediciones, 2012.

Ricoeur, Paul. *Figuring the Sacred: Religion, Narrative, and Imagination.* Translated by Donald Pellauer. Minneapolis: Fortress Press, 1995.

—. *Time and Narrative*, Vol. 1. Translated by Kathleen Mclaughlin and David Pellauer. Chicago and London: University Press of Chicago, 1984.

Rieger, Joerg. *Christ and Empire: From Paul to Postcolonial Times.* Minneapolis: Fortress Press, 2007.

—. *Globalization and Theology, Horizons in Theology.* Nashville: Abingdon Press, 2010.

—. *No Rising Tide: Theology, Economics, and the Future.* Minneapolis: Fortress Press, 2009.

Rieger, Joerg and Kwok Pui-lan. *Occupy Religion: Theology of the Multitude.* Lanham, MD: Rowman and Littlefield, 2012.

Ringelblum, Emmanuel. *Notes from the Warsaw Ghetto.* Edited and translated by Jacob Sloan. New York: Schocken Books, 1958.

Roald, Anne Sofie. *Women in Islam: The Western Experience.* New York: Routledge, 2001.

Robinson, George. *Essential Judaism: A Complete Guide to Beliefs, Customs, and Rituals.* New York: Pocket Books, 2001.

Romero, Oscar, "Georgetown Address: Address of Archbishop Romero on the Occasion of His Academic Investiture as a Doctor of Humanities, Honoris Causa, in the Cathedral of San Salvador, 14 February 1978." In *Archbishop Oscar Romero: Voice of the Voiceless—The Four Pastoral Letters and Other Statements*, translated by Michael J. Walsh, 162–167. Maryknoll: Orbis Books, 1985.

Rosales, Gaudencio and C. G. Arevalo, eds. *For all the Peoples of Asia: Federation of Asian Bishops' Conferences Documents from 1970 to 1991.* Maryknoll: Orbis Books, 1992.

Rosenblüth, Pinchas E. "Exil II." In *Theologische Realenzyklopädie*, Vol. 10, edited by Gerhard Krause and Gerhard Müller, 714. Berlin: Walter de Gruyter, 1982.

Sadiqi, Fatima and Moha Ennaji. "The Feminization of Public Space: Women's Activism, the Family Law and Social Change in Morocco." *Journal of Middle East Women's Studies* 2.2 (Spring 2006): 86–115.

Sadri, Mahmoud and Ahmad Sadri, eds. *Reason, Freedom and Democracy in Islam, Essential Writings of Abdolkarim Soroush*. Oxford: Oxford University Press, 2000.

Sangharakshita. *The Bodhisattva Ideal: Wisdom and Compassion in Buddhism*. Birmingham: Windhorse Publications, 1999.

Schmidt-Leukel, Perry. "*Den Löwen brüllen hören*." *Zur Hermeneutik eines christlichen Verständnisses der buddhistischen Heilsbotschaft*. Paderborn-München-Wien-Zürich: Schöningh, 1992.

—. *Understanding Buddhism*. Edinburgh: Dunedin Academic, 2006.

Schneider, Peter. *The German Comedy: Scenes of Life after the Wall*. London: I.B. Tauris, 1992.

Schuchardt, Erika. *Why Me? Learning to Live in Crises*. Geneva: WCC Publication, 2005.

Schumann, Hans Wolfgang. *Der historische Buddha. Leben und Lehre des Gautama*, rev. edn. Kreuzlingen und München: Hugendubbel, 2004.

Semprún, Jorge. *Literature or Life*. Translated by Linda Coverdale. New York: Viking, 1997.

Sen, Amartya. *The Idea of Justice*. London: Allen Lane, 2009.

Shaikh, Sa'diyya. "Transforming Feminisms: Islam, Women and Gender Justice." In *Progressive Muslims, On Justice, Gender and Pluralism*, edited by Omid Safi, 147–162. Oxford: OneWorld, 2003.

Shakespeare, William. *The Riverside Shakespeare*. Boston: Houghton Mifflin, 1974.

Sharma, Arvind. *Hinduism and Its Sense of History*. Oxford: Oxford University Press, 2003.

Shepherd, Robin H. E. *The Velvet Revolution and Beyond*. London: Macmillan, 2000.

Shinran. *The Collected Works of Shinran* Vol. 1. Edited by Dennis Hirota, Hisao Inagaki, Michio Tokunaga, and Ryushin Uryuzu. Kyoto: Jōdo Shinshū Hongwanji-ha, 1997.

Sillato, María del Carmen. *Diálogos de amor contra el silencio. Memorias de prisión, sueños de libertad* (Rosario-Buenos Aires, 1977–1981). Cordoba: Alción Editora, 2006.

—. *Huellas: Memorias de resistencia (Argentina 1974–1983)*. San Luis: Nueva Editorial Universitaria, 2008.

Skalli, Loubna H. "Communicating Gender in the Public Sphere: Women and Information Technologies in the Mena." *Journal of Middle East Women's Studies* 2.2 (Spring 2006): 35–59.

Sobrino, Jon. "Presentation at the Second International Congress of Philosophy Xabier Zubiri at the José Simeón Cañas Universidad de Central America." *Revista Latinoamericana de Teología* 66 (2005): 209–228.

—. "Redeeming Globalization through Its Victims." In *Globalization and Its Victims*, edited by Jon Sobrino and Felix Wilfred, 105–114. London: SCM Press, 2001.

Solomon, Normon. *The Talmud: A Selection*. Penguin: London, 2009.

Spadaro, Antonio. "A Big Heart Open to God." *America*. September 30, 2013.

St John of the Cross. *The Dark Night of the Soul*. New York: Barnes and Noble Publishing, 2005.

Strassberg, Gavriel b. Yehoshua of Raisha. "How Can I Lift My Face?" In *Sefer HaDema'ot* (*The Book of Tears*), edited by Simon Bernfeld, 3: 179–184. 3 vols. Berlin: Eschkol Publishers, 1924–1926.

Strong, John S. *The Buddha: A Short Biography*. Oxford: OneWorld, 2001.

Sugirtharajah, R. S. "Charting the Aftermath: A Review of Postcolonial Criticism." In *The Postcolonial Biblical Reader*, edited by R. S. Sugirtharajah, 7–32. Oxford: Blackwell, 2006.

Tamez, Elsa. *Amnesty of Grace: Justification by Faith from a Latin American Perspective.* Translated by Sharon H. Ringe. Nashville: Abingdon Press, 1993.

Tanner, Kathryn. *Theories of Culture: A New Agenda for Theology.* Minneapolis: Fortress Press, 1997.

Thucydides. *History of the Peloponnesian War.* Translated by Rex Warner. London: Penguin, 1972.

Timerman, Jacobo. *Prisoner without a Name, Cell without a Number.* New York: Vintage, 1982.

Torberg, Friedrich. "Seder, 1944." In *Voices within the Ark: The Modern Jewish Poets*, edited by Howard Schwartz and Anthony Rudolf, 980–981. New York: Avon Books, 1980.

Turner, Victor Y. *The Forest of Symbols: Aspects of Ndembu Ritual.* Ithaca, NY: Cornell University Press, 1967.

Verdugo, Patricia, "Los Protagonistas." In *De la tortura no se habla: Agüero versus Meneses*, edited by Patricia Verdugo, 17–44. Santiago: Catalonia, 2004.

Volf, Miroslav. *The End of Memory: Remembering Rightly in a Violent World.* Grand Rapid: Eerdmaans, 2006.

Weil, Simone. *The Simone Weil Reader.* Edited by George Panichas. New York: David McKay, 2007.

Wetzell, David, ed. *From the Berlin Museum to the Berlin Wall: Essays on the Cultural and Political History of Modern Germany.* Westport, CT and London: Praeger, 1996.

Wheaton, Bernard and Zdenek Kavan. *The Velvet Revolution: Czechoslovakia, 1988–1991.* Boulder, CO: Westview Press, 1992.

Wiesel, Elie. *From the Kingdom of Memory: Reminiscences.* New York: Summit Books, 1990.

Wilfred, Felix. *Asian Public Theology. Critical Concerns in Challenging Times.* Delhi: ISPCK, 2010.

Yaakov, Menachem b. "Woe Unto Me." In *Sefer HaDema'ot* (*The Book of Tears*), edited by Simon Bernfeld, 1: 239–240, 3 vols. Berlin: Eschkol Publishers, 1924–1926.

Yerushalmi, Yosef Hayim. *Zakhor: Jewish History and Jewish Memory.* Seattle: University Press of Washington, 1996.

Zweig, Connie and Jeremiah Abrams, eds. *Meeting the Shadow: The Hidden Power of the Dark Side of Human Nature.* New York: Penguin, 1991.

Index

CPSIA information can be obtained
at www.ICGtesting.com
Printed in the USA
LVHW011937090720
660251LV00004B/66